The DARK SIDE of CALVINISM

A biblically based
examination,
evaluation,
and refutation
of the Reformed Doctrine
of Redemption
and Reprobation.

The **DARK SIDE**
of **CALVINISM**
THE CALVINIST CASTE SYSTEM

GEORGE L. BRYSON

The Dark Side of Calvinism
The Calvinist Caste System

Copyright © 2004 by George Bryson

Published by Calvary Chapel Publishing (CCP)
a resource ministry of Calvary Chapel of Costa Mesa
3800 South Fairview Rd.
Santa Ana, CA 92704

First printing 2004

1-931667-88-8

Printed in the United States of America.

If you represent a church, a church related organization, a Bible college, seminary, etc., and would like information on scheduling George to speak on the topic of Calvinism, please call 1-800-332-2276.

DEDICATED TO ...

the memory of Bob Passantino, who went to be with our Lord on November 17, 2003. Along with Gretchen, his wife and very capable ministry partner of many years, Bob proved to be a major help and encouragement to me in the seven years I took to do the research and write *The Dark Side of Calvinism.* Without their help and encouragement, I am not certain that I would ever have finished.

FOREWORD

I N *The Dark Side of Calvinism,* George Bryson has shined the light of Scripture and scripturally based reasoning upon some very important and disturbing problems with the distinctive doctrines of Reformed Theology. As George documents, John Calvin asserts:

> By predestination we mean the eternal decree of God, by which he determined with himself whatever he wished to happen with regard to every man. All are not created on equal terms, but some are preordained to eternal life, others to eternal damnation; and, accordingly, as each has been created for one or other of those ends, we say that he has been predestined to life or death.[1]

Despite the unscriptural and radical nature of such a position, George demonstrates that this is the position promoted by the leading proponents of Calvinism today. While Calvinists are prone to accent the less negative features of Calvinism, even the best of what Calvin taught about salvation logically leads to the worst of what Calvinism teaches. While Calvinists prefer to talk about election, they know that the other side of unconditional election is a very troubling and unscriptural doctrine of unconditional reprobation. Typically, a contemporary advocate of Calvinism, James White says:

> God elects a specific people unto Himself without reference to *anything they do.* This means the basis of God's choice of the elect is *solely* within Himself: His grace, His mercy, His will. It is not man's actions, works, or *even foreseen faith,* that "draws" God's choice. God's election is unconditional *and final.*[2]

The doctrinal distinctive of Reformed Theology cannot be reconciled with what we know about God from His holy Word. Scripture has taught me to believe that God is loving and absolutely just. Could and would such a God allow a man to be born who has no possibility to be saved? Would the God of love and Scripture have me tantalize unsavable men with the offer of salvation? Would the God of all hope punish a man for all eternity for rejecting the offer of salvation, if that man was decreed by God to reject that salvation in the first place?

The God introduced to us by Calvin seems to be far removed and very different from the God who said, "And whosoever will, let him take the water of life freely" (Rev. 22:17, KJV). Would I not be lying to a non-elect man if I offered him eternal life based on what Christ did for him on the cross? For if Calvinism is true, Christ did nothing of redemptive value for the non-elect. Why are we commanded to preach the gospel to every creature (Mark 16:15)? If Calvinism is true, and I affirm to a man that Jesus loves him and died on the cross to redeem him from his sins, I may be offering nothing more than a false hope. Can I, with a clear conscience, really do this in the name of the God of all truth, knowing full well that it may not be true? Perhaps this explains why evangelism is so neglected in much of the Reformed community!

Assuming Calvinism is true, if I urge men to receive Jesus as their Lord that they might be saved, would this not be nothing more than a cruel tease for many of those to whom I speak (Acts 2:36–39)? Why would the God of all truth, who speaks so sternly against lying, send His servants out to promote such a lie? If God has no saving concern for many (perhaps even most), why should I? Why would God call upon a man to make a choice as to which God he would serve as He did with Joshua and Elijah? If it is impossible for men to choose because they have been pre-ordained by God to be saved or lost, is it not rather cruel and deceitful to hold out the offer of the gospel to them if it is impossible for them to accept it? Conversely, if a man is ordained by God to be saved, with no real responsibility on his part, then why spend time and resources seeking to bring the gospel to the world? If they have been irrevocably chosen to be saved, then they cannot possibly be lost; therefore, where then is the incentive to take the gospel to them? On the other hand, if they have been predestined to be irrevocably lost, then it is cruel to hold out to them the hope of the gospel.

How can you declare that God is love, if He has unconditionally destined men to the eternal torment of hell? If I follow the referenced position of James White, I would have to accept that a man's "faith" in Jesus Christ has nothing to do with getting saved. In stark contrast, when our Lord was asked, "What shall we do, that we might work the works of God?" Jesus responded, "This is the work of God, that ye believe on him whom he hath sent" (John 6:28–29, KJV). When the Philippian jailor asked, "what must I do to be saved?" Paul and Silas said, "Believe on the Lord Jesus Christ, and thou shalt be saved. ..." (Acts 16:30–31, KJV).

According to Calvinism, it is futile to try to convert the lost who are not predestined to be saved. Perhaps this explains why so many Calvinists are spending so much time and energy trying to win the already saved to Calvinism. What this means is that Calvinists want other Christians to believe in their convoluted theology, which if fully understood, destroys the gospel to every creature.

No matter what your position on the subject of Reformed Theology, George is going to force you to think it through. This is a must-read for all who have wrestled with Calvinism.

Chuck Smith
Senior Pastor, Calvary Chapel Costa Mesa

CONTENTS

ACKNOWLEDGMENTS

W HEN you take seven years to write a book, as I did with this one, it is very difficult to even remember all the people that helped you along the way. Perhaps some of those left unmentioned will take comfort in the fact that it may be best not to be acknowledged in a book that is certain to be controversial. Since Chuck Smith, senior pastor of Calvary Chapel of Costa Mesa, wrote the foreword for me, I doubt saying thanks to Chuck for doing so will expose him to any more criticism than he will already be subject to. I would also like to thank Pastor Brian Brodersen and his skilled staff at Calvary Chapel Publishing for the very important part they played in getting this book into readable print. Special thanks must go to Romy Godding for her skills as an editor, who can see what a book can be (and help it become that) long before it takes its final form. Also, I want to say thanks to Neil Godding for the cover design that clearly captures and communicates what I tried to say throughout the book. Thanks must also go to Christine Scheller, whose skill as a writer helped make *The Dark Side of Calvinism* quantitatively smaller but qualitatively better.

I must also mention Debbi, my dear wife of thirty-five plus years, who with the patience of Job listened (in the midst of her own very busy ministry schedule) as I read what I wrote and then rewrote (and rewrote) many times over these many years. Thanks Deb. My daughter Esther, who just happens to have a very handy degree in English, also read the manuscript from beginning to end and provided very helpful suggestions (as well as other kinds of very time consuming and patience producing help) that will explain why at least some of what I wrote will be understood by those who understand the English language. (I knew that college education was a good idea.) Thanks also to Esther's husband Matt DeWitt, who, along with Esther, works with me full time in our church-planting mission to Russia. If he did not do what he does, I could not do all that I do.

Finally, I must say thank you to several people who have provided a great deal of encouragement to me in general and in the writing of this book in particular. First, there is my friend and co-laborer in Christ for more than three decades, Ken Ortize, who just happens to be the senior pastor of Calvary Chapel of Spokane, Washington. Then there is Roger Stahlut, senior pastor of Calvary Chapel of Open Door in Anaheim, California, who along with Pastor Ken, shares my heart for reaching Russia with the love and grace of our Lord and Savior, Jesus Christ. Were it not for the labor of love (and considerable language skills) of Christina Dixon and Shannon Bruns, two very dedicated missionaries working with me in Russia, this book may have taken an additional seven years to write.

Oh yes, I cannot fail to mention my two precious grandchildren, Hannah Faith (9) and Jonathon Matthew (7). While they did not assist me in the writing or editing of the book, they helped fill the last seven years with a great deal of joy.

INTRODUCTION

THE CASE AGAINST CALVINISM

> There are some people ... who ... assert that God is, in himself,
> the cause and author of sin. ... If I should attempt to refute them,
> it would be like inventing a long argument to prove that God is not
> the Devil. (John Milton, De Doctrina Christiana)

DESPITE formal denials from some Calvinists and documents such as *The Westminster Confession of Faith,* John Calvin and the system of theology he championed, does "... assert that God is, in himself, the cause and author of sin. ..." According to Calvin, it is all happening according to the perfect plan and purpose of God. Everything is as it should be. All Evangelicals would agree that God is ultimately going to have His way. Of that, there should be no doubt. But is everything as it should be—or just as important as God determined it to be? What about the wrong that men do? Can we trace moral evil back to God in the same way we can good things? Insofar as Calvin was concerned, even the first sin and its terrible consequences were orchestrated by God. Thus, Calvin could say:

> God not only foresaw the fall of the first man, and in him the ruin
> of his posterity; but also at his own pleasure arranged it.[3]

As to how this kind of sovereign control and divine direction (of all things—even human choices) affects the eternal destiny of Adam's posterity, Calvin reasoned:

> ... some are preordained to eternal life, others to eternal damnation; and, accordingly, as each has been created for one or other of those ends, we say that he has been predestined to life or death.[4]

The key to understanding Calvin is not only in the words "predestined to" but in the words "created for." *Where* you go when you die, is, according to Calvin, determined by *why* God created you in the first place. It is possible, according to Calvin, that God created you *for eternal life.* Calvin also taught that it was equally possible that God created you *for eternal death.* Thus, for Calvin, there is both a bright side and a dark side to the destiny question (where will you go when you die?). If you are one of those individuals that God created for *life,* then your future (whether you know it or not) is indeed very bright. If, on the other hand, you are one of those individuals that God created for *death,* then your future (even if unknown to you) is dark indeed. That is, if Calvin is right:

> ... God ... arranges all things by his sovereign counsel, in such a way that individuals are born, who are doomed from the womb to certain death ...[5]

Only if you understand and agree with these statements of John Calvin (and the sentiments they represent) can it be correctly said that you are a true Calvinist. You do not have to agree with everything that Calvin said or taught to be a Calvinist. To be a true Calvinist, however, you do have to understand and agree with the central tenets and doctrinal distinctives of the Reformed faith. To be a true Calvinist, you must also believe much more than the doctrinal distinctives of Reformed Theology. As professor R. Laird Harris says:

> It must not be forgotten that Calvinism holds, besides its distinctives, to those doctrines common to all historic Christianity, such as the full truthfulness of Scripture, the Trinity, the deity of Christ, His supernatural miracles, bodily resurrection, etc. Without these basic and fundamental doctrines a theology cannot properly be called Calvinist or Reformed.[6]

It is the "distinctives" of the Reformed faith that are of concern to me and are the focus of this book. It may seem ironic, but one reason I *go after* Calvinism as I do in this book is precisely *because* those who embrace it (or who may be tempted to take a turn down the theologically-Reformed road) are sincere and devout believers. While I am clearly opposing Calvinism as a theological system, I do not consider Calvinists to be the enemy. In fact, I view Calvinists as the victims of Calvinism. The fact that many Calvinists are both sincere in what they believe and devoted to the Lord is not disputed in this book and has never been called into question by me.

Both my sincere appeal to Calvinists and harsh criticism of Calvinism are to some extent motivated by the very fact that I consider true Calvinists to be true Christians. While the issues that will be addressed in this book are serious and represent cause for great concern among the people of God, for me this is a "family" or "in-house" discussion and should not be interpreted in any other way.

In light of the disturbing things that Calvinism says about God and a host of other related and very important topics, the fact that this is a "family matter" only makes the discussion all the more urgent and serious. For example, the Calvinist scholar John Feinberg admits:

> Sometimes it would be easier not to be a Calvinist. An intellectual price tag comes with any conceptual scheme, but the one that comes with Calvinism seems beyond the resources of human intelligence to pay. Calvinists hold views that appear at very least counterintuitive. This is especially so with respect to Calvinist accounts of God's sovereign control in relation to human freedom and moral responsibility for evil.

> If Calvinists are right about divine sovereignty, there seems to be little room for human freedom. If freedom goes, so does human moral responsibility for sin. Worst of all, if Calvinists are right, it appears that God decides that there will be sin and evil in our world, maybe even brings it about that there is such evil, and yet, according to Calvinists, is not morally responsible for any of it. We are.

> If this is Calvinism's God, Calvinism seems not only intellectually but also religiously bankrupt. Who would worship this God? Moreover, if atheists understand this portrait of God as paradigmatic of traditional Christianity, no wonder they are repulsed by Christianity. Although committed atheists will not likely abandon their atheism for any concept of God, at least the Arminian portrayal of God seems more attractive than the Calvinist portrayal.[7]

Notice that Feinberg seems most concerned about how Calvinism presents itself. In other words, the problem is with the accurate "portrayal" to which he refers. Conversely, it is not in a misrepresentation of that "portrayal" by non-Calvinists that troubles him. Though I doubt that Feinberg would say it quite this way or concede so much, it is Calvinism, accurately understood and fairly represented, that poses the greatest intellectual, emotional, spiritual, theological, and scriptural challenge, even and perhaps especially to those who call themselves Calvinists.

Given the fact that Feinberg has dedicated at least some of his life to promoting and defending Calvinism, what he admits here has not caused him to abandon Reformed Theology for the "Arminian portrayal of God." Thus, despite what Feinberg concedes, he still believes that Calvinism is the "portrayal of God" found in Scripture. How this can be, if what he says about Calvinism is true, is difficult for me to fathom. Of course, Feinberg believes that Calvinism can be rescued from most of the criticism that even he has leveled against what he calls "the Calvinist portrayal." Feinberg has worked very hard to resolve as many apparent problems inherent in Reformed Theology as he can. Nevertheless, there is, according to Feinberg, a portrait *by Calvinists* of Calvinism that he is not willing to accept. That is, Feinberg says:

> Unfortunately, some Calvinists, because of their understanding of God's sovereignty, have denied that humans are free. Yet some of those Calvinists maintain that we are morally responsible for our sin, while God, who decreed our sin, is not morally accountable. When asked how this can be true, they respond that it is a paradox that nonetheless must be true because Scripture demands it.[8]

Evidently, the Calvinists that Feinberg refers to here are, according to Feinberg, just *copping out.* I must confess that I cannot see any real difference in the faulty "understanding" of Calvinism that Feinberg seems to reject and the accurate "portrayal" he seems to accept. Regardless, it would appear that Edwin Palmer is representative of the kind of Calvinism that Feinberg finds objectionable. According to Palmer:

> To say on one hand that God has made certain all that ever happens, and yet to say that man is responsible for what he does ...[is] nonsense! It must be one or the other ... So the Calvinist has to make up his mind. What is his authority? His own human reason or the Word of God?[9]

These words must be very painful to the ears of someone like Feinberg who worries about how Calvinism appears to the rest of us. What Palmer does here is give us two choices. We can embrace:

1.   "Nonsense"

Or:

2. Our "own human reason"

The "nonsense," according to Palmer, is *Calvinism*. "Human reason" is anything contrary to "nonsense." I sympathize with Feinberg and can see why these kinds of statements trouble him. Yet, it cannot be argued that Palmer is not onto something, and that what he says is much more representative of true Calvinism than what men like Feinberg will concede. Upon close inspection, Palmer is really only saying what Feinberg says. He just does so with less sophistication and less concern about how Calvinism may appear to others. As with Feinberg, for Palmer the conflicts in Calvinism are also only "apparent." Thus he says:

> ... The apparent paradox between the sovereignty of God and the responsibility of man belongs to the Lord our God and we should leave it there. We ought not probe into the secret counsel of God.[10]

Are these conflicts in Calvinism really only an "apparent paradox," or are they hopeless contradictions, with absolutely no hope of reconciliation in this life or the next? Even though some Calvinists make a valiant attempt to rescue Calvinism from its own internal contradictions and inconsistencies, they all fail, as they must. They must fail because the contradictions and inconsistencies in Reformed Theology are not merely apparent, but very real. No amount of wishful thinking will make them go away, in time or eternity. This should be of concern to anyone seriously thinking about becoming a Calvinist. Even if we were to ignore the contradictions and inconsistencies of Calvinism, which I do not think it wise to do, we still need to ask the question: is Calvinism compatible with Scripture? While it is *not possible* for a theological system to be self-contradictory *and* true, it is possible for it to be internally consistent and not true or not true to Scripture. It is the contention of this writer that the Calvinist is saddled with the double burden of being under a system which is both contradictory *and* unscriptural.

You may have noticed that I use the terms Calvinism and the Reformed faith interchangeably. You may also remember that Harris, a staunch Calvinist, used the terms "Calvinist" and "Reformed" in the same way. For all practical purposes, they are one and the same designation or label and will be used as such throughout this book. For Calvinist Paul Enns is right when he says:

> To speak of Calvinism is to speak of the Reformed faith. The term
> Reformed is today basically synonymous with Calvinism and dis-
> tinguishes the Calvinist churches ...[11]

The distinctive doctrines about which I am concerned and that we will consider in *The Dark Side of Calvinism* are *the Calvinist doctrines* of salvation and damnation. Calvinism as an entire system of theology is about much more than the doctrines of salvation and damnation. I am not concerned in this book about those other issues, no matter how important they may be. Often when Christians consider the Calvinist or Reformed doctrines of salvation and damnation, they have in mind the Calvinist doctrine of predestination. There is a good reason for equating the Calvinist doctrines of salvation and damnation with the Calvinist doctrine of predestination. For all practical purposes, the advocacy and promotion of the Calvinist doctrine of predestination is advocacy and promotion of the Calvinist doctrines of salvation and damnation. To say (as I do) that many Calvinists are extremely zealous in their commitment to win non-Calvinists (especially non-Calvinist Evangelicals) over to the Reformed version of the Christian faith would be to put it very mildly. In *Chosen by God*, R. C. Sproul says:

> They say there is nothing more obnoxious than a converted drunk.
> Try a converted Arminian. Converted Arminians tend to become
> flaming Calvinists, zealous for the cause of predestination.[12]

Sproul goes on to admit:

> You are reading the work of such a convert.[13]

In saying that "flaming Calvinists" are by definition "zealous for the cause of predestination," Sproul was no doubt attempting to inject a little humor into an otherwise serious topic. Nevertheless, the point he humorously makes should be cause for even greater concern. The reason Sproul speaks of "converted Arminians" is due both to his personal conversion from Arminianism to Calvinism and to the widespread and errant view held by Calvinists that all non-Calvinist Evangelicals are by definition Arminian in their theological convictions. Believing they are doing all non-Calvinists a favor by winning them over to Calvinism, many Calvinists have become proselytizers for the Reformed faith. Although some Calvinists are very "good" at winning non-Calvinist Christians into the Reformed faith, there are some obstacles in their way. For as Sproul says:

The very word *predestination* has an ominous ring to it. It is linked to the despairing notion of fatalism and somehow suggests that within its pale we are reduced to meaningless puppets. The word conjures up visions of a diabolical deity who plays capricious games with our lives. We seem to be subjected to the whims of horrible decrees that were fixed in concrete before we were born.[14]

But why does the word "predestination" make people think these terrible thoughts? Ironically, it is due (at least in part) to the fact that Calvinists promote a view of predestination which reduces (in their thinking and theology) *all* people "to meaningless puppets" and subjects *some* people "to the whims of horrible decrees that were fixed in concrete before" they "were born." In other words, the very Calvinist doctrinal distinctives that Sproul is "zealous for" and all consistent Calvinists embrace give "predestination" an "ominous ring." For all practical purposes, Calvinism amounts to *Theistic Fatalism*. A theist believes in a personal God. A fatalist believes the future (especially regarding the destiny of individuals) is fixed. A Theistic Fatalist believes that a personal God unconditionally determines where individuals go when they die, that is, whether they go to heaven or hell.

Lawrence Vance, one of America's leading critics of Calvinism, says:

Although Calvinists go out of their way to distance themselves from fatalism, they are in essence teaching the same thing. When a philosopher believes "what is to be will be" it is called determinism. When a stoic believes "what is to be will be" it is called fate. When a Moslem believes "what is to be will be" it is called fatalism. But when a Calvinist believes "what is to be will be" it is called predestination.[15]

Wayne Grudem, while attempting to defend Calvinism from the charge of fatalism, gives a very good definition of what I have in mind when I speak of fatalism. Unwittingly, he also concedes Calvinism to be a fatalistic system. According to Grudem:

By fatalism is meant a system in which human choices and human decisions really do not make any difference. In fatalism, no matter what we do, things are going to turn out as they have been previously ordained. Therefore, it is futile to try and influence the outcome of events or the outcome of our lives by putting forth any effort or making any significant choices, because these will not make any difference anyway.[16]

I have never read a better description of the Calvinist doctrine of predestination than this. When I say that Calvinism amounts to Theistic Fatalism or that it has a dark side, it is not for the purpose of offending Calvinists, though some will no doubt take offense at my use of these words. I use the label Theistic Fatalism because it perfectly describes Reformed Theology. I use the words *dark side,* because Calvinism has, as a central tenet, a very dark and disturbing distinctive. Everyone seriously considering a theological move in the direction of Reformed Theology deserves to know about Calvinism's dark side before they make a commitment to Calvinism. Considering Calvin's own admissions with regard to his doctrine of predestination (i.e., he called it a "horrible" or "dreadful decree") as it relates to damnation, I am not convinced that Calvin would object to the title of a book called *The Dark Side of Calvinism* that focused on his distinctive doctrines of reprobation and damnation.

I am also convinced that understanding Calvinism's dark side before making a commitment to Reformed Theology is the surest way to discourage a thoughtful and scripturally literate Christian from becoming a Calvinist. So there you have it. No hidden agenda. If you are not now a Calvinist, I have written this book with the conviction that given sufficient and accurate information about Reformed Theology, it is not likely you will ever become a Calvinist. If you already are a Calvinist, all I can hope and pray is that you will read through this book with both an open Bible and an open mind.

The truth is, some Calvinists do not want non-Calvinists to know the full implications of Calvinism until after they have become committed Calvinists. Even in the context of a church committed to the Reformed faith, some Calvinists think it unwise to introduce a new believer to the truly distinctive doctrines of Reformed Theology early on. From a pragmatic point of view, that is probably a wise course of action. Ethically speaking, it raises some serious questions. Loraine Boettner explains at least one of the reasons (or rationalizations) behind the reluctance of some Calvinists to initially lay it all out on the table early on:

> In preaching to ... those who are just beginning the Christian life ... At that early stage little need be said about the deeper truths which relate to God's part. As in the study of Mathematics we do

not begin with algebra and calculus but with the simple problems of arithmetic ...[17]

"The deeper truths" to which Boettner refers are the distinctive doctrines of Calvinism. If it were only a matter of spiritual milk versus spiritual meat, and what could be described as spiritually *age-appropriate* information, it would not really be an issue. That is not the case, however. As will be documented in the pages that follow, there is *danger* and not just *difficulty* in the theological deep of Reformed doctrine. Some Calvinists are not only less than totally up-front, but they are not even being altogether honest with the non-Calvinists whom they are targeting. In the promotion of doctrines, what is held back or not expressed (relative to those doctrines) can be very misleading. One *Reformed* Southern Baptist pastor, in an article entitled "Instructions for Local Church Reformation," advises other Calvinist pastors as follows:

> Don't tackle the whole church at one time. Choose a few men who are sincere, teachable and spiritually minded and spend time with them in study and prayer. They will help you to reform. ... In the pulpit, don't use theological language that is not found in the Bible. Avoid terms such as Calvinism, reformed, doctrines of grace, particular redemption, etc. Most people will not know what you are talking about. Many that do will become inflamed against you.[18]

Whatever the reason or reasons, many Calvinists, when promoting Reformed Theology to a potential convert to Calvinism, typically limit the discussion to those features that *seem* positive to the uninitiated. As in so many other areas of life, however, it is what they *do not* tell you that you really need to know in order to make a truly informed decision. Packaged just right, a little Calvinism may serve as a lure into the Reformed faith. When the dark side of Calvinism is exposed early on, it serves as a very strong deterrent. Most leading proponents of Calvinism know this all too well.

If the distinctives of Calvinism are as unscriptural as I believe (and will prove them to be), then *Calvinism undermines the scriptural doctrine of salvation* (John 5:16–18, 1 Tim. 2:4, 2 Pet. 3:8, etc.). That being the case, I just cannot leave the matter alone. By extension, Reformed Theology must also represent a *serious threat to at least some of the people for whom that salvation was provided by Christ's death on the cross* (1 John 2:2, 1 Tim. 2:5–6, Heb. 2:9, etc.). The salvation that is provided is also the salvation that is *offered to them in a truly scriptural proclamation of the gospel* of our Lord and Savior, Jesus Christ (1 Cor. 15:1–3).

These factors alone more than justify the kind of probe into Reformed Theology that *The Dark Side of Calvinism* is meant to be. I would, therefore, be spiritually derelict not to impress upon the reader the seriousness of this misguided, no matter how well intended, theological system called Calvinism. As most if not all Calvinists will agree, a great deal is at stake in the debate over the issues involved in this controversy. How we understand the doctrines of salvation and damnation in general, and the gospel of Jesus Christ in particular, is of great biblical, spiritual, and practical importance. In fact, this is the very argument often used by Calvinists to persuade other Christians to reconsider their non-Reformed views in favor of Reformed Theology. So Calvinists should not cry foul when their views are subjected to the same scrutiny for reasons they feel justified in challenging alternative and competing views. Besides, those who advocate Reformed Theology are typically not the *"can't we all just get along?"* or *"you believe what you believe and I will believe what I believe"* kind of Christians. While the temperament of individual Calvinists may cause some to keep their theological convictions a relatively private matter, Calvinism tends to make its adherents more theologically aggressive and spiritually hostile to non-Calvinists than they might otherwise be.

It should, therefore, be emphasized that the doctrinal differences that divide equally sincere and devout believers on both sides of the Calvinist controversy are substantial and serious. To suggest, as some have, that the differences between Calvinists and other Evangelicals are merely semantic and superficial reveals a serious misunderstanding of the core issues involved in this long-standing controversy. Without fear of contradiction, I can confidently say that all knowledgeable Calvinists agree with non-Reformed Evangelicals that the issues this book addresses are central to biblical Christianity. There should be no question or controversy on this point. Everyone should also agree that the differences between equally devout Christians on this matter are very pronounced. I have never met a serious and seasoned Calvinist who did not agree with me on at least this much. If you grant these two points (i.e., these issues are central and our differences are substantial) and couple them with the also indisputable fact that many Calvinists feel a need to reach *out to* and *into* the non-Calvinist world of Evangelical believers, you should also understand that there is simply no reasonable way to avoid this controversy.

Having said this, I would like to stress that my response to Calvinism is not intended to be and should not be interpreted as a personal attack on anyone. It is unfortunate but understandable that some on both sides of the Calvinist divide will be troubled by the fact that I openly and publicly challenge the views of individuals that are undoubtedly sincere in what they believe. I also realize that naming names is, for many, a Christian writer's *no-no*. Ironically, John MacArthur, a five-point Calvinist, comes to my defense (theoretically speaking). First, he asks:

> Is it inherently unkind or condemnatory to say someone else's view is errant?[19]

He then answers:

> Not if one has biblical authority for saying so. In fact, to remain silent and allow error to go unexposed and uncorrected is an abdication of the elder's role (Titus 1:9). The apostle Paul publicly called Peter a hypocrite for compromising biblical principles (Gal. 2:11–15). Peter had been publicly hypocritical; it was right that he be rebuked publicly (cf. 1 Tim. 5:20). To disagree with or critique someone's published views does not constitute a personal attack.[20]

MacArthur goes on to say:

> If the Church cannot tolerate polemic dialogue between opposing views—especially if Christian leaders cannot be held accountable for whether their teaching is biblical—then error will have free reign.[21]

On this we agree. Let there be no mistake, however, about one thing. In the world of contemporary evangelicalism, at least as far as American Christendom goes, if anyone is on the attack, it is the Calvinist. If I am right in my assessment of Calvinism relative to the Reformed doctrines of redemption and reprobation, it is my scriptural and spiritual obligation to defend the truth of Scripture from the distortion and challenge of Reformed doctrine. My contention is that Calvinism is not simply a protest or correction of the errors of the Roman Catholic Church, as so many mistakenly believe. Instead, it is a challenge to all Christians everywhere who believe God has a *saving love for* and *saving interest in* all of mankind, as expressed in John 3:16, 1 Timothy 2:4, 2 Peter 3:9, and elsewhere throughout the pages of Scripture.

As is thoroughly documented in the pages that follow, in Reformed Theology, God's redemptive love is not only minimized but also outright denied to untold millions of desperately lost souls. God's holy character and nature, however unwittingly, is also called into question. Not only so, but the very cross of Christ is *theologically robbed* of all *value* for countless millions of people who desperately need the forgiveness and cleansing that can only come from the Savior's *precious* blood (1 Pet. 1:18–19). The Reformed doctrine of a limited atonement, if it says anything at all, says this.

According to Reformed Theology, the world that God loved with a saving love is not as big as one might think from a reading of Scripture. Even those Calvinists who believe God loves *all* people have redefined that love, in their thinking and theology, to exclude any kind of saving grace for some of the people they say God loves. I know these are serious charges. Be assured that I do not make them lightly and, in fact, take no pleasure in making them. Realizing how serious these charges are, I have gone to great lengths in order to support them with irrefutable facts. I know that on every matter of substance and importance defended in this book there will be those who *dispute* what I say. I am equally confident that they will not be able to *refute* what I say. The reason I can say this without fear of contradiction is that I have carefully compared what Calvin and his followers teach with what our Lord and His apostles taught. It will, of course, be up to you to decide for yourself whether or not I have done my homework. It will also be up to you to decide if you believe the evidence supports my contention that Calvinist distinctives contradict scriptural doctrine.

If for some sad and unfortunate reason you believe the subject of God's saving love for mankind is unimportant, the matters that this book addresses will not likely hold your interest. If, however, you believe that nothing could be more important to the entire population of this planet in general and that nothing should be more important to the people of God in particular, then you should also understand how serious this matter is. We can take John 3:16 at face value or we can allow Calvinism to devalue, in our thinking and theology, the wonderful truth contained and conveyed in this and many other precious, important, and powerful passages of Scripture. We cannot do both.

What if Calvinists were content to simply win the lost to Christ and then build them up in the Reformed faith? If that were all that Calvinists were doing, they would hear little or nothing from me. Contemporary champions of Calvinism—men like R. C. Sproul, John Piper, James R. White, John MacArthur, and a host of others—are not simply *promoting* Reformed Theology among those new believers that *they have led to Christ* or that *have come to them* for spiritual guidance. Instead, as noted earlier, Calvinists are zealously proselytizing for the Reformed faith. If you are a part of a non-Reformed Evangelical Christian church or affiliation of churches, it is very likely that Calvinists have their sights set on winning you. Ready or not, they are coming for you and your church or church group (if they have not already arrived).

So much of the energy expended by Calvinists, energy that could and should be spent winning the lost to the Savior, is spent trying to win non-Calvinist Christians into the Reformed faith. Some Calvinists evidently see this as their sacred duty and primary calling in life. National organizations and nationally-syndicated radio programs have been established to aggressively challenge the views of any Christian or Christian church that does not agree with the distinctive doctrines of Calvinism, no matter what their commitment to the essentials of the historic and orthodox Christian faith is. Apparently, some Calvinists see themselves on the front lines of a spiritual and theological battle. They see themselves as Calvinists (and for Calvinism) fighting for the hearts and minds of the greater Evangelical Christian community. They desire to liberate non-Calvinist Christians from a Reformed-free faith. They actually view and treat many of the most dearly held convictions of non-Calvinist Evangelicals as symptomatic of a spiritual and theological disease, of which Reformed Theology is supposedly the *CURE.*[22]

Sproul and a number of other proponents of Calvinism have managed to work themselves into historically non-Calvinist communities (some say stealthily). They do this by offering help in what can be considered theologically neutral areas of general concern to Christians of all theological persuasions. They may present themselves as defenders of biblical inerrancy or experts on the dangers of the cults, but it is their Calvinist paradigm that they are most passionate to promote among those individual Christians and churches not already committed to the Reformed faith.

Without a doubt, some Calvinists really do want to help non-Calvinists on matters that are unrelated to Calvinism. Without hesitation, I would include Sproul in that company. All that I know of him and have read about him suggests that he is a man of impeccable integrity. I can only wish that

Sproul and all other Calvinists were a little more up-front about what does sometimes turn out to be a hidden agenda. Once the Calvinist gains the confidence of the non-Calvinist or the non-Calvinist church (often endearing himself in the process), he may be given the freedom to discuss the Calvinist worldview—what might otherwise be an unwelcome topic.

Why, might you ask, do Calvinists want non-Calvinists to become Calvinists? One reason is that Calvinism is by nature more or less evangelistically sterile, depending on how consistently the Calvinist applies his Calvinism. Thus, for Calvinist churches to grow, they need to bring non-Calvinists into the Reformed faith. Despite the many and loud protests of Calvinists to the contrary, Calvinism as a system of theology is not all that encouraging to evangelism and Calvinists are typically not all that effective (and sometimes not even all that interested) in winning the lost to Christ. Another reason is more theological in nature and perhaps motivated from genuine but misguided charity toward the non-Calvinist. That is, many leading advocates for the Calvinist cause and crusade are convinced that only Calvinists believe in and embrace *the doctrines of grace.* If Calvinists were to qualify this view by saying that only Calvinists believe in the Calvinist *version* of grace, I would agree. For it cannot be reasonably denied that Calvinists hold to a distinctive definition of grace. Whether or not they are right in the way they define grace is an altogether different matter. Nevertheless, Loraine Boettner, in *The Reformed Doctrine of Predestination* (a textbook for many in Reformed academia), boasts:

> The doctrine that men are saved only through the unmerited love
> and grace of God finds its full and honest expression *only* in the
> doctrines of Calvinism.[23]

Does this mean that non-Reformed Evangelicals embrace a partial and dishonest doctrine of salvation? Surely, such claims call for a critical examination and evaluation of Calvinism in light of Scripture. That is exactly what this book offers. I neither pull any theological punches in *The Dark Side of Calvinism,* nor do I hit below the spiritual belt. I am absolutely convinced that a factually and scripturally based refutation of Calvinism is impossible without a fair and accurate representation of Calvinism. While I will be accused by some of misrepresenting Calvinism, a fair and objective reading of this book will prove otherwise. If you are a convinced and committed Calvinist, I know that it will be difficult (though not impossible) for you to stay with me long enough to find out for yourself that what I call Calvinism is in fact the real thing. Can you objectively listen to the scripturally based arguments and evidence against Reformed Theology? If you can, I believe it is very likely that you will discover that Calvinism is in serious conflict with the truth of God's Word on a number of important matters related to the great and gracious saving work of God.

WHAT WE AGREE ON

Despite the sometimes serious and substantial differences between Calvinists and non-Calvinists, all Evangelicals agree, at least *in principle,* on the importance and priority of Scripture. As Sproul says:

> A brief glance at church history reveals that the debate over pre-destination is not between liberals and conservatives or between believers and unbelievers. It is a debate among believers, among godly and earnest Christians.[24]

All devout believers have a formally agreed upon standard by which to judge and evaluate all doctrines which they claim to be biblical. It is not Calvin's *Institutes of the Christian Religion, The Canons of Dort, The Westminster Confession of Faith,* or *The Heidelberg Catechism* that should be the determining factor as to what we believe.[25] It is not Augustine, Calvin, or Edwards[26] that we are to rely upon for our understanding of the truth. I wholeheartedly agree with the reformers, Calvinist and non-Calvinist, in affirming *Sola Scriptura.* Every Christian not only has the right, but the responsibility to personally *search the Scriptures* to discern what they mean by what they say (2 Tim. 2:15–17, 2 Pet. 1:20–21, Acts 17:11, Matt. 22:29). As Christians, we can and should learn from our spiritual elders. We are not bound, however, to what they taught unless it passes the objective test of scriptural truth. Since many pioneers of Reformed Theology disagreed so seriously among themselves, they do not always serve as a reliable guide in the pursuit of biblical truth. The widely acclaimed Calvinist writing team of David Steele and Curtis Thomas correctly states:

> The question of supreme importance is not how the system under consideration came to be formulated into five points, or why it was named Calvinism, but rather *is it supported by Scripture?* The final court of appeal for determining the validity of any theological system is the inspired, authoritative Word of God. If Calvinism can be verified by clear and explicit declaration of Scripture, then it must be received by Christians; if not, it must be rejected.[27]

Loraine Boettner could not be more right than when he says:

> The Scriptures are the final authority by which systems are to be judged.[28]

Not only so, but:

> In all matters of controversy between Christians, the Scriptures are accepted as the highest court of appeal.[29]

Charles Hodge accurately speaks for all thoughtful Evangelicals when he says:

> It is the duty of every theologian to subordinate his theories to the Bible, and teach not what seems to him to be true or reasonable, but simply what the Bible teaches.[30]

In *principle* then, I would agree with Calvinists as to how to evaluate a theological system or any of the distinctives of that system. This principle can be stated as follows: All Christians are obliged to believe and embrace all views that agree with the teaching of Scripture. Conversely, if the distinctives of a theological system are found to be in conflict with the teaching of God's holy and infallible Word, that system or the errant distinctives of that system ought to be rejected. Orthodoxy can ask nothing more or less.

With all of my heart, I embrace the grace of God and the fundamental and foundational truth that salvation is by grace and grace alone (Eph. 2:8–10). Unbelievers are absolutely and utterly dependent upon the grace of God to *save* them. Believers are absolutely and utterly dependent upon the grace of God to *sustain* them. I am insulted by the Calvinist's distinctive definition of grace, but not because I oppose salvation by grace alone. With all that is within me, I believe and rejoice in God's saving and sustaining grace. I am deeply troubled over the Reformed version of grace because through it, the precious and scriptural truths concerning grace are so maligned. I reject Reformed Theology because in it I find a scripturally distorted, spiritually offensive, and thoroughly unsatisfying substitute for God's saving grace.

All this is to say that the true grace of God is neither promoted nor protected in the distinctives of Reformed Theology. At best, Reformed Theology misrepresents God's saving grace in order that it may appear to correspond and conform to the equally disturbing *Reformed views* of sovereignty and predestination. For example, for those in a hopeless *caste* of humanity that

Calvinists call the reprobate, Reformed Theology denies even the existence of a grace intended to save them. (The term *caste* is appropriate, not *class,* since one is inexorably bound in one's *caste,* but can move from one *class* to another.) Calvinists, of course, contend that the grace of God is not insufficient to save the unsavable caste. The Calvinist will rightly say that it is not the fault of the *grace* of God that many people cannot be saved. Calvinists wrongly say or suggest that it is the *God* of grace Himself that is ultimately responsible (or to blame) for the plight of the reprobate. Blaming God for the damnation of those who end up in hell is either explicit or implicit in all forms of authentic Calvinism.

The charges I have leveled against Calvinism are true and are well documented in the writings of its most respected champions. If you do not like what I say about Calvinism, take it up with your Calvinist friends. This is what I have done. I have carefully read the writings of leading Calvinists both past and present. I know the difference between Calvinists who are considered *mainstream* and those who are considered *extreme.* Like Spurgeon, I can honestly and accurately say that when I speak of Calvinism:

> I speak of it as I find it in Calvin's Institutes, and especially in his Expositions. I have read them carefully. I take not my views of Calvinism from common repute but from his books.[31]

Reformed professor and pastor, Douglas Wilson, is one of several contributors to *Back to Basics: Rediscovering the Richness of the Reformed Faith.* In a review of my earlier book, Wilson, to the consternation of many Calvinists, says:

> George Bryson is a very unusual non-Calvinist. He is able to describe the doctrinal position of Calvinism without putting any extra eggs in the pudding. His descriptions are fair and accurate, and he clearly knows his subject. The first portion of the book, the place where he does all this, is very good. ... The name of this book is *The Five Points of Calvinism: Weighed and Found Wanting.*[32]

Although Wilson then criticizes the second half of the book, here he acknowledges several important facts with regard to my understanding and treatment of Calvinism. For this I am grateful. I especially appreciate the fact that he did not play the *Arminian card* but was able to simply refer to me as a non-Calvinist. While such a label does not tell you much about what I believe, it is, as far as it goes, accurate. The label that Calvinists attach to non-Calvinist Evangelicals almost universally is that of *Arminianism.* In my case, as in the case of hundreds of thousands, if not millions, of non-Calvinist Evangelicals, the *Arminian* label is simply not accurate.[33]

EITHER/OR?

The idea that an Evangelical could be neither Calvinist nor Arminian, or some kind of theological hybrid called a *Calminian,* is simply unthinkable to most leading Calvinists. Boettner speaks for most leading advocates of Reformed Theology when he says:

> It must be evident that there are just two theories which can be maintained by evangelical Christians upon this important subject; that all men who have made any study of it, and who have reached any settled conclusions regarding it, **must be either Calvinists or Arminians**. There is no other position which a "Christian" can take.[34]

According to Reformed theologian G. T. Shedd:

> Ultimately, there can be only two alternatives in evangelical understanding of the Christian Faith, the Calvinistic and the Arminian.[35]

Shedd also reasoned that for Christian believers, these two views are the only options that are:

> ... Logically possible ... [and] in the future, as the past, all evangelical believers will belong either to one dogmatic division or the other.[36]

In other words, if your conclusions are the result of study, assuming you are a Christian, you will agree with Boettner and Shedd. This approach apparently makes it easier for some Calvinists to dismiss any case against Calvinism. It does so by virtue of the fact that Calvinists are satisfied that Arminianism has been refuted. Just like those who mistakenly supposed that Jesus was born in Galilee and used that as their excuse not to accept Him as the Messiah of Israel, so Boettner and Shedd conclude all non-Calvinist Evangelicals must be Arminians. This results from the fact that either many Calvinists choose not to hear what non-Reformed mainstream Evangelicals are saying or they do not evidently understand what they are saying.

For the record, it is precisely because I have carefully studied this matter *as a Christian* that I am neither a Calvinist nor an Arminian. I cannot speak for every mainstream Evangelical, but I can speak for myself. I know what I believe and I know what James Arminius believed. I know the views of the Remonstrance.[37] I also understand the views of the many contemporary derivatives in the Arminian tradition, especially those most heavily influenced by the architect of modern day Arminianism, John Wesley.

Although I do not agree with even one of the distinctives of Calvinism, I disagree with all of the distinctives of Arminianism as well. This does not mean that I do not agree with them on some important issues related to the biblical doctrines of salvation and damnation. I do. For example, I believe strongly that Arminians are right about the universal provision of an atonement that makes salvation possible for all, but applicable only for those who believe. That is, I believe God has provided through Christ on the cross an atoning substitutionary sacrifice, so all *can be* saved. With Arminians, I also believe that the redemptive and atoning benefits of Christ's death are effectively restricted to those who *through faith alone in Christ alone* become both:

- *Justified by God alone* (Rom. 8:33)

And:

- *Regenerated by God alone* (John 1:12–13)

While the Calvinist doctrine of a limited atonement, which says Christ died redemptively *only* for some, is a distinctive of Calvinism, it is not the case that a universal atonement is a distinctive of Arminianism. That is, belief in a *provisionally* unlimited atonement does not set Arminians apart from most other believers. A universal atonement, provisionally speaking, is common to almost all, if not all, other orthodox believers.

To confuse all non-Calvinist views with Arminianism is as careless as confusing Calvinism with Roman Catholicism by virtue of the fact that Calvinists and Catholics both agree with the teachings of the Trinity, the virgin birth of Christ, and a host of other important doctrinal matters. Even so, Calvinists should not confuse all non-Calvinist Evangelicals with Arminians by virtue of the fact that they share some important theological views. Even the well-established fact that both Romanism and Calvinism have historical and theological roots in the thinking and theology of one man, Augustine, would not justify the silly notion that Calvinists are Roman Catholics or that Roman Catholics are Calvinists. Their respective views are simply too divergent to make such a claim.

I not only agree with some aspects of Arminian theology on salvation, I also agree with Calvinists on some important matters related to the biblical doctrine of salvation. For example, I am persuaded that all true believers are absolutely secure in Christ. This is in contrast to what Arminians believe and in agreement with what Calvinists teach. This, however, does not mean I believe in the Calvinist doctrine of perseverance of the saints, a truly distinctive doctrine of Calvinism, which is often confused with, but actually undermines, what I believe to be a truly biblical doctrine of eternal security.

While I find much to agree with in the teachings of Calvinists and Arminians, I cannot rightly claim to be either and should not be accused of or confused with either. For I disagree with all of the *distinctives* of both theological systems. The fact is that Arminians and Calvinists agree with each other on some matters of theological importance, even matters related to the great and gracious saving work of God.

It should be apparent to all thoughtful Christians that agreements between Calvinists and Arminians do not necessarily make Calvinists partly Arminian or Arminians partly Calvinists any more than they make me a Calvinist, Arminian, or *Calminian.* Now, if I subscribed to one or more of the distinctives of either one or both of these theological systems, it would be a different matter. I simply have no *reasonable* right, however, to call myself a Calvinist if I deny all of the distinctives of Calvinism. So too, Calvinists have no *reasonable* right to call me an Arminian. This, of course, will not keep some from doing so.

SCRIPTURALLY SOUND ALTERNATIVE

There is a scripturally sound and logically consistent alternative to both Calvinism and Arminianism. With a little theological tongue in cheek, though not much, I will refer to that alternative, at least initially, as *Biblicism.* This would make me a Biblicist. If you stay with me through the end of this book, you will know what I believe and why I believe it. For a Biblicist, the errors and extremes of any system can only be fully appreciated and properly evaluated in contradistinction to the truth of God's Word. Thus, the reader will not be left to wonder what I believe Scripture actually teaches on the most important issues with which this book is concerned.

For most Christians, even without a fully developed and systematically stated alternative to Calvinism, a simple and *unbiased* comparison of what Calvinism teaches with what Scripture says is sufficient to raise all kinds of theological red flags. You can test my thesis as follows: Take any important passage directly addressing the doctrine of salvation. Read it carefully, keeping in mind the immediate and greater contextual considerations. Then on a piece of paper, write down what you think the meaning of that passage is. Then look at what Calvin and other Reformed luminaries have to say about the same passage. It is highly unlikely that you will be able to see what they see unless and until they show it to you. Even then, they may have to be very persuasive and do some theological arm twisting to get you to agree with them.

1

IS CALVINISM THE GOSPEL?

F OR a Calvinist, the doctrinal distinctives of Calvinism (sometimes called the "doctrines of grace") are nothing more or less than the gospel of Jesus Christ found throughout the pages of the New Testament. Calvinists also equate these so-called doctrines of grace with the five points of Calvinism. The much-loved "Prince of Preachers," Charles Spurgeon, boasts:

> There is no such thing as preaching Christ and him crucified, unless you preach what … is called Calvinism … It is a nickname to call it Calvinism; Calvinism is the gospel, and nothing else.[38]

The very enthusiastic *Reformed* Baptist, John Piper, claims:

> The doctrines of grace (Total depravity, Unconditional election, Limited atonement, Irresistible grace, Perseverance of the saints) are the warp and the woof of the biblical gospel that so many saints have cherished for centuries.[39]

A little later, and on multiple occasions, we will consider this claim. Despite, however, their equating of Calvinism with the gospel, I have yet to meet a Calvinist who claims to have embraced the five points of Calvinism when he turned in faith to Jesus Christ. For some, the time span between conversion to Christ and conversion to Calvinism may be many years, even decades. Does this mean that they were not really saved before they came to understand and accept Reformed Theology *as* the gospel? If the five points of Calvinism can be equated with the gospel, which is *the power of God unto salvation for everyone who believes* (Rom. 1:16), why don't we hear Calvinists talking to the unsaved about the five points? If the Calvinist version of the doctrines of grace is equivalent to the true gospel, and if believing the true gospel is necessary to salvation, why is it that most true Calvinists

avoid any discussion of these so-called doctrines of grace when they are trying to win the lost to faith in Christ? These are very important questions that
demand an honest and straightforward answer.

To many Christians from a wide range of theological persuasions and
traditions, nothing could be more important than fidelity to the gospel of
Jesus Christ. In my many years as a Christian, I have known very few professing Christians who have abandoned the faith by overtly rejecting the
gospel of God's grace. Sadly, I have known many Christians who have fallen
prey to those who would distort the truth of the glorious gospel of our Savior.
To the Galatians, the apostle Paul says:

> *I marvel that you are turning away so soon from Him who called*
> *you in the grace of Christ, to a different gospel, which is not anoth-*
> *er; but there are some who would trouble you and want to pervert*
> *the gospel of Christ. But if we, or an angel from heaven, preach any*
> *other gospel to you than what we have preached to you, let him be*
> *accursed. (Gal. 1:6–8)*

To be sure, these are harsh words representing a serious and sobering
problem. Even so, it is possible, according to the apostle Paul, to *turn from*
the Lord after you have *turned to* the Lord. The question I would like to
put to my Calvinist friends is this: *Is the gospel of Calvinism, or the so-*
called five points of Calvinism, the gospel that Paul preached and that the
Galatians believed when they turned to the Lord? I ask this question because
many Calvinists confuse the five points of Calvinism with the gospel of
Jesus Christ. We know that the apostle Paul was:

> *... not ashamed of the gospel of Christ, for it is the power of God*
> *unto salvation to everyone who believes. (Rom. 1:16)*

When you first came in faith to Christ, or if you prefer, came to Christ
in faith, did you believe in the five points of Calvinism? Or did you simply
believe in and personally embrace the truths of Scripture in which we are
told that Christ died for our sins and then rose victorious from the grave?
The apostle Paul says:

> *I declare to you the gospel which I preached to you, which also*
> *you received and in which you stand, by which also you are saved,*
> *if you hold fast that word which I preached to you—unless you*
> *believed in vain. For I delivered to you first of all that which I also*

> *received: that Christ died for our sins according to the Scriptures,
> and that He was buried, and that He rose again the third day ac-
> cording to the Scriptures. (1 Cor. 15:1–4)*

If the gospel you believed in at your conversion was the true gospel of
1 Corinthians 15:1–4, what does that make the five points of Calvinism?
You probably did not even know about the five points until some time later.
Remember also that this so-called gospel of Calvinism totally altered your
understanding of the gospel of Jesus Christ when you converted to Calvinism.
Is it possible that you were saved by believing in the true gospel and then
got seriously sidetracked by later accepting the five points of Calvinism *as*
the gospel? Or is it possible that you did not really hear and heed the gospel
proclamation and invitation until after you were introduced to the five points
of Calvinism? Some outside (or barely inside) Reformed circles have suggested that I am overstating the case in accusing the Calvinist of equating
Calvinism with the gospel. A large body of Reformed literature and the testimony of leading Calvinists everywhere support this charge.

Reformed theologian Herman Hoeksema says that:

> ... for me the truth of the gospel and the Reformed faith are
> *synonymous.*[40]

According to Calvinist David Engelsma:

> Calvinism is the Gospel. Its outstanding doctrines are simply the
> truths that make up the Gospel.[41]

Similarly, Calvinist Arthur Custance says:

> Calvinism is the Gospel and to teach Calvinism is in fact to preach
> the Gospel. It is questionable whether a dogmatic theology which
> is not Calvinistic is truly Christian.[42]

If you are a Calvinist now, *when* did the truth of the gospel and the
Reformed faith become synonymous to you? Odds are it was some time
after you at least thought you had received Christ as Lord and Savior. The
question is, could you really have been saved believing that which turned
out not to be the true gospel after all? It is clear from his own testimony that
Spurgeon did not even know about the five points or the so-called doctrines
of grace until he was introduced to them some time after coming to faith in
Christ. If we must believe the gospel to be saved, as Calvinists concede, are

all Calvinists lost between the period when they thought they received Christ as Lord and Savior and when they became convinced of Calvinism?

According to Loraine Boettner:

> ... the Reformed faith ... is beyond all doubt the teaching of the Bible and of reason.[43]

Presumably speaking for most, if not all Calvinists, Boettner also says:

> ... we ... hold that a **full** and **complete** exposition of the Christian system can be given only on the basis of the truth as set forth in the Calvinistic system.[44]

Thus, according to Boettner, your Christian system is, at best, only *partial* and *incomplete* if it is not in accordance with Calvinism. Boettner does not beat around the theological bush when he says:

> The Bible unfolds a scheme of redemption which is Calvinistic from beginning to end, and these doctrines are taught with such inescapable clearness that the question is settled for all those who accept the Bible as the Word of God.[45]

That's it. You either believe that the Bible teaches the Reformed doctrine of redemption, and by extension, the Reformed doctrine of reprobation, or you do not accept the Bible as the Word of God. If you think this sounds a bit extreme, brace yourself. The Calvinist claims for Reformed Theology go much further than even this. For example, a theological giant to many Calvinists, B. B. Warfield, says:

> ... Calvinism is just Christianity ... nothing more or less than the hope of the world.[46]

Calvinists Kenneth Talbot and Gary Crampton express what I mean when they say:

> ... any compromise of Calvinism is a step towards humanism.[47]

Boettner goes so far as to say that:

> There is no consistent stopping place between Calvinism and atheism.[48]

To say that Calvinists take their Calvinism seriously would be a serious understatement. If Calvinism is what they believe it to be—the gospel, Christianity, the hope of the world, etc.—then *they should* take it very seriously.

Based on their conviction that *Calvinism is the gospel,* it might seem logical that Calvinists would deny that non-Calvinists could be true Christians, or that they would believe that only Calvinists could be saved. Logically that would be a safe assumption. Calvinists, however, are not usually bound by the logical implications of their theological system. Most Calvinists do not go so far as to deny that non-Calvinist Evangelicals are true Christians. Only the most extreme—those on the fringes of Calvinism—would go so far as to say that only Calvinists are or will be saved. Boettner even says that:

> As Calvinists we gladly recognize as our fellow Christians any who trust Christ for their salvation, regardless of how inconsistent their other beliefs may be. We do believe, however, that Calvinism is the only system which is wholly true.[49]

- If, as Calvinists believe, Calvinism is equal to the gospel,

And:

- If, as Calvinists agree, a lost person must believe the true gospel in order to become a saved person,

And:

- If, as Calvinists contend, non-Calvinists do not believe in the true gospel,

Then:

- How can Calvinists accept non-Calvinists as saved?

Logically they can't. But, in fact, they do. As far as I can tell, mainstream Calvinists do not even try to explain how this can be. The way many leading advocates of Calvinism view non-Calvinists is probably best captured in the words credited to F. E. Hamilton by Boettner. According to Boettner, Hamilton says:

> A blind, deaf and dumb man can, it is true, know something of the world about him through the senses remaining, but his knowledge

will be very imperfect and probably inaccurate. In a similar way, a Christian who never knows or never accepts the deeper teachings of the Bible which Calvinism embodies, may be a Christian, but he will be a very imperfect Christian, and it should be the duty of those who know the whole truth to attempt to lead him into the only storehouse which contains the full riches of true Christianity.[50]

That would mean that all non-Reformed Evangelicals, men like Billy Graham, C. S. Lewis, John Wesley, D. L. Moody, Charles Ryrie, Chuck Swindoll, Chuck Smith, Charles Stanley, as well as the untold millions of others that they represent, are spiritually *blind, deaf, and dumb*. It is amazing that given this deplorable spiritual condition of the non-Reformed, the Calvinist George Whitefield could have put up with John Wesley for so long.

Even what appear on the surface to be conciliatory statements made by Calvinists about other Evangelicals often turn out to be backhanded compliments. I emphasize the word *backhanded*. For example, Boettner approvingly quotes an early editor of *Christianity Today,* S. G. Craig, as saying:

> The Calvinist ... does not differ from other Christians in kind, but only in degree, as more or less good specimens of a thing differ from more or less bad specimens of a thing.[51]

If that is supposed to make us feel better, I cannot imagine what a statement meant to offend would sound like. Likewise, Boettner says:

> We are not all Calvinists as we travel the road to heaven, but we shall all be Calvinists when we get there.[52]

In like manner, Charles Spurgeon says:

> I do not ask whether you believe Calvinism. It is possible you may not. But I believe you will before you enter heaven.[53]

Does this mean that Spurgeon believed that all non-Calvinists would, during their earthly sojourn, eventually be persuaded that Calvinism is true? If not, how is it that a Christian who is never convinced of or converted to Calvinism in this life will become a Calvinist before he enters the next life? Because, according to Spurgeon:

> God ... will wash your brains before you enter heaven.[54]

Thus, unless you are a Calvinist, you are more or less a bad specimen of a Christian in need of a theological brainwashing. With these convictions, the Calvinist can rationalize the proselytizing of other Christians, including the splitting of non-Calvinist churches, as nothing more than assisting God in the brainwashing process. Admittedly, sometimes what Calvinists say about other Christians is not meant to make *us* feel bad or to put us down. Rather, it is meant to make *them* feel good about themselves and *their* Reformed faith. The fact that they do so at our expense is, for many Calvinists, as unfortunate as it is unavoidable.

A true Calvinist believes not only that the five points of Calvinism represent the true gospel and the doctrines of grace taught in Scripture, but also that these doctrinal distinctives of Calvinism embody what they call *the deeper truths* of Scripture. These are *not* the common doctrines that Calvinism *shares* with Christianity in general, but the *distinctives* that *separate* them from the greater Christian world. Supposedly, the doctrinal *distinctives* of Calvinism are taught with such "inescapable clearness" in the pages of Scripture that virtually anyone should be able to see them by reading Scripture alone. Spurgeon tells us:

> A learned lord, an infidel, once said to Whitfield, "Sir I am an infidel, I do not believe the Bible, but if the Bible be true, you are right, and your Arminian opponents are wrong. If the Bible be the Word of God, the doctrines of grace are true"; adding that if any man would grant him the Bible to be the truth, he would challenge him to disprove Calvinism.[55]

Spurgeon goes on to say:

> The doctrines of original sin, election, effectual calling, final perseverance, and all those great truths which are called Calvinism— though Calvin was not the author of them, but simply an able writer and preacher upon the subject—are, I believe, the essential doctrines of the Gospel that is in Jesus Christ.[56]

He also claims:

> It is no novelty ... I am preaching; no new doctrine. I love to proclaim these strong old doctrines, which are called by nickname Calvinism, but which are surely and verily the revealed truth of God as it is in Christ Jesus.[57]

Understandably, given the mutually exclusive explanations as to why the Calvinist and non-Calvinist Evangelicals believe some go to heaven and others to hell, it is extremely difficult, if not impossible, for Reformed theologians to make a case *for* Calvinism without making a case *against* all other forms of Evangelicalism. I do not fault them for doing so. I readily acknowledge that an explanation and defense of the views of a Biblicist is to some degree an attack on Calvinism as a system. This can be true even when Calvinism is not the primary subject at hand.

As noted earlier, while some Calvinists only grudgingly admit that a non-Calvinist can be a true Christian, others gladly accept us as fellow believers and joint heirs with Christ. Even among those who are apparently happy to count us as *family,* however, many suggest that we may not really love the Lord or His Word with the same fervency or depth as they do. For example, D. James Kennedy, a man not usually considered hostile to non-Calvinists, says:

> I am a Calvinist precisely because I love the Bible and the God of the Bible. The doctrines of the Calvinist theological system are the doctrines of the Bible. When you get to know what we actually believe you may find you too are a Calvinist, especially if you love the Lord Jesus Christ and desire with all your heart to serve Him.[58]

I hate to impugn motives, but in reading this, it seems reasonable to conclude that Kennedy is using a bit of spiritual psychology. After all, what Christian does not want to *love the Lord Jesus and desire with all his heart to serve Him?* I know I do. If Kennedy was right, I should want to become a Calvinist immediately. Or perhaps I should have been a Calvinist all along. I do not pretend to know Kennedy's heart or motive for saying what he says here. His words, however, come across as so very condescending to me. Can you imagine the protests if a non-Calvinist were to reverse all of this? Suppose I were to say:

- As Biblicists, we gladly recognize as our fellow Christians any who trust Christ for their salvation, regardless of how inconsistent their other beliefs may be. We do believe, however, that Calvinism as a system is very defective.

- A blind, deaf, and dumb man can, it is true, know something of the world about him through the senses remaining, but his knowledge will be very imperfect and probably inaccurate. In a similar way, a Calvinist, who never knows or accepts the deeper teachings of the Bible which Calvinism does not include, may be a Christian, but he will be a very imperfect Christian, and it should be the duty of all Biblicists, because we know the truth, to attempt to lead the misguided Calvinist into the only storehouse which contains the full riches of true Christianity.

- The Biblicist does not differ from Calvinist Christians in kind, but only in degree, as more or less good specimens of a thing differ from more or less bad specimens of a thing.

- We are not all Biblicists as we travel the road to heaven, but I believe before we enter heaven, we shall all become Biblicists and therefore cease to be Calvinists.

- I am a Biblicist and not a Calvinist precisely because I love the Bible and the God of the Bible. The doctrines of the Biblicist theological system are the doctrines of the Bible. When you get to know what we actually believe you may find you too are a Biblicist, especially if you love the Lord Jesus Christ and desire with all your heart to serve Him.

- Before you get into heaven, if you are a Calvinist, God will wash your brains of Reformed dogma and you will become a Biblicist.

While Calvinists equate and therefore confuse Calvinism with the gospel of Jesus Christ, Calvinism is most definitely not the gospel of our Lord and His grace. If you think it is, my challenge to you is to keep reading for scriptural evidence to the contrary.

THE AUGUSTINIANISM OF CALVINISM

Although the five points of Calvinism are most closely associated with the sixteenth century Protestant Reformer John Calvin (and for good reason), they did not originate with him. Calvinists would, first and foremost, contend that the five points faithfully represent the teaching of the New Testament in general, and of the apostle Paul in particular. Obviously, I do not agree with this contention. I do, however, agree with Calvinists when they point out that Calvin was not the first notable figure in church history to champion the views that led to what is today the Calvinist or Reformed system of theology. Just as the *Synod of Dort,* which first formally presented these points as the five points of Calvinism, was a Calvinist synod, so John Calvin was an Augustinian.

This is especially true with regard to the later Augustinian view of predestination and its bearing upon the salvation of the elect and the damnation of the reprobate. Norman Geisler makes the point that Augustine held two contradictory views, reflecting a change of thought over time. According to Geisler, it is the views of Augustine in the latter part of his Christian life that had such an influence on Calvin and many other Calvinists down through the centuries. This is especially so with regard to the Reformed view of salvation and damnation.[59] Lawrence Vance makes the case that Augustine was at once both the father of Roman Catholicism and of Reformed Theology.[60]

Because of Augustine's association with the Roman Catholic Church, there are some uninformed Calvinists who believe that Calvin was not influenced by Augustine and that to make this connection is nothing more than a smear tactic on the part of anti-Calvinists. Calvin's repeated references to Augustine, however, reveal that he gave a lot of weight to what Augustine taught and was in fact echoing Augustine on the most central tenets of Reformed doctrine. Because some Calvinists object to the assertion that Calvin relied upon Augustine to develop and defend his doctrinal distinctives, I will quote from a wide variety of leading Calvinists to establish this statement. Herman Hanko, as non-Roman Catholic as one can be, says:

> In fact, our fathers at Dordrecht knew well that these truths set forth in the Canons could not only be traced back to the Calvin Reformation; they could be traced back to the theology of Saint Augustine who lived almost a millennium before Calvin did his work in Geneva. For it was Augustine who had originally defined these truths. Calvin himself, again and again, pays tribute to the work of Augustine and points out that what he is saying has been said before him by the Bishop of Hippo. The Synod of Dordrecht was conscious of this.[61]

In agreement, Loraine Boettner says:

> It was Calvin who wrought out this system of theological thought with such logical clearness and emphasis that it has ever since borne his name. He did not, of course, originate the system but only set forth what appeared to him to shine forth so clearly from

the pages of Holy Scripture. Augustine had taught the essentials of the system a thousand years before Calvin was born, and the whole body of the leaders of the Reformation movement taught the same. But it was given to Calvin with his deep knowledge of Scripture, his keen intellect and systematizing genius, to set forth and defend these truths more clearly and ably than had ever been done before.[62]

Calvinist theologian, R. Laird Harris, also agrees when he points out that:

Although Calvin gave the Reformed doctrine its most thorough formulation, the theology had long been held. Calvin would have been the first to deny its novelty. ... Indeed Calvinism is often called Augustinianism.[63]

Boettner went so far as to say:

The Reformation was essentially a revival of Augustinianism ...[64]

J. I. Packer echoes this sentiment saying:

The Reformation was an Augustinian Revival.[65]

Edwin Palmer explains:

The name Calvinism has often been used, not because Calvin was the first or sole teacher, but because after the long silence of the Middle Ages, he was the most eloquent and systematic expositor of these truths.[66]

For these reasons and some others, Calvin gets the lion's share of credit for what he did with the teachings of Augustine. According to Boettner:

Inasmuch as it was Calvin who first formulated these principles into a more or less complete system, that system, or creed, if you will, and likewise those principles which are embodied in it, came to bear his name.[67]

Boettner explains the Reformed view of Calvin's role in Calvinism as follows:

Calvin's active and powerful intellect led him to sound the depths of every subject which he touched. In his investigations about God and the plan of redemption he went very far, penetrating into mysteries concerning which the average man seldom if ever dreams. He brought to light a side of Scripture which has as yet been very much in the shade and stressed those deep truths which in the ages preceding the Reformation had comparatively escaped notice in the Church. He brought to light forgotten doctrines of the apostle Paul, and fastened them in their full and complete sense upon one great branch of the Christian Church.[68]

Spurgeon probably speaks for all authentic Calvinists when he says:

That doctrine which is called "Calvinism" did not spring from Calvin; we believe that it sprang from the great founder of all truth. Perhaps Calvin himself derived it mainly from the writings of Augustine. Augustine obtained his views, without doubt, through the Spirit of God, from the diligent study of the writings of Paul, and Paul received them of the Holy Ghost, from Jesus Christ the great founder of the Christian dispensation. We use the term then, not because we impute any extraordinary importance to Calvin having taught these doctrines. We would be just as willing to call them by any other name, if we could find one which would be better understood, and which on the whole would be as consistent with fact.[69]

William S. Reid, in the *Evangelical Dictionary of Theology,* says:

John Calvin, often regarded as "the systematizer of the Reformation," was a second generation Protestant Reformer of the sixteenth century who brought together biblical doctrine systematically, in a way that no other Reformer before him had done ... all Reformed and Presbyterian churches look back to him as the founder of their biblical-theological doctrinal position. ... Although Calvin was the systematizer of the Reformation theology, since his day those who have accepted his structure of theology have continued to develop many of his ideas. During his own lifetime he himself developed his thought in the successive editions of his *Institutes of the Christian Religion.* With the writing of various Calvinistic confessions as the Heidelberg Catechism (1563), and the Canons of Dort (1618), and the Westminster Confession and

Catechisms (1647–48) additions to and further developments in theological thought have appeared.[70]

While Reformed Theology—the theology of Calvin and Calvinism itself—is often thought of as the theology of the Reformation, this is imprecise at best. In fact, church historian Bruce Shelly says:

> Calvin's leadership ... shaped a third reformation tradition. Today we call it Reformed or Calvinistic Christianity. It includes all Presbyterians, Dutch and German Reformed Churches, and many Baptists and Congregationalists.[71]

In fairness, I should point out that when Reformed denominations become liberal they lose their Calvinism along with their part in biblical Christianity. Thus, one could qualify the Calvinists among these groups as Evangelical or even Conservative Presbyterians, Congregationalists, etc. I should also point out that while there have always been Calvinist Baptists, variously called Reformed, Particular, or even Sovereign Baptists, etc., Baptists as a whole tend not to buy in to Reformed Theology. Still, in all of the mainstream Baptist denominations, there are those who are mounting a major effort to turn all Baptists (or as many as possible) into Reformed or Calvinist Baptists. Some even believe that a non-Reformed Baptist is not a true Baptist. One only needs to read *The Other Side of Calvinism* or the materials available through the *Baptist Fire* web page[72] to see how wrong it is to equate Reformed Theology with the theology of mainstream Baptists.

THE FIVE POINTS OF CALVINISM

So what is meant by Reformed Theology? What does the Calvinist theologian have in mind when he refers to the Reformed gospel or the gospel of Calvinism? What is it that the Calvinist apologist/proselytizer so desperately seems to want all non-Calvinist Evangelicals to believe and embrace? According to Boettner:

> The Calvinistic system especially emphasizes five distinct doctrines. These are technically known as "The Five Points of Calvinism," and they are the main pillars upon which the super-structure rests.[73]

Due to the logical interdependence between the five points, most Calvinists argue, and I believe rightly so, that you cannot reasonably embrace one point without also embracing the other four. That is, most leading proponents of Calvinism say that to be consistent, we must embrace *all* of the points if we embrace *any* of them.

HAPPY INCONSISTENCY

In *Chosen by God,* R. C. Sproul is right when he says:

> To be a four-point Calvinist one must misunderstand at least one of the five points ...[74]

While not everyone who calls himself a Calvinist is a Calvinist, there are some among those who call themselves four-point Calvinists who are nevertheless true, albeit inconsistent Calvinists. One of the more notable four-point Calvinists is A. H. Strong, creator of the *Strong's Exhaustive Concordance of the Bible.* As Sproul says:

> There always is the possibility ... of the happy inconsistency by which people hold incompatible views at the same time.[75]

Nevertheless, Boettner explains that:

> These are not isolated and independent doctrines but are so inter-related that they form a simple, harmonious, self-consistent system; and the way in which they fit together as component parts of a well-ordered whole has won the admiration of thinking men of all creeds. Prove any one of them true and all the others will follow as logical and necessary parts of the system. Prove any one of them false and the whole system must be abandoned. They are found to dovetail perfectly one into the other.[76]

While I take issue with the view that Calvinism as a complete system (even relative to the doctrines of salvation and damnation) is self-consistent, I cannot see how or why one could believe in one or more of the five points without also (logically speaking) believing in all of the five points of Calvinism. In fewer words, Joseph Wilson says essentially the same thing as Boettner. That is:

> The five doctrines form a harmonious whole. Not one of them can be changed without giving disharmony to the whole and causing confusion as to how men are really saved.[77]

The issue is more than consistency. These points not only agree with one another, they imply and require one another, as they are understood in Calvinism. Charles W. Bronson says that:

> In order for one to be consistent he must hold all five points of Calvinism.[78]

Grover Gunn says:

> The five points are logically related such that any one of them implies the other.[79]

Gise J. Van Baren reasons:

> The five points of Calvinism are closely related. One point presupposes the others.[80]

Arthur Custance reasons as follows:

> Granted any one of these five points, the rest must follow inevitably; deny any one of them and the whole structure is endangered. One cannot satisfactorily defend some points but not the others.[81]

Edwin Palmer says:

> The Five Points of Calvinism all tie together. He who accepts one of the points will accept the others.[82]

As to the importance of the five points to the Calvinist or Reformed community, Herman Hoeksema says:

> All five points of Calvinism … are important. Indeed if any one of the five points of Calvinism is denied, the Reformed heritage is completely lost.[83]

REALLY ONLY ONE POINT

J. I. Packer cautions:

> The very act of setting out Calvinistic soteriology in the form of five distinct points (a number due merely to the fact that there were five Arminian points for the Synod of Dort to answer) tends to obscure the organic character of Calvinistic thought on this subject. For the five points, though separately stated, are really inseparable.

They hang together; you cannot reject one without rejecting them all, at least in the sense in which the Synod meant them. For to Calvinism there is really only one point to be made in the field of soteriology.[84]

Soteriology is the technical term used by theologians to refer to the doctrine of salvation. Insofar as an affirmation of any one of the five points is concerned, it does not matter where you begin, according to Calvinism. Logically:

- If these points are indeed "inseparable";

- If one point "presupposes the others";

- If there is really "only one point to be made" in the Calvinist doctrine of salvation;

And:

- If you accept any point of Calvinism,

Then:

- You will eventually, if you are consistent, become a five-point Calvinist.

The views stated above represent the entire Calvinist community of believers. Those who understand and follow through with the implications of any one of the points, no matter what they call themselves at the outset, must logically, and will eventually, embrace the *entire* doctrinal system of salvation and damnation in Calvinism. Although all of the points are logically inter-related, if any one point stands out above the others, it is the second point—unconditional election. Even so, most Calvinists emphasize the importance of embracing all five points. Fred Phelps says:

> If you do not know the Five Points of Calvinism, you do not know the Gospel, but some perversion of it.[85]

Phelps also charges:

> If you do not have a thorough knowledge and understanding of the Five Points of Calvinism you are truly in darkness and ignorance of all divine truth. And if you do not have an intelligent belief in

and love for the Five Points of Calvinism, you have no rational religion, but are bound up in superstition and religious lies.[86]

While many mainstream Calvinists would not like the way Phelps states the Calvinist position, what he says *is* the position of Calvinism. It may make some Calvinists uncomfortable to hear this, but Phelps is just laying it all out on the table.

2

UNCONDITIONAL ELECTION/ REPROBATION

EXPLAINED

ARGUABLY, the most important and foundational distinctives of Reformed Theology are to be found in the Calvinist doctrines of sovereignty and predestination. I say this because it is sovereignty and predestination *as defined by* Calvin and Calvinists that the non-Calvinist community takes issue with. Sovereignty and predestination, defined in a way that corresponds to what Scripture says, pose no real problem for the non-Calvinist Evangelical. Chapter Twelve was written to specifically address these very important scriptural truths. For now, it should be understood that these concepts, as defined in Calvinism, serve as the theological and philosophical basis and justification for the Calvinist doctrines of unconditional election and reprobation.

HYPER-CALVINISM VERSUS HYPO-CALVINISM

For this discussion, it is essential to understand that regarding salvation and damnation there are basically two kinds of Calvinists. Don't let the technical sounding nature of these terms trouble you. The concepts and positions they represent are not all that difficult to understand. A majority of Calvinists are what can be called hypo-Calvinists.[87] *Webster's Dictionary* defines *hypo* as "less than normal." The dictionary also makes it clear that this term is often used as a pejorative and says that it refers to something that is "denoting a lack or deficiency." The Greek form of this word is *hupo*. A hypo-Calvinist is accused (by hyper-Calvinists) of *stopping short* of totally embracing the *implications* of the teachings of John Calvin.

A lesser, but significant, number of Calvinists are what can be called hyper-Calvinists.[88] *Webster's* defines "hyper" as "more than normal; excessive." It is made up of two Latin words, *hax* and *par*. *Hax* is the word for "more," while *par* is the word for "normal." Hence, when hyper is affixed to a word, as in hyperactive, hypersensitive, or hypercritical, it means that a person so labeled is more active, more sensitive, or more critical than what is normal. The Greek form of the word is *huper.* A hyper-Calvinist is accused (by hypo-Calvinists) of *going beyond* the *explicit* teachings of John Calvin.

According to the widely read and highly respected Church Historian (who also happens to be a Calvinist) Phillip Schaff:

> Calvinism ... starts with a double decree of predestination, which antedates and is the divine program of human history. This program includes the successive stages of the creation of man, a universal fall and condemnation of the human race, a partial redemption and salvation: all for the glory of God and the display of His attributes of mercy and justice. History is only the execution of the original design. ... The beginning and the end, God's immutable plan and the issue of the world's history, must correspond.[89]

Schaff shines a light on the dark side of Calvinism by asking the questions:

> What will become of the immense majority of human beings who live and die without God and without hope in the world? Is this terrible fact due to the eternal counsel of God, or to the free agency of man?[90]

He then explains:

> The Calvinistic system involves a positive truth: the election to eternal life by free grace, and the negative inference: the reproba-tion to eternal death by arbitrary justice.[91]

Is "arbitrary justice" an oxymoron? Is it possible to speak rationally of a justice that is arbitrary? A thoughtful reflection on the meaning of these terms suggests that they cannot go together without a serious redefinition of at least one of them. Arbitrary justice is the equivalent of "dry water" or an "innocent criminal." Most Calvinists would object to the use of the word arbitrary in this context, but Schaff is only pointing out a built-in contradiction of Calvinism that should be *evident to* all Calvinists and *admitted by* all Calvinists.

PREDESTINATION AS ELECTION/REPROBATION

Often when a Calvinist uses the term "predestination," with which Calvinism is most closely identified, he has in mind the so-called second point of Calvinism, which logically must include reprobation, which results in eternal damnation. In his advocacy of Calvinism, Sproul says:

> Our study focuses on predestination in the narrow sense, restricting it to the ultimate question of predestined salvation or damnation, what we call *election* and *reprobation*.[92]

The reason Sproul limits his discussion of predestination to *"election and reprobation"* is because together these are the most important examples of predestination in Reformed Theology. According to Calvinism, election and reprobation are simply the outworking of sovereignty and predestination as they are brought to bear on the salvation of the elect and the damnation of the reprobate. This equation of predestination with election *and* reprobation is stated plainly by Calvin as follows:

> By predestination we mean the eternal decree of God, by which he determined with himself whatever he wished to happen with regard to every man. All are not created on equal terms, but some are preordained to eternal life, others to eternal damnation; and, accordingly, as each has been created for one or other of those ends, we say that he has been predestined to life or death.[93]

In a discussion of how Calvin and the early Calvinist reformers used the term predestination, the hyper-Calvinist scholar Herman Hoeksema says:

> By predestination was meant God's decree concerning the eternal destiny of His rational, moral creatures. And this counsel of predestination was distinguished again according to the different objects as election and reprobation.[94]

What Hoeksema says here is not only strikingly similar to what Calvin said, but also essentially the same as what the hypo-Calvinist Loraine Boettner says about election and reprobation. According to Boettner:

> The doctrine of absolute Predestination of course logically holds that some are foreordained to death as truly as others are foreordained to life. The very terms "elect" and "election" imply the terms "non-elect" and "reprobation." When some are chosen out others are left not chosen. The high privileges and glorious destiny

of the former are not shared with the latter. This, too, is of God. We believe that from all eternity God has intended to leave some of Adam's posterity in their sins, and that the decisive factor in the life of each is to be found only in God's will.[95]

Despite the fact that many hypo-Calvinists prefer to sharply distinguish between an election that is to salvation and a reprobation that is to damnation, such distinctions are not compatible with a consistent Reformed Theology. Many just do not want to face or admit the dark side of their theological system. Those included in the two castes of Calvinism are simply chosen for two very different destinies. The former are *elect to* salvation and the latter are, in a manner of speaking, *elect to* damnation. Notice that Boettner says that: "some are foreordained to death *as truly* as others are foreordained to life." If foreordination to life is an election to salvation, it follows that foreordination to reprobation is an election to damnation.

From a reading of popular Christian literature, however, it is obvious that many Evangelicals are either confused, or they are in *denial*, about the meaning and implication of unconditional election and its flip side, unconditional reprobation. *The Westminster Confession of Faith* says:

> By the decree of God, for the manifestation of his glory, some men and angels are predestined unto everlasting life; and others are foreordained to everlasting death. (III) These angels and men, thus predestined and foreordained, are particularly and unchangeably designed, and their number so certain and definite, that it cannot be either increased or diminished. (IV)

As will be considered in more detail later, it is not what a man is, was, or will do that moves God to accept (elect) him or reject (reprobate) him. For as *The Westminster Confession of Faith* also says:

> God, from all eternity, did by the most wise and holy counsel of his own will, freely, and unchangeably ordain whatsoever comes to pass. ... (I) Although God knows whatsoever may or can come to pass upon all supposed conditions, yet hath he not decreed anything because he fore-saw it as future, or as that which would come to pass upon such conditions. (II)

Not long ago, an article on Calvinism was published in the popular Evangelical magazine *Christianity Today*. The article focused on a possible split among Southern Baptists over Calvinism. Drawing the greater Christian community's attention to this matter is a very good thing. Rather than help the reader understand the reasons for this possible split, however, the author only contributed to the already serious misunderstanding behind the controversy. He did so by equating the doctrine of unconditional election to the scriptural truth that "salvation is without merit." It is, of course, true that Calvinists believe that "salvation is without merit," but so do all Evangelicals. Many non-Calvinist Evangelicals just as strongly believe and contend that salvation in the biblical sense is without merit. This does not necessarily entail, however, a belief that God saves and damns unconditionally. "Salvation without merit" belongs in the category of doctrines that are held in common by all Evangelical believers and not just Calvinists.

Calvinists should take partial responsibility for this confusion because they suggest that only Calvinists embrace a salvation without merit. Many non-Calvinist Evangelicals, however, should also take some responsibility for not paying closer attention to how Calvinists explain what they mean by unconditional election. One does not have to be theologically sophisticated to see the rather substantial difference between the Calvinist view of election and reprobation and what Scripture teaches on the topic of salvation and damnation. Before we take a closer look at the Reformed doctrine of election and reprobation, it should be understood that a rejection of this Calvinist distinctive does not mean that we should deny that Scripture teaches a doctrine of election. As Boettner says:

> Every Christian must believe in some kind of election; for while the Scriptures leave unexplained many things about the doctrine of Election, they make very plain the FACT that there has been an election.[96]

In fact, as most Calvinists would agree, Scripture uses the word "election" and related forms of this same word in more than one way. With the distinctively Calvinist doctrine of *unconditional* election in mind, the Reformed scholar and hyper-Calvinist Herman Hanko explains:

> ... it is certain that the truth of unconditional election stands at the foundation. ... This truth is the touchstone of the Reformed faith. It is the basis of the truth of God concerning our salvation. It is the very heart and core of the gospel. It is the basis of all the comfort and assurance of the people of God in the midst of the world. It

alone inspires in the hearts of the faithful the burning hope of life everlasting. No doubt it is precisely for this reason that no other single truth in all of the history of the church has been so viciously and consistently attacked as the truth of unconditional election. But no man can claim to be either Calvinistic or Reformed without a firm and abiding commitment to this precious truth.[97]

Hanko also says:

> ... if there was one reason why Calvin was hated it was because he maintained so unswervingly the truth of unconditional election.[98]

He then adds:

> We are generally accustomed to trace this truth of unconditional election back to the Calvin Reformation. And yet it was not Calvin who was the first to develop this truth. But, just as with the truth of total depravity, so also with this truth, St. Augustine, who lived more than a millennium ago in the Fifth Century A.D., was the first to speak of it. If we consider this a moment, this is not surprising. Augustine took the position that man is totally depraved. By this he meant that man is incapable of doing any good. And, most emphatically, that man is incapable of doing anything, which would contribute to his salvation.[99]

He goes on to say:

> In answer, therefore, to the question of how men are saved, Augustine answered that the power of salvation is to be found only in the power of sovereign, unmerited grace. There is no other power of salvation but that. But immediately the question arises: if the power of salvation is the power of sovereign, unmerited grace, not dependent in any respect upon man, how is it then that some men are saved and others are not? The answer to that question Augustine found in the decree of election and reprobation.[100]

To Hanko and all Calvinists, a great deal hangs on an affirmation of the *unconditional* nature of election. He says:

> The fact is that unless we maintain unconditional election, there is no election at all ... because then the power of sovereign grace is denied as the power by which God saves those whom He has cho-

sen to be His own.[101]

This is an extremely important point in Calvinism. According to Reformed Theology, unless you affirm the unconditional aspect of an election to salvation, you must *in effect* deny the sovereignty *and* grace of God in salvation. To the Calvinist, a denial of *sovereign grace* is a denial of sovereignty *and* grace. This view which says sovereignty and grace necessitate the unconditional nature of election to salvation is a theological and logical sore spot for many hypo-Calvinists because they say or suggest that God:

- *Unconditionally* elects some people to salvation,

And yet:

- *Conditionally* reprobates all other people to damnation.

Using Calvinist logic, this would mean that God is only sovereign with regard to the elect but not so with regard to the reprobate. We will revisit this issue many times throughout this book. For now it is enough to stress that according to Calvinism, in order for a lost person to become a saved person, he must be among a special *caste* of humanity called *the elect*. While the caste system of Reformed Theology transcends the earthly distinctions of humanity (i.e., rich, poor, black, white, Jew, Gentile, highly cultured, lowly peasants, etc.), it is an undeniable feature of Calvinism. In fact, the eternal castes of the elect and reprobate necessarily include representatives of all temporal distinctions. James White, while focusing on the election side of the election/reprobation coin, says that:

> God elects a specific people unto Himself without reference to *anything they do*. This means the basis of God's choice of the elect is *solely* within Himself: His grace, His mercy, His will. It is not man's actions, works, *or even foreseen faith*, that "draws" God's choice. God's election is unconditional *and final*.[102]

While White may or may not appreciate what I am going to say, logically White's view, at the very least, implies that *God reprobates a specific people away from Himself without reference to anything they do.* In fact, although this is hushed up or even denied in at least some hypo-Calvinist circles, Calvinism maintains an unconditional election to damnation as much as it does an unconditional election to salvation. All Calvinists *shout* about their doctrine of unconditional election. Most, however, *whisper* when talking about unconditional reprobation, if they speak of it at all. They boast of the former while they are seemingly embarrassed about the latter.

Sproul argues that the term "unconditional election" can be very misleading. Instead he prefers to use the term "sovereign election to unconditional election." As a leading proponent of hypo-Calvinism, and like so many of his Calvinist contemporaries, Sproul is also in a kind of *theological denial* of the full implications of a consistent Calvinism. While I can understand why Sproul does not want to admit to (or face) the dark side of Calvinism, I cannot understand how he can deny it. Of all people, Sproul should be the first to recognize the logical link and relationship between election and reprobation in Reformed Theology. Sproul does say:

> Unconditional election ... is decided by God according to His purpose, according to His sovereign will. It is not based upon some foreseen condition that some of us meet and others fail to meet.[103]

The "foreseen condition" that Sproul refers to and that he claims election "is not based upon" is *faith in Christ*. Logically, however, it would be just as Calvinistic to say that *unconditional reprobation is decided by God according to His purpose, according to His sovereign will.* That is, election to salvation and election to damnation are both *unconditional,* according to a consistent Calvinism. A little later Sproul says:

> When we say that election is unconditional we mean that the original decree of God by which He chooses some people to salvation is not dependent upon some future condition in us that God foresees.[104]

The "future condition" that Sproul speaks of is also *faith in Christ*. That is, election and the salvation that some (but not all) are elected to does not *require* faith *from* the elect but *results* in faith *for* the elect, according to Reformed Theology. H. Wayne House says election is:

> That aspect of God's eternal purpose whereby he certainly and eternally determines by means of unconditional and loving choice who will believe. This is not merely the intention of God to save all who may believe; rather, it determines who will believe.[105]

He also says:

> Election is an expression of God's sovereign will and is the cause

of faith.[106]

House goes on to further define election as:

> The unconditional and love choice of God by which He determines
> who must believe. It is the cause of man's faith.[107]

Steele and Thomas, with one theological eye open to reprobation,
explain:

> The doctrine of election declares that God, before the foundation
> of the world, chose certain individuals from among the fallen
> members of Adam's race to be the objects of His undeserved favor.
> These, and these only, He purposed to save. ... He chose to save
> some and exclude others. His eternal choice of particular sinners
> unto salvation was not based upon any foreseen act or response on
> the part of those selected, but was based solely on His own good
> pleasure and sovereign will. Thus election was not determined by,
> or conditioned upon, anything that men would do, but resulted en-
> tirely upon God's self-determined purpose.[108]

Thus, according to Steele and Thomas, God not only "chose to save
some" but He also chose to "exclude others." This means that in Calvinism
there is an election of *inclusion* and an election of *exclusion,* both unconditional in nature. According to Calvinism, God determines the destiny of both
the *included* and the *excluded* without consideration of, or factoring in, faith
or unbelief. While many hypo-Calvinists want to deny this fact, the Calvinist
doctrine of unconditional reprobation *blames God* at least implicitly, if not
explicitly, for the damnation of the reprobate. In Calvinism God gets as
much *blame* for reprobation and damnation as He does *credit* for election
and salvation. In the case of the elect, God chose to save them. In the case of
the reprobate, God chose to exclude them from salvation, that is, by definition, to include them in damnation. A consistent Calvinist traces reprobation to God in the same way that he traces election to God. W. R. Godfrey,
the highly respected professor of church history at Westminster Seminary
in California, represents the Augustinian doctrine of predestination (from
which Calvinism traces its roots) as follows:

> The reason that some sinners are saved and others lost must be in
> God. It is according to God's sovereign purpose, His eternal decree
> that some sinners are rescued and others are left in their sin. The

foundation of this divine decree is simply the good pleasure or will of God.[109]

Notice that "the reason that some sinners are ... lost must be in God." Given the faulty premise upon which Reformed Theology is based, logically what Calvinists say about salvation in this regard must also be as true about damnation. Understandably, most Calvinists prefer to focus on election to salvation *versus* reprobation to damnation. The dark side of Calvinism in some Calvinist circles is just *too bitter a theological pill to swallow.* The following words of Steele and Thomas are typical of the way hypo-Calvinists like to represent the Calvinist doctrine of election. That is:

> God's choice of certain individuals unto salvation before the foundation of the world rested solely in His own sovereign will.[110]

However, a consistent Calvinist could, just as easily, logically, and theologically, say:

> God's choice of certain individuals unto *damnation* before the foundation of the world rested solely in His own sovereign will.

Best-selling author Jay Adams, in his booklet, *Counseling and the Five Points of Calvinism,* is also typical of hypo-Calvinists in remaining silent about the reprobate when he says:

> God has chosen some to be saved. ... The choice was unconditional ... The choice was made entirely within God. ... The selection of some for eternal life was made on the basis of unrevealed factors known to God alone.[111]

Consistency would, however, allow or even require Adams to also say:

> God has chosen some to be *damned.* ... The choice was unconditional. ... The choice was made entirely within God. ... The selection of some for eternal *death* was made on the basis of unrevealed factors known to God alone.

There is just no way to avoid the fact that a consistent view of unconditional election also logically leads to an unconditional view of reprobation. This is a serious bone of contention between hyper-Calvinists and hypo-Calvinists. Although this point is both denied and affirmed in a variety of ways by many, if not most hypo-Calvinists, it is clearly the flip side of unconditional election. Nevertheless and understandably, much more is said about election than reprobation in books by Calvinists promoting Calvinism. People don't mind getting something for nothing (election). It is being punished for nothing (reprobation) that they find difficult to accept. It is enough, many believe, to zero in on the unconditional aspect of election. If one is *really* willing to turn the coin over, however, it is not difficult to see reprobation as plainly as election to salvation can be seen on the other side. In *TULIP,* the acronym for the five points of Calvinism, Calvinist Duane Spencer says:

> The Apostle Paul declares that the ground of election is in God Himself, which is to say in His will and purpose, and not in an act of faith or some "condition." ... Election is unconditional.[112]

A consistent Calvinist could also say:

> The ground of *reprobation* is in God Himself, which is to say in His will and purpose, and not in an act of *sin* or some "condition." ... *Reprobation* is unconditional.

Some hypo-Calvinists go to great lengths to suggest that you can believe in unconditional election without believing in unconditional reprobation. That is, however, like saying you can believe in unconditional election and not in limited atonement. This is logically impossible. Steele and Thomas are representative of Calvinism when they say that God's:

> ... choice of particular sinners was not based on any foreseen response or obedience on their part, such as faith, repentance, etc. On the contrary, God gives faith and repentance to each individual whom He selected. These acts are the result, not the cause of God's choice. ... Thus, God's choice of the sinner, not the sinner's choice of Christ, is the ultimate cause of salvation.[113]

Logically, a consistent Calvinist would also have to say that God's:

> ... rejection of particular sinners was not based on any foreseen response on their part, such as unbelief, a refusal to repent, etc. On the contrary, God withheld faith and repentance from each individual He rejected. These are the result, not the cause of God's choice to reject. ... Thus, God's rejection of the sinner, and not the sinner's rejection of Christ, is the ultimate cause of damnation.

Sproul claims that only a hyper-Calvinist could say such a thing. He equates hyper-Calvinism with unorthodox, anti,—or even sub-Calvinism. We will consider the legitimacy of this charge a little later.

Even though Calvin and Calvinism plead ignorance as to why God chooses to save some or why He chooses to damn others, or even why this pleases God, Calvin believed that regardless of the reason behind God's decision to damn the reprobate, it must be their fault. In other words, God's choice is completely within Himself and not because of the individual, and yet, contradictorily, the "fault" continues to lie *not with God, but with the individual.* Thus, Calvin could say that although mankind's:

> ... perdition depends on the predestination of God, the cause and matter of it is in themselves.[114]

Such a proposition is double talk. I mean Calvin no disrespect, but he is speaking here from both sides of his mouth, and it is hard to imagine that such a brilliant man did not realize what he was doing. In the Calvinist scheme of things, the human cause that leads to damnation is only secondary to the divine cause that ultimately is the cause of sin in the sinner. According to Calvin and a consistent Calvinism, whatever is in man, God put there in the first place. However, unwittingly, Reformed Theology makes God the primary cause of that which leads to sin and the damnation that follows for all but the elect. This is where the Calvinist, especially the hypo-Calvinist, accuses me of misunderstanding Calvin and Calvinism. My key witness in this contention, however, is Calvin himself. Nevertheless, in saying that man is to be blamed for his own doom, Calvin was making it clear that he did not believe that God was being unjust in His treatment of those He doomed.

Some will say that the reason the reprobate can be unconditionally "passed over" or even unconditionally "hardened," as Reformed Theology teaches, without calling into question the justice of God is because they are sinners who deserve what they are going to get. Although Calvin clearly believed that reprobates are sinners deserving divine retribution, this is not the reason that Calvin believed God condemns them. Calvin simply never explained how God could be just in damning the lost and admitted that this was "incomprehensible" to him.

If God did reject the reprobate for this reason (i.e., their sinfulness), how can we explain why God chose the elect? Certainly the elect, before conversion, are just as sinful and just as deserving of divine retribution as their reprobate counterparts. To identify *sinfulness* or even *unbelief* as the cause of reprobation would create insurmountable problems for Calvin's view of salvation by grace in general, and of Calvin's views of sovereignty and predestination in particular. While Calvin may have talked a lot about the depravity of man and how undeserving man is, he could not use these factors when trying to explain non-election, reprobation, or damnation.

Some Calvinists say God elects some to salvation because He chose to love them. But that only begs the question, why some and not others? Certainly the elect are no more lovable before regeneration than the reprobate. Note carefully what Calvin said on this very point:

> Predestination is nothing else than a dispensation of divine justice, secret indeed, but *unblamable,* because it is certain that those predestined to that condition were not unworthy of it, it is equally certain, that the destruction consequent upon predestination is also most just.[115]

To Calvin, the justice in damnation is certain, but it was certainly not evident to him. That is what Calvin meant by "secret indeed." Whatever the reason the reprobate will be punished for all eternity, Calvin believed it was the result of, or at least in accordance with, "divine justice." For His part, God is "unblamable." The reprobate man was "not unworthy of it." "The destruction" of the reprobate is "just." If it had anything to do with the sin or sinfulness of the reprobate, it would not be a "secret," and it would apply to the elect as well. The closest Calvin got to what some might consider an explanation of why God chooses to unconditionally condemn some and unconditionally save others equally deserving of damnation is when he says that God has the right and desire to show His mercy and His judgment in whatever way He wants.

According to Reformed Theology, someone has to be saved for God to show how merciful He can be and someone has to be condemned to show how severe He can be. Since all the people God has to choose from are equally undeserving of His mercy, anyone He chooses not to be merciful to is only getting what he deserves. Calvin also made it clear that although the reprobate is deserving of hell, that is not the reason for his ultimate rejection by God. Rather, he who ends up in hell is there because this is what pleases God and where He unconditionally sends him.

The sinfulness of the reprobate, as a result of the fall of the first man, is not only *not* a reason for ultimate punishment, but is itself the result of a "just" decision of God, according to Calvin. How it is that a man could be deserving of something that ultimately lands him in hell without regard to anything he did or was going to do—or that God caused him to do—is just another one of the many mysteries in Reformed Theology. Immediately after the above admission, Calvin went on to say:

> The first man fell because the Lord deemed it meet that he should:
> why he deemed it meet, we do not know now, it was certain, how-
> ever that it was just ...[116]

It is evident, therefore, that Calvin believed that both the fall and the consequences of the fall are *just* punishments from God. Human sin, in this scenario, is not so much the *root* of the problem but the *fruit* of the problem. The underlying problem itself is totally unknown, except that this is the way God wanted it to be. If the theological chicken is God's decree to damn and the theological egg is man's sin, what would Calvin say to the question, "Which came first (causally speaking), the chicken or the egg?" In effect, Calvin said both are first, depending upon your vantage point. From the human perspective, sin is what leads to damnation and therefore it is man's fault if he goes to hell. From the divine perspective, man originally sinned and even continues to sin because God decreed that he would and should. Clearly, Calvin turns the *fall of man* into a *push from God.*

Why God would push man into sin, and how this can be without making God the author (or cause) of sin, is evidently a part of the same *mystery* that Calvinists so often appeal to and even hide behind. Calvin leaves us with hopeless *contradictions* that Calvinists call *mysteries.* Even the logically minded R. C. Sproul says:

> God wills all things that come to pass. ... God desired for man to
> fall into sin. I am not accusing God of sinning; I am suggesting that
> God created sin.[117]

If this is what the mainstream Calvinist really believes, then there is not much room to differentiate between the *extreme* and the *mainstream.* I would love to hear Sproul explain how God could create sin without being the cause or author of sin, and therefore a sinner. If God is the creator of sin and no one or nothing caused God to create sin, then God is the cause of sin. If He is the cause of sin, He must also be responsible for the sin He caused.

The hypo-Calvinist Edwin Palmer represents Calvin and Calvinism as making God and His predestination the cause of:

> ... the moving of a finger, the beating of a heart, the laughter of a girl, the mistake of a typist—*even sin.* [118]

Calvinists articulate a view which not only calls into question the indiscriminate love of God, but the justice and character of God as well. As non-Calvinists, we are not even supposed to ask how this can be squared with Scripture. To do so, says the Calvinist, is to challenge God Himself. In fact, when it suits Calvin, he seems to make ignorance of these matters a virtue. It is, however, Calvin who creates the theological system that makes God out to be guilty of wrongdoing. When we question that system, he conveniently turns the table on us. Calvin clearly understood his detractors' objections to the extreme and seemingly illogical position he had taken. Consider the questions they were asking, as reported to us by Calvin himself:

> Why should God blame men for things the necessity of which he has imposed by his own predestination? What could they do? Could they struggle with his decrees? ... It is not just ... to punish them for things the principal cause of which is in the predestination of God. [119]

Assuming Calvin is right to consider the divine decree as the ultimate and primary cause of all that is and will be, these are perfectly reasonable questions, reflecting perfectly justified concerns. Instead of acknowledging the logic of such questions or attempting a reasonable answer to them, Calvin simply charges that:

> This ... is the scoffing language which profane tongues employ. [120]

Calvin's answer is *theological intimidation* and is destitute of *scriptural illumination.* Herein lies a serious problem. Calvin and Calvinists say so much more about predestination than Scripture does, and even contradict what Scripture says about predestination. Yet we are supposed to unquestioningly accept what they say, no matter how much it impugns the love, justice, and character of God. It is Calvin who introduced so many foreign and scripturally incompatible doctrines while calling them biblical truths. Calvin is the pot calling the kettle black. He is the one who does what he chides others for doing.

In Reformed Theology, the concepts of election and reprobation are so bound together that whenever you try to give a reason for one thing, such as why God condemns the reprobate, it backfires on the doctrine of Calvinism. For as soon as you say "because," you are trapped. That is, if whatever you say about the reprobate is also true of the elect—sinners, undeserving of salvation, deserving of hell, etc.—then those things cannot be factors. Allow me to illustrate with an excerpt from my primer on the five points of Calvinism:

> Suppose you are offered some chocolates from a box of chocolates. While gazing into the box, you decide there is nothing in any of the chocolates to make you want to pick one chocolate over another. Nevertheless, you choose some of the chocolates and some of the chocolates you do not choose. You may have a reason for picking some and not others, but the reason has nothing to do with the individual chocolates themselves. It stands to reason then, if there is nothing in the chocolates that affected your decision to pick one piece of chocolate over the others, there is also nothing in the ones you do not pick to affect your decision to *not* pick them.[121]

After reading this analogy in my earlier book, some Calvinists protested that it was a total misrepresentation of what Calvin said or implied. Calvin, however, used exactly the same logic when he said in reference to Romans Chapter Nine:

> If we cannot assign any reason for his bestowing mercy on his people, but just that it so pleases him, neither can he have any reason for his reprobating others but his will. When God is said to visit in mercy or harden whom he will, men are reminded that they are not to seek for any cause beyond his will.[122]

With this same portion of Scripture in mind, Calvin said:

> … hardening is not less under the immediate hand of God than mercy.[123]

He also said:

> … the hidden counsel of God is the cause of hardening.[124]

The "not to seek for any cause beyond his will" phrase rules out the fall, sin, depravity, unbelief, or anything else true of man after the fall. Hanko explains:

> First of all (and negatively) this means that in the decrees of election God chose *not* according to anything found in man. He did not base His choice on man in any way. Not on man's goodness, works, faith, holiness; not on man's faithfulness to the gospel. There could not be found in man any good thing. It was a free choice, a sovereign choice of God. He made it without any consideration of man whatsoever.[125]

The hyper-Calvinists are more likely to acknowledge the flip side to this point than their hypo-Calvinist counterparts. That is, they seem more inclined than most hypo-Calvinists to accept the implication of Calvinism which says that the choice for damnation is "made ... without any consideration of man whatsoever." Logically, this is an inescapable conclusion in Calvinism, which also creates insurmountable problems for the notion of divine justice and human culpability. For if the reason a man is damned has nothing to do with that man, then whatever is *hidden* in the *mystery* cannot point to the man. To blame the man, as Calvinists do, for what Calvinism implicitly says God is really responsible for doing does not get God off the moral hook that Calvinists put Him on. Many Calvinists of the hypo-variety seemingly cannot accept what Calvinism implies about the ultimate reason for the damnation of the reprobate or the reprobation of the damned. This is why Spurgeon contradicts a consistent Calvinism and says:

> It is the uniform doctrine of Calvinism, that God creates all for his own glory; that he is infinitely righteous and benignant [without malice], and that where men perish it is only for their sins.[126]

Calvinists can say these kinds of things. A consistent Calvinism, however, cannot allow it. While Calvin did not care (or perhaps was unable) to resolve the many logical, theological, and scriptural problems his teaching created, he was not unaware of the "dreadful" implications of his views concerning reprobation. Nevertheless, his commitment to a particular and unscriptural view of sovereignty and predestination left him no other option. The doctrinal and logical dilemma in which Calvin put himself (and all consistent Calvinists) can be discerned when he says:

> I ... ask how it is that the fall of Adam involves so many nations with their infant children in eternal death without remedy unless that it so seemed meet to God? ... The decree, I admit, is, dreadful;

and yet it is impossible to deny that God foreknew what the end of man was to be before he made him, and foreknew, because He had so ordained by his decree. ... God not only foresaw the fall of the first man, and in him the ruin of his posterity; but also at his own pleasure arranged it.[127]

Calvin believed and taught that the fall and ruin of Adam and his posterity, including the hopeless (i.e., "without remedy") and dreadful fact that infant children are unconditionally doomed to eternal death, was according to God's own decree. For Calvin, this is also to say it was God's doing. Can God arrange something at His own pleasure and then not be responsible for what He arranges? Logically, He cannot. Yet this is what the hypo-Calvinist, at least by implication, wants us to believe. Calvin and many, if not most, of his followers try to have it both ways. Calvin repeatedly said that the fall was caused by God's decree. Then Calvin would also say that it is a man's own fault and according to justice when a man ends up unconditionally in hell. Calvin is not the only one to face, or refuse to face, the logical problems posed by Reformed Theology. Sproul puts the best possible spin on the Calvinist doctrine of reprobation. Upon close inspection, it is still just spin. In *Chosen by God*, Sproul initially appears to want to lay it all out on the table. For example, he explains:

Though there is strong sentiment to speak of single predestination only, and to avoid any discussion of double predestination, we must still face the questions on the table. Unless we conclude that every human being is predestined to salvation, we must face the flip side of election. If there is such a thing as predestination at all, and if that predestination does include all people, we must not shrink from the necessary inference that there are two sides to predestination. It is not enough to talk about Jacob; we must also consider Esau.[128]

Elsewhere Sproul says:

Every coin has a flip side. There is a flip side to the doctrine of election. Election only refers to one aspect of the broader question of predestination. The other side of the coin is the question of reprobation.[129]

I would have applauded Sproul's willingness to face the flip side had he actually done so. What he did, however, was distance himself from the flip side of election as far as his genius and command of the English language would allow. It is the Calvinist understanding of God's view of Esau that creates so many headaches for them and is so offensive to the rest of us. Remember that according to Calvinism, single predestination refers to the Calvinist doctrine that says God unconditionally elects some to salvation but does not unconditionally condemn others to damnation. This is the view of men like Charles Spurgeon as well as a lot of new converts to Calvinism. It is not, however, a fully developed or consistent view of Reformed Theology. It leaves the Calvinist theologically and logically stranded.

The doctrine of double predestination, to which Sproul refers and at least formally agrees, affirms that God also predestines the reprobate to damnation. All those who try to be consistent Calvinists believe in and embrace double predestination (in some form or fashion) whether they call it that or not. The problem is that when many hypo-Calvinists get around to really explaining themselves in terms that can be understood, their explanation amounts to a denial of what double predestination really affirms. No amount of semantic gymnastics can, however, shield the Calvinist from the dark side of Calvinism. Sproul and many mainstream Calvinists simply do not seem to *understand* or *accept* the full implications of the dark side of Calvinist doctrine.

We know that according to Calvinist logic, sovereign election to salvation and sovereign reprobation to damnation must stand or fall together. Still, it is just too harsh an implied *truth* of Reformed Theology for many Calvinists to contemplate—that God damns millions merely because of His own secret pleasure, not because of anything they have done, will do, or even would do if they had the opportunity. Despite what Sproul says and what he may truly have intended to do, he does anything but face the flip side of Calvin's doctrine of election. Instead, he compares what he purports to be a more extreme view of double predestination with his own seemingly more moderate view of double predestination, thereby making it seem as though his view is not extreme. Sproul explains:

> There are different views of double predestination. One of these is
> so frightening that many shun the term altogether, lest their view
> of the doctrine be confused with the scary one. This is called the
> equal ultimacy view.[130]

Sproul then distances himself from this view by explaining:

Equal ultimacy is based on a concept of symmetry. It seeks a complete balance between election and reprobation. The key idea is this: Just as God intervenes in the lives of the elect to create faith in their hearts, so God equally intervenes in the lives of the reprobate to create or work unbelief. ... Equal ultimacy is not the Reformed or Calvinist view of predestination. Some have called it "hyper-Calvinism." I prefer to call it "sub-Calvinism" or, better yet, "anti-Calvinism." Though Calvinism certainly has a view of double predestination, the double predestination it embraces is not one of equal ultimacy.[131]

Having sided with the hypo-Calvinist camp, Sproul goes on to explain:

To understand the Reformed view of the matter we must pay close attention to the crucial distinction between positive and negative decrees of God. Positive has to do with God's active intervention in the hearts of the elect. Negative has to do with God's passing over the non-elect. The Reformed view teaches that God actively or positively intervenes in the life of the elect to insure their salvation. The rest of mankind God leaves to themselves. He does not create unbelief in their hearts. That unbelief is already there.[132]

Sproul also says:

God's "hardening of hearts" is itself a just punishment for sin that is already present.[133]

Although Sproul fails to acknowledge how this sin came to be "already present" (it was unconditionally decreed by God according to Calvin), he calls this "hardening of hearts" "passive hardening." He says:

Passive hardening involves a divine judgment upon sin that is already present. All that God needs to do to harden the heart of a person whose heart is already desperately wicked is "give him over to his sin."... All that God has to do to harden people's hearts is to remove the restraints. He gives them a longer leash. Rather than re-stricting their freedom, He increases it. He lets them have their own way. In a sense He gives them enough rope to hang themselves.[134]

It is difficult for me to believe that Sproul could have missed so much. The point is not about whether the reprobate is worthy of damnation. He most certainly is. But so is the individual God elects for salvation. In effect, Sproul gets sidetracked and changes the topic. What, may I ask, is the *mystery* in the *justice* when a man (for obvious reasons) gets what he deserves?

When convenient to do so, Sproul seems to disconnect the Calvinist notion of a decree of God with what follows inevitably from that decree. Even the term "double predestination" can be misleading. Calvinists constantly hammer away at the notion that all things are sovereignly determined, decreed, and destined by God in such a manner that God is the primary and responsible cause of whatever comes to pass. If the eternal destiny of a reprobate person is included as one of the "all things" that God predestines (and it must be so) in the Calvinist sense, it stands to reason that the reprobate go to hell primarily and ultimately because of God. According to Reformed Theology, people simply do not go to hell for any reason that can be traced to them. Oliver Buswell speaks for all consistent Calvinists when he says:

> The decrees of God may be regarded as one complex decree, including all things.[135]

John Gill explains that all things pertaining to a man are:

> ... according to the determinate counsel and will of God.[136]

More narrowly focused, John Giradeau says:

> Predestination includes two parts, election and reprobation, the predetermination of both the good and the wicked to their final end ...[137]

Ultimately, when it comes to the bottom line, even Sproul admits:

> There is ... a kind of equal ultimacy. The reprobate, who are passed over by God, are ultimately doomed by God, and their damnation is as certain and sure as the ultimate salvation of the elect.[138]

"Kind of equal ultimacy"? Sproul should know that it is equal or it is not equal. Two things that are unequal, no matter how close to equal they may be, cannot, by definition, be "kind of equal." Sproul the logician has to know this. Sproul the Calvinist must have forgotten it. Sproul objects to the notion that says:

God is equally responsible for election and reprobation.[139]

He says that this is characteristic of hyper-Calvinism. Sproul still concedes that God is responsible, albeit to a lesser degree, for the damnation of the reprobate. How can this be without making God less sovereign, according to Calvinist logic? As far as I can tell, Sproul never attempts to explain this dilemma. To make God responsible to any degree for the damnation of the reprobate is, however unwittingly, an attack on the character of God.

Is God wholly, partly, or not responsible at all for the damnation of the reprobate? A hyper-Calvinist would say (or at least strongly imply) that God is *as* responsible for the damnation of the reprobate, as He is for the salvation of the elect. Some hypo-Calvinists, such as Spurgeon, argue that damnation is wholly of man. The implication of the position taken by Sproul and other hypo-Calvinists is that God is not *as* responsible for damnation as He is for salvation. That is, God is not *as responsible* for damnation, though He is still responsible. Another way to state this view is to say that God is not responsible for damnation *to the same degree* as He is for salvation.

Unless we weaken or even deny the implications of a divine decree that is in keeping with Calvinism, no matter what means is used, that which follows is necessarily linked to and ultimately caused by that decree. Even if we can distinguish between a negative and positive decree, as Sproul does, it would still be God that decrees reprobation. Reprobation is still (in the Calvinist view) primarily and ultimately the result of a divine decree. To deny that the primary and ultimate cause of anything is anyone or anything but God is to deny a fundamental tenet of a consistent Calvinism. Thus, the distinction between a negative and positive decree in Calvinism not only *does not* clear up the matter, it compounds the confusion. Moreover, it flies in the face of so much that Calvin and Calvinists of all kinds say. With election and reprobation in mind, Douglas Wilson also challenges us to:

> Turn the coin over and look at the other side: if God chooses those who are saved, and not everyone is saved, then God also chooses *not* to give salvation to some—those who ultimately remain lost. One side of the coin is called election, while the other is called hardening—the process by which God passes by those who are not elect. Coming to grips with what the Bible says about hardening is crucial if we are to understand election. ... If, as some argue, God does not harden the non-elect, then we must reject the notion of

election that God chooses the elect, since hardening is simply the flip side of election.[140]

"God passes by," a favorite phrase used by the Calvinist, is a cosmetic effort to distance God from damnation, and is therefore misleading. For the hardening process that leads to reprobation and ultimately damnation is, according to Calvinism, the work of God, as is the irresistible grace of God that leads to salvation for the elect. Moreover, it is God alone who hardens. Ultimately, there are no co-hardeners and co-condemners in a consistent Calvinism. All Calvinists say that it is not God *with* man's help who saves the elect, but God and God alone who elects to save from all eternity to all eternity and that He does so unconditionally. It is also God and God alone who actually saves the elect in time. Further, a consistent Calvinism says that it is not God *with* man's help that condemns the reprobate or that reprobates the damned. God alone unconditionally elects to condemn the reprobate, and it is God alone who ultimately brings to pass the condemnation of the reprobate.

Calvinists constantly argue that if anyone but God has a say about anything, especially in matters relating to ultimate destinies, then God is not sovereign. They imply that God and God alone is the reason some go to heaven and others end up in hell. The reason God does this, according to Calvinism, is unknown and unknowable on this side of glory. Logically, even on the other side of glory, a consistent Calvinism says that we will not be able to make the case that an eternally condemned man was the cause of his own condemnation any more than we could credit an eternally saved man with the fact that he is saved. In other words, the mystery will have to remain a mystery for all of eternity.

Wilson appears to have gone further than Sproul in "coming to grips with" the hardening process by which God passes by those who are reprobate. All Calvinists agree that God *hardens* those ultimately lost, but they hold to differing views as to what this means and what its implications are. To dismiss those who at least try to be consistent as sub-Calvinists or anti-Calvinists, as Sproul does, will simply not do. The way Sproul uses words like "passive," "active," "positive," and "negative" only serves to obscure the bottom line. Although Sproul insists that the Reformed view of hardening is only "passive," Calvin explained:

> The word hardens, when applied to God in Scripture, means not only permission, (as some washy moderators would have it,) but

> also the operation of the wrath of God: for all those external things, which lead to the blinding of the reprobate, are the instruments of his wrath; and Satan himself, who works inwardly with great power, is so far his minister, that he acts not, but by his command. ... Paul teaches us, that the ruin of the wicked is not only foreseen by the Lord, but also ordained by his counsel and his will ... not only the destruction of the wicked is foreknown, but that the wicked themselves have been created for this very end—that they may perish.[141]

It is as if Calvin was looking into the future and labeling Sproul, and those who agree with him, as "washy moderators" or "weak exegetes," as another translation renders it. Surely then, Sproul must object to Calvin when Calvin objected to:

> ... the distinction between will and permission, the object being to prove that the wicked perish only by the permission, but not by the will of God.[142]

Is that not what Sproul tries to do? To Calvin, whether it is passive or not:

> ... The will of God is necessity ...[143]

Calvin explained:

> There is no random power, or agency, or motion in the creatures, who are so governed by the secret counsel of God, that nothing happens but what he has knowingly and willingly decreed ... the counsels and wills of men are so governed as to move exactly in the course which he has destined.[144]

Here Calvin is talking about Adam before he even had a sinful nature. Thus, the reason Adam sinned could not be blamed on the fact that he was a sinner. According to Calvin, what is true of the fall of Adam is also true of the destiny of Adam's posterity. That is, people end up in heaven *or hell* because that is where God wants and ordains them to go, and for no reason or reasons that can be traced to them. This is a very disturbing thought if you happen to be one of the many reprobates (or if you care about them) God created for the very purpose of condemning to eternal torment. This is not a misrepresentation of Calvinism but the very unambiguous teaching of John

Calvin himself. Remember, Calvin reasoned:

> ... Since the arrangement of all things is in the hand of God, since to him belongs the disposal of life and death, he arranges all things by his sovereign counsel, in such a way that individuals are born, who are doomed from the womb to certain death, and are to glorify him by their destruction. ... I, for my part, am willing to admit, that mere prescience [foreknowledge] lays no necessity on the creatures ... the dispute is superfluous since life and death are acts of the divine will rather than of prescience. If God merely foresaw human events, and did not also arrange and dispose of them at his pleasure, there might be room for agitating the question, how far his foreknowledge amounts to necessity; but since he foresees the things which are to happen, simply because he has decreed that they are so to happen, it is vain to debate about prescience, while it is clear that all events take place by his sovereign appointment.[145]

I did not put the words "doomed from the womb" into Calvin's mouth. I am not responsible for the view that says God arranges for the disposal of men "at his pleasure." I am not reading into the teachings of Calvin something he did not say. On the contrary, I am letting Calvin speak for himself. If this troubles you, then Calvinism troubles you. The point is hard to miss. God saves, God condemns. Why He does either is unknown and unknowable as far as Calvinism is concerned. I have no doubt that men, especially those as capable as Sproul, can find ways to seemingly soften what Calvin says and call the *softer-sounding* position "orthodox Calvinism." They can also call what appears on the surface to be the authentic views of Calvin, "hyper." If, however, the principle of authorial intent means anything, then the so-called sub-Calvinists of today are at least as authentically Calvinist as are their *softer-sounding* counterparts on this central issue. I would say that at least on this issue, the hyper-Calvinists stand theologically closer to Calvin than their hypo-Calvinist detractors. To say that "individuals are born, who are doomed from the womb" is about as hard a position as one can take. A much-respected expert on the life and teachings of John Calvin, Alister McGrath, is exactly right when he says:

> For Calvin, logical rigour demands that God actively chooses to redeem or to damn. God cannot be thought of as doing something by default. He is active and sovereign in His actions. Therefore

God actively wills the salvation of those who will be saved and the damnation of those who will not be saved.[146]

Although Sproul and many other hypo-Calvinists try very hard to restate Calvinism so as to distance themselves from its dark side, A. A. Hodge, also a hypo-Calvinist, admits that:

... All the world knows that as a predestinarian [Calvin] went to the length of Supralapsarianism*, from which ... the Synod of Dort, and the Assembly of Westminster, recoiled.[147]

Loraine Boettner explains:

Among those who call themselves Calvinists there has been some difference of opinion as to the order of events in the Divine plan. The question here is, When the decrees of election and reprobation came into existence were men considered as fallen or as unfallen? Were the objects of these decrees contemplated as members of a sinful, corrupt mass, or were they contemplated merely as men whom God would create? ... According to the supralapsarian view the order of events was: (1) to elect some creatable men (that is, men who were to be created) to life and to condemn others to destruction; (2) to create; (3) to permit the fall; (4) to send Christ to redeem the elect; and (5) to send the Holy Spirit to apply this redemption to the elect. The question then is as to whether election precedes or follows the fall.[148]

Do not let these long words intimidate you. Supralapsarianism is different from infralapsarianism only in ways that do not really matter or make a difference. If I were to say that three times six is eighteen and you were to say that six plus six plus six is eighteen, we would be in agreement. It would seem rather silly if we argued about the differing means, such as multiplication versus addition, which led us to the same correct conclusion.

---

* A supralapsarian is a Calvinist who believes that election to salvation and reprobation to damnation was decreed by God without regard to the first sin of man or the subsequent sinfulness of man. That is, both salvation and damnation are unconditional in nature. In contrast, an infralapsarian says that God factored in the fall and the sinfulness of mankind when He chose to elect some to salvation and reprobate others to damnation. Thus, the elect are saved unconditionally while the non-elect or reprobate are damned conditionally. Most (if not all) hyper-Calvinists are supralapsarians though not all supralapsarians are hyper-Calvinists. Most (if not all) infralapsarians are hypo-Calvinists.

More to the point, Calvin explained as much about why reprobates are condemned as the system of theology he espoused would allow. He was, however, very critical of those Christians who could not admit the *dark side* of Calvinism for fear that it would subject God to an unflattering accusation. Thus, Calvin chided:

> Many professing a desire to defend [God] from an invidious charge admit the doctrine of election, but deny that any one is reprobated. … This they do ignorantly and childishly, since there could be no election without its opposite reprobation. God is said to set apart those whom he adopts for salvation. It [is] most absurd to say, that he admits others fortuitously, or that they by their industry acquire what election alone confers on a few. Those therefore whom God passes by he reprobates, and that for no other cause but because he is pleased to exclude them from the inheritance which he predestines to his children.[149]

When most Calvinists explain their doctrine of reprobation, more often than not, they try to make it sound as though reprobation is effectively the sinner hanging himself with his own sins. This is what Sproul and most other hypo-Calvinists do. But how can we reconcile such a notion with Calvin's words?

> Those … whom God passes by he reprobates, and that for no other cause but because he is pleased to exclude them …[150]

Remember what Calvin also said:

> … each has been created for one or other of these ends, [therefore] we say that he has been predestined to life or to death.[151]

There was nothing, according to Calvin, in or about Adam to explain his fall. As we have seen, Calvin repeatedly asserts this while at the same time arguing the contradictory notion that Adam's fall was Adam's fault and not God's. Consider Calvin's reasoning, when referring to his detractors. He said:

> They deny that it is ever said in distinct terms, God decreed that Adam should perish by his revolt. As if the same God, who is declared in Scripture to do whatsoever he pleases, could have made the noblest of his creatures without any special purpose. They say

that, in accordance with free-will, he was to be the architect of his own fortune, that God had decreed nothing but to treat him according to his desert. If this frigid fiction is received, where will be the omnipotence of God, by which, according to his secret counsel on which everything depends, he rules over all? But whether they will allow it or not, predestination is manifest in Adam's posterity. It was not owing to nature that they all lost salvation by the fault of one parent. Why should they refuse to admit with regard to one man that which against their will they admit with regard to the whole human race? Why should they in caviling lose their labour? Scripture proclaims that all were, in the person of one, made liable to eternal death. As this cannot be ascribed to nature, it is plain that it is owing to the wonderful counsel of God.[152]

This notion that God could not have a special purpose in mind for His creatures unless He caused them in the person of Adam to sin is reiterated in a slightly modified form even by hypo-Calvinists. To be honest, I do not see the logic here. Nevertheless, this is how it breaks down:

- Adam did not have a free choice to sin or not to sin.

- It was not the nature of man that led to or resulted in the first sin.

- It was the decree, purpose, plan, wonderful counsel, and will of God that was the ultimate cause of Adam's sin and the terrible consequences of the fall.

- Nevertheless, it is not God's fault.

In other words, God, by His decree, pushed man into sin by which man fell and took the entire future human race with him, and yet, somehow, it is still man's fault, not God's. Remember what Sproul says:

God wills all things that come to pass. ... God desired for man to fall into sin. ... *God created sin.*[153]

Sproul asks:

Why does God only save some?[154]

He then says:

The only answer I can give to this question is that I don't know. I have no idea why God saves some but not all. ... I know that He does not choose to save all. I don't know why.[155]

Very much to the point, Sproul says:

> It was certainly loving of God to predestine the salvation of His
> people, those the Bible calls the "elect or chosen ones." It is the
> non-elect that are the problem. If some people are not elected unto
> salvation then it would seem that God is not all that loving toward
> them. For them it seems that it would have been more loving of
> God not to have allowed them to be born. *That may indeed be the*
> *case.*[156]

"Not all that loving toward them" may be one of the greatest theological
understatements of all time. According to Calvin, God created the reprobate
for the very purpose of condemning them to the torments of hellfire for all
eternity. That is (according to Reformed Theology) God's "special purpose"
for them. Not all that loving toward them? Imagine a science fiction story in
which in a future time an advanced group of scientists learn how to create
human-like creatures. Imagine that some of these creatures are created to be
tortured for the pleasure of these scientists. Would we not conclude that the
scientists in our fictional story were immoral, cruel, and even sadistic for
doing such a thing? Has not the Calvinist painted an even worse portrait of
God?

WHERE IS THE LOVE?

Concerning "the words of Christ himself in John 3:16," in which our Savior
says that "God so loved the world that He gave His only begotten Son," the
hyper-Calvinist John Gill explains:

> All the individuals in the world are not loved by God in such a
> manner.[157]

Gill wants us to believe that God loves some individuals in the world "in
such a manner," just not all the individuals in the world. How odd that Jesus
did not say anything to support such a view.

Charles Spurgeon followed as the pastor of the same church that Gill
had pastored many years earlier. Spurgeon distanced himself as much as he
was able from the hyper-Calvinism of Gill.

Whereas Gill denies that God loved the *whole* world, Spurgeon, along with all other hypo-Calvinists, denies a *saving* love for the reprobate of the world. Gill insists that God only loves some and therefore only saves some. In fact, Gill and others of the same Calvinist camp argue that it was the fact that God only saves some that proves He only loves some. Spurgeon insists that God loves everyone but that He does not love everyone with an *electing* love. Spurgeon appeals to his listeners to see a divine love for all the lost and not just those who could, by virtue of election, become saved. Spurgeon also argues that God has a broader and non-redemptive love for everyone and a more narrowly focused, saving love for the elect. Thus Spurgeon could be heard saying:

> Beloved, the benevolent love of Jesus is more extended than the lines of his electing love … That … is not the love which beams resplendently upon his chosen, but it is true love for all that.[158]

Spurgeon says God's electing love:

> … is not for all men … There is an electing, discriminating, distinguishing love, which is settled upon a chosen people … and it is this love which is the true resting place for the saint.[159]

In his book titled *The God Who Loves,* MacArthur apparently follows the lead of Spurgeon and says:

> An important distinction must be made: God loves believers with a particular love. … It is an eternal love that guarantees their salvation from sin and its ghastly penalty. … We know from Scripture that this great love was the very cause of our election (Eph. 2:4). Such love clearly is not directed toward all of mankind indiscriminately, but is bestowed uniquely and individually on those whom God chose in eternity past.[160]

MacArthur perfectly illustrates how incredibly inconsistent some Calvinists can be. For example, MacArthur goes to great lengths to distance himself from those who deny the universality of God's love and marshals a great deal of scriptural evidence against the view that says God only loves the elect. In his book, *The Love of God,* MacArthur explains:

> One of the deep concerns that has prompted me to write this book is a growing trend I have noticed—particularly among people committed to the biblical truth of God's sovereignty and divine

election. Some of them flatly deny that God in any sense loves those whom He has not chosen for salvation. ... I am troubled by the tendency of some—often young people newly infatuated with Reformed doctrine—who insist that God cannot possibly love those who never repent and believe.[161]

MacArthur goes on to explain that those with whom he vehemently disagrees contend:

If God loved everyone, He would have chosen everyone unto salvation. Therefore, God does not love the non-elect.[162]

MacArthur then reasons:

Those who hold this view often go to great lengths to argue that John 3:16 cannot really mean that God loves the whole world.[163]

MacArthur then rejects the view that says:

... ("For God so loved the *world* ...") refers to *the world of believers* (God's elect), in contradistinction from *"the world of the ungodly."*[164]

As we will see in a subsequent chapter, MacArthur argues that the word "world" cannot be *all-inclusive* of everyone in the world when Scripture says Christ died for the whole world. When Scripture says that God loves the whole world, he says the world cannot be *exclusive* of anyone in the world. Setting this aside for now, is MacArthur's view of a non-redemptive universal love any better or any less unscriptural than Gill's denial of a divine love which is universal and all-inclusive? In some respects it is worse. While MacArthur affirms God's love for everyone, he reduces that love to a non-redemptive love. It is simply not a *saving love.*

This is the equivalent of saying Christ died for the reprobate, but not redemptively—which, by the way, MacArthur also says. If the love mentioned in John 3:16 is for everyone, as MacArthur rightly insists, then it must be a redemptive love, *period!* How could MacArthur have missed this? While MacArthur is worried about some in the Reformed community denying the love of God for all, he is just as troubled by those he perceives to read too much into the fact that God loves everyone. It should come as no surprise, then, that MacArthur would say:

> D. L. Moody ... was undoubtedly guilty of an over emphasis on
> divine love.[165]

I would love to hear what it is that Moody said that made him "guilty of an over emphasis on divine love." MacArthur argues that where a person ultimately ends up, whether that is heaven or hell, corresponds directly to whether or not God loves or hates him. MacArthur also argues for the contradictory view that it is not really whether or not God loves or hates you that really matters. For according to MacArthur the person in danger of hellfire is a person God both loves and hates. MacArthur explains:

> I am convinced from Scripture that God's hatred toward the wicked
> is not a hatred undiluted by compassion, mercy, or love. We know
> from human experience that love and hatred are not mutually ex-
> clusive. It is not the least bit unusual to have concurrent feelings
> of love and hatred directed at the same person. We often speak
> of people who have love-hate relationships. There is no reason to
> deny that in an infinitely purer and more noble sense, God's hatred
> toward the wicked is accompanied by sincere, compassionate love
> toward them as well.[166]

MacArthur is not saying, as we often hear, that God hates the sin but loves the sinner or that He hates the sin because He loves the sinner. God actually hates at least some sinners, and every sinner He does not love with a special or electing love, according to MacArthur, will end up in hell. Immediately after saying that God loves and hates those He has no interest in saving and no saving love for, he goes on to say:

> The fact that God will send to eternal hell all sinners who persist in
> sin and unbelief proves His hatred toward them.[167]

According to MacArthur, if God loves and hates a person, that person has no hope. Whatever good may result from being loved by God, if God also hates you, the love God has for you will do you no saving good. Diluting the condemning hate God has for you with His non-saving love will be of no benefit; you will still be irredeemable. No matter how sincere and compassionate God's love for you may be, it cannot overcome the fact that God's hatred for you has destined you to hell forever. Is this the love of John 3:16 that Jesus says is for the world?

Recall the words of Jesus, "*God so loved the world that He gave His only begotten Son, that whoever believes in Him should not perish but have everlasting life"* (John 3:16). MacArthur is rightly convinced that the love of John 3:16 is not restricted to the elect but is extended to everyone in the world. If this love ascribed to God for man is not a redemptive love, what would be? Why should MacArthur be so concerned to defend a non-saving, non-redemptive love? Surely, it does not ultimately matter that God loves some people for whom He has no saving love or saving interest. If the non-saving love of God for the reprobate is coupled with a hate that is responsible for sending all sinners who persist in sin and unbelief to hell, why defend it at all? As evidence of this non-redemptive love that God has for the reprobate, MacArthur argues rightly that God is sincere in His offer of eternal life in a gospel proclamation to all. He says:

> God freely and indiscriminately offers mercy to all who will come to Christ.[168]

He then goes on to say:

> Let us honestly admit that on the face of it, the universal love of God is difficult to reconcile with the [Reformed] doctrine of election.[169]

If we were talking about a saving love it would be impossible, not just "difficult." This gospel offer of eternal life for all those who believe cannot by any stretch of the imagination be a sincere offer to the reprobate if MacArthur and other Calvinists are right. Let us go back to the point Sproul makes about double predestination. That is, in some sense he believes God predestines some to salvation and in some sense he believes God predestines some to damnation. As we read, however, Sproul sees another view of double predestination that is "scary and frightening." He calls this "hyper-Calvinism" and "sub-Calvinism." Sproul also distinguishes between what he calls "equal ultimacy, symmetry, a complete balance between election and reprobation" and his view. Sproul's view could therefore be described as the less frightening and friendlier view of unequal ultimacy, non-symmetry, and a non-balanced view between election and reprobation.

According to Sproul, however, as well as almost all Calvinists, we only know that it is God's will that the elect are elected to salvation and that the reprobate are condemned to damnation. We do not and cannot know why this is God's will, except that it pleases Him. Why this pleases God, we do not and cannot know. We also know, according to Reformed Theology, that for whatever reason God willed these things; we cannot point to anything in a man to explain his ultimate destiny.

Thus, the words "equal, symmetry, and balance," insofar as what we know is concerned, do logically apply. Man simply does not enter into the equation as to why God sends him to one place or the other, according to a consistent Calvinism. And if everything works out in accordance with the predetermined will of God in the sense that the Calvinist claims and that their view of sovereignty and predestination demands:

- Unbelief in the heart of the reprobate must also be the sovereign work and will of God, just as Calvinists claim that faith in the elect is the sovereign work and will of God.

Otherwise, God is not sovereign or not as sovereign over the heart of the reprobate, according to Calvinist logic, as He is over the heart of the elect. Calvinists have backed themselves into a theological and logical corner from which they simply cannot escape. Even if we were to say that God did something for no particular reason, a silly thing to say for sure, He would still be responsible for what He did. Not even the first sin could be a factor for reprobation according to Calvinism. For if we can point to that first sin, then:

- It is not a mystery,
- It involves the elect as much as the reprobate,

And,

- It would base a divine decision to reprobate on a human decision to sin.

If God factors something in, such as faith or unbelief, then man is conditionally destined. If man is destined unconditionally, then he simply cannot legitimately be blamed for where he spends eternity. That is, nothing he has done or is going to do could be considered a factor. Even if you could argue that these reprobates are still only getting what they deserve, you could not argue that they are getting what they deserve *because they deserve it.* But even this kind of argument fails to account for the extreme and unbiblical view of sovereignty and predestination found in Calvinism. Ironically, as we have repeatedly seen, the Calvinist has to deny the sovereignty of God for the reprobate in order to affirm the sovereignty of God for the elect, if indeed a sovereign choice must be an unconditional choice. Simply hiding behind a *mystery* will not do. Too much is already on the table. Spurgeon argues that we know that salvation is all of God and that damnation is all of man. For example, Spurgeon says:

> The first thing is, THE GREAT DOCTRINE—that God "only is our rock and our salvation." If any one should ask us what we would choose for our motto, as preachers of the gospel, we think we should reply, "God only is our salvation." The late lamented Mr. Denham has put at the foot of his portrait, a most admirable text, "Salvation is of the Lord."[170]

Now what thinking Christian could disagree with this scriptural affirmation? If that were all Calvinism was saying, no Evangelical would protest. Spurgeon and all hypo-Calvinists leave out half of what Calvinism is saying, when they say, "God only is our salvation." The other half, the dark side, says "God only is our damnation." Consider how Spurgeon elaborates on this same point:

> Now, that is just an epitome of Calvinism; it is the sum and the substance of it. If any one should ask you what you mean by a Calvinist, you may reply, "He is one who says, salvation is of the Lord." I cannot find in Scripture any other doctrine than this. It is the essence of the Bible. "He only is my rock and my salvation." Tell me anything that departs from this and it will be a heresy; tell me a heresy, and I shall find its essence here, that it has departed from this great, this fundamental, this rocky truth, "God is my rock and my salvation."[171]

It is rather remarkable that Spurgeon was unable or unwilling to see that the Calvinist version of "Salvation is of the Lord" forces upon the consistent Calvinist the view that says "Damnation is also of the Lord." Election to salvation in the Calvinist sense can be likened to a firefighters' rescue mission that was intended to save only some of the people caught in a fire that was about to consume all of the people. Imagine one hundred people trapped in a burning building and the fire captain saying to his crew:

> I know you can save all of the people trapped in this building, but I have no interest in saving them all. For reasons that I will not divulge at this time, or perhaps for reasons you cannot now understand, I want you to let seventy-five of these people perish in the flames. It is not our fault they are in this predicament, and we owe them nothing. It is their own fault that they are now about to

> go down in flames. But that is not why I am going to leave them to burn to death. I have chosen to express my love and show mercy only on twenty-five of them. As for the rest, let them burn.
>
> Here is the list of the people I want you to save. Now go save them and leave the rest to perish. My choice is simply to save some and not to save others. Those I have chosen to save, I have also chosen to use in the fire department once they are rescued. Once we get them out of harm's way, I will give them their working assignments and all the tools they will need to do the job I will give them.

In some ways, the Calvinist scheme is even more sinister in that it has God setting the very fire from which He chooses, for His own pleasure, not to rescue some people. Now suppose a different rescue mission takes place at sea. Suppose a hundred people have been swept overboard in a terrible storm. Suppose they put themselves in harm's way, by going out onto the deck when they were specifically warned not to do so. Suppose that when this perilous situation comes to the captain's attention, with compassion and a sense of urgency in his voice, he immediately tells his rescue crew:

> Make every effort to reach every person with a life preserver and to bring him or her back to safety.

The captain then tells his crew:

> Make no distinction between those overboard. Throw life preservers to everyone. Once they get aboard ship, I will give each person rescued an assignment on the ship with all the tools he will need to do the job I will give him to do.

Suppose the crew rises to the occasion and successfully gets a life preserver to everyone overboard. Suppose, however, that for whatever reason, some of those overboard choose not to accept the help offered to them. Suppose some want to commit suicide and others simply believe they can save themselves by some other means.

In both stories, some are saved and some are lost. In the first story, however, things turn out just the way the captain wants them to. The ones he wants to save, he saves. The ones he does not want to save perish. In the second story, the captain really wants to save everyone and makes provision to do so. The only thing he does not do is force anyone to accept the help he offers.

In the first story, the elect are saved because they are elect. That is, they are saved because the captain elects to save them. In the second story, the saved are elected to serve because they are saved. The captain wants to save everyone, but chooses to use all of those that are saved in accordance with the fact that they received the help offered in the saving process. While no analogy is perfect, the fire captain represents the God of Calvinism and the ship's captain represents the God of the Bible.

Of course, the hypo-Calvinist can object to the first characterization because they, as believer-evangelists, are told to preach the message of salvation contained in the gospel of Jesus Christ to everyone without distinction. The reason they are told to preach salvation or even offer salvation to everyone is, however, not because everyone can be saved, but because they do not know who (among the many) God has chosen to save. Calvinists insist that God has decreed that only some of all those in need of saving can or should be saved. John MacArthur and John Piper believe that God really wants to save the lost; He just chose not to do so. It is still God, they say, who decreed not to save them and therefore decreed to unconditionally damn them.

It can all be reduced to this: damnation is not based on any moral or spiritual failure on the part of man. The ultimate reason some go to hell is to be found in the unrevealed—and therefore hidden—will of God. It cannot, according to Reformed Theology, be found in the obvious and manifest sinful rebellion of man. It is in the glorious, divine nature of God, not the depraved human nature of man, that the Calvinist must find the answer to the question of why some will be damned.

The hypo-Calvinist will not like the above fire captain analogy because it makes God seem heartless and callous toward those He chooses to condemn. The fact is, this is the shoe that fits, and Calvinism must wear it. Moreover, Calvinism makes God out to be even more heartless and callous because it portrays Him as not only unconditionally condemning so many poor, desperate people, but according to a consistent Calvinism, it is God who caused them to put themselves in harm's way in the first place.

Some hypo-Calvinists have tried to find fault in my reasoning because they say I rely too heavily upon logic in my evaluation and refutation of Calvinism. They claim that they are just affirming what Scripture says, and if that is illogical, then so be it. Yet Calvinists constantly boast about how logical Calvinism is. They also charge all non-Reformed views as being hopelessly illogical. Calvinists should not be allowed to have it both ways. They should not be allowed to commend Calvinism as logical and then hide behind their misapplication of Scriptures such as *"His thoughts are higher than our thoughts"* whenever it suits their fancy or whenever they back themselves into logical and theological corners. Ironically MacArthur says:

> I want to state as clearly as possible that I am in no way opposed to logic. I realize there are those who demean logic as if it were somehow contrary to spiritual truth. I do not agree; in fact, to abandon logic is to become irrational, and true Christianity is not irrational. The only way we can understand any spiritual matter is by applying careful logic to the truth that is revealed in God's Word. ... There is certainly nothing whatsoever wrong with sound logic grounded in the truth of Scripture; in fact, logic is essential to understanding.[172]

Once more, I find myself in agreement with these sentiments as expressed by MacArthur. I can only wish his handling of Scripture corresponded to this affirmation. It is not the case that one can be "too logical," nor is it the case that God's wonderful plan of redemption is illogical. Many truths are simply not of a logical nature. Just as the tools of a historian do not help in the solving of mathematical problems, so logic or logical consistency is not a factor in evaluating everything a Calvinist teaches. If Calvinism embraces doctrines which conflict with other doctrines they teach or with something taught in Scripture, then it is legitimate to reject those doctrines on that basis alone. However, even if Calvinism was logically consistent in what it teaches (which it is not), it still must pass the test of Scripture. For although an illogical statement cannot be true, a logical statement is not necessarily true. For example, there is nothing illogical about the heresy of Unitarianism, but it is, according to Scripture, a false doctrine.

3

UNCONDITIONAL ELECTION/ REPROBATION

SCRIPTURALLY REFUTED

Most Calvinists will admit that there are a number of passages in the New Testament that seem to pose a problem for their view of unconditional election and/or reprobation. Sometimes these passages are referred to as the pillars of Arminianism. My contention is that these two, as well as similar passages, are pillars of the truth regarding salvation. If that agrees with the Arminian view (or, in fact, any other non-Calvinist view), so be it.

One of these passages is found in Paul's first pastoral letter to Timothy. Paul tells us:

> *God ... desires all men to be saved and to come to the knowledge of the truth. (1 Tim. 2:3–4)*

With this verse in mind, Spurgeon says that:

> It is quite certain that when we read that God will have all men to be saved it does not mean that he wills it with the force of a decree or a divine purpose, for, if he did, then all men would be saved.[173]

No non-Calvinist Evangelical that I know believes that God's *desire* here is the same as a *decree*. That is, all non-Calvinist Evangelicals would agree with Spurgeon in saying that what God wants in this sense is not what He will get. And no Evangelical would argue that God determined that all would be saved. Had He done so, we would all agree that everyone would eventually and inevitably be saved. If, however, God decrees the damnation of the reprobate, in the Calvinist sense, then there is a conflict between what God desires and what He decrees. In a futile and convoluted attempt to resolve the conflict between what God *desires* and the Calvinist view of unconditional election, MacArthur reasons:

> The Gr. word for "desires" is not that which normally expresses God's will of decree (His eternal purpose), but God's will of desire. There is a distinction between God's desire and His eternal saving purpose. … Ultimately, God's choices are determined by His sovereign, eternal purpose, not His desires.[174]

It is true that there are many things that do not happen that God desires to happen, or that do happen that God desires not to happen. For example, God desires that Christians always tell the truth. Yet few, if any, always tell the truth, no matter how honest they typically may be. So, unless you argue that Christians always do what God desires them to do, you must agree that God does not always get what He desires.

MacArthur, however, seems to be confused about this desire/decree dilemma. Suppose we get to heaven and find out that although we were told that God did not desire us to lie, He actually decreed that we should and would lie. That is, what if we found out that the primary reason we lied when we lied is that God determined this is what we would do? First and foremost, He decrees that we will lie, and then as a consequence to that decree, we actually do lie. God could allow or permit us to lie without being responsible for our lies. God could not make us lie, however, by way of a Calvinist kind of decree, without being responsible for our lie. This is the kind of problem MacArthur faces with his desire/decree explanation. It is not as though God cannot desire one thing and then permit another. He can and does. He cannot, however, desire one thing and then decree, in the Calvinist/MacArthur sense, another thing, without being morally responsible for whatever comes to pass in correspondence to that decree.

God is and must be responsible for what we do; and He must be responsible for what He does not desire us to do—if indeed His decree is what makes us do what He does not desire us to do. God can and does decree that a man may be *able* to lie. God can and does permit the telling of lies. In the Calvinist sense, however, the decree of something *to be* is the primary and responsible cause of that which *is to be*. While Calvinists are not required to agree with Calvin on every minutiae of doctrine, it is still instructive to see how Calvin interpreted the word *desire* in 1 Timothy 2:4. Calvin said that the *desire* of this text *is* God's *decree*. Thus Calvin asked:

> What is more reasonable than that all our prayers should be in conformity with this decree of God?[175]

If this were all that Calvin said on this matter it would mean that MacArthur cannot be right in contrasting God's desire with His decree and at the same time be in agreement with Calvin. It is not, however, the entirety of what Calvin said on this matter. John Piper goes to great lengths to get God off the moral hook that Calvin and Calvinists have put Him on by arguing that there is no necessary conflict in a desired versus a decreed will of God in the Calvinism scheme. This is why he says:

> ... unconditional election ... does not contradict biblical expressions of God's compassion for all people, and does not nullify sincere offers of salvation to everyone who is lost among all the peoples of the world.[176]

The only way this can be true is if we do to Piper's words what Calvinism does with Scripture. That is, the words *all people* must refer to *all kinds of people*. The sincere offer must *only* be to *everyone* who is among the elect and still lost. If we assume that what God desires in this text is not what God decrees, the argument has no merit. For if the *decreed will of God* is the primary reason that the *desired will of God* is unfulfilled, then God has not decreed in accordance with what He desires, but He has decreed *contrary to* what He desires.

Remember that, according to MacArthur and Piper, God desires that all men be saved and decrees that some men be damned. According to Calvinism, however, the desire of God only comes to pass when God decrees that it will. Of course, the same is true of everything else, according to a consistent Calvinism. That is, if it happens, it is because God decreed it to be so. God, according to Calvinism, decrees what He decrees always and only because it pleases Him to do so. Are we to believe that God is pleased to do what He decrees but is not pleased to do what He desires? Someone help me please!

As we have already read, however, in Calvinism damnation is just as much determined by what pleases the Lord as is salvation. That is, according to Calvin and Calvinism, insofar as we know, those ultimately damned are damned for the same revealed reason those ultimately saved are saved—it pleases God. The Calvinist can reasonably argue that God permits what He would rather not have happen without being inconsistent or unscriptural. The Calvinist cannot, however, reasonably argue that something turns out a certain way because this is what pleases God or because He has decreed it, and then turn around and say that God really desires something else.

By pitting what God desires against what pleases God, Calvinists have created an even more serious logical and scriptural problem. The hypo-Calvinist cannot embrace an unconditional love that is universal and an unconditional election, which is anything *but universal*. The hypo-Calvinist wants what a consistent and seemingly less compassionate Calvinism will not let him have. John Piper may be responsible for one the strangest attempts made by a Calvinist to rescue Calvinism from the hopeless contradiction that Reformed Theology has created. Piper says:

> I affirm with John 3:16 and 1 Timothy 2:4 that God loves the world with a deep compassion that desires the salvation of all men. Yet I also affirm that God has chosen from before the foundation of the world whom he will save from sin. Since not all people are saved we must choose whether we believe (with Arminians) that God's will to save all people is restrained by his commitment to human self determination or whether we believe (with Calvinists) that God's will to save all people is restrained by his commitment to the glorification of his sovereign grace.[177]

Note that this "deep compassion" to which Piper refers is that God "desires that all men be saved." In these words Piper thereby affirms what MacArthur denies, namely that God also loves the reprobate with a saving love. Nevertheless, immediately after pitting *God's will to save all men* against *His will to glorify His sovereign grace,* Piper goes on to say:

> God's will for all people to be saved is not at odds with the sovereignty of God's grace in election. That is, my answer to the question about what restrains God's will to save all people is his supreme commitment to uphold and display the full range of his glory through the sovereign demonstration of his wrath and mercy for the enjoyment of his elect and believing people from every tribe and tongue and nation.[178]

"Restrains God's will"? What Piper says is that God has a supreme will that will result in the glorification of His sovereign grace and which is to display the full range of God's glory through the sovereign demonstration of His wrath *and* mercy, etc. Accordingly, God also has a *less* than supreme will, which is to save all men. According to Piper, God cannot have it both ways. God therefore chooses to fulfill His *supreme* will rather than His *less* than supreme will. Remember that Piper set out to rescue Calvinism from the charge that it says God's *sovereign* will is at odds with His *saving* will. His supposed solution continues to put at odds the two wills of God—he simply invents a "supreme" will and "less than supreme" will. Piper has not refuted the charges against Calvinism; he has affirmed and added to them.

It is incredible to think that Piper can believe he has somehow helped the Calvinist case. Perhaps he could use the favorite Calvinist "synonym" for contradiction—mystery. And Piper makes it so easy to choose! You can choose to agree with those Arminians who are so *man-centered* or with the Calvinists who are so *God-centered*. Referring to what Piper calls the "Arminian pillar texts," he reasons that they:

> ... may indeed be pillars for universal love, nevertheless they are not weapons against electing grace.[179]

Unlike MacArthur, who believes God loves everyone, just not with a saving love, Piper sees the love that God has for everyone as a saving love. Piper calls this saving love a "universal love." It is a saving love for everyone, not just the elect. Thus, it is a saving love for the reprobate just as it is a saving love for the elect. God does not have one kind of love for the elect and another love for the reprobate. For "God loves the world with a deep compassion that desires the salvation of all men."[180] That saving love that is directed toward the reprobate, however, inevitably runs up against, or is contrary to, God's electing grace as well as His need or desire to demonstrate His wrath and the full range of His glory.

If, however, God elects those He elects because He chooses to savingly love them, as most mainstream Calvinists contend, then the love involved in 1 Timothy 2:4 or 2 Peter 3:9 cannot be universal. That is, the love implicit in these pillar texts *is* a weapon against unconditional election if it is a saving love and if it is universal. Piper also seems to want what his doctrines of salvation and damnation will not allow him to have. He's just a little more creative in trying to get it. (A little later, we will hear directly from Calvin on this very matter.) After arguing that God has no saving interest in much, if not most of mankind, with 1 Timothy 2:4 in mind, Hagopian admits:

> At first glance, this passage appears to contradict everything we have said up to this point.[181]

Without getting into the specifics of what Hagopian was proposing just before this statement, he, like most hypo-Calvinists, believes that God is only interested in saving some of mankind and not all of mankind. He also believes, with all Calvinists, that Christ only died savingly for those in whom God has a saving interest. Obviously, a passage such as 1 Timothy 2:4 will at least appear to contradict him. To remove this apparent contradiction in the mind of the potential convert to Calvinism, Hagopian reasons:

> … This passage teaches either that God desires that many be saved, which is perfectly true, or that He desires all kinds of men to be saved … God wants all kinds of men to be saved. … "all kinds of men" is a perfectly legitimate translation of the word *pas* [all] in 1 Timothy 2:4. … Christ did not come for the Jews alone; He came for all kinds of men. Christ did not come for the rich alone; He came for all kinds of men. Christ did not come for the poor alone; He came for all kinds of men. And this is the point made in 1 Timothy 2:4, as well as in similar passages that teach that Christ died for all.[182]

Thus, Hagopian says that the issue is not with what God desires, but with the meaning of the word "all." Accordingly, the word "all" could mean "many" or "all kinds" rather than every single one. God really desires what Scripture says He desires. We just need a Calvinist to tell us what the word *all* really means. White agrees with Hagopian and says:

> … It is perfectly consistent with the immediate and broader context of Paul's writings to recognize this use of "all men" in a generic fashion … [as in] all kinds of men.[183]

While it is certainly true that Christ came for "all kinds of men," the all kinds of men He came to save are *the lost kind*. Referring to Himself, Jesus said *"the Son of Man has come to save that which was lost"* (Matt. 18:11). It follows that whatever else may be true of a man, whether he is a Jew, Gentile, Greek, or German, if that man is a lost man, Jesus came to save him. Calvinists, however, taking their cue from Calvin, must read into Scripture their theological convictions, since those convictions cannot be found in the text. While MacArthur and Piper distinguish between what God desires and what He decrees, Hagopian, like Calvin, referred to God's desire as His decree or at least leading to God's decrees. Commenting on the subsequent words: *"And may come to the acknowledgment of the truth,"* Calvin argued that this:

... Demonstrates that God has at heart the salvation of all, because he invites all to the acknowledgment of this truth. This belongs to that kind of argument in which the cause is: proved from the effect; for, if "the gospel is the power of God for salvation to every one that believeth" (Romans 1:16), it is certain that all those to whom the gospel is addressed are invited to the hope of eternal life.[184]

Before you conclude that Calvin interpreted these words to mean that anyone may come in faith to Christ and be saved, consider what Calvin went on to say:

The Apostle simply means, that there is no people and no rank in the world that is excluded from salvation; because God wishes that the gospel should be proclaimed to all without exception. Now the preaching of the gospel gives life; and hence he justly concludes that God invites all equally to partake of salvation. But the present discourse relates to classes of men, and not to individual persons; for his sole object is, to include in this number princes and foreign nations. That God wishes the doctrine of salvation to be enjoyed by them as well as others, is evident from the passages already quoted, and from other passages of a similar nature. ... In a word, Paul intended to shew that it is our duty to consider, not what kind of persons the princes at that time were, but what God wished them to be. Now the duty arising: out of that love which we owe to our neighbor is, to be solicitous and to do our endeavor for the salvation of all whom God includes in his calling, and to testify this by godly prayers.[185]

With just a few strokes of the quill, Calvin was able to reduce the saving interest of God *for all* in the world *to some* in the world. In other words, according to Calvin, "the present discourse relates to classes of men, and not to individual persons." Calvinists have been using this argument to accomplish the same purpose (i.e., a narrowing and restricting of the saving interest of God to an elect *caste* of men) ever since. The Calvinist interpretation can be stated as a salvation syllogism:

- God wishes all to be saved. Only some are saved. The all He wishes to save, therefore, equals the some He does in fact save.

Or:

- God wishes all to be saved. All of the elect are saved. All He wishes to save, therefore, equals the elect that He does in fact save.

Initially, it appears that Calvin recognized that God has a saving interest in all of mankind. Given a little time to explain what he meant, Calvin managed to limit that saving interest, in his thinking and theology, into a saving interest in the elect of mankind only. While Calvinists will argue among themselves about the nature of the love of God for the reprobate, all Calvinists end up denying that God has anything that could be considered a real saving interest in those He does not choose to save. With 1 Timothy 2:4 in mind, Spurgeon had some very critical comments to those who interpreted the "all" in this passage as a *relative* "all." That is:

> "All men," say they; "that is, *some men*": as if the Holy Ghost could not have said "some men" if he had meant some men. "All men," say they; "that is, some of all sorts of men": as if the Lord could not have said "All sorts of men" if he had meant that. The Holy Ghost by the apostle has written "all men," and unquestionably he means all men. I know how to get rid of the force of the "alls" according to that critical method which some time ago was very current, but I do not see how it can be applied here with due regard to the truth.[186]

Spurgeon was locked in a decades-long theological battle with the hyper-Calvinists of his day. This is the way they treated 1 Timothy 2:4. Ironically, this is exactly the way many of Spurgeon's most loyal fans treat (or mistreat) this passage today. I am not sure that Spurgeon was aware that what he says here in criticism of some Calvinists applies equally to what we just read by Calvin. Since he read Calvin's *Institutes* and *Commentaries* he should have known this.

Despite the fact that most Calvinists insist that all the men God wills to save must be limited to those He actually does save, the context of 1 Timothy 4 gives us a number of reasons to believe otherwise. Calvinists agree that there is only one Savior. Yet, in 1 Timothy 4:10, the apostle Paul says:

> ... *We trust in the living God, who is the Savior of all men, especially of those who believe.*

A straightforward reading of this verse seems to suggest that the God we trust is the Savior, at least in some sense, of two classes of men. He is the Savior of believers and unbelievers. No Calvinist, however, would say that He is the Savior of unbelievers *in the same sense* that He is the Savior of the believer. Another way of saying this is to say that God is not the Savior of all in the same sense that He is the Savior of some. He is the Savior in both cases. So what is the difference? The difference is that God, the only possible Savior of all, only actually saves those who believe in His Son and accept His Son's sacrifice on their behalf. Some Calvinists will say that if God does not actually save an unbeliever, He cannot be that unbeliever's Savior. That is, however, like saying that the subject of a king must be in subjection to that king in order for the king to be that subject's king. It would also be like saying that God, who is Lord over all, is not Lord over those in rebellion to His Lordship. God is and can be the Savior of those He does not save, just as He is the Lord of those who do not willingly serve Him.

Clearly, there is a difference between affirming the Lordship of Christ over those who have submitted their lives to His rule, and affirming His Lordship over those who reject Him and His rule. Just so, there is a difference between saying that God is the only Savior of those who have met the only God-ordained condition of salvation, and saying He is the Savior of those who have not or never will trust Him to save them. That is why Paul says that God is the Savior of those that believe, or believers, in a special or distinctive sense. To avoid the problems faced by a denial of the fact that this Scripture says God is the Savior of all men, some Calvinists, such as MacArthur, see God saving the elect, in an eternal and complete sense, and the reprobate, in a temporal and incomplete sense. God provides a *temporal atonement* (as MacArthur calls it) for the reprobate in "spill over" or "overflow" benefits from the salvation provided for the elect. (See MacArthur's notes on 1 Tim. 4:10 and 1 Jn 2:2 in his Study Bible.) John Piper, seemingly always willing to do whatever is necessary to accommodate Scripture to Reformed Theology, says:

> … Christ is the Savior of all men … he is *especially* the Savior of those who believe … The death of Christ actually saves from *all* evil those for whom Christ died especially.[187]

The text, however, does not say that Christ died especially for those He saves. Rather, it says He is the Savior in a special sense of those who believe. It is therefore the absence of faith in Christ and not the absence of an atonement by Christ for some that matters. If Christ did not die redemptively for those that are ultimately lost, how can Piper say that He is their Savior in any meaningful sense? Surely, Christ cannot even be the possible or potential Savior of those on whose behalf He did nothing of a saving nature. If Christ must die for a person for that person to be saved, it follows that those He did not savingly die for cannot be saved. It also follows that Christ cannot be called the Savior, in any sense, of such a person. Even though He can be the Lord of those who do not voluntarily submit to His Lordship in this life, He cannot be the Savior of those He has no saving interest in and for whom He has done nothing of a saving nature. What could Piper possible mean when he refers to "those for whom Christ died especially?" Is he suggesting that Christ died for the reprobate—just not especially?

SEEKING TO SAVE THE LOST

According to Luke, Jesus, referring to Himself and His purpose for coming, says:

> *"The Son of Man has come to seek and to save that which was lost." (Luke 19:10)*

If Calvinism is true, it would be more precise, if not more accurate, to say, the Son of Man has come to seek and to save *the elect lost*. In his now classic sermon entitled *Good News for the Lost,* Charles Spurgeon ministered to the unsaved attending one of his services as follows:

> I would have all anxious hearts consider HOW THE OBJECTS OF MERCY ARE HERE DESCRIBED—"The Son of Man is come to seek and to save that which was lost." I feel inexpressibly grateful for this description—"that which was lost!" There cannot be a case so bad as not to be comprehended in this word, "lost." I am quite unable to imagine the condition of any man so miserable as not to be contained within the circumference of these four letters—"lost."[188]

Spurgeon went on to exhort the "lost" in his listening audience with these very encouraging and non-Calvinist words:

> Beloved Friends, "The Son of Man is come to seek and to save that which was lost." Does not the description suit you? Are you not among the lost? Well then, you are among such as Jesus Christ came to save.[189]

These and similar words got Spurgeon in hot water with the hyper-Calvinists of his day. If you take the time to read their criticism of Spurgeon, however, they were only asking him to be consistent. To be consistent with

Calvinism would be to deny so much that Scripture says and that Spurgeon believed. It is simply not possible, logically speaking, to say *you are among such as Jesus Christ came to save* merely because *you are among the lost* and, at the same time, embrace unconditional election. Are we to believe that Spurgeon was using the words *among* and *such as* to say that if you are lost and reprobate, you are only *like* those who can be saved? That is, since you are lost and not elect, you cannot be saved. If that is what Spurgeon wished to communicate, he certainly had a very odd way of doing so. How would a lost, but non-elect person find comfort in the fact that they were lost, since they would not be one of those whom the Lord came to save? To be merely *like* one of those the Lord came to save would hardly be comforting to the reprobate. Such a notion would be a reasonable basis for despair and hope-lessness, not consolation and comfort. If you are only *among those* that are lost and can be saved and not *one of those* who are lost and can be saved, Spurgeon could not be preaching news that was *any good for you*. And if the news is not *truly* good, it is not the *true* gospel.

Spurgeon, like so many hypo-Calvinists, could not follow through and become a consistent Calvinist without also giving up on so much that Scripture says. So Spurgeon tried to do the impossible. He tried to embrace the five points of Calvinism as well as the teachings of John Calvin and also remain faithful to all that Scripture says. This resulted in Spurgeon appeal-ing to everyone to receive Christ, even though he believed that Christ really did not come to save everyone. Despite his universal appeals to anyone and everyone, and the grief he received from the hyper-Calvinists of his day for such appeals, it was Spurgeon's posture and not his position that really distinguished him from the hyper-Calvinists. In other words, it was what Spurgeon chose to *emphasize* that set him apart from the hyper-Calvinists, at least as much as what he really believed. Let us compare what we just read Spurgeon saying to the lost with what he explains elsewhere about our Lord's mission to the lost:

> Our Lord's mission was not so much to save all whom he ad-dressed, as to save out of them as many as his Father gave him.[190]

While Spurgeon tells *all* the lost there is hope because Christ came to save the lost, he did not believe Christ *elected, efficaciously calls,* or *died for all* the lost. Still and inconsistently, like many other Calvinists of the hypo-variety, Spurgeon believed that while God unconditionally elects those ultimately saved, those ultimately damned have only themselves to blame.

Thus Spurgeon saw no problem saying:

> From the Word of God I gather that damnation is all of man, from
> top to bottom, and salvation is all of grace, from first to last. He that
> perishes chooses to perish; but he that is saved is saved because
> God has chosen to save him.[191]

Reprobation, however, is as most Calvinists reason, the logical flip side
of unconditional election. And if anything is clear, it is that unconditional
reprobation makes lostness a hopeless situation for countless numbers of
people who were *passively* not elected, or *actively* reprobated. If we were to
allow Calvinists to help out Luke a little, we could rewrite the words of Jesus
to agree with Calvinism:

> The Son of Man has come to seek and save *the elect lost.*

The other passage that Piper referred to as a pillar of Arminianism
comes to us through the apostle Peter. Like so many other passages of
Scripture, if you did not come to the text already convinced that Calvinism
is true, you could never interpret 2 Peter 3:9 as does the Calvinist. If,
however, you come to this text convinced of Calvinism, you must find
a way to explain away what Peter clearly says. Without equivocation or
qualification, Peter tells us:

> *The Lord ... is longsuffering toward us, not willing that **any** should
> perish but that **all** should come to repentance. (2 Pet. 3:8–9,
> emphasis added)*

Ordinarily, most Evangelicals would agree with the interpretive
principle:

> When the plain sense makes good sense, seek no other sense.

When the plain sense does not conform to the Calvinist sense, however,
the Calvinist will need to ask, as does Sproul:

> How can we square this verse with [the Calvinist view of]
> predestination? ... What is the antecedent to *any*?[192]

Sproul then answers:

> It is clearly us. ... I think that what he is saying here is that God
> does not will that any of us (the elect) perish.[193]

This is a textbook example of *eisegesis,* reading into a text what it does not say or suggest, not *exegesis,* getting out of the text what it does say and suggest. MacArthur agrees with Sproul when he says:

> "Us" is the saved, the people of God. He waits for them to be saved. ... He is calling and redeeming His own. ... The "any" must refer to those whom the Lord has chosen and will call to complete the redeemed, i.e., the "us" ... "All" ... must refer to all who are God's people who will come to Christ to make up the full number of the people of God.[194]

Thus, for MacArthur and other Calvinists, the people of God include all the elect people still unsaved. In other words, in the most basic sense, we do not become the people of God when we believe. Rather, it simply becomes manifest that we already are and have always been God's people. Spencer asks:

> Why is the Lord longsuffering regarding His promised coming?[195]

He then answers:

> For the simple reason that He is: ... not willing that any of (US) should perish, but that all of (US) should come to repentance.[196]

James White argues:

> ... This passage is not speaking about salvation as its topic. The reference to "coming to repentance" in 3:9 is made in passing.[197]

Even if this passage is not speaking about salvation as its topic, what it says about salvation, passing or otherwise, must be true if the apostle Peter is telling the truth. Even so, White is in agreement with Hagopian and most other hypo-Calvinists in the way he interprets this passage. He explains:

> Peter writes to a specific group, not to all of mankind. ... There is nothing in chapter three that indicates a change in audience, and much to tell us the audience remains exactly the same. ... Therefore, the "not wishing any should perish" must be limited to the same group already in view: the elect. In the same way, the "all to come to repentance" must be the very same group. In essence Peter is saying the coming of the Lord has been delayed so that all the elect of God can be gathered in. Any modern Christian lives

and knows Christ solely because God's purpose has been to gather in His elect down through the ages to this present day. There is no reason to expand the context of the passage into a universal proclamation of a desire on God's part that every single person come to repentance. Instead, it is clearly His plan and His will that *all the elect* come to repentance, and they most assuredly will do so.[198]

No matter who the audience might be, it does not alter what Peter actually says:

> *The Lord ... is longsuffering toward us, not willing that any should perish but that all should come to repentance. (2 Pet. 3:9)*

It is not the context that determines the meaning of Peter's words for the Calvinist. It is the Calvinist doctrines of salvation and damnation that leads him to interpret the words *any* and *all* to mean any and all *of us*. If they did not already believe in the Reformed view, I am convinced that these otherwise very astute scholars would understand these words in the same way that the rest of us do. Commenting on this verse, Calvin said:

> So wonderful is [God's] love towards mankind, that he would have them all to be saved, and is of his own self prepared to bestow salvation on the lost. But the order is to be noticed, that God is ready to receive all to repentance, so that none may perish; for in these words the way and manner of obtaining salvation is pointed out. Every one of us, therefore, who is desirous of salvation, must learn to enter in by this way.[199]

Once again, however, what Calvin gave, he also took away. Thus he immediately went on to say:

> But it may be asked, if God wishes none to perish, why is it that so many do perish? To this my answer is, that no mention is here made of the hidden purpose of God, according to which the reprobate are doomed to their own ruin, but only of his will as made known to us in the gospel. For God there stretches forth his hand without a difference to all, but lays hold only of those, to lead them to himself, whom he has chosen before the foundation of the world.[200]

If you only know God's "will as made known to us in the gospel," you don't have the whole story, according to Calvin. You need to factor in "the

hidden purpose of God, according to which the reprobate are doomed ..."
If you can see what is hidden, you can see what Calvin and Calvinism is
saying. I will confess that I find it difficult to see that which is hidden. I also
confess, if it is not made known in the *not hidden* pages of Scripture, it is
very difficult for me to see it.

Picture, if you will, a hand stretched out *to all*. Then, picture that hand
only grabbing hold of some of those that the hand has been stretched out
to. This is what Calvin was saying about God. He is stretching out a hand
that makes it appear that He is interested in rescuing all because His hand is
stretched out to all. But that same stretched out hand conceals a hidden purpose, in which the One with the stretched out hand is interested only in saving some to whom He is stretching out His saving hand. What I can clearly
see is that it is the hidden purpose or the secret counsel of God that guides
the Calvinist in his understanding (or misunderstanding) of what Scripture
says, relative to why some are saved and others are damned.

At best, this portrays God as teasing the reprobate. If anyone of us did
this, we would rightly be accused of a cruel and deceptive practice. Suppose
a hundred Calvinists were swimming in rough waters and were about to go
under. Suppose some lifeguards stretched out their hands to all of them, but
only intended to rescue fifty of them (even though they could have saved
all of them). It would not be difficult to imagine that at least fifty Calvinists
would find something troubling about the morality of lifeguards who would
behave in such a manner.

What if these same lifeguards decided to save fifty Arminians and let
fifty Calvinists drown? Would the Calvinists object? The lifeguards could
argue that they have the right to save anyone they desire to save and to let
drown whomever they want to see drown. They could claim that they owe
no one anything, and so they can be merciful to whomever they want and
merciless to whomever they want. They could even say that although they
only chose to save the Arminians and not the Calvinists, it had nothing to do
with the swimmers' theological convictions.

Suppose the lifeguards say that it is not anyone else's business, or it
is over the head of everyone else, or even an incomprehensible mystery.
I do not see much difference in this scenario and that which is inherent in
Reformed Theology. The *all* in 2 Peter 3:9, or those whom Calvin believed
God would cause to come to repentance, are no more or no less than the

elect that He actually does save. More specifically, to Calvin, it was the elect among those that were *wandering and scattered* that Peter had specifically written this letter to. That is:

> God would have all, who had been before wandering and scattered, to be gathered or come together to repentance.[201]

With the dark side of Calvinism in mind, we can also see that:

> The Lord is willing that *all* but the elect should perish and that all but the elect should not come to repentance.

If, however, you come to this text without a Calvinist bias, the Calvinist interpretation is very difficult, if not impossible, to discern. The Lord is longsuffering toward *us* and this is why we could be saved. For indeed, in verse 15 of the same chapter Peter says:

> *Account that the longsuffering of our Lord is salvation. (KJV)*

It is the same longsuffering Lord who does not want *any* to be lost. It would have been a rather simple matter to say the Lord is not willing that any of the elect perish. Instead, however, he says the Lord is not willing that *any* should perish. The fact that the Lord is writing to believers, as White points out, is true of much, if not most of the New Testament, with perhaps the exception of the four Gospels. That does not mean that He cannot be writing *about* non-believers while writing *to* believers. Turning the *any* from the lost community into an elect *us* of the saved community may be required of Calvinism, but it is only *evident* to those who subscribe to Reformed Theology. In effect, the Calvinist concepts of election/reprobation are a divine excuse for the lost.

To illustrate, suppose a student is caught outside a class while class is in session. Suppose the one who catches him demands an explanation. Suppose the child pulls out a note from the principal saying that this child is excused from class. Suppose the note goes on to say *the principal does not want this child in school and never did.* Suppose the principal said he should not be allowed in the classroom because it is only for a group of select young people of which he is *not now, never was, nor ever will be* among. Should the student then be punished for not being in class? Is this not what Calvinists have done with election/reprobation? What better excuse could we give a lost person than the Calvinist view of election/

reprobation? If a person remains lost, he can pull out his *note from God* that says:

> I did not want to save this person. I did not choose to save him. I did not do anything to make it possible for him to be saved. He is up the eternally *bleak creek* without a paddle.

Logically, if Calvinism is true, those who ultimately perish have a very good excuse for not being saved. Let us continue with our analogy of the principal and the student. Suppose the same principal that excludes a student from the classroom punishes the student for not attending class. First, he provides an excuse for not attending class and actually bars the student from attending class. Then he punishes him for not being in class and says that this punishment is just, and that the student's absence from class is inexcusable. When the defenders of this principal are asked to explain how this can be, they say that it cannot now be understood. That is the Calvinist view of reprobation/damnation. This also perfectly illustrates why it is that Calvinists need to appeal to or hide behind an *apparent mystery* so often. Jesus tells us that no one knows:

> *"... The Father except the Son, and the one to whom the Son wills to reveal Him." (Matt. 11:27)*

Calvinists believe that this verse is a very strong *proof text* for unconditional election. As someone said, however, *every text out of context is a pretext.* If you continue reading, our Lord identifies those to whom He *wills* to reveal the Father. With obvious compassion, He says:

> *"Come to Me, all you who labor and are heavy laden, and I will give you rest." (Matt. 11:28)*

Are we supposed to believe that *only* the elect-lost *labor and are heavy laden*? Or are we to assume that the Lord was insincere in inviting *all* who labor and are heavy laden to come to Him for rest? Or perhaps He was only inviting all kinds of people who labor and are heavy laden. At first glance, we might think we only have two choices here.

CALVINISM

- Christ was inviting all that labor and are heavy laden.

- Only the elect (while lost) labor and are heavy laden.

SCRIPTURE

- Christ was inviting all that labor and are heavy laden.

- All the lost labor and are heavy laden.

There is a third option, or a different way to word the first option, that would satisfy some Calvinists:

- Christ was inviting all kinds of people who labor and are heavy laden.

- The all kinds of people He invited to come for rest were the elect kind.

While most Calvinists will vehemently disagree with this characterization, the Calvinist view of unconditional election/reprobation says that a man will be saved or lost *for* all eternity because he is saved or lost *from* all eternity. It amounts to nothing more than an eternal caste system that condemns a very large number of people to eternal misery with no recourse or remedy. As the reprobate do not and cannot have any hope of salvation, the elect, according to Calvinism, have never had any real reason to be concerned about damnation. In an article entitled *I'm Going to Heaven Someday,* Joseph Wilson explains:

> In actuality, not one of the elect has ever for a moment been in real danger of going to hell. No man can truly believe in sovereign grace and question this statement. God's elect were, from eternity, predestined to be conformed to the image of Jesus Christ. They were ordained to eternal life. They were chosen to be saved. ... In reality, they were as safe while living in sin and rebellion against God as they are now.[202]

Consistent Calvinists can also say:

> In actuality, not one of the reprobate, which is everyone who is not one of the elect, has ever for a moment had any hope of going anywhere but hell. No man can truly believe in sovereign predestination and question this statement. God's reprobate were, from eternity, predestined to damnation. They were ordained to reprobation. They were chosen to be damned from all eternity to all eternity.

Compare this despairing and disturbing view with the hope-filled message of John 3:16, 1 Timothy 2:4, and 2 Peter 3:9. You can see why I suggested in my primer on Calvinism that you can have John 3:16 or you can have John Calvin, but you cannot logically have both. With this in mind, let us now take a close look at some of those other passages that Calvinists rely upon to support unconditional election. Keep in mind that for Calvinists, a sovereign unconditional election to salvation rules out the possibility of a sovereign condition for salvation. Faith in Christ, therefore, must ultimately be a *consequence* of a sovereign election by God versus a sovereign *condition* of salvation for man. Jesus says:

> *"... many are called, but few are chosen." (Matt. 22:14)*

Surely, says the Calvinist, *these words at least imply an unconditional election to salvation.* Steele and Thomas, in a chapter of their book written to define, defend, and document unconditional election, offer this verse as evidence. So does Hagopian. Commenting on verse 14, Reformed pastor and professor Douglas Wilson says:

> *Elect* does not mean "elector." *Chosen* does not mean "chooser." The Bible's teaching on this subject is so plain that denying it involves standing the words of Scripture on their head. When a man is chosen, he is not the one performing the action; that is, he is not the one who is choosing.[203]

Wilson's reasoning here is flawless. Does the context of this passage, however, support the Calvinist doctrine of an unconditional election to salvation and its flip side, an unconditional reprobation to damnation? Read and decide for yourself. Backing up a few verses, Jesus says:

> *"The kingdom of heaven is like a certain king who arranged a marriage for his son, and sent out for his servants to call those who were invited to the wedding; and they were **not willing to come**. Again, he sent out other servants, saying, 'Tell those who are invited, "See, I have prepared my dinner; my oxen and fatted cattle are killed, and all things are ready. Come to the wedding." ' But they made light of it and went their ways, one to his own farm, another to his business. And the rest seized his servants, treated them spitefully, and killed them. But when the king heard about it, he was furious. And he sent out his armies, destroyed those murderers, and burned up their city. Then he said to his servants, 'The wedding is*

*ready, but those who were invited were not worthy. Therefore go
into the highways, and as many as you find, invite to the wedding.'
So those servants went out into the highways and gathered together
all whom they found, both bad and good. And the wedding hall was
filled with guests.*

*"But when the king came in to see the guests, he saw a man there
who did not have on a wedding garment. So he said to him, 'Friend,
how did you come in here without a wedding garment?' And he was
speechless. Then the king said to the servants, 'Bind him hand and
foot, take him away, and cast him into outer darkness.' ... For many
are called, but few are chosen." (Matt. 22:2–14, emphasis added)*

WHY ARE SOME EXCLUDED AND OTHERS IN-CLUDED?

Is there a correlation between those invited but unwilling to come and the
many who are called? Or are we to conclude that this whole story leading
up to the statement "many are called, but few are chosen," is something akin
to a *filler*? Is there a correlation between those who were invited and that
became guests and the few who were chosen from among the called? Are
we to understand this latter group was not willing or that their willingness
was irrelevant? Or perhaps we should conclude some were invited, but not
allowed to say no as did the former group. Now if the king was happy that
this latter group came to the wedding and that they came to the wedding
only because he made them come or made them want to come, he certainly
could have done the same for the former. If Calvinism in general, and unconditional election in particular, is true, you should be excused for asking:
why all the fuss?

I am not suggesting here that everything in a story is necessarily ger-
mane to the main point of the story. Certainly, however, some things are.
What is it in this story that will help us understand the concluding statement,
"many are called, but few are chosen"? It seems obvious that the "called"
refers both to the former and latter group, or all who were invited. Only the
latter group, however, corresponds to the "chosen," and they are the ones
who accepted the invitation and dressed appropriately for the occasion. The
responsibility or culpability for attending or failing to attend the wedding
belonged to the one invited, not the king who did the inviting. The provision
and offer was entirely the king's. The responsibility to respond and respond

appropriately to the invitation belonged entirely to the ones invited.

The Calvinist doctrine of unconditional election makes the king out to be insincere, since he invites individuals to come but did not choose them to come, thereby making it impossible for them to accept the invitation. That would of course make the invitation a tease at best. There is no way that such an invitation could be considered a serious or sincere invitation. It could even be considered a fraudulent scam. It makes much more sense to see the chosen ones as guests already and not chosen to be guests. In other words, they were chosen because they were invited guests, not invited to be guests. All were invited *to be guests*, but only those who became guests because they accepted the invitation given them to attend the wedding were chosen *as guests*.

This distinction is crucial. They were invited or called to the wedding and accepted the invitation. They could then be chosen as guests. The others, with the exception of the one who came in unacceptable apparel, were invited, refused the invitation, and therefore did not even show up to be chosen. In reality, they excluded themselves from being guests by refusing to come to the wedding, for only guests at the wedding feast were chosen. In Chapter Twenty of Matthew's Gospel, we see this phrase used again in the context of yet another parable. Jesus says:

> *"For the kingdom of heaven is like a landowner who went out early in the morning to hire laborers for his vineyard. Now when he had agreed with the laborers for a denarius a day, he sent them into his vineyard. And he went out about the third hour and saw others standing idle in the marketplace, and said to them, 'You also go into the vineyard, and whatever is right I will give you.' So they went. Again he went out about the sixth and the ninth hour, and did likewise. And about the eleventh hour he went out and found others standing idle, and said to them, 'Why have you been standing here idle all day?' They said to him, 'Because no one hired us.' He said to them, 'You also go into the vineyard, and whatever is right you will receive.'*
>
> *"So when evening had come, the owner of the vineyard said to his steward, 'Call the laborers and give them their wages, beginning with the last to the first.' And when those came who were hired about the eleventh hour, they each received a denarius.*

> *But when the first came, they supposed that they would receive
> more; and they likewise received each a denarius. And when they
> had received it, they complained against the landowner, saying,
> 'These last men have worked only one hour, and you made them
> equal to us who have borne the burden and the heat of the day.'
> But he answered one of them and said, 'Friend, I am doing you
> no wrong. Did you not agree with me for a denarius? Take what
> is yours and go your way. I wish to give to this last man the same
> as to you. Is it not lawful for me to do what I wish with my own
> things? Or is your eye evil because I am good?' So the last will be
> first, and the first last. For many are called, but few are chosen."
> (Matt. 20:1–16)*

It would seem that the *so* and *for* of 20:16 identify the last in this life
with the "called" who are also "chosen." The question is this: what were they
called to and *chosen for*? The answer is that they were called to and chosen
for the work of the kingdom. Clearly this is not even remotely related to the
kind of unconditional election to salvation found in Calvinism. There is, of
course, a Scripture in which Jesus comes right out and says:

> *"Ye have not chosen me, but I have chosen you." (John 15:16,
> KJV)*

Concerning this verse, Boettner says:

> Christ explicitly declared to His disciples, "Ye did not choose me,
> but I chose you, and appointed you, that ye should go and bear
> fruit," John 15:16, by which He made God's choice primary and
> man's choice only secondary and a result of the former.[204]

Spencer goes so far as to say:

> The bluntest affirmation that man does not do the choosing of God,
> since his depraved nature is capable of being "positive" only to-
> wards Satan, is that of Jesus who said: *"Ye have not chosen Me, but
> I have chosen you"* (John 15:16, cf. v. 17).[205]

Before we consider this verse and what it says and does not say, let us be
clear about one thing. The Calvinist is not denying that there is not a sense
in which we do not choose Christ. They believe we choose Christ, and often
say so, after we are born again and as a result of the new birth, new nature,

saving faith, etc. In fact, they believe that choosing Christ is inevitable for the elect because it is irresistible for the elect. As Sproul says:

> To be sure, a human choice is made, a free human choice, but the choice is made because God first chooses to influence the elect to make the right choice.[206]

This influence is defined by Sproul as *forces, coerces,* or *drags.*[207] If, however, this verse says we do not choose Christ relative to salvation, it also says we *never* do so. That is, it does not say *you chose Me because I chose you*, anymore than it says what an Arminian would say, which is *I chose you because you were going to choose Me*. Unless we read into this verse a Calvinist assumption, it offers no more support for the Calvinist view than it does the Arminian view.

In whatever sense He says the disciples do not choose Him, *they never choose Him*. Otherwise He would have said something like *you did not choose Me first*. He plainly says to His disciples, however, *"you did not choose Me, but I chose you."* I think we can take this verse at face value, keeping in mind the context. What is the context? What is it He chose them for? If it was not for salvation, regeneration, justification, glorification, etc., then what was it for? There can be no doubt that it was *for service*.

By way of analogy, consider a conversation between the owner of a company and an employee of the company. Suppose the owner of a company initially recruited and eventually hired an employee for a specific job. Later in a conversation with that same employee, the owner says, "you did not hire me, but I hired you" for the purpose of producing a lot of widgets.

The employee could not hire the owner. He could accept the offer of a job, but he could not hire himself. Even so, the things God gives us to do for Him, including the abilities, gifts, and opportunities to do them, is really and only from God. We can refuse to do the job He gives us. We can refuse to do a good job relative to the job He gives us to do. We can choose to do the job and choose to do it well. We cannot, however, *choose the job* we are called or elected to do, since it is His and His alone to assign to us.

The job in this case is the sacred ministry, given to each disciple by the Lord Himself. It is first and foremost *service to Him* and as a result, it is *service for Him*. The choosing is always and only His prerogative. Calvinists and non-Calvinists alike at least formally agree that we have some choices to make both in terms of salvation and service. The kind of choice referred to by our Lord in John 15:16–17, however, is a choice that only He can make, by definition of who and what He is in relation to us. In like manner, it is not a choice we can make by definition of who and what we are in relation to Him.

Paul did not choose to be an apostle. Nor indeed could he, any more than an eye could choose to be the member of the body *capable of sight*. We will return to this matter a little later in the context of a discussion of the closely related issue of *calling* and the various ways in which Scripture uses this and similar terms. No matter how you state it, a Calvinist view of this passage is, at best, incapable of consistency. It also fails to take into account the different kinds of *choices* referred to in the New Testament. The Calvinist almost always assumes that when the Bible speaks of God choosing a believer for service, He is referring to a choice made by God on behalf of an unbeliever for salvation.

While most Calvinists will concede that the word "election" can be used in a variety of ways, for all practical purposes, most make an attempt to see an unconditional election to salvation wherever they find a form of the word "election" in Scripture. Show a Calvinist how a particular use of the word "elect" or "election" cannot, according to the context, be an election to salvation—unconditional or otherwise—and he comforts himself with the conviction that somewhere else it will refer to an unconditional election to salvation.

A lawyer who has no single piece of evidence to prove his case may present to the jury and judge a whole host of facts, which on the surface may seem like evidence. When it turns out that after a careful examination of the facts, they do not to prove or even support the case he is trying to make, he just turns to more facts that do not prove his case. The hope is that the jury will just see a bunch of facts, the sheer volume of which must prove something. Sometimes, a whole lot of non-evidence can, when taken together, appear to turn into evidence. It never really does.

So it is with the word "election." If the individual instance in which the word "elect" or "election" is used does not refer to an unconditional election to salvation, the total sum of such instances cannot provide scriptural support for the Calvinist doctrine of unconditional election.

Consider another scriptural use of the word "chosen" that Calvinists use as evidence of an unconditional election to salvation. Jesus says to His disciples:

> *"Did I not choose you, the twelve, and one of you is a devil?"*
> *(John 6:70)*

Obviously, a person can be designated elect, because God has given him something to do; something He has elected him to do. God can elect someone without unconditionally electing him to salvation, for one of those He chose or elected was a devil. No Calvinist I know of believes God unconditionally elects devils to salvation. No Calvinist that I know believes God unconditionally elected Judas to salvation. Yet, the text clearly indicates that Judas was chosen in the same way and for the same purpose as the other eleven disciples. With this verse in mind, White admits:

> Of course the word "chosen" is used in more than one way. No one
> is arguing that "chosen" always has the same meaning.[208]

No matter what Scripture says in a given context, however, the Calvinist is so convinced of unconditional election or what they call sovereign election, and so desperate to find evidence of this view, that there is often a *theological knee-jerk reaction* to the word "election." For example, also with this verse in mind, MacArthur says:

> In response to Peter's words that the disciples had come to believe
> in Jesus, He reminds them that He sovereignly chose them (vv. 37,
> 44, 65). Jesus would not allow even a whisper of human pretension
> in God's sovereign selection.[209]

Does MacArthur see evidence of the Calvinist version of sovereign and unconditional election to salvation in Judas? Of course, Jesus sovereignly chose the disciples. Everything a sovereign Lord does, He does sovereignly. By definition, our Lord's choice of the twelve, for whatever reason He chose them, was a sovereign choice. His choice of Judas was just as sovereign as His choice of Peter. This just goes to show how wrong the Calvinists can be about the meaning and implications of a sovereign choice. Did MacArthur not notice that this sovereign choice included Judas? It is almost impossible not to notice Judas, since he is the only one identified by name, in this text, as chosen by our Lord.

No, MacArthur did not miss the identity of Judas as one of the chosen, as is evident in the time and attention he gave to the diabolical character and conduct of Judas. Regardless, if so many of the passages used to support the Calvinist doctrine of unconditional election do not actually teach this doctrine, the Calvinist has to introduce it wherever he can. Commenting on this verse and specifically the elect of this verse, Calvin said:

> When Christ says that he has CHOSEN or ELECTED *twelve,* he does not refer to the eternal purpose of God; ... but, having been *chosen* to the apostolic office. ... He used the word *chosen*, therefore, to denote those who were eminent and distinguished from the ordinary rank.[210]

The apostle Peter says:

> ... *giving all diligence, add to your faith virtue, to virtue knowledge, to knowledge self-control, to self-control perseverance, to perseverance godliness, to godliness brotherly kindness, and to brotherly kindness love. For if these things are yours and abound, you will be neither barren nor unfruitful in the knowledge of our Lord Jesus Christ. For he who lacks these things is shortsighted, even to blindness, and has forgotten that he was cleansed from his old sins.*
>
> *Therefore, brethren, be even more diligent to make your call and election sure, for if you do these things you will never stumble; for so an entrance will be supplied to you abundantly into the everlasting kingdom of our Lord and Savior Jesus Christ.*
>
> *For this reason I will not be negligent to remind you always of these things, though you know and are established in the present truth. (2 Pet. 1:5–12)*

In context, Peter is exhorting his readers to live a life in concert with their "call and election." In reference to the word "election," Calvin automatically concluded that Peter refers here to an unconditional election to salvation. Calvin explains this passage as follows:

> The meaning then is, labor that you may have it really proved that you have not been called and elected in vain. ... Now a question arises. Whether the stability of our calling and election depends on good works, for if it be so, it follows that it depends on us. But the

whole Scripture teaches us, first, that God's election is founded on His eternal purpose; and second, that calling begins and is completed through His gratuitous goodness ...

If anyone thinks that calling is rendered sure by men, there is nothing absurd in that; we may however, go still farther, that everyone confirms his calling by leading a holy and pious life ... this does not prevent election from being gratuitous, nor does it shew that it is in our own hand or power to confirm election. For the matter stands thus,—God effectually calls whom He has preordained to life in His secret counsel before the foundation of the world; and He also carries on the perpetual course of calling through grace alone. But as he has chosen us, and calls us for this end, that we may be pure and spotless in his presence; purity of life is not improperly called the evidence and proof of election ...[211]

I am simply amazed that such a brilliant man, as Calvin no doubt was, could not see or was willing to overlook the many and serious problems with this view. First of all, Calvin had to know that it is meaningless to appeal to men to do what they cannot help but do (i.e. "God ... carries on the perpetual course of [effectual] calling ..."). Second, it is silly to ask a man to confirm what he is incapable of confirming, which is the case for the reprobate, according to Calvin. Third, how could an effectual calling or unconditional election be in vain? If you are called and elect, according to Calvinism, all the other links in the chain of redemption will inevitably and irresistibly follow.

If you could somehow prove your calling and election were in vain in the Calvinist sense of calling and election, you would only prove you were not called or elected, according to Calvinism. That would also prove you had no calling or election to prove, one way or the other. It would be like trying to prove that words have no meaning with words. If words have no meaning, you could not meaningfully prove such a theory with words.

According to the apostle Peter, an awful lot hangs on making your calling and election sure. Viewing this calling and election, in this context, as the calling and election of a believer (and the service or even character development he is called to and elected for) makes sense. It makes no sense to view this calling and election as an unconditional election to salvation for the unbeliever. It is my contention that a careful look at the way Scripture uses the term election does not support any notion of an election to salvation for the unbelieving lost—unconditional or conditional. That is, insofar as the New Testament is concerned, the issues involving election are always and only issues that concern believers. Unbelievers are not referred to as the elect of God or the called of God in the New Testament.

Now there is an invitation-type "calling" that both Calvinists and non-Calvinist Evangelicals acknowledge. The calling, which is most often associated with election in Scripture, is not an invitation to salvation but a calling in the sense of vocation, Christian service, character development, or even our ultimate destiny as believers. Christians are elected for and called to a variety of things, in keeping with the purposes of a holy God. Show me an elect person in the post-Pentecost period (as this term is related to the New Testament saints), and I will show you a Christian. Conversely, show me a non-Christian and I will show you a person that is not one of the elect of God or one of the called of God. Does God elect believers as Scripture seems to say, or does He make the elect believe as Calvinism teaches?

MacArthur identifies another verse that he believes *clearly* supports the Calvinist view of unconditional election. He says:

> In 2 Thessalonians … chapter 2 verse 13, [Paul says] "But we should always give thanks to God for you." Why should we always thank God? "Brethren, because God has chosen you from the beginning for salvation."[212]

Paul says to the Thessalonian believers:

> *But we are bound to give thanks to God always for you, brethren beloved by the Lord, because God from the beginning chose you for salvation through sanctification by the Spirit and belief in the truth, to which He called you by our gospel, for the obtaining of the glory of our Lord Jesus Christ. (2 Thess. 2:13–14)*

- We know from this text that the one doing the choosing for this salvation is God.

- We know that God made this choice from the beginning.

- We know that this salvation is faith-based.

- We know that the calling related to this salvation was the open and even audible proclamation of the gospel. It was not a hidden, secret, or inward calling.

- We know that nothing even remotely related to an unconditional election to salvation for unbelievers is mentioned in these verses.

The Calvinist will argue erroneously that if God's choice to save a particular man is conditioned upon that man believing, then it is man and not God who is in control. At best this is misleading, for it is God who determines what the condition of salvation for a man will be, and even that there will be a condition. Man is in no position to dictate to God that He will or will not condition salvation on faith in Christ. If God decided that salvation would not be conditioned on anything, that would have been His choice and no one could contest it.

If God chose to condition salvation on faith in Christ, as I am convinced Scripture teaches, it is no less God who decides how He would go about His work of saving the lost and under what, if any, conditions He would do so. Sovereignty is not denied because it is God doing what He wants to do, the way He wants to do it. Grace is not denied if the condition is not meritorious, or a work. Admittedly, such a salvation could not be gracious if the condition was anything but faith. Since, however, it is *through faith,* it can be and is *by grace* (Eph. 2:8–10).

The Calvinist contends that the elect believe because they are in Christ, while Scripture makes it clear that we are in Christ because this is where God places the believer when he believes. All Evangelicals agree that in Christ, God provides much for the believer and promises much for the believer. As the apostle Paul says:

> *If in this life only we have hope in Christ, we are of all men the most pitiable.*

> *But now Christ is risen from the dead, and has become the firstfruits of those who have fallen asleep. For since by man came death, by Man also came the resurrection of the dead. For as in Adam all die, even so in Christ all shall be made alive. But each one in his own order: Christ the firstfruits, afterward those who are Christ's at His coming. (1 Cor. 15:19–23)*

The context of this passage does not allow us to think of this life as the life of regeneration, but of resurrection, which are admittedly two ends of the same saving work of God. Thus, all that are alive in the regeneration sense will be made alive in the resurrection sense. We have life *here and now* and we are looking forward to life *there and then*. In Adam, the entire human family was born into spiritual death. In Adam, the entire human family is also on the road to physical death. We are born spiritually dead and then a few years later we physically die. In Christ, all members of the family of God have received life through the new birth. Most still die physically, but physical death has no permanent hold on them because in Christ, all will be resurrected to glory. The significance of this privileged position of the believer cannot be overstated. As to our present spiritual condition, Paul says:

> *If anyone is in Christ, he is a new creation; old things have passed away; behold, all things have become new. (2 Cor. 5:17)*

Concerning how blessed believers are and will be "in Christ" and because we are "in Christ," Paul says:

> *Blessed be the God and Father of our Lord Jesus Christ, who has blessed us with every spiritual blessing in the heavenly places in Christ, just as He chose us in Him before the foundation of the world, that we should be holy and without blame before Him in love, having predestined us to adoption as sons by Jesus Christ to Himself, according to the good pleasure of His will, to the praise of the glory of His grace, by which He made us accepted in the Beloved.*
>
> *In Him we have redemption through His blood, the forgiveness of sins, according to the riches of His grace which He made to abound toward us in all wisdom and prudence, having made known to us the mystery of His will, according to His good pleasure which He purposed in Himself, that in the dispensation of the fullness of the times He might gather together in one all things in Christ, both which are in heaven and which are on earth—in Him. In Him also we have obtained an inheritance, being predestined according to the purpose of Him who works all things according to the counsel of His will, that we who first trusted in Christ should be to the praise of His glory. (Eph. 1:3–12)*

- The choice that is referred to here was made by God.

- The choice was made by God "before the foundation of the world."

- The choice made by God "before the foundation of the world" was made of individuals that were "in Him."

- The purpose of the choice made by God "before the foundation of the world" of individuals "in Him" was that those so chosen would "be holy and without blame before Him in love."

- To accomplish this purpose God "predestined us [those in Christ] to adoption as sons by Jesus Christ to Himself."

- All this is "according to the good pleasure of His will, to the praise of the glory of His grace."

- This grace which is glorified is the same grace "by which He has made us accepted in the Beloved."

According to Reformed Theology, these individuals are not *chosen in Him* but *chosen to be in Him*. This distinction is crucial. To be chosen *in Him* is to be chosen as a *believer*. Chosen *to be* in Him is to be chosen as an *unbeliever*.

Notice that this text does not speak of the unregenerate being predestined to be children of God through regeneration. Rather, this text refers to those "in Him." If they are "in Him," they are already regenerate children of God or viewed as regenerate children of God. It is therefore regenerate children of God that are predestined to adoption as sons. That is, Reformed Theology says that this text is talking about non-sons being predestined to become sons through adoption. However, this text refers to sons being predestined to adoption as sons. What then does it mean to be predestined to adoption as sons? Fortunately, the answer to this question is not only found here in this immediate context but in several different places in the New Testament. Notice that:

> *In Him also we have obtained an inheritance, being predestined according to the purpose of Him who works all things according to the counsel of His will, that we who first trusted in Christ should be to the praise of His glory. (Eph. 1:11–12)*

Adoption relates to our inheritance. We are now heirs. The day is coming when we will receive what is ours by virtue of our relationship to Christ.

We have already "obtained an inheritance" and have already received the Spirit of adoption. We have not, however, actually received what is in our inheritance as we will on the day of our glorification. It is the full realization of adoption, and all that this implies for our inheritance, to which we still have to look forward.

There is nothing in this text even remotely similar to what Calvinists have in mind when they speak of an unconditional election to salvation or an unconditional reprobation to damnation. There is nothing related to what they have in mind when they speak about an elect lost person being predestined to become an elect saved person.

ORDAINED TO ETERNAL LIFE

The Authorized Version (KJV) of Acts 13:48 reads as follows:

> ... as many as were ordained to eternal life believed.

Jamieson, Fausset, and Brown say that this is:

> ... a very remarkable statement, which cannot, without force, be interpreted of anything lower than this, *that a divine ordination to eternal life is the cause, not the effect, of any man's believing.*[213]

In *The 1599 Geneva Bible Notes* we read that:

> ... either all were not appointed to everlasting life, or either all believed, but because all did not believe, it follows that certain ones were ordained: and therefore God did not only foreknow, but also foreordained, that neither faith nor the effects of faith should be the cause of his ordaining, or appointment, but his ordaining the cause of faith.[214]

In representing the view of Charles Spurgeon, and all hypo-Calvinists, Iain Murray says in reference to Acts 13:48:

> All men are equally condemned in sin but, for reasons unknown to us and to the praise of his grace, God does not deal equally with those who are equally undeserving. The testimony of Scripture ought to be unmistakable: "as many as were ordained to eternal life believed" (Acts 13:48).[215]

John MacArthur, in his study notes on Acts 13:48, says that this is:

One of Scripture's clearest statements on the sovereignty of God in salvation. God chooses man for salvation, not the opposite. ... Faith itself is a gift from God.[216]

Many Calvinists view Acts 13:48 as the most powerful evidence of Calvinism in general and unconditional election in particular. For some Calvinists, any interpretation of this verse that does not support Reformed Theology does not deserve serious consideration. It may surprise even some Calvinists to know that there are some respected scholars who are not so certain that this verse lends support to the case for Calvinism. Due to the fact that so much weight is given (by most Calvinists) to this verse, we will look very closely at the arguments for and against a Calvinist interpretation of Acts 13:48, giving special consideration to the context in which these words were spoken.

All serious students of Scripture will agree that the context of what is said here is that of a very intense time of gospel preaching for Paul and Barnabas. On one hand, many Gentiles were responsive, in a very positive and enthusiastic way, to the gospel message preached by Paul and Barnabas. In contrast, many of the Jews were negative to the point of hostility. Beginning with verse 46, Luke tells us:

> *Paul and Barnabas waxed bold, and said, It was necessary that the word of God should first have been spoken to you: but seeing ye put it from you, and judge yourselves unworthy of everlasting life, lo, we turn to the Gentiles. For so hath the Lord commanded us, saying, I have set thee to be a light of the Gentiles, that thou shouldest be for salvation unto the ends of the earth. And **when the Gentiles heard this, they were glad, and glorified the word of the Lord: and as many as were ordained to eternal life believed.** (Acts 13:46–48, KJV, emphasis added)*

The problem with MacArthur's statement is not that he says God is sovereign in salvation. God is sovereign in all things. If God were not absolutely sovereign in every way and over everything, He would not be God as we understand God in Scripture. The problem is not that God chooses man for salvation. Obviously, God does choose to save men. Not only so, if God did not choose to save men, men would not be saved because only God can, and therefore, only God does, save. Unless God does what He does without choosing to do so, then anyone saved by God must have also been chosen by God for salvation. Just because God chooses to save, however, does not mean He cannot and does not require that a man make a choice that conditions salvation on whatever He sovereignly determines that condition to be.

So what can be said about Acts 13:48? Does this verse teach us that faith is logically the result of being appointed to or ordained to eternal life, as Calvinists believe? Is Luke telling us that an eternal choice by God is the cause for which faith, in time, is the effect? Or is there a more reasonable and biblically sound interpretation? In a discussion of this verse and its meaning, *Vine's Dictionary* says:

> ... Those who having believed the gospel, *"were ordained to eternal life."*[217]

The New Testament Greek Scholar, Henry Alford, believes that it should read:

> As many as were *disposed* to eternal life believed.[218]

The highly acclaimed New Testament Greek scholar, A. T. Robertson, says:

> The word "ordain" is not the best translation. ... There is no evidence that Luke had in mind an *absolutum decretum* of personal salvation ...[219]

In similar fashion, *The Expositor's Greek New Testament* states:

> There is no countenance here for the *absolutum decretum* of the Calvinists.[220]

J. Oliver Buswell says:

> Actually the words of Acts 13:48, 49, do not necessarily have any reference whatever to the doctrine of God's eternal decree of election.[221]

The Presbyterian commentator Albert Barnes explains:

> There has been much difference of opinion in regard to this expression. One class of commentators have supposed that it refers to the doctrine of election—*to God's ordaining* men to eternal life; and

another class, to their being *disposed themselves* to embrace the gospel—to those among them who did not reject and despise the gospel, but who were *disposed* and *inclined* to embrace it.[222]

Barnes goes on to say:

> The main enquiry is, what is the meaning of the word rendered *ordained?*[223]

According to Barnes, the word "ordain" could just as accurately be rendered *appoint,* as is found in some newer translations. Even so, this does not directly help the case of either of the two interpretive schools mentioned above. That does not mean that Barnes believes that men *dispose themselves to embrace the gospel* either. According to Barnes:

> The word is *never* used to denote an internal *disposition* or *inclination* arising from one's own self. It does *not* mean that they *disposed themselves* to embrace eternal life. ... It does not properly refer to an eternal decree, or directly to the doctrine of election ...[224]

While the scholars can legitimately debate about what is the best rendering of this verse, I will assume for our present discussion that the Authorized Version's "ordained" is a perfectly good translation of the original Greek word. I will also interpret it to mean appoint, as many scholars on both sides of the Calvinist divide have done. As always, to correctly understand a verse of Scripture, we should carefully consider its context. So what is the context of this verse? While preaching to the Jews, Paul says:

> *"Men and brethren ... through this Man* [Jesus Christ] *is preached to you the forgiveness of sins; and by Him **everyone who believes** is justified from all things from which you could not be justified by the law of Moses ... "*

> *So when the Jews went out of the synagogue, the Gentiles begged that these words might be preached to them the next Sabbath. Now when the congregation had broken up, many of the Jews and devout proselytes followed Paul and Barnabas, who, speaking to them, persuaded them to continue in the grace of God.*

> *On the next Sabbath almost the whole city came together to hear the word of God. But when the Jews saw the multitudes, they were filled with envy; and contradicting and blaspheming, they opposed*

*the things spoken by Paul. Then Paul and Barnabas grew bold and said, "It was necessary that the word of God should be spoken to you first; but **since you reject it**, and judge yourselves unworthy of everlasting life, behold, we turn to the Gentiles. For so the Lord has commanded us: 'I have set you as a light to the Gentiles that you should be for salvation to the ends of the earth.' " Now when the Gentiles heard this, they were glad and glorified the word of the Lord. And as many as had been appointed to eternal life believed. (Acts 13:26, 38b, 42–48, emphasis added)*

First, it should be noted that Paul proclaims the gospel as truly to the Jews who *reject* its message as to those who *accept* it. That is, the gospel proclamation appears to be a very genuine offer of eternal life, no matter who the audience happens to be or how they respond to it. Paul seems convinced that they *could* believe if they *would* believe. Thus, he gives them all kinds of evidential and scriptural reasons why they *should* believe. The heart of the message is:

*... Through this Man [Jesus Christ] is preached to you the forgiveness of sins; and by Him **everyone who believes is justified** from all things from which you could not be justified by the law of Moses. (v. 38, emphasis added)*

It is reasonable, therefore, to conclude that they could have been forgiven and justified had they simply and sincerely believed in Jesus Christ. Even so, many of the Jews rejected this good news, evidenced by their unbelief in the gospel message and their rejection of the offer of eternal life contained and conveyed therein. Their loss was due to their rejection of what God offered them in Christ. Paul then turns to the Gentiles and proclaims the gospel to them. Many of the Gentiles accepted the offer of eternal life that came to them in this proclamation of the gospel, as evidenced by their very enthusiastic and believing response to it.

Paul's *alternative message* (alternative to the gospel) to the unbelieving Jews was that *since you reject* Christ, you forfeit eternal life. In contrast to these unbelieving Jews, many of the Gentiles "were glad and glorified the word of the Lord" because the offer of salvation in the gospel proclamation included them just as it did the Jews. Moreover, the Gentiles were offered eternal life on the same basis, or with the same condition that was set forth for the Jews. That is, they could have eternal life through faith in Jesus

Christ. The believing Gentiles therefore happily received what the unbelieving Jews tragically rejected.

The context of this verse makes the Calvinist interpretation very difficult to maintain. The Calvinist interpretation of this verse makes the rejection of the unbelieving Jews the result of God's lack of a saving interest in them and His prior decision to reject them unconditionally. The Calvinist would have us believe (based on their understanding of this verse) that these Gentiles only believed the gospel because they had been unconditionally appointed or ordained to eternal life. To say as Scripture says that those appointed to eternal life believed is not however to say that they believed *because* they were appointed to eternal life. Nothing is said in this verse or anywhere in Scripture that says or suggests that an appointment to eternal life *causes* faith. Even if we assume the strongest possible meaning for the word "ordain" or "appoint," it does not necessarily follow from what is said in this text that those ordained or appointed believed *because* they were ordained or appointed.

Of course, God appointed or ordained them to eternal life. That is not in dispute. If we assume that this appointment refers to an appointment that was made in eternity as opposed to an appointment that was made in time (not a necessary assumption), then they were appointed to eternal life before they actually believed in Christ. When they were appointed, however, is not the issue. The question is not *when* they were ordained or appointed to eternal life (i.e., eternity versus time), but *why* they were ordained or appointed to eternal life. That is, it is not the chronological relationship of this appointment to faith that should concern us.

Rather, it is the logical relationship of this appointment to faith that is of importance. Everyone that is ordained or appointed to eternal life is appointed or ordained to eternal life *because* God in Christ provides and offers salvation to all who through faith turn to Christ for salvation. The Calvinist wrongly argues that people are unconditionally ordained or appointed to eternal life, and therefore believe as a consequence of that appointment. The abundant and unequivocal testimony of Scripture is that a person is ordained or appointed to eternal life on condition that they believe in Jesus Christ, making faith *logically*, but not necessarily *chronologically* before this appointment, as a prerequisite to receiving eternal life.

Like Barnes, however, I am not persuaded that the words in question support either the Calvinist or the non-Calvinist position, or that they were intended to do so. To argue one way or the other from these brief words misses the point. I do believe, however, that the immediate context (as well as many other passages of Scripture) teaches that faith in Christ is a prerequisite (logically, even if not chronologically) to an appointment to eternal life.

Luke's purpose seems to be to point out what is at stake here. That is, this is a serious matter with a great deal to be gained or lost depending upon how one responds to the gospel. The Reformed interpretation of these words paints a picture of "whatever will be, will be," or *Que Sera, Sera.* That is just the opposite of what we get out of the very intense time spent by Paul and Barnabas on the spiritual battlefield that we call the mission field. If little is offered, little is lost by a rejection of what is offered. Even so, if much is offered, much is lost if it is rejected.

If faith is the God-ordained means, and the only God-ordained means by which we can receive eternal life, then to believe or not to believe makes an eternal difference. To be appointed or not appointed to eternal life is no light matter. Therefore the decision to believe or not to believe should be made with a full understanding of what is gained by faith and lost by unbelief. To Luke, everything hinges on how you respond to the gospel provision, proclamation, invitation, and offer. In Reformed Theology, everything is simply working out the only way it can. The Calvinist interpretation of this verse is a *what was* (i.e., ordained to eternal life or not) determines what *will be* (i.e., believing response to the gospel or not) proposition. There is nothing you can say to the lost that will make any real difference in the Calvinist scenario. They will or will not believe in Christ in the realm of time, based on whatever God decided unconditionally for them in the realm of eternity. Luke tells us that:

> ... *When the Gentiles heard this* [the gospel preached by Paul and Barnabas], *they were glad and glorified the word of the Lord. And as many as had been appointed* [or ordained] *to eternal life believed. (Acts 13:48)*

Their positive response to the good news seems to be very important to Luke. Calvinism makes it incidental at best. Notice their three-fold response to the gospel proclamation they heard. From these words we know:

• The Gentiles were glad about what they heard concerning the Word of the Lord.

- The Gentiles evidenced their gladness concerning the Word of the Lord in that they glorified the Word of the Lord.

- The Gentiles ... believed the Word of the Lord.

Thus, putting it all together we know:

- As many as were appointed or ordained to life eternal, rejoiced, glorified the Word of the Lord, and believed.

It would seem almost too obvious that what they heard was the gospel or at least contained the gospel. Thus, what they were glad about and believed was the gospel. The Calvinist, like other Evangelical Christians, accepts that these Gentiles:

- Rejoiced over what Paul said concerning salvation being for the Gentiles as well as the Jews,

- Glorified the Word of the Lord, which in this context was the message of the Old Testament about salvation being for the Gentiles as well as for the Jews, and

- Believed the salvation message Paul and Barnabas preached and which, in some way, gave rise to their gladness about and glorification of the Word of the Lord.

The typical interpretation the Calvinist gives to this passage, however, suggests or even requires that these Gentiles responded as they did *because,* and *only because,* God from eternity past ordained or appointed them to eternal life. As evidence that they were appointed or ordained to eternal life from eternity past, Calvinists say that they eventually and inevitably trusted in Christ. In other words, faith in Christ is, according Calvinism, caused by that appointment or ordination to life.

Remember, in the Calvinist scheme of things, they did not rejoice and did not glorify the word of the Lord because they became *convinced* that this message of salvation was true or good or even from God. Rather, they became convinced and believed that it was true because God *chose them unconditionally* from eternity past, regenerating them in time, giving them faith in Jesus Christ in the process. In other words, they believed *because*

God *made them believe* or *made them believers*. According to Calvinism, the fact that they believed the message was not a choice *they* made based upon anything they heard or saw, but solely upon a choice made by *God*, and all that inevitably followed that choice. To accept this Calvinist interpretation one must redefine everything that seems to be stated plainly in the passage.

A non-Calvinist approach to this passage is simpler, more reasonable, and more straightforward. A non-Calvinist approach also corresponds to everything else we know about God's saving purpose and process from Scripture. This approach would affirm:

Paul preaches to the Jews.

Many of the Jews reject in unbelief what he says.

Paul turns to the Gentiles. He preaches a salvation message to them and demonstrates to them from the Old Testament Scriptures that God has a saving interest in the Gentiles, just as He does in the Jews.

Many of these Gentiles respond in faith to that message, evidenced by their gladness concerning the salvation message they were hearing and their glorification of the Word of the Lord through which that message came.

Since salvation is by grace through faith, and since it is true that those who believe in the Lord Jesus will be saved, these Gentiles were ordained or appointed, along with all Jewish believers, to eternal life.

When they were ordained or appointed is therefore irrelevant, insofar as this text is concerned. *Why* they were ordained or appointed (i.e., because of faith alone in Christ alone) is really all that matters and is the very motivation for all true gospel preaching. That is, when we preach we are asking unbelievers to believe in the message of the gospel, assuming that they are *able* (or *enabled* by God) to do so. If we are not doing this, then we have no business preaching.

The cause of their salvation is the God who ordains or appoints believers to eternal life.

The God-ordained condition for receiving all that is offered in the gospel is faith in Christ.

Only God saves.

Therefore only God can be the ultimate and primary cause of salvation.

The God who causes men to be saved does so when they meet the condition for salvation ordained by Him, which is to believe in Jesus Christ.

The text clearly says that those who believed were ordained to eternal life. Conversely, the text also says that those who were ordained to eternal life believed. That is, believers are one and the same as those ordained or appointed to eternal life. It does not say they believed *because* they were ordained to eternal life. Setting aside for now the issue as to *when* they were ordained or appointed to eternal life, if you show me someone ordained to eternal life, I will show you a believer. While it clearly identifies the believing ones with those ordained or appointed to eternal life, the text does not suggest the cause/effect relationship (i.e., God ordained the Gentiles to eternal life; therefore they believed) suggested by the Calvinist interpretation.

Calvinism says:

> These Gentiles who believed the gospel when it was preached to them believed in time because God unconditionally ordained or appointed them to eternal life before time. Their appointment to eternal life is the *cause* of their faith and their faith is an *effect* of their appointment to eternal life.

Scripture teaches:

> These Gentiles who believed the gospel when it was preached to them did so because they were persuaded by the case Paul and Barnabas made on behalf of the gospel. They were ordained or appointed to eternal life because God has purposed that all who believe in His Son will have everlasting life.

While hypo-Calvinists attempt to prove unconditional election from Acts 13:48, consistency requires that they see unconditional reprobation as well. Wendel Francois in *Calvin: The Origins and Development of His*

Religious Thought, states what should be obvious to everyone familiar with the teachings of Calvin both in his *Institutes* and *Commentaries*. He says:

> Calvin was never content with the statement that God, in his goodness, elected to salvation a certain number of men taken from the mass of sinners; he thought that those who had not been chosen had also been the object of a special decree, that of reprobation.[225]

Williston Walker, in his book *John Calvin,* says:

> To Calvin's thinking, election and reprobation are both alike manifestations of the divine activity. ... Calvin's severe logic, insistent that all salvation is independent of merit, led him to assert that damnation is equally antecedent to and independent of demerit. ... The sole cause of salvation or of its loss is the divine choice.[226]

By any meaningful definition of terms, if unconditional election is a good thing, unconditional reprobation is a bad thing. That is why I call it the dark side of Calvinism. If, however, you cannot have an unconditional election to salvation without an unconditional reprobation to damnation, then Calvinists should admit the dark side in their quest for converts to Calvinism. I can understand why Calvinists are so shy to talk about the dark side; that being said, no Calvinist can rationally deny it.

Remember that the apostle Paul says:

> [God] *desires all men to be saved and to come to the knowledge of the truth. (1 Tim. 2:4)*

Remember also that the apostle Peter says:

> *The Lord is ... longsuffering toward us, not willing that any should perish but that all should come to repentance. (2 Pet. 3:9)*

This is why Jesus said of Himself:

> *"The Son of Man has come to seek and save that which was lost." (Luke 19:10)*

It is also undoubtedly why Jesus, speaking of His Father, says:

> *"God so loved the world that He gave His only begotten Son, that whoever believes in Him should not perish but have everlasting life.*

> *For God did not send His Son into the world to condemn the world,*
> *but that the world through Him might be saved." (John 3:16–17)*

In light of both Scripture and logic, there is simply no way to make sense out of Calvinism, even when expressed (perhaps especially) by it most moderate and mainstream advocates. Of his hero, Charles Spurgeon, Iain Murray says:

> He refused to explain how men could be held accountable for not trusting in a Saviour in whom they were never chosen, on the grounds that Scripture itself offers no explanation.[227]

There is no possible scriptural explanation for the Calvinist version (hypo or hyper) of reprobation because there is no scriptural affirmation of the Calvinist version of reprobation. To see in Scripture sinners being "held accountable for not trusting in a Saviour in whom they were never [unconditionally] chosen," you must be able to see that which is "hidden." Evidently that is just what a good pair of Calvinist-colored glasses will allow you to do.

4

LIMITED ATONEMENT

EXPLAINED

A CCORDING to Reformed Theology, for those unconditionally elected to salvation, like the old gospel song says, it is "nothing but the blood of Jesus" that provides atonement, propitiation, or satisfaction for sin. The dark side of Reformed doctrine says that for the reprobate, there is *nothing in the blood of Jesus* to atone for sin. Ironically, the most widely *understood* and yet the most *disputed* distinctive in the Calvinist doctrines of redemption and reprobation is the third point of Calvinism. Commonly it is referred to as *limited atonement*. It may also be called *particular redemption* or *definite atonement*. Perhaps so many question or even reject the third point precisely *because* they understand it.

Certainly one of the reasons that so many understand this point is that no matter how one states it, it is difficult to miss the bottom line. That is, if Christ died for anyone, He either died for *all* or He only died for *some*. Reformed Theology *denies* the scriptural teaching that Jesus died for *all* and *affirms* the very unscriptural teaching that says He only died for *some*. To the question, "Did Jesus die for everyone?" Sproul says:

> One of the most controversial points of Reformed theology concerns the L in TULIP. L stands for *Limited Atonement*.[228]

Sproul goes on to say:

> It has been such a problem doctrine that there are multitudes of Christians who say they embrace most of the doctrines of Calvinism but get off the boat here. They refer to themselves as "four-point" Calvinists.[229]

Sproul also says:

I prefer to use the term *definite* atonement to the term *limited* atonement. The doctrine of definite atonement focuses on the question of the *design* of Christ's atonement. It is concerned with God's intent in sending Jesus to the cross.[230]

Sproul is correct when he reasons:

> Anyone who is not a Universalist is willing to agree that the effect of Christ's work on the cross is limited to those who believe. That is, Christ's atonement does not avail for unbelievers. Not everyone is saved through His death. Everyone also agrees that the merit of Christ's death is sufficient to pay for the sins of all human beings. Some put it this way: Christ's death is sufficient for all, but efficient for only some. This however, does not get at the heart of definite atonement.[231]

The question that must be asked is this: who did Christ die for? Despite what Scripture so often says about Christ dying for the whole world, Calvinists constantly tell us that these many verses cannot mean that Christ died for everyone in the whole world. For example, Sproul speaks for most Calvinists when he says in reference to the word *world* in John 3:16:

> The world for whom Christ died cannot mean the entire human family. It must refer to the universality of the elect (people from every tribe and nation).[232]

Sproul should have said that "The world for whom Christ died cannot mean the entire human family, if Calvinism is true." Palmer explains what he believes John 3:16 must mean, despite what it actually says. That is:

> Because God has so loved certain ones ... these particular ones will be saved, He sent His Son to die for them, to save them, and not all of the world.[233]

Every unbiased person will concede that it is a major and daring (perhaps reckless) leap from *God so loved the world* to *God so loved certain ones*. Every Christian who becomes a consistent Calvinist must make this leap. Many, if not most Calvinists, have to make this leap every time they read passages like John 3:16. Of course, if Calvinists are right about unconditional election, Christ could, by definition only have savingly died for the elect. If every individual Christ died for necessarily becomes a believer, and yet not every individual who lives becomes a believer, then logically, Christ must not have died for those who do not become believers. Given the Calvinist premise of unconditional election, logic forces the Calvinist conclusion. (In fact, non-Calvinists disagree with the part of the equation that says those for whom Christ died *necessarily* become believers.) Many say that the doctrine of limited atonement did not gain widespread acceptance among the greater Reformed community until the *Synod of Dort* (1618–1619) affirmed it half a century after Calvin's death. Regardless of whether or not this is so, the framers of the response to the Arminian Remonstrance left no doubt as to what their convictions on this point were. That is:

> This was the Sovereign counsel and most gracious will and pur-
> pose of God the Father, that the quickening and saving efficacy of
> the most precious death of His Son should extend to all the elect,
> for bestowing upon them alone the gift of justifying faith, thereby
> to bring them infallibly to salvation …[234]

The dark side of this view says:

> This was the Sovereign counsel and most incomprehensible but just
> will and purpose of God the Father, that the quickening and saving
> efficacy of the most precious death of his Son should not extend
> to all people, thereby to withhold from all but the elect the gift of
> justifying faith, thereby to bring them infallibly to damnation …

Some have accused the Synod of paying too much attention to what they believe was implicit in the teachings of Calvin as opposed to what Calvin explicitly taught. It is difficult to deny that some of what Calvin said makes it seem as though he believed that the atonement was potentially or provision-ally unlimited. It is equally clear that his overall theological system in gen-eral and his *unswerving* commitment to unconditional election in particular, led his followers to believe in an atonement which was potentially, provi-sionally, and actually for the elect alone. Despite a great deal of scriptural evidence to the contrary, John Owen says:

> The Scripture nowhere says Christ died for all men.[235]

Sometimes I cannot help but wonder if men like John Owen had a spe-cial Calvinist version of the Bible that left out many of the passages I find in all of the translations of the Bible that I use. A little later, we will consider a number of passages of Scripture and even a few admissions from well-known Calvinists that contradict Owen. Berkhof, however, is exactly right when he says:

> The Reformed position is that Christ died for the purpose of actu-
> ally and certainly saving the elect, and the elect only. This is the
> equivalent to saying that He died for the purpose of saving only
> those to whom He actually applies the benefits of His redemptive
> work.[236]

Berkhof is exactly wrong when he claims:

> Scripture repeatedly qualifies those for whom Christ laid down his
> life in such a way as to point to a very definite limitation.[237]

Concerning those that the atonement was designed for, Boettner says:

> Calvinists hold that in the intention and secret plan of God Christ
> died for the **elect only** ..."[238]

It would appear to all but the "initiated" that the Calvinist "secret plan" and God's revealed Word are often at odds. An example of one of the passages most often used by Calvinists to defend limited atonement is Mark 14: 24. There we read that Jesus says to His disciples:

> *"This is My blood of the new covenant, which is shed for many."*

It is argued that if the blood of Christ were shed for *all*, Scripture would not have used the word "many." Ironically, some Calvinists insist that the word "all," when referring to the saving interest and saving work of God, must always mean or imply less than everyone, but then say that the word "many," when referring to the saving interest and work of God, can never mean *all*. With this verse in mind, Tom Ross says:

> Jesus plainly tells His disciples that His blood was not shed for all,
> but for many.[239]

Does Jesus plainly tell His disciples that "His blood was *not* shed for all but for many"? Just because His blood was shed for many, it does not mean it was not shed for all. All, with regard to the human population is always many even if many is not always all. Thus, while it is true that the word "many" can, and at times does, refer to less than all, it is not true that the word "many" cannot refer to all. The context, in which a word like *many* is used, is the key to understanding how it should be understood. Seemingly in support of those that believe Calvin held to a potentially and provisionally unlimited atonement in the death that Christ died, Calvin explained that in this text:

> The word many does not mean a part of the world only, but the whole human race.[240]

For Calvin, however, as well as most Calvinists, the words, "whole human race" do not necessarily refer to *every individual* in the whole human race.

Commenting on the meaning or implication of Colossians 1:14, where we read "in whom we have redemption through His blood, the forgiveness of sins," Calvin interpreted what the apostle Paul says as follows:

> … Redemption was procured through the *blood of Christ,* for by the sacrifice of his death all the sins of the world have been expiated. Let us, therefore, bear in mind, that this is the sole price of reconciliation …[241]

To Calvinists, the fact that Christ may have died for "all the sins of the world" cannot mean that He died for *all* or even *any* of the sins of some in the world. Calvinism will allow that Christ died for every kind of sin in the world because it allows that Christ died for every kind of sinner in the world. Calvinism cannot, and therefore does not, allow that Christ died for every sin in the world because it does not allow for what Scripture actually says. That is, Calvinism cannot say with Scripture that Christ died for *every sinner* in the world. While some Calvinists believe Christ died in a non-redemptive sense for everyone, all Calvinists agree that He died redemptively *only* for the elect. Garner Smith admits:

> There is a … class of passages, which seem to belong together and which may indeed be interpreted to signify a certain universalistic aspect of the Lord's death, which cannot be denied, but which in no way conflicts with the doctrine of Limited Atonement as formulated by the Reformers.[242]

Non-Calvinist Evangelicals can and do believe that Christ redemptively died for all those that the Calvinist says He redemptively died for. We can and do believe that Christ died redemptively *for us* as truly as Calvinists say Christ died redemptively *for us*. We believe Christ died for us, because in fact Scripture says He died *for us*. The system of Calvinism, however, does not allow Calvinists to accept the plain teaching of Scripture when and where it says that Christ died redemptively *for all* or *for them*. The Calvinist doctrines of redemption and reprobation put an eternal and impenetrable wall between *them* and *us*. There is no crossing over from the caste of the reprobate into the caste of the redeemed.

In the most important sense, where you begin is where you end. Nothing ever really changes from what it has always been determined to be. For as Calvinism teaches that God only elected to save some, so it teaches the corresponding doctrine that God only sent Christ to die as a sin-substitute for the elect. Conversely, Calvinism teaches that God did not send Christ to die as a sin-substitute for the reprobate. Jesus says:

> *"The Son of Man ... [came] ... to give His life a ransom for many."*
> *(Mark 10:45)*

Boettner says that we should:

> Notice, this verse does not say that He gave His life a ransom for
> **all**, but for **many**.[243]

Does this mean, as Calvinists insist, that the "many" Christ died for cannot equal the world and everyone that has ever lived in the world? The apostle Paul tells us:

> *For as by one man's disobedience **many** were made sinners, so also*
> *by one Man's obedience **many** will be made righteous. (Rom. 5:19,*
> *emphasis added)*

Every Calvinist would agree that *all* of Adam's posterity (with the exception of our Savior) is included in and among the *"many"* that were made sinners. Every Calvinist would also agree that *all* those who believe in Christ are included in and among the *many* that were made righteous through Christ. In fact, Calvinists would agree that the many in both of these instances could have been referred to as "all" without changing the meaning of the verse. Thus, the Calvinist has to agree that "many" can and sometimes does refer to "all." If I were to refer to the total number of stars in the heavens, I could use the word "many." For example, I could say that the many stars God created serve a celestial and terrestrial purpose. Using the logic of some Calvinists, someone could then say that I said that only some and not all of the stars serve a celestial and terrestrial purpose.

Godfrey correctly represents the Reformed view when he says:

> Those that hold that the atonement is limited or definite in extent teach that Christ died to save only those whom the Father had predestined to eternal life. Therefore the atoning work of Christ is applied in due time to all for whom it was accomplished.[244]

I agree with Godfrey's reasoning when he says:

> If the Father has elected [in the Calvinist sense] some sinners to eternal life and if the Holy Spirit applies the saving work of Christ only to the elect, then Christ, in harmony with the purpose of the Father and the Spirit, died on the cross for the elect alone.[245]

I agree with the logic of Boettner when he says:

> ... that this doctrine necessarily follows from the doctrine of election. If from eternity God has planned to save one portion of the human race and not another, it seems to be a contradiction to say that ... He sent His Son to die for those whom He had predetermined not to save, as truly as ... those whom He had chosen for salvation. These two doctrines must stand or fall together. We cannot logically accept one and reject the other. If God has elected some and not others to eternal life, then plainly the primary purpose of Christ's work was to redeem the elect.[246]

I also fully agree with Sproul when he says:

> I have often thought that to be a four-point Calvinist one must misunderstand at least one of the five points. It is hard for me to imagine that anyone could understand the other four points of Calvinism and deny limited atonement. There always is the possibility, however, of the happy inconsistency by which people hold incompatible views at the same time.[247]

I would add that if you really understand the Calvinist doctrine of unconditional election, you should easily be able to see how the Calvinist doctrine of limited atonement logically and necessarily follows. Sproul goes on to say:

The question is, "For whom was the atonement *designed?*" ... Some argue that all limited atonement means is that the benefits of the atonement are limited to believers who meet the necessary condition of faith. That is, though Christ's atonement was sufficient to cover the sins of all men and to satisfy God's justice against all sin, it only *effects* salvation for believers. The formula reads: Sufficient for all; efficient for the elect only. ... The doctrine of limited atonement goes further than that. It is concerned with the deeper question of the Father's and the Son's *intention* in the cross. It declares that the mission and death of Christ was restricted to a limited number ...[248]

In lockstep, White says:

A common, but not fully Reformed, assertion is that Christ's death was sufficient to save every single human being, but efficient to save only the elect. While the statement carries truth, it misses the most important issue: whether it was Christ's intention to make full and complete atonement for every single individual ...[249]

White argues, as do all five-point Calvinists, that it was Christ's intention to make a full and complete atonement for the elect and the elect alone. He also believes that Christ made no redemptive atonement, complete or otherwise, for many or most of the individuals in the world. John Murray asks:

Did Christ come to make the salvation of all men possible, to remove obstacles that stood in the way of salvation, merely to make provision for salvation? ... Did He come to put all men in a savable state? Or did He come to secure the salvation of all those who are ordained to eternal life? Did He come to make men redeemable? Or did He come effectually and infallibly to redeem? ... The doctrine of "limited atonement" ... we maintain is the doctrine which limits the atonement to those who are heirs of eternal life, [that is] to the elect.[250]

John Owen says:

... Jesus Christ, according to the counsel and will of his Father, did offer himself upon the cross ... with this intent and purpose; that all the things so procured by his death, might be actually and infallibly bestowed on, and applied to, all and every one for whom he died according to the will and purpose of God.[251]

The dark side of Calvinism is:

> ... Jesus Christ, according to the counsel and will of His Father, did *not* offer Himself upon the cross for all men. ... He had no saving intention or purpose for all men; nothing of a saving nature was procured by His death for many if not most men.

Boettner explains:

> Calvinists do not deny that mankind in general receive some important benefits from Christ's atonement. ... Many temporal blessings are thus secured for all men, although these fall short of being sufficient to insure salvation.[252]

Redemptively, however, Boettner says:

> Christ died not for an unorderly mass, but for His people, His Bride, His Church.[253]

There are some Calvinists, especially among the hyper-variety and the supralapsarians, who deny any benefits from the death of Christ to those for whom He did not die redemptively. Hyper-Calvinist Herman Hoeksema reasons:

> If Christ died for the elect only, then there are no possible benefits in that death of Christ for anyone else but those for whom He died.[254]

Regardless, the Calvinist doctrines of election and reprobation more than imply the Calvinist doctrine of a limited atonement. In one very real and necessary sense, the Calvinist version of election and reprobation includes the Reformed doctrine that says Christ did not die redemptively for millions upon millions of people on this planet. For if God includes only some and excludes all others (i.e., the reprobate) by an unconditional election and reprobation, then no matter what Christ did on the cross, it could not lead to, or result in, the salvation of the reprobate. Hence, His atonement relative to the reprobate would be no atonement at all. If we allow for the Calvinist definition of "sovereign election," Herman Hoeksema is right on target when he says:

It is in this truth of limited atonement that the doctrine of sovereign election ... comes into focus.[255]

Spencer also reasons as does Boettner when he says:

If you believe the Bible teaches that God is sovereign, His plan is immutable, His election unconditional, you must conclude that the atonement is limited to those whom He freely willed to make the objects of His grace.[256]

Walter A. Ewell, in the *Evangelical Dictionary of Theology*, correctly says:

The doctrine that Jesus died for the elect in particular; securing their redemption, but not for the world, arose as the implications of the election ... theory of the atonement developed immediately following the Reformation.[257]

Boettner says:

Concerning this doctrine *The Westminster Confession* says: "... Wherefore they who are elected ... are redeemed in Christ. ... Neither are any other redeemed by Christ ... but the elect only."[258]

Sproul is not the only Calvinist who does not like to use the word *limited* in connection with the atonement. To many Calvinists it seems as though the word is used by its detractors to undermine or distort the true meaning of the Reformed view of the atonement. Spurgeon says:

We beg your pardon, when you say we limit Christ's death. ... We say Christ so died that he infallibly secured the salvation of a multitude that no man can number, who through Christ's death not only may be saved, but are saved, must be saved and cannot by any possibility run the hazard of being anything but saved.[259]

The very thought of a universal or unlimited atonement or an atonement in which the saving benefits were conditioned upon faith in Christ is anathema to Spurgeon, who says:

That Christ should offer an atonement and satisfaction for the sins of all men, and that afterwards some of those very men should be punished for the sins of which Christ had already atoned, appears to me to be the most monstrous iniquity ...[260]

But where is the *good* in the news proclaimed to the reprobate caste for whom Christ did not die? How can it be *good* for the person for whom Christ did not shed His precious blood? For them, can it be said that His blood is precious or that it has redemptive value? If it is the gospel we are to preach to everyone (and by definition the gospel is a proclamation of news that is good), how can this be squared with a limited atonement? Unwittingly, Spurgeon points out the impossible predicament placed on the evangelist by a limited view of the atonement:

> The chief aim of the enemy's assaults is to get rid of Christ, to get rid of the atonement, to get rid of his suffering in the place of men. Some say they can embrace the rest of the gospel. But what "rest" is there? What is there left? A bloodless, Christless gospel is neither fit for the land nor for the dunghill. It neither honors God nor converts men.[261]

Spurgeon went so far as to say:

> A bloodless gospel, a gospel without the atonement, is a gospel of devils.[262]

If the *gospel* preached to the reprobate has no Christ sent *for them* or to die and shed His precious and redeeming blood *for them*, then that gospel, if we dare call it a gospel, cannot be the power of God to salvation *for them*. When Spurgeon proclaimed the gospel to the reprobate, according to his Calvinist logic, he was preaching a "monstrous iniquity," a "Christless gospel," and "bloodless gospel," "neither fit for the land nor for the dunghill," "a gospel of devils." J. I. Packer unwittingly challenges the very notion that Calvinism even can preach the true gospel to the reprobate. After spending considerable time and effort rightly pointing out the centrality of the atonement in the true gospel, Packer says:

> A gospel without propitiation at its heart is another gospel.[263]

Whatever it is that Packer preaches to the reprobate, by definition, it excludes *propitiation*. By his own definition, then, Packer and all those who believe in limited atonement must be preaching *another gospel* when preaching to the reprobate. I am not accusing Packer of preaching *another gospel*. I am only pointing out a problem that Packer and other Calvinists seem to ignore. For Packer, and all five-point Calvinists, when Jesus says, "It is finished," He had accomplished *nothing of a saving nature* for the reprobate. He did *nothing of redemptive value* for millions upon millions of lost people and never intended to do so. There is nothing *good* in the gospel for the reprobate, and therefore, no true gospel can be truly preached to the reprobate. A limited atonement, at the very least, limits and distorts a gospel proclamation. Steele and Thomas state this doctrine accordingly:

> Christ's redeeming work was intended to save the elect only and actually secured salvation for them. His death was a substitution-ary endurance of the penalty of sin in the place of certain speci-fied sinners. In addition to putting away the sins of His people, Christ's redemption secured everything necessary for their salva-tion, including faith which unites them to Him. The gift of faith is infallibly applied by the Spirit to all for whom Christ died, thereby guaranteeing their salvation.[264]

Steele and Thomas explain:

> All Calvinists agree that Christ's obedience and suffering were of infinite value, and that if God had so willed, the satisfaction ren-dered by Christ would have saved every member of the human race. It would have required no more obedience, nor any greater suffer-ing for Christ to have secured salvation for every man, woman, and child who ever lived than it did for Him to secure salvation for the elect only. But He came into the world to represent and save only those given to Him by the Father. Thus Christ's saving work was limited in that it was designed to save some and not others, but it was not limited in value for it was of infinite worth and would have secured salvation for everyone if this had been God's intention.[265]

For those doomed from and to all eternity, the blood of Christ is of no value to redeem and it has no power to save. Steele and Thomas are correct in saying:

> Historical or main line Calvinism has consistently maintained that Christ's redeeming work was definite in *design* and *accomplish-ment*—that it was intended to render complete satisfaction for cer-tain specified sinners and that it actually secured salvation for those individuals and for no one else.[266]

A. A. Hodge says:

Christ died with the intention of saving all [and only] those whom he actually does save.[267]

Hodge, as well as most hypo-Calvinists, cannot, however, seem to admit that a limited atonement nullifies a valid offer of eternal life for the reprobate. Speaking for most (if not all) hypo-Calvinists, Hodge illogically reasons:

The question [of a limited atonement] does *not* relate to the UNIVERSAL OFFER in perfect good faith of a saving interest in Christ's work on the condition of faith.[268]

At best, unconditional election and reprobation makes the "universal," "good faith" offer seem just a little disingenuous. Could you imagine, for example, "universal" health care that only covers politicians and their families? Or a "good faith" offer to pay off a loan that cannot be paid on behalf of the one for whom it is promised? Hoeksema speaks for all Calvinists when he explains the meaning of a limited atonement as follows:

… It means this, that Christ died and atoned *for the elect, and for them only.*[269]

Hoeksema is also exactly right when he says:

The doctrine of limited atonement is the Reformed doctrine concerning the death of Christ …[270]

One of the more common arguments against an unlimited atonement by many if not most Calvinists involves what is called *double jeopardy.* Custance explains:

No man can be held accountable for a debt that has already been paid for on his behalf to the satisfaction of the offended party. But a double jeopardy, a duplication of indebtedness, is indeed involved if the non-elect are to be punished for sins which the Lord Jesus Christ has already endured punishment.[271]

Likewise Boettner reasons:

For God to have laid the sins of all men on Christ would mean that as regards the lost He would be punishing their sins twice, once in Christ, and then again in them.[272]

Wayne Grudem says:

> Reformed people argue that if Christ's death actually paid for the sins of every person who ever lived, then there is no penalty left for *anyone* to pay, and it necessarily follows that all people will be saved, without exception. For God could not condemn to eternal punishment anyone whose sins are already paid for: that would be demanding double payment, and it would therefore be unjust.[273]

Besides the clear statements of Scripture, many of which we will consider momentarily, this reasoning fails to distinguish between an atonement provided and an atonement appropriated. By way of analogy, most Calvinists recognize that it is possible that a person be perfectly righteous in a positional sense and less than perfectly righteous in a practical sense. As God views Christians regarding salvation, we are "positionally" righteous in Christ. Nevertheless, Christians still sin and God still allows us "practical" consequences for our sinning (such as excluding the brother from the Corinthian congregation until he repents and stops sleeping with his stepmother—1 Cor. 5:1–13). No biblically literate Christian grounded in Scripture and reality would deny these two propositions. Even so, the atonement provides for the forgiveness of all of our sins, although some do not appropriate that provision. The atonement that is rejected is as real as the atonement that is accepted. In fact, it is the same exact atonement. As certain conditions must be met by the seller of a home before he can get his money out of escrow, so there is a condition a lost person must meet in order to receive what has been provided in the atonement and offered in the gospel.

Atonement in the Calvinist sense "inherently saves." In this view, the elect are actually saved at the time Christ died to save them. The rest is just a formality, adding nothing necessary to the salvation process. Faith, and everything else that appears to be required of the elect, are already provided for the elect by the very fact of Christ's atoning work on their behalf. The Calvinist dismisses even the possibility that God could, much less would, provide forgiveness of sins on the condition that the sinner trusts the sin-bearer for the salvation offered through His sacrifice for sin on the cross. In doing so, the Calvinist must dismiss the very language in which God communicates the meaning of the cross and how it is we can receive what He offers us, by virtue of Christ and His death on our behalf.

If we accept the Calvinist premise that Christ's death must actually save those whom He dies to save, we must also accept the premise that if God elects to save us, we are saved when He elects us. This would, of course, make the cross of Christ itself just a formality, adding nothing that makes a difference. In effect, the Calvinist cross is not so much a saving instrument as it is a reflection of unconditional election, the real saving work of God. The view that says that Christ's death inherently or automatically saves those Christ died for can also be expressed as the *efficacy factor*. According to Erickson:

> The underlying issue here is the question of the efficacy of the atonement. Those who hold to limited atonement assume that if Christ died for someone, that person will be saved. By extension they reason that if Christ in fact died for all persons, all persons would come to salvation; hence the concept of a universal atonement is viewed as leading to the universal-salvation trap. The basic assumption here, however, ignores the fact that our inheriting eternal life involves two separate factors: an objective factor (Christ's provision for salvation) and a subjective factor (our acceptance of that salvation). In the view of those who hold to an unlimited atonement, there is the possibility that someone for whom salvation is available may fail to accept it.[274]

Crenshaw admits:

> Some have said ... nowhere does scripture say that Christ did **not** die for the reprobate or that He died **only** for the elect. This is true ...[275]

Despite this admission, he immediately goes on to say:

> ... As we survey, consider the following logic:
>
> Christ's death inherently saves.
>
> If Christ died for all, then all are saved.
>
> Not all are saved.
>
> Therefore, Christ did not die for all.[276]

Crenshaw then says:

> If one is going to deny the logic of these statements, he must object to the first premise, for the two middle premises no one would deny, and the conclusion is forced by the premises.[277]

Crenshaw is, of course, exactly right in zeroing in on the *first premise* as the problem. Where in Scripture do we find the first premise? Where do we find that "Christ's death inherently saves"? That is, where do we find in Scripture that the price paid by Christ on the cross for the salvation of the lost is effective or efficacious without regard to faith, or that its effectiveness is unconditional? For that is exactly what the Calvinist is claiming when he says Christ's death *inherently saves*. I would suggest a different kind of reasoning and one that is in keeping with what Scripture actually does say:

Christ died provisionally for all (1 John 2:2).

Only those who trust Christ for salvation redemptively profit from God's saving work (John 3:16).

Everyone is invited to trust Christ for salvation (John 20:30–31 and 1 Tim. 2:3–6).

Those who end up lost forever will not be lost forever because Christ did not die for them, but because they refused to trust Christ for salvation (John 3:18).

Using the same logic as Crenshaw, while relying on what Scripture says, versus what it does not say, we can safely conclude that Christ died for all sinners and not just for some sinners.

5

LIMITED ATONEMENT

SCRIPTURALLY REFUTED

IF Christ died for the elect only, why does the apostle Paul tell Timothy:

*There is one God and one Mediator between God and men, the Man Christ Jesus, who gave Himself a ransom **for all**. ... (1 Tim. 2:5–6, emphasis added)*

Evidently, John Owen could not see how this apostolic affirmation contradicts the doctrine of a limited atonement and his own words when he says, "The Scripture nowhere says Christ died for all men."[278] Should this read, "a ransom for *all the elect* men"? Commenting on this very verse, MacArthur says:

Not all will be ransomed ... only the many ... for whom the actual atonement was made. ... the substitutionary aspect of His death is applied to the elect alone.[279]

MacArthur's words have confused some (on both sides of the Calvinist controversy) and have left them scratching their heads. MacArthur believes that the atonement was only made for the elect and not made for the reprobate. For MacArthur, however, Christ died for everyone in a non-redeeming sense and with no interest or intention of redeeming many for whom He died. Some of those for whom He died, He actually died to save. He refers to this as "the substitutionary aspect of His death." Take "the substitutionary aspect" out of the cross of Christ for many people, as MacArthur does, and you make the cross of Christ of no redeeming value or saving benefit to them. This is what Calvinism requires. For these individuals, Christ did not savingly die. To them, He is just another martyr who died a death of no lasting consequence.

It is true that "not all will be ransomed." Only the Universalist would say otherwise. Did, however, Jesus really give "Himself a ransom for *all,*" as Paul says, or did He not, as MacArthur suggests? Only those men and women who *believe* will *receive* the saving benefits of what Christ did on the cross. No one is disputing this. The question then is not will all be ransomed? Rather, was the ransom paid for all? The Calvinist always answers this question incorrectly. The doctrines of unconditional election and limited atonement make sure that he does. Again, notice that the text does not say all were ransomed, and only the Universalist would say it does. It does, however, say, "Christ Jesus ... gave Himself a ransom *for all.*" There is simply no reason to say that Christ did not give Himself as a ransom for all just because not all will be ransomed, unless, of course, you are trying to make scriptural truth conform to Calvinist dogma.

MacArthur often uses the term "believer" in the same way other Calvinists use the word "elect." He means, however, exactly what they mean. While all Evangelicals would agree that only believers will be ransomed, MacArthur, like all Calvinists, would argue that only those who are elect can believe. My guess is that many with a longer association with Reformed doctrine will not like the way MacArthur tries to make both camps happy, and may not even accept that he really believes in the third point of Calvinism (limited atonement). On the other side of the Calvinist divide, I suspect that he has found a way, in the minds of some, to bridge the gap between limited and unlimited atonement. Regardless of MacArthur's intentions, or what he believes he has done, he does not believe that Christ did anything on the cross that could be considered redemptive in any ultimate sense for much, if not most, of mankind.

God did not love some in the world enough to send Christ to savingly die for them or give them the faith to believe in the one who died, according to MacArthur in particular and the greater Reformed community in general. With 1 John 2:2 in mind, MacArthur says our Lord's ...

> ... sacrifice was sufficient to pay the penalty for all the sins of all whom God brings to faith. But the actual satisfaction and atonement was made only for those who believe.[280]

The key to understanding what MacArthur is saying is to be found in the words "sufficient to pay the penalty for all the sins *of all whom God brings to faith.*" To the contrary, the apostle John says that Jesus ...

> ... *is the atoning sacrifice for our sins, and not only for ours but also for the sins of the whole world. (1 John 2:2, NIV)*

Concerning the words "not only for ours," Calvin said that John:

> ... Added this for the sake of amplifying, in order that the faithful might be assured that the expiation made by Christ, extends to all who by faith embrace the gospel.[281]

Calvin immediately added:

> Here a question may be raised, how have the sins of the whole world been expiated? I pass by the dotages [foolishnesses] of the fanatics, who under this pretense extend salvation to all the reprobate. ... Such a monstrous thing deserves no refutation. They who seek to avoid this absurdity, have said that Christ suffered sufficiently for the whole world, but efficiently only for the elect. This solution has commonly prevailed in the schools. Though ... I allow that what has been said is true, yet I deny that it is suitable to this passage; for the design of John was no other than to make this benefit common to the whole Church. Then under the word *all* or whole, he does not include the reprobate, but designates those who should believe as well as those who were then scattered through various parts of the world.[282]

So now we know that a word (i.e., world) that is often used in Scripture as almost antithetical to the word "church" is really a synonym for the word "church." The whole world is the whole church, or perhaps the whole church world. It is a good thing we have Calvin to tell us this, otherwise we may never have noticed. According to Calvinism, it would also have been theologically correct had the apostle John said that Christ died, *also for the sins of the whole world of the elect.* Regarding those Scriptures that tell us that Christ died *for the whole world,* MacArthur says:

> This is a generic term, referring not to every single individual, but to mankind in general. ... The passages which speak of Christ's dying for the whole world must be understood to refer to mankind in general (as in Titus 2:11). "World" indicates the sphere, the beings toward whom God seeks reconciliation and has provided propitiation.[283]

It only *must* mean what MacArthur says it means if Calvinism is *assumed* to be true. Are you buying this? If you are, you are able to pay more of what Feinberg calls an *intellectual price tag* than I can afford, or more importantly, than I think Scripture requires. That is, however, the price Calvinism demands. With this passage in mind, Gill says:

> Now let it be observed, that these phrases, *all the world*, and *the whole world*, are often in scripture to be taken in a limited sense … in this epistle of John, the phrase is used in a restrained sense … in the text under consideration, it cannot be understood of all men … what may be observed and will lead more clearly into the sense of the passage before us, is, that the apostle John was a Jew, and wrote to Jews: and in the text speaks of them, and of the Gentiles, as to be distinguished; and therefore says of Christ, *he is* the propitiation *for our sins; and not for ours only,* for the sins of us Jews only; but for the sins of the whole world; of the Gentiles also, of all the elect of God throughout the Gentile world …[284]

It *cannot* mean what it seems to mean only if we assume Calvinism is true, as Gill obviously does. Those of us who do not assume Calvinism to be true, are free to interpret the words "whole world" in a *less strained sense*. The Calvinist believes he can see beneath the plain meaning of Scripture and therefore often appeals to the *deeper things,* the *hidden purposes,* or the *secret counsel* of God to justify his reading into a text what is not otherwise evident. Often an imagined context is appealed to, but the result is the same. With reference to the sins of the whole world, as seen in 1 John 2:2, Albert Barnes explains:

> This is one of the expressions occurring in the New Testament which demonstrate that the atonement was made for all people, and which cannot be reconciled with any other opinion. If he had died only for a part of the race, this language could not have been used. The phrase, "the whole world," is one which naturally embraces all people; is such as would be used if it be supposed that the apostle meant to teach that Christ died for all people; and is such as cannot be explained on any other supposition.[285]

Calvinists such as Sproul will admit:

> On the surface this text seems to demolish limited atonement.[286]

With a little imagination or insight into the hidden purposes of God, Calvinists can see what non-Calvinist Evangelicals cannot see. Or could this be a case of *The Emperor's New Clothes*? If you believe the "whole world" of 1 John 2:2 can be understood as or reduced to the whole church or the whole world of the elect, ask yourself how you discerned this. Did you simply study the text and see this? Or did a Calvinist friend or mentor point it out to you? Did you come to this verse convinced of Calvinism and then unconsciously interpret it from a Calvinist perspective? Without a previous commitment to Calvinism, no one could discern in 1 John 2:2 what is so plain to see for the Calvinist.

If someone were to deny that Christ died for the church (Eph. 5:25), a Calvinist would go theologically ballistic if they justified it by saying that sometimes the word "church" is used to designate a gathering of ordinary folk. Calvinists would rightly say that if you look at the context, it is clear that most of the time when the word "church" is used in the New Testament, the context requires that we interpret it to mean God's family of believers, whether local or universal. But why should Calvinists be able to do essentially the same thing with the word "world" just because it does not fit into their theological scheme? Again with 1 John 2:2 in mind, MacArthur says:

> God has mitigated His wrath on sinners temporarily, by letting them live and enjoy earthly life (see note on 1 Tim. 4:10). In that sense, Christ has provided a brief, temporal propitiation for the whole world. But He actually satisfied fully the wrath of God eternally only for the elect who believe.[287]

Since MacArthur references 1 Timothy 4:10, let us consider what this so-called temporal propitiation is in that context as well. Writing to Timothy, Paul says:

> *We trust in the living God, who is the Savior of all men, especially of those who believe.*

MacArthur says:

> The Gr. word translated "especially" must mean that all men enjoy God's salvation in some way like those who believe enjoy His salvation. The simple explanation is that God is the Savior of all men, only in a temporal sense, while of believers in an eternal sense. Paul's point is that while God graciously delivers believers from sin's condemnation and penalty because He was their substitute (2 Cor. 5:21), all men experience some earthly benefits from the goodness of God.[288]

I am not arguing that this is not a simple explanation. Not every simple explanation is, however, the right explanation. MacArthur's use of the word "must" is telling. This answer *must* be the right answer only if we buy into the whole Calvinist scheme of things. Why does MacArthur avoid the common Calvinist answer, which says the "whole world" means "some" of the world, or the church, or the elect—specifically when it refers to the saving purpose and provision of God? Why, in almost every text in which the words, "all," "everyone," the "whole world," etc., appear, does MacArthur suggest the *relative all?* Yet in 1 Timothy 4:10, why does he opt for an absolute versus a relative salvation? The reason is simple. The typical Calvinist approach simply does not work and MacArthur knows it. James White provides the more common Reformed explanation of 1 John 2:2 as follows:

> The Reformed understanding is that Jesus Christ is the propitiation for the sins of all the Christians to which John was writing, and not only them, but for all Christians throughout the world, Jew and Gentile, at all times and in all places.[289]

James Boice explains:

> If John, as a Jew, is actually thinking of the propitiatory sacrifice as it was practiced in Israel, particularly on the Day of Atonement—and how could he not?—then it may well be of himself and other Jews as opposed to Gentiles that he uses the word "us" or "we" in this phrase. The contrast would therefore be, not between Christians and the as-yet-unsaved world, but between those Jews for whom Christ died and those Gentiles for whom Christ died, both of whom now make up or eventually will make up the church.[290]

Now if Christ did not die for everyone, why would the writer to the Hebrews say of Christ that He:

> ... *suffered death, so that by the grace of God he might* **taste death for everyone.** *(Heb. 2:9, NIV, emphasis added)*

Should this read, *"taste death for everyone who is elect"*? Referring to this verse, Calvin said:

> By saying *for every man* ... he means that Christ died for us, and that by taking upon him what was due to us, he redeemed us from the curse of death.[291]

Thus, Calvin told us what the word "for" refers to. That is, as all Evangelicals would agree, Christ died on the cross *for us*. It is the word "everyone" that poses a problem for Reformed Theology. While I am not sure that Calvin intended for us to conclude that *everyone* refers to *every elect one*, as Calvinism does, his continual use of the word "us" may have provided his followers with the boldness to interpret many of the *every/all* passages of Scripture as referring to those of *us* who are elect. MacArthur is unambiguous. He says that the phrase, "taste death for everyone" means:

> Everyone who believes, that is.[292]

How easy it would have been for the writer of this letter to qualify "everyone" by saying that everyone is "everyone who believes." I think it is safe to assume that the phrase, "taste death for everyone" is what Jesus was referring to when He said God "gave His only begotten Son." If so, assuming MacArthur is right, we could paraphrase John 3:16 to read:

> For God so loved the elect of the world that He gave His only begotten Son for the elect, that everyone who believes in Him, which is **only** and **all** of the elect, might not perish but have everlasting life.

In my representation of Calvinism, I have used this and similar restatements of John 3:16 to illustrate the implications of a Calvinist view of salvation and damnation. I have been seriously rebuked by Calvinists for doing so. Why, however, would Calvinists object to this? I have repeatedly documented that this is exactly what Reformed Theology forces the Calvinist to do. Consider the very telling words of Palmer:

> It was because God so loved the world of the elect sinners that He sent His only begotten Son that the world might be saved through Him (John 3:16–17). In this passage, "world" does not mean every single person, reprobate as well as elect, but the whole world in the sense of people from every tribe and nation.[293]

Why can Palmer restate John 3:16 this way and I can't? As we found in our consideration of unconditional election, Calvinists dismiss the universality of God's saving interest in mankind, including the manifestation of His saving work on behalf of the lost, which is the cross of Christ, by replacing the *all* men and *every* man passages of Scripture with the words *all kinds of men* and *every kind of man*. Steele and Thomas sum up this Calvinist explanation as follows:

One reason for the use of these expressions was to correct the false notion that salvation was for the Jews alone. Such phrases as the "the world," "all men," "all nations," and "every creature" were used by the New Testament writers to emphatically correct this mistake. These expressions are intended to show that Christ died for all men without *distinction* (i.e., He died for Jews and Gentiles alike) but they are not intended to indicate that Christ died for all men without *exception* (i.e., He did not die for the purpose of saving each and every lost sinner).[294]

If eternal and unconditional redemption for the elect and eternal and unconditional damnation for the reprobate does not constitute a *distinction*, I cannot imagine what would. In fact, it is obvious that if there is an elect caste versus a reprobate caste, a sure-to-be-saved caste versus a certain-to-be-damned caste, that would constitute the greatest and most important distinction imaginable. Moreover, if Christ did not die for those ultimately lost as well as those ultimately saved, who is Peter talking about when he refers to those that were "… denying the Lord who bought them …" (2 Pet. 2:1)?

As we will see in a consideration of the fifth point of Calvinism, if Calvinists are right about perseverance, these words cannot refer to back-slidden Christians. If Calvinists are right about limited atonement, Christ could not have died for them. If He *bought them,* what price did He pay for them? If the price He paid was not payment for their salvation, then what was it for? Did Christ pay one price for the elect, by dying as a substitute on the cross for the elect, and another *non-redeeming* price for the non-elect? MacArthur dismisses what seems to be the rather straightforward meaning of the words "the Lord who bought them" by saying:

> The terms which Peter used here are more analogical than theological. … they are probably claiming that they were Christians, so that the Lord had bought them actually and personally. With some sarcasm, Peter mocks such a claim by writing of their coming damnation.[295]

While MacArthur may very well be right (and I happen to believe he is) that these false teachers were not true believers, there is nothing in the text to suggest that they were not really bought by the Lord they were denying. This is another case of reading into a text what it does not say or imply, based upon and necessitated by a Calvinist conviction. Giving this phrase an *ana-*

logical interpretation provides nothing more than a semantic cover so that a theological interpretation consistent with Calvinism can be imposed upon this text. Besides, Peter does not say that those to whom he refers *claim* the Lord *bought* them. He unequivocally says the Lord *did* buy them.

Therefore, if the Lord did not actually buy them, Peter is wrong. It seems to me that we must choose between the apostle Peter's teaching and John MacArthur's Calvinism. I do not see how we can have both. Reading this passage without a Calvinist bias would lead one to believe that the Lord really had bought these false teachers. There is no more reason to believe that the words "who bought them" are any more analogical than the words "denying the Lord" are analogical. Theological convictions aside, there is every reason to believe He really bought them as there is every reason to believe they really did deny Him.

Though he makes no mention of an analogical interpretation of 2 Peter 2:1, Hoeksema agrees with MacArthur's conclusions. The primary reason for rejecting what seems to be the obvious meaning of this passage is, however, purely theological and not exegetical. That is, Peter could not mean what he actually says if Calvinism is true. With this much I agree. Hoeksema sees in this verse a connection to 1 John 2:19 (KJV). There we read:

> *They went out from us, but they were not of us; for if they had been*
> *of us, they would no doubt have continued with us: but they went*
> *out, that they might be made manifest that they were not all of us.*

This, however, misses the point of the text. The question is not: were they really Christians? I agree that they were not. The question is: did Christ die for them? Were they, as Peter says, bought by the Lord they were denying? Hoeksema explains:

> This verse certainly cannot mean that those false teachers were
> bought by the blood of Christ and that now they fell away from
> grace.[296]

Again Hoeksema misses the point. The point is not: did they fall from grace? That assumes they had actually been saved by grace in the first place. The question is: did the Lord buy them? Hoeksema can't see them falling from grace if Christ died for them, otherwise the atonement would not have automatically saved them, as those who subscribe to a limited atonement believe. Hoeksema cannot see them falling from grace if the Calvinist doctrine of perseverance of the saints is true. So Hoeksema has to come up with an alternative to work with Calvinism, even if it contradicts what the text clearly says. So if this verse *cannot mean* what it seems to mean, what does it mean? Hoeksema says:

> It must mean that although formerly and nominally they were reck-
> oned to belong to the church of Christ in the world, they became
> enemies and denied the atoning blood of Christ.[297]

That, however, does not address the question as to why Peter said that the Lord bought them. This phrase will simply not go away because it does not fit into one's theological scheme. Calvin seems to accept what this text is saying. Thus he conceded:

> It is no small matter to have the souls perish who were bought by
> the blood of Christ.[298]

For Calvin, the purchase price paid for those who deny Him *and* that ultimately perish is the same as the purchase price paid for those of us who are ultimately redeemed. Remember Peter says:

> *You were not redeemed with corruptible things, like silver or gold,*
> *... but with the precious blood of Christ, as of a lamb without blem-*
> *ish and without spot. (1 Pet. 1:18–19)*

Thus, if we can conclude that the purchase price of a soul is Christ on the cross on behalf of that soul, then we must also conclude that Christ died for some that will perish. If there are only two categories of people—those who ultimately perish and those who are (or ultimately will be) saved—then the atonement was an atonement provided for but rejected by the ultimately lost, as well as an atonement provided for and accepted by the ultimately saved.

John Gill proposes another solution to this problem passage for the Calvinist. Gill also disagrees with John Calvin, but for different reasons than does John MacArthur or Herman Hoeksema. Gill agrees with MacArthur and Hoeksema that Christ did not shed His blood for the reprobate or those that ultimately perish, and he agrees with Calvin that some who perish were really bought by the Lord. Gill disagrees with MacArthur, Hoeksema, and Calvin when they say that the price the Lord paid for those who perish was Christ on the cross and His shed blood for the remission of sins. In fact, Gill and White disagree with Calvin and MacArthur that the Lord referenced in

2 Peter 2:1 is Christ the Lord. Although Gill and White do not tell us what kind of purchase price this was or what it was paid for, Gill and White believe this price was paid for those that ultimately will perish. Gill is very clear about who the Lord of this verse is. He explains:

> It is concluded that such as are bought by Christ, may be destroyed; but Christ is not here spoken of, but God the Father; and of him the word (*despotace*—Lord) is always used, when applied to a divine Person, and not of Christ; nor is there anything in this text that obliges us to understand it of him; nor is there here anything said of Christ dying for any persons, in any sense whatever; nor of the redemption of any by his blood; and which is not intended by the word *bought*: where Christ's redemption is spoken of, the price is usually mentioned ...[299]

The most common word for Lord in the New Testament, whether speaking of the Son or the Father, is *Kurios*. Because a different word for Lord is used in this verse, however, does not mean a different Lord is referred to. Even if, however, we could speak of the Father as the one who made this purchase, it does not mean that He did not do so with the blood of Christ. Certainly, everyone would agree that the price Christ paid for our sins is in some sense the price the Father paid for our sins as well.

God was in Christ reconciling the world to Himself. (2 Cor. 5:19)

The fact that God is triune allows Paul to speak of:

... the church of God which He purchased with His own blood. (Acts 20:28)

If it was the Father who sent the Son to die on the cross, there was indeed a price the Father paid as well. The very nature of the relationship between the Father and Son suggests that the sacrifice of one is in some sense the sacrifice of the other. None of this even hints of the heresy of *patripassianism* (confusing the Person of the Father with the Person of the Son; specifically declaring that the Father suffered on the cross with the Son). The only real problem for the Calvinist with this passage is that it does not fit the Calvinist doctrine of a limited atonement. If a person were not already convinced of the Calvinist view of the atonement, this passage would pose no problem to solve. Calvinists just cannot allow Scripture to say what it seems to be saying. If they did, Calvinism would be indefensible. Albert Barnes says:

The only arguments to show that it refers to God the Father would be, (1) that the word used here … is not the usual term … by which the Lord Jesus is designated in the New Testament; and (2) that the admission that it refers to the Lord Jesus would lead inevitably to the conclusion that some will perish for whom Christ died. That it does, however, refer to the Lord Jesus, seems to me to be plain from the following considerations: (1) It is the obvious interpretation; that which would be given by the great mass of Christians, and about which there could never have been any hesitancy if it had not been supposed that it would lead to the doctrine of general atonement.[300]

In other words, the Calvinist cannot accept what the text plainly says because it is believed by the Calvinist to contradict the Calvinist doctrine of limited atonement. Calvinists can defend their position on limited atonement only because they are so willing to bend what Scripture says to conform to Reformed Theology. Even with all the bending they are willing to do, they still cannot make it work for some passages like 2 Peter 2:1. Nevertheless, while drawing his listeners' attention to the person of Jesus Christ, John the Baptist said:

> Behold! The Lamb of God who takes away the sin of the world! (John 1:29)

A Calvinist reading of this verse could be, "Behold! The Lamb of God who takes away the sin of the world *of the elect*!" But, Calvin said of this verse that John the Baptist:

> … Uses the word sin in the singular number, for any kind of iniquity; as if he had said, that every kind of unrighteousness which alienates men from God is taken away by Christ. And when he says, the sin OF THE WORLD, he extends this favor indiscriminately to the whole human race; that the Jews might not think that he had been sent to them alone. But hence we infer that the whole world is involved in the same condemnation; and that as all men without exception are guilty of unrighteousness before God, they need to be reconciled to him.

> John the Baptist, therefore, by speaking generally of the sin of the world, intended to impress upon us the conviction of our own misery, and to exhort us to seek the remedy. Now our duty is, to

embrace the benefit which is offered to all, that each of us may be convinced that there is nothing to hinder him from obtaining reconciliation in Christ, provided that he comes to him by the guidance of faith. Besides, he lays down but one method of taking away sins ...

I own, indeed, that all the spurious rites of a propitiatory nature drew their existence from a holy origin, which was, that God had appointed the sacrifices which directed men to Christ; but yet every man contrived for himself his own method of appeasing God. But John leads us back to Christ alone, and informs us that there is no other way in which God is reconciled to us than through his agency, because he alone takes away sin. He therefore leaves no other refuge for sinners than to flee to Christ; by which he overturns all satisfactions, and purifications, and redemptions, that are invented by men ...[301]

Statements like this encourage some four-point Calvinists to argue that Calvin did not teach or believe in limited atonement. If Calvin did believe in unlimited atonement, which I am not convinced he did, it would not help the reprobate sinner, according to Calvinism. For Calvin also taught that God has no real saving interest in the reprobate. Assuming unconditional election to be true, unlimited atonement would simply be the ultimate tease for the reprobate. Most Calvinists, however, cannot leave this verse as it is. They must see Christ as the Lamb of God who really only takes away the sin of His elect sheep. Nevertheless, the apostle Paul tells us:

God was in Christ reconciling the world to Himself. (2 Cor. 5:19)

MacArthur says:

The word "world" should not be interpreted in any universalistic sense, which would say that everyone will be saved, or even potentially reconciled.[302]

Why shouldn't the word "world" be interpreted to mean that anyone can "be potentially reconciled"? It is because this would be to deny Reformed Theology in general and limited atonement in particular. This is another way of saying that the plight of some sinners, which is all of the reprobate sinners, is so miserable and hopeless that they are beyond the saving love, grace, and reach of God. If the Calvinist is right, this could and perhaps should be rendered, *God was in Christ reconciling **the elect** of the world to Himself.* It is the position of the apostle John that:

> ... *the Father has sent the Son as Savior of the world. (1 John 4:14)*

A Calvinist-corrected reading would be, *the Father has sent the Son as Savior of **the elect** of the world.* For the Calvinist, whenever the word "world" is used in reference to the saving interest or work of God, it must *always* mean *some* of the world and must *never* mean *all* of the world. The apostle Paul also tells us:

> ... *Christ died for the ungodly. (Rom. 5:6)*

To be consistent with Calvinism, Paul could or maybe even should have said that *Christ died only for the ungodly elect.* For no matter who Scripture says Christ died for, limited atonement forces the Calvinist to add the limiting word elect (in their thinking and theology) to that person or group. Despite the fact that Spurgeon held to limited atonement, he nevertheless rightly (but inconsistently) argues:

> Self-righteousness is a folly, and despair is a crime, since Christ died for the ungodly. None are excluded hence but those who do themselves exclude; this great gate is set so wide open that the very worst of men may enter, and you, dear hearer, may enter now.[303]

If Christ did not die for *all* of the ungodly, as Spurgeon believes, then by virtue of this fact alone, Spurgeon should also believe that some were excluded by God and were not simply excluding themselves. Instead of "you, dear hearer, may enter now," Spurgeon could also say "you, dear hearer, may not enter now or ever."

WHAT DOES GOD DESIRE?

Earlier we considered the scriptural affirmation, which says:

> ... *God our Savior ... desires all men to be saved and to come to the knowledge of the truth. (1 Tim. 2:3–4)*

We discussed this verse in our focus on unconditional election. Let us now look at this verse and its immediate context relative to limited atonement. Notice that just a few verses earlier Paul wrote:

This is a faithful saying and worthy of all acceptance, that Christ
Jesus came into the world to save sinners. ... (1 Tim. 1:15)

I take this to mean that if you are a sinner, He came to save you. The
reason that the apostle Paul can say with such confidence that God desires to
save *all men* and to have *all men* come to the knowledge of the truth is even
more devastating to the notion of limited atonement. That is, as we have
already seen, he can say this because:

There is one God and one Mediator between God and men, the
*Man Christ Jesus, who gave Himself **a ransom for all**. (1 Tim.*
2:5–6 emphasis added)

Paul says that Christ, the only Mediator, mediated *for all*. If as every
Calvinist would agree, Christ did His primary and most important mediating work on the cross, then it follows that what He did on the cross (to give
Himself as a ransom), He did *for all* sinners. Notice also that this teaching
about our Lord's mediating work, which paid the ransom for all, is mentioned immediately after Paul tells us about God's desire to save all men.
God's intentions toward all sinners could not be stated more clearly. Why
can't the Calvinist see this?

The Calvinist view is necessarily distorted by insisting that *all* must
mean *some* whenever it refers to the saving interest, purpose, and work of
God. To allow even one *all* to mean an unqualified *all* when referring to
the saving interest and work of God, would bring the Calvinist doctrine of
limited atonement to its logical knees. Like all other distinctive doctrines
of Calvinism, limited atonement is not affirmed because it is clearly taught
in Scripture but because it logically follows some other assumption of
Calvinism. Concerning the history of the doctrine of limited atonement,
Godfrey explains:

This view emerged clearly among the followers of Augustine as
a consequence of his teaching on sovereign, particular grace in
salvation. ... John Calvin did not explicitly teach the doctrine, but
it seems implicit in his work. His successors made it explicit and
made it part of the Reformed confessional in the Canons of Dort
and the Westminster Confession of Faith.[304]

It is fair to ask: if limited atonement follows so clearly from the doctrine
of unconditional election, as I agree it does, and if it is also clearly taught

from Scripture, as Calvinists since the *Synod of Dort* contend, why does Calvin not just come right out and teach this doctrine? Perhaps A. A. Hodge, as convinced as anyone of limited atonement could be, has the answer. Hodge says:

> ... Let the fact be well noted ... that Calvin does not appear to have given the question we are at present discussing a deliberate consideration, and has certainly not left behind him a clear and consistent statement of his views.[305]

Still, White is right when he says:

> It makes no sense for Christ to offer atonement for those the Father does not entrust to Him for salvation. Obviously, a person who does not believe the Father entrusts a particular people (the elect) to the Son has no reason to believe in particular redemption.[306]

For White, then, if you do not believe in the Calvinist doctrine of unconditional election, you have no reason to believe in the Calvinist doctrine of limited atonement. Conversely, to White, if you believe Christ died for all sinners, then you have no reason to believe in the Calvinist doctrine of unconditional election. I have no argument with his logic, only with the truthfulness of his premise. Remember the admission of Crenshaw:

> Some have said ... nowhere does scripture say that Christ did **not** die for the reprobate or that He died **only** for the elect. This is true ...[307]

Remember also what Calvin said:

> It is no small matter to have the souls perish who were bought by the blood of Christ.[308]

Earlier, I said that Sproul speaks for most Calvinists when he says in reference to the word "world" in John 3:16:

> The world for whom Christ died cannot mean the entire human family. It must refer to the universality of the elect (people from every tribe and nation).[309]

I then followed this quote with another quote from Palmer who reasons:

> Because God has so loved certain ones … these particular ones will
> be saved, He sent His Son to die for them, to save them, and not all
> of the world.[310]

While it is true that these statements represent Calvinism, insofar as the bottom line is concerned, they still pose serious problems for many Calvinists. That is, while no Calvinist that believes in limited atonement can allow for the word "world" in John 3:16 to really mean that everyone in the world can potentially be saved, the way Sproul and Palmer handle this verse is objected to by many Calvinists, including MacArthur. MacArthur and many others believe that the world in this instance really does include everyone. It does, according to MacArthur, imply that everyone is loved and not just the elect. It cannot, however, mean that everyone in the world is loved with a redemptive love, according to MacArthur. Concerning John 3:16, he argues:

> Those who approach this passage determined to suggest that it
> *limits* God's love miss the entire point. There is no delimiting lan-
> guage anywhere in the context. It has nothing to do with how God's
> love is distributed between the elect and the rest of the world. It
> is a statement about God's demeanor toward mankind in general.
> It is a declaration of *good* news, and its point is to say that Christ
> came into the world on a mission of salvation, not a mission of
> condemnation.[311]

What good does the "demeanor" of God do for those who are not re-demptively loved by God? Can we really reduce the powerful and precious implication of this passage to a question of God's demeanor toward the world in general? How can this be? If the love referred to is for the entire world and not just the elect of the world, and if the good in the good news has any relationship to that love with which God loves the world, then it would follow that the message of salvation would be for all in the world and not just the elect of the world. If Calvinism is true, however, the news is not good for any but the elect, because He only savingly loves the elect. The fact that Christ did not come to condemn the world is of no comfort or good to the reprobate because they must remain in the condemnation to which they were assigned, unconditionally, by God from all eternity to all eternity.

Suppose I were to say to an absolute pauper: *Do not worry, I have not come to take away your money.* The pauper would be excused for saying:

Big deal, I have no money for you to take from me. Even so, is it not reasonable for the reprobate to say to Christ (assuming Calvinism is true): *So what that You did not come to condemn me? I am already condemned and must remain condemned for all eternity. What good could there be in Your incarnation and crucifixion, as far as my plight is concerned?* At best, a limited atonement strips the gospel of the good that it contains for untold millions. Fortunately, it only does so in the minds and hearts of the consistent Calvinists.

Remember:

> *There is one God and one Mediator between God and men, the Man Christ Jesus, who gave Himself a ransom for all. (1 Tim. 2:5–6)*

> [Jesus] *is the atoning sacrifice for our sins, and not only for ours but also for the sins of the whole world. (1 John 2:2, NIV)*

> *God was in Christ reconciling the world to Himself. (2 Cor. 5:19)*

> [Jesus is] *the Lamb of God who takes away the sin of the world! (John 1:29)*

> *Jesus ... suffered death, so that by the grace of God he might taste death for everyone. (Heb. 2:9, NIV)*

> *We trust in the living God, who is the Savior of all men, especially of those who believe. (1 Tim. 4:10)*

> *"For God so loved the world that He gave His only begotten Son, that whoever believes in Him should not perish but have everlasting life." (John 3:16)*

The message or "gospel" of Calvinism is not even potentially good for a large number of people. For these same people it is outright bad news. If the message we preach to a man has no good in it and if it has nothing but bad in it, how can we call it "Good News"?

6

IRRESISTIBLE GRACE

EXPLAINED

A CCORDING to *The Westminster Confession of Faith*:

> All those whom God hath predestinated unto life, and those only,
> He is pleased, in His appointed time, effectually to call, by His
> Word and Spirit, out of that state of sin and death, in which they are
> by nature to grace and salvation, by Jesus Christ; enlightening their
> minds spiritually and savingly to understand the things of God, tak-
> ing away their heart of stone, and giving unto them a heart of flesh;
> renewing their wills, and by His almighty power, determining them
> to that which is good, and effectually drawing them to Jesus Christ:
> yet so, as they come most freely, being made willing by His grace
> (X:1).

Is it possible to "come most freely" when you are "made willing"? Once
you truly understand what Calvinism means by being "made willing," it is
clearly a logical contradiction to say that a person comes to faith in Jesus
Christ freely. This is the reason Calvinists use the word *irresistible* when
speaking of saving grace. Although some Calvinists will use the term irresistible grace in both a broad and a narrow sense, in this chapter we will,
for the most part, limit ourselves to a consideration of grace as it relates to
salvation in the most basic and narrow sense. Sometimes Calvinists refer to
this as saving grace as opposed to sustaining grace or some other theological
distinction. Spurgeon referred to this irresistible saving grace as:

> The mighty, overwhelming, constraining force of a divine
> influence. ...[312]

Can you freely resist a *mighty, overwhelming, constraining force*?
Sproul explains the difference between an inward call to salvation, which

is a synonym for irresistible grace, and an outward call, which is a gospel proclamation and invitation, as follows:

> When I was a boy my mother used to stand at the window and call me into the house for dinner. Usually I came at the first summons, but not always. If I delayed, she would call a second time, usually with greater volume. Her first call was not always effective. It failed to gain the desired effect. Her second call usually was effective; I hurried into the house.[313]

This illustration is misleading in that it put the onus on young Sproul to heed the call of his mother, even if he did not do so the first time she called. In Reformed Theology, the one who fails to respond to the outward call was never the recipient of an inward or effective call. Still there is some value in this illustration. Sproul is trying to make the point that a call that is positively responded to is a saving call. If the call is not positively responded to, it is not a saving call. It is not, however, an *effective* call because it is *responded to*, as it was with the young Sproul. Rather, according to Reformed Theology, it is positively *responded to* because it is an *effective* call.

In Sproul's childhood illustration, his mother probably expected young Sproul to heed the call the first time just as he actually did the second time. The *only* difference that mattered was in young Sproul's *response* to his mother's two calls. Unlike the call of Sproul's mother (who intended her son to respond to both the effective and the ineffective call to dinner), in the Reformed view, only the saving call of God is intended to bring a lost person to salvation. The non-saving call (i.e., the gospel proclamation) of God is not intended to bring a lost man to salvation unless it is accompanied by a hidden, secret, and inward saving call. As for the place of preaching the gospel, insofar as the effective or saving call is concerned, Sproul says:

> The preaching of the gospel represents the outward call of God. This call is heard audibly by both the elect and the non-elect. A human being has the ability to resist and refuse the outward call. He will not respond to the outward call in faith unless or until the outward call is accompanied by the effectual inward call of the Holy Spirit.[314]

Again, in Calvinism the call is effective *not* because it is responded to. It is responded to *because* it is the effective or irresistible kind of call. Sproul explains:

There is a call of God that is effective. When God called the world into being, the universe did not hesitate to comply with the command. God's desired effect in creation came to pass. Likewise, when Jesus called dead Lazarus from his grave, Lazarus came to life.[315]

This distinction is very important. Allow me to explain it this way. Suppose a soldier is called upon by his commanding officer to return to his post. As long as the soldier has the option or ability to disobey that order it would not be an effective, efficacious, or irresistible command. Only if the commanding officer was able to force or make the soldier obey, taking away the option to disobey, could it be said that this was an effective command in the Calvinist sense.

The most important thing about this call, as with most every other issue central to Calvinism, is that only God has a meaningful say in what takes place as a result of the call. Man does not and cannot have a say. Generally speaking, it can be argued that all forms of Calvinism embrace something that can be called *monovolitionism.* That is, only one being (God) has a will that makes a difference. While Calvinism implicitly teaches this in a general sense, it is especially prominent in Calvinism with regard to where a person ends up—whether that be in heaven or hell. As an uncreated object can have no say in its own creation and as a dead man can have no say in his resurrection to life, even so the Calvinist argues that a spiritually dead man cannot, while spiritually dead, respond positively with true and saving faith to God. That is, he cannot voluntarily receive eternal life offered to him in the gospel on the condition of faith while he is still unregenerate. This is also to say that he cannot believe in God's Son for salvation until he is born again and given faith with his new life in Christ. The dark side says that the reprobate has only one "choice" when the gospel is preached to him, and that is to reject the gospel in unbelief. Sproul goes on to explain:

> Effectual calling is related to the power of God in regenerating the sinner from spiritual death. It is sometimes called "irresistible grace." … When Paul teaches that those whom He predestines, He calls, and those He calls, He justifies, the call to which He refers is the effectual call of God.[316]

Sproul then says:

> The effectual call of God is an inward call. It is the secret work of

quickening or regeneration accomplished in the souls of the elect by the immediate supernatural operation of the Holy Spirit. It effects or works the inward change of the disposition, inclination, and desire of the soul. Before the inward effectual call of God is received, no person is inclined to come to Him. Everyone who is effectually called is now disposed to God and responds in faith. We see then that faith itself is a gift from God, having been given in the effectual call of the Holy Spirit.[317]

Since a man cannot choose to believe in Christ before regeneration, according to Reformed Theology, logically he cannot choose to repent of sin, especially the sin of unbelief. So that the elect can and will repent, the irresistible call of Calvinism is also an irresistible call to repentance just as it is an irresistible call to faith. John Piper explains:

When a person hears a preacher call for repentance he can resist that call. But if God gives him repentance he cannot resist because the gift is the removal of the resistance. Not being willing to repent is the same as resisting the Holy Spirit. So if God gives repentance it is the same as taking away the resistance. This is why we call this work of God "irresistible grace."[318]

This is also why I say that an irresistible call cannot be responded to freely. An irresistible call to faith and repentance equals a forced response in faith and repentance. Erickson represents Calvinism in saying:

Because all humans are lost in sin, spiritually blind, unable to believe ... some action by God must intervene between His eternal decision and the conversion of the individual within time. This activity is termed special or effective calling. ... Special calling means that God works in particularly effective ways with the elect, enabling them to respond in repentance and faith, and rendering it certain that they will. ... Special or effectual calling ... involves an extraordinary presentation of the message of salvation. It is sufficiently powerful to counteract the effects of sin and enable the person to believe. It is so appealing that the person will believe.[319]

Sproul says:

The term irresistible grace is misleading. Calvinists believe that all men can and do resist the grace of God. ... [God's grace] is irresist-

ible in the sense that it achieves its purpose. It brings about God's
desired effect. Thus I prefer to use the term *effectual grace*.[320]

In other words, those who resist the grace of God are only fulfilling
God's purpose for them. This is the desired effect grace is supposed to have
on them. More often than not, a Calvinist uses the term "irresistible grace"
with the elect in mind, and the divinely desired effect or purpose is their salvation, initially in terms of regeneration and then justification. In Reformed
Theology, regeneration precedes and produces faith. Faith then results in
justification. Spencer says:

> The Calvinist insists that salvation is based on the free will of God,
> and since God is omnipotent, His will cannot be resisted.[321]

Thus, if salvation occurs, it is God's will. If it does not occur, it is not
God's will. Translated in terms of the elect, it is God's will that they be
saved. In terms of the reprobate, it is God's will that they be damned. Also
speaking of irresistibility in the narrower or pre-conversion sense (i.e., leading up to and bringing about salvation initially), Curtis Crenshaw says:

> ... that God decides who will be saved and when, [and] that man
> does not have a "free will" and that God's grace is irresistible (a
> free gift).[322]

He also says:

> The Bible speaks against "free will" ...[323]

And:

> God irresistibly enables us to believe the Gospel.[324]

The difference between the Calvinist and the non-Calvinist (i.e., Biblicist)
view is not in the fact that Calvinists say that God irresistibly enables us to
believe the Gospel. Rather, it is that they say God irresistibly makes us (the
elect) believe, or, if you prefer, makes us believers. The Calvinist view is also
differentiated in two ways. Calvinists deny that many sinners are enabled by
God to believe. They also affirm (by implication) that some are decreed by
God to unbelief and its horrible consequences for all eternity.

To help make this very important distinction as clear as possible, consider the following analogy. Suppose there is a man stranded on an island

without water or food. Suppose that the pilot of a plane flies over the island and drops (by parachute) water and food to the stranded man. Without the water and food supplied by the pilot, the stranded man would have died in just a matter of a few days. Without the help of the pilot, the stranded man is not able to drink or eat. With the help of the pilot, the stranded man is able to drink and eat. The ability of the stranded man to drink and eat is directly related to and dependent upon the provisions dropped onto the island by the pilot. If the stranded man is to benefit from those provisions and live, however, he must choose to drink the water and eat the food. The fact that he *can* do so does not guarantee that he *will* do so. This is how the non-Calvinist views the offer of salvation. All lost men can believe and be saved and in fact are called upon to do so. Happily some do and tragically some don't.

Now suppose, there is a man in a hospital unconscious and dying of dehydration and starvation. In such a helpless state, the doctor on duty decides to rehydrate and feed the man intravenously. Only after this man is revived is he able to drink and eat on his own. This is how the Calvinist views the salvation process. You do not choose to believe but you are chosen to believe. According to Reformed Theology, if a man believes it is because he was chosen to believe. The choice a man makes to believe is merely the effect of which the prior choice by God is the cause.

Calvinists believe that if man could be free to accept or reject the salvation that God offers by grace through faith in His Son, salvation could not be a gift and could not be sovereignly bestowed. Calvinists have imagined that a relatively free man would be the undoing (theoretically speaking) of an absolutely free and sovereign God. They have also concluded that a freely or graciously given gift would not be a gift at all if the one offered the gift were able to freely receive it. Contrary to Scripture and logic, W. E. Best says:

> The idea of free grace and free will are diametrically opposed. All who are strict advocates for free will are strangers to the grace and sovereignty of God.[325]

While I agree that God irresistibly *enables* us to believe, nowhere in Scripture do we find the notion that God *makes* us believe (or makes us believers) as Calvinism teaches. I am also a little mystified as to why a free gift must be an irresistible gift. I would love to hear the *Scriptures* or *logic* that leads to such a conclusion. Steele and Thomas explain:

In addition to the outward general call to salvation, which is made
to everyone who hears the gospel, the Holy Spirit extends to the
elect a special inward call that *inevitably* brings them to salvation.
The external call (which is made to all without distinction) can be,
and often is, rejected; whereas the internal call (which is made only
to the elect) *cannot be rejected*; it always results in conversion. By
means of this special call, the Spirit *irresistibly* draws the sinner
to Christ. He is not limited in His work of applying salvation by
man's will, nor is He dependent upon man's cooperation for suc-
cess. The Spirit graciously causes the elect sinner to cooperate, to
believe, to repent, to come freely and willingly to Christ. God's
grace, therefore, is invincible; it never fails to result in the salvation
of those to whom it is extended.[326]

According to Calvinism, therefore, salvation results when saving grace
is extended to the unbelieving elect. The unbelieving elect are then irresistibly and supernaturally *turned into* the believing elect. Thus, the gospel
invitation extends a call of salvation to some (i.e., all *but* the elect) without
the necessary saving grace that is required to produce the salvation of those
called to that salvation. On the one side, Calvinism teaches that there is a
caste of men who are unconditionally elect from all eternity and therefore
inwardly and irresistibly called in time. On the other side, the dark side, it
teaches that there is a caste of men who are unconditionally reprobated from
all eternity and therefore not called inwardly in time.

While heavily criticized by their so-called hypo-Calvinist counterparts,
the hyper-Calvinists should be applauded for at least attempting to be a
little more consistent with the implications of Calvinism. One breakaway
Reformed church association called the *Presbyterian Reformed Church*
(PRC) says:

The objection of the PRC to the offer is not at all that the offer requires that the gospel be preached to all, or that the offer insists that
all be called to believe on Christ. But the objection is that the offer
holds that this preaching and calling are *grace to all*.[327]

Obviously, if the gospel proclamation cannot be believed by reprobates,
then there can be nothing gracious about the offer. The problem with this
view, besides the fact that it is patently unscriptural, is that it cannot give a
reasonable explanation for making an ungracious offer in the first place. To

say God says so and that settles the matter does not amount to a reasonable explanation. It just makes God responsible for the unreasonable and ungracious offer. Why offer to give to a person what the person cannot receive? To use ignorance of who can and cannot receive the gift of eternal life made in the offer is not a good answer. God, the one on behalf of whom the gospel preacher is making the offer, is certainly not ignorant of the one to whom He is making the offer. Nevertheless, hyper-Calvinism is a slight improvement over hypo-Calvinism, insofar as consistency is concerned, because it admits that the offer of Reformed Theology is not a *well-meant offer*. Steele and Thomas, representing the mainstream or hypo-Calvinism, explain:

> The gospel invitation extends a call to salvation to everyone who hears its message. It invites all men without distinction to drink freely of the water of life and live. It promises salvation to all who repent and believe. But this outward general call, extended to the elect and un-elect alike, will not bring sinners to Christ. Why? Because men are by nature dead in sin and are under its power. They are of themselves unable and unwilling to forsake their evil ways and to turn to Christ for mercy. Consequently, the unregenerate will not respond to the gospel call to repentance and faith. No amount of external threatening or promises will cause blind, deaf, dead, rebellious sinners to bow before Christ as Lord and to look to Him alone for salvation. Such an act of faith and submission is contrary to the lost man's nature.[328]

Boettner says:

> As the bird with a broken wing is "free" to fly but not able, so the natural man is free to come to God but not able.[329]

Some freedom! Augustinianism, the precursor to Calvinism, says that man is so bound by sin that all that a man can do is sin. Erickson, reflecting on Augustine's views, explains:

> This is not to say that man is not free. Man has options, but those options are all sinful in nature. He is free to choose, but merely to engage in one sin or the other.[330]

Here we have an excellent explanation as to what the Calvinist has in mind when he says that a lost man is a free man. According to this view, the lost sinner cannot do the right thing. He can only do the wrong thing.

Spurgeon illustrates the difference between the ineffectual or general call that comes as the gospel proclamation to the reprobate, and the effectual and directed call that is meant only for the elect as follows:

> The general call of the gospel is like the common "cluck" of the hen which she is always giving when her chickens are around her. But if there is any danger impending, then she gives a very peculiar call, quite different from the ordinary one, and the little chicks come running as fast as they can, and hide for safety under her wings. That is the call we want, God's peculiar and effectual call to his own.[331]

In *Spurgeon's Catechism,* he connects the application of redemption, which is the actual time when the elect are saved as well as the method by which they are saved, to the Calvinist notion of irresistible grace or effectual calling. That is:

28. Q. How are we made partakers of the redemption purchased by Christ?

A. We are made partakers of the redemption purchased by Christ, by the effectual application of it to us (John 1:12) by his Holy Spirit (Titus 3:5–6).

29. Q. How does the Spirit apply to us the redemption purchased by Christ?

A. The Spirit applies to us the redemption purchased by Christ, by working faith in us (Eph. 2:8), and by it uniting us to Christ in our effectual calling (Eph. 3:17).

30. Q. What is effectual calling?

A. Effectual calling is the work of God's Spirit (2 Tim. 1:9) whereby, convincing us of our sin and misery (Acts 2:37), enlightening our minds in the knowledge of Christ (Acts 26:18), and renewing our wills (Ezek. 36:26), he does persuade and enable us to embrace Jesus Christ freely offered to us in the gospel (John 6:44–45).

31. Q. What benefits do they who are effectually called, partake of in this life?

A. They who are effectually called, do in this life partake of justification (Rom. 8:30), adoption (Eph. 1:5), sanctification, and the various benefits which in this life do either accompany, or flow from them (1 Cor. 1:30).

The Calvinist can and sometimes does say that a person must choose to be saved, but he cannot say that an unregenerate person must or even can choose to come to Christ. For it is only after regeneration that a man is made to believe and only after regeneration that a man is made willing, according to Calvinism. Crenshaw, referring to an illustration he borrowed from Boice, says:

Preaching the Gospel is like tossing torches in 55-gallon drums. You toss the torch in one drum and there is water in the drum so the torch goes out. The same happens with another drum. Then the torch is cast into a drum with gunpowder in it—boom! An explosion occurs. So it is with preaching. We preach and preach and nothing happens; the word falls on deaf ears that cannot—and will not—hear. Then God regenerates one and boom, conversion occurs.[332]

Sproul says:

The Calvinist view of predestination teaches that God actively intervenes in the lives of the elect to make absolutely sure that they are saved.[333]

He then says:

Of course the rest are invited to Christ and given an "opportunity" to be saved *if they want to* ...[334]

Putting the word "opportunity" in quotes and the words *if they want to* in italics is Sproul's way of nodding that he understands that these are just words without substance in light of what Calvinism says about unconditional election, irresistible grace, limited atonement, etc. In other words, it is not a genuine opportunity to reprobates and as reprobates they *cannot* want to be saved. This is in full accord with the decree of God concerning their destiny. Thus he is quick to add:

Calvinism assumes that without the intervention of God no one will ever want Christ. Left to themselves, no one will ever choose Christ.[335]

It must be remembered that Calvinism requires more than a pre-salvation intervention of enablement on the part of God. It requires that the pre-faith intervention include a regenerating of the lost, which in turn brings with it a saving faith. Sproul explains the Calvinist logic as follows:

> Fallen man is still free to choose what he desires, but because his desires are only wicked he lacks the moral ability to come to Christ. As long as he remains ... unregenerate, he will never choose Christ.[336]

This notion that nothing short of regeneration will enable and/or make a man believe is central to the Calvinist doctrine of salvation in general and of their doctrine of irresistible grace in particular. Virtually all Calvinists agree that believers are supposed to preach the gospel without distinction for two primary reasons:

- Because we cannot be sure who the elect are and are not; and

- Out of obedience to God who commands that we do so.

They are divided as to whether or not this call to believe can be a valid offer of eternal life when proclaimed to the reprobate. The hypo-Calvinists have somehow convinced themselves that such an offer is valid. The hyper-Calvinists do not believe it is a *real* or a *valid* offer of eternal life to the reprobate. In this instance, the hyper-Calvinist is compelled by the logic of Reformed Theology to accept the implications of a Calvinist offer of eternal life to the reprobate. Evidently, the hypo-Calvinist ignores the logical implications of his views.

While hypo-Calvinists are affirming only what Scripture affirms with regard to the validity of the offer in a gospel proclamation, it is difficult to see how such an offer—in keeping with the implications of unconditional election, irresistible grace, and limited atonement—can be viewed as a valid offer of eternal life. In fact, it is more than difficult. Unless you are wearing special Calvinist-colored glasses, it is impossible. Mainstream or hypo-Calvinists continue to insist that the offer of eternal life proclaimed in the gospel to the reprobate is valid, despite the fact that reprobates cannot accept the offer due to the decree of God concerning their ultimate damnation. Berkhof explains the hypo-Calvinist view in light of the hyper-Calvinist objection. He says:

There is an objection derived from the *bona fide* offer of salvation. We believe that God "unfeignedly," that is, sincerely or in good faith, calls all those who are living under the gospel to believe, and offers them salvation in the way of faith and repentance. ... The offer of salvation in the way of faith and repentance does not pretend to be a revelation of the secret counsel of God, more specifically, of His design in giving Christ as an atonement for sin. It is simply a promise of salvation to all those who accept Christ by faith.[337]

Berkhof goes on to explain:

This offer, in so far as it is universal, is always conditioned by faith and conversion. Moreover, it is contingent on a faith and repentance such as can only be wrought in the heart of man by the operation of the Holy Spirit.[338]

Not only so but:

The universal offer of salvation does not consist in the declaration that Christ made atonement for every man that hears the gospel. ... It consists in (a) an exposition of the atoning work of Christ as in itself sufficient for the redemption of all men ...[339]

If that is the Calvinist version of a *bona fide* offer, I will have to think twice before doing business with a Calvinist. The *catch* in this offer is not even in small print. It is altogether hidden from view, in that it can only be discerned by a "secret counsel of God." Anticipating the obvious questions that inevitably come from detractors like me, Berkhof says:

It is not the duty of the preacher to harmonize the secret counsel of God respecting the redemption of sinners with His declarative will as expressed in the universal offer of salvation.[340]

At least Berkhof seems to acknowledge that one cannot harmonize both the Calvinist view of a divine decree which unconditionally condemns untold millions to eternal damnation without remedy, and also a scriptural declaration that God would have all to be saved. Still, some Calvinists obey the command to preach to everyone with the full assurance that the damnation of some is set in the same spiritual and eternal cement as is the salvation of others.

The only way we can be reasonably sure an elect person has been the recipient of irresistible grace, according to Calvinism, is when he positively responds to or no longer rejects the gospel. While the preaching of the gospel is not always accompanied with an irresistible grace leading to salvation, irresistible grace is never received apart from the gospel, according to many if not most contemporary Calvinists. As already noted, hypo-Calvinists do not say that all grace is irresistible or that it always leads to salvation. Rather, they say that *saving grace* is irresistible and therefore always leads to salvation. It should, however, be evident that irresistible grace, as defined in Calvinism, suffers from many of the same logical, practical, and scriptural problems, as does unconditional election. Keep in mind that, according to Reformed Theology:

If you are among the elect caste of humanity, you will necessarily come under the irresistible grace of God and eventually must/will be saved.

If you are not one of the elect, you will not come under the influence of the irresistible grace of God and will not/cannot be saved.

Thankfully, the offer of eternal life, expressed in a variety of ways and in many different contexts, is much more straightforward and less complicated to understand in the New Testament than it is in Reformed Theology. The scriptural response evident among those who hear the gospel and thereby receive or reject the gift of eternal life offered in the gospel is also far less complicated than how it is presented in Reformed Theology.

According to H. Wayne House, the general calling (in contrast to the effectual calling):

… involves the presentation of the Gospel in which the individual is offered the promise of salvation in Christ by faith in order to receive the forgiveness of sins and eternal life.[341]

He also says that the general calling:

… reveals the great love of God to sinners in general.[342]

Is the "individual" truly "offered the promise of salvation in Christ by faith" if the individual cannot have faith because that faith is withheld from him by God? I have to ask (along with Dave Hunt) "What love is this?"

IRRESISTIBLE GRACE

To the entire city of Jerusalem, our Lord says:

> *"O Jerusalem, Jerusalem! ... How often I wanted to gather your children together, as a hen gathers her chicks under her wings, but **you were not willing!**" (Matt. 23:37, emphasis added)*

Couldn't He just as easily have said they were *unable*? If they were unwilling only because they were unable, their unwillingness is not a matter of choice, but a matter of having no choice. Is it possible that Christ was sad, not because they were unwilling, but because they were not elect? Now if they were among the elect, they would have been willing, according to Calvinism (in fact, they would have been *compelled* to be willing!). That would, of course, mean that He was sad that He had not chosen them in the first place. So how does the Calvinist avoid what seems to be the obvious meaning and implication of the Lord's words and concern? Commenting on this verse and its immediate context, White says that:

1. It is to the leaders that God sent prophets.

2. It is to Jewish leaders who killed the prophets and those sent to them.

3. Jesus speaks of "your children," differentiating those to whom He is speaking from those that the Lord desired to gather together.

4. The context refers to the Jewish leaders, scribes, and Pharisees.[343]

White goes on to explain:

> A vitally important point to make here is that the ones the Lord desired to gather are not the ones who "were not willing"! Jesus speaks

to the leaders about their children that they, the leaders, would not allow Him to "gather." Jesus was not seeking to gather the leaders, but their children. ... The "children" of the leaders would be Jews who were hindered by the Jewish leaders from hearing Christ. The "you would not" then is referring to the same men indicated by the context: the Jewish leaders who "were unwilling" to allow those under their authority to hear the proclamation of the Christ.[344]

According this view, the leaders of the city (or those in authority) were the guilty ones. They represent those that killed the prophets. They also kept their victims, the people of the city, from hearing Christ speak about His saving love and grace for them. Their children, the regular folk of the city, those under the authority of the leaders, were not representative of those guilty of killing the prophets. They were not the unwilling ones and were the ones Christ had a saving love and interest in. That would lead to the conclusion that these leaders were not elect. It would also lead to the conclusion that those under their authority (those they were hindering) were elect. It would also lead to the conclusion that the irresistible grace needed to save a lost person is not for those who were "unwilling," but for those who were not "unwilling." Why would the willing need irresistible grace? If anyone needs irresistible grace, it is the unwilling. Are you confused yet? Calvinist John Gill explains:

> The persons whom Christ would have gathered are not represented as being unwilling to be gathered; but their rulers were not willing that they should. The opposition and resistance to the will of Christ were not made by the people, but by their governors.[345]

So, we have the resisters or obstructionists and the people under their awful control. God desires, according to White/Gill, to save the latter and has no saving interest in the former. So much for the total depravity of all! Now if our unwillingness is due to total depravity, then everyone should be unwilling until after they are born again. So much for the "no difference" between the unregenerate elect and the unregenerate reprobate insofar as their spiritual condition is concerned. Though acknowledging differing degrees of culpability between the leaders and the people in general, Calvin did not seem to agree with his future followers. Calvin reasoned:

> If in *Jerusalem* the grace of God had been merely rejected, there would have been inexcusable ingratitude; but since God attempted

to draw the Jews to himself by mild and gentle methods, and gained nothing by such kindness, the criminality of such haughty disdain was far more aggravated. There was likewise added unconquerable obstinacy; for not once and again did God wish to gather them together, but, by constant and uninterrupted advances, he sent to them the prophets, one after another, almost all of whom were rejected by the great body of the people.[346]

Here we have an irresistible God attempting *to draw* and wishing *to gather* people of an *unconquerable obstinacy*. Sounds very much like Calvin believed Christ was going after the ones White and Gill see as reprobate. Can there really be an *unconquerable obstinacy* if there is an *irresistible grace* of God? Sounds suspiciously like the silly notion that an immovable object met an irresistible force.

In light of the Calvinist view of saving grace, what are we to make of Stephen's words to the men who eventually stoned him? That is:

> *You men who are stiff-necked and uncircumcised in heart and ears are always resisting the Holy Spirit. (Acts 7:51, NASU)*

These men are indeed most pitiful—not simply because they were rejecting Jesus Christ (evidenced by their stoning of Stephen), but because they were doing the only thing they were able to do, according to Calvinism. The writer to the Hebrews says:

> *Today, if you will hear His voice, do not harden your hearts. (Heb. 4:7)*

Calvinism teaches that ultimately the non-elect caste must harden their hearts, or more precisely, their hearts must be hardened. They cannot and never will hear His voice. It also says that the elect caste ultimately and inevitably hears His voice and will ultimately and inevitably be unable to harden their hearts. So why the exhortation: *do not harden your heart?* And what are we to make of the words Jesus says to the Samaritan woman? Probably to her utter amazement, He says:

> *"If you knew the gift of God, and who it is who says to you, 'Give Me a drink,' you would have asked Him, and He would have given you living water." (John 4:10)*

In this context, it is clear that the living water to which Jesus refers is the salvation that comes, as the Calvinist would agree, by grace. For Jesus also says:

> *"Whoever drinks of this* [well] *water will thirst again, but whoever drinks of the water that I shall give him will never thirst. But the water that I shall give him will become in him a fountain of water springing up into everlasting life." (John 4:13–14)*

FOR THE ASKING

Yet Jesus says it is hers *for the asking* if only she knew who He was and what He was offering. How could she know who He was and what He was offering? He could tell her. And that is just what He does. She, in turn, went to town in what turned out to be an evangelistic endeavor. After the Samaritan woman got the townspeople interested in Jesus by raising the possibility that He could be the Messiah, we are told:

> *Many of the Samaritans of that city believed in Him because of the word of the woman who testified, "He told me all that I ever did." So when the Samaritans had come to Him, they urged Him to stay with them; and He stayed there two days. And many more believed because of His own word.*
>
> *Then they said to the woman, "Now we believe, not because of what you said, for we ourselves have heard Him and we know that this is indeed the Christ, the Savior of the world." (John 4:39–42)*

Moving forward in John's Gospel a couple of chapters, we come to a portion of Scripture that many Calvinists of all stripes see as the most powerful proof text confirming that grace is irresistible for the elect. In Chapter Six, Jesus says:

> *"All that the Father gives Me will come to Me, and the one who comes to Me I will by no means cast out." (v. 37)*
>
> *"This is the will of the Father who sent Me, that of all He has given Me I should lose nothing." (v. 39)*
>
> *"No one can come to Me unless the Father who sent Me draws him; and I will raise him up at the last day." (v. 44)*

> *"I have said to you that no one can come to Me unless it has been granted to him by My Father." (v. 65)*

Calvinists attempt to use these verses as if they were a weapon against any notion that gives man a say in where he will spend eternity. In fact, some Calvinists see this chapter as irrefutable evidence for irresistible grace. As soon as you put these words into their biblical context, however, a Calvinist interpretation of these words is forced (no pun intended) at best. Backing up to verses thirty-five and thirty-six of John Chapter Six, Jesus says:

> *"I am the bread of life. He who comes to Me shall never hunger, and he who believes in Me shall never thirst. But I said to you* [those that were opposing Him] *that you have seen Me and yet do not believe." (John 6:35–36)*

The failure of the Jews to believe was their forfeiture of spiritual food and drink, and it was their fault as well. It is in this context that Jesus goes on to say:

> *"All that the Father gives Me will come to Me, and the one who comes to Me I will by no means cast out." (John 6:37)*

NEITHER REJECTED NOR EJECTED

Those who believe in Jesus Christ are one and the same as those whom the Father gives to Him. In like manner, in coming to Christ in faith, the sinner can be assured that he will neither be rejected *(kept out)* nor ejected *(kicked out)* of the kingdom of God. Jesus is making the lost aware of how secure in Him they *will be* if they come to Him in faith. He is also making the saved aware of how secure in Him *they are* because they have come to Him in faith. To further demonstrate that this is indeed our Lord's purpose, consider the next two verses.

> *"For I have come down from heaven, not to do My own will, but the will of Him who sent Me. This is the will of the Father who sent Me, that of all He has given Me I should lose nothing, but should raise it up at the last day." (John 6:38–39)*

Once again, the context makes it evident that the ones given to the Son by the Father are the ones who believe in Christ and therefore come to Him in faith. For in the next verse He says:

*"This is the will of Him who sent Me, that everyone who sees the
Son and believes in Him may have everlasting life; and I will raise
him up at the last day." (John 6:40)*

Those who remained lost may have seen the Lord, but did not see and
believe in Him. Those who saw *and* believed received eternal life and a
guarantee of a resurrection to life, according to the will of God. While it is
very clear that those who are given to the Lord are believers and therefore
have come to Christ in faith, it is not clear, as Calvinists want us to believe,
that those given to the Son by the Father *believed because they were given.*
Those given to Christ are given to Christ because "God so loved the world
that He gave His only begotten Son, that whoever believes in Him should
not perish but have everlasting life" (John 3:16). The reason a lost man can
be and is in fact saved, is because of who God is, what God is like, and what
God did for the lost in the person of His Son. Jesus died for their sins and
then rose from the dead to die no more. The God-ordained condition for salvation, or that which a man must do to be saved, is to believe in Jesus Christ
(Acts 16:31).

Logically, faith in Christ is *necessary* to being *given* to Christ.
Chronologically, faith in Christ is *simultaneous* to *coming* to Christ. When
a lost person believes in Christ in time, He is given to Christ for time and
eternity. Otherwise we have unbelievers given to Christ. It is believers and
not unbelievers who *come* to Christ. It is believers and not unbelievers who
are given to Christ. Even if we accept that there is a sense in which the one
who believes in time was already given to Christ in eternity, those given
must be viewed as believers, before they actually believe, and are given as
believers to the one they will eventually believe in. Calvinists go adrift, in
part, because they have *factored out* the all-important faith factor.

None of the above is meant to suggest that an unbeliever does not need
supernatural enablement to believe. It does not mean that faith in Christ produces that which follows faith, whether we are talking about regeneration or
justification. Only God can and does regenerate the spiritually dead. Only
God can and does justify the ungodly. Referring to John 6:39–40, Sproul is
on the mark and makes my case when he says:

In this passage Jesus makes it clear that He is concerned about
every believer being raised up at the last day. This qualifies His
statement about what the Father has given Him that would never be

lost. It is believers that are given to Christ by the Father, and these believers will never be lost. This affirmation builds on what Jesus declared only moments earlier (John 6:36–38).[347]

Notice that Sproul admits, "it is believers that are given to Christ." It is, therefore, not unbelievers who are given to Christ. On this we could not be more agreed. Nevertheless, Sproul, commenting on John 6:65, asks:

Does God give the ability to come to Jesus to all men?[348]

According to Sproul and all knowledgeable Calvinists:

The Reformed view of predestination says no.[349]

"The Reformed view ... says no," but the scriptural view says *yes*. In John 6:65, Jesus says (as also quoted by Sproul):

"Therefore ... no one can come to Me unless it has been granted to him by My Father." (John 6:65)

We will be forgiven for asking the question, "To what does 'therefore' refer?" While speaking to those that opposed Him, Jesus says:

"There are some of you who do not believe. ... Therefore I have said to you that no one can come to Me unless it has been granted to him by My Father." (John 6:64–65)

That is, to those who believe in Christ, it is granted by the Father that they come to Christ. You must, therefore, come to Christ in faith or you cannot come to Christ at all. If you do come to Christ in faith, you will neither be *rejected* nor *ejected*. At this point the Calvinist is likely to ask, "How is it that an utterly lost, totally depraved, and, yes, spiritually dead sinner is able to believe in Christ?" By God's grace and with God's help—that's how. I completely agree with Sproul when he concludes from a reading of John 6:65:

The meaning of Jesus' words is clear. No human being can possibly come to Christ unless something happens that makes it possible for him to come. ... Man does not have the ability in and of himself to come to Christ. God must do something first. This passage teaches at least this much; it is not within fallen man's natural ability to come to Christ on his own, without some kind of divine assistance.

One thing is certain; man cannot do it on his own steam without some kind of help from God.[350]

Where we differ is over the answer to the questions:

What kind of help is required? How far must God go in order to overcome our natural inability to come to Christ?[351]

The Calvinist insists that this help must *irresistibly* lead to faith, and not just give the ability or capacity to believe. Furthermore:

It takes much more than the Spirit's assistance to bring a sinner to Christ—it takes regeneration by which the Spirit makes the sinner alive and gives him a new nature.[352]

By what logic, or from what Scripture, does the Calvinist conclude that the Spirit's assistance would not be enough, unless it included irresistibly making an unbeliever a believer or regenerating the lost before he believes, so that he can and will—indeed *must*—believe? Often the Calvinist says, or implies, that one must either believe that the Calvinist version of irresistible grace is necessary to salvation, or one must believe grace is not at all necessary to the process of bringing a sinner to faith in Christ. This is an incredible and unreasonable leap out of logic, or into illogic (i.e., an example of what is called the complex fallacy), as well as a tragic distortion of Scripture. There is another logical and scriptural option that the Calvinist either ignores or rejects. We must be born again to *see* or *enter* the kingdom of God. Of that there should be no question. Coming to Christ, however, requires that we simply and truly believe in Christ. When we do, God gives us a new life and that new life is eternal. That is, God regenerates the believer when an unbeliever turns from his unbelief and believes.

Faith in Christ does not regenerate or justify the spiritually dead sinner—God does. God, however, *only* and *always* regenerates and justifies a lost person *when* the lost person believes in His Son.

THE FATHER DRAWS

The fact that God offers the kind of help that an unregenerate unbeliever needs so that he can choose to believe in Christ for salvation is to be found in the very context that we are now considering. That is, Jesus says:

"No one can come to Me unless the Father ... draws him; and I will raise him up at the last day." (John 6:44)

The Calvinist says that because God must draw (*elko*) many (if not most) people cannot believe and be saved. In doing so they give the unsaved an excuse for their unbelief and lostness. As we will see, Jesus suggests that God draws so that all can believe and be saved and so that no one will have an excuse for not believing. Both the Calvinist and the non-Calvinist Evangelical recognize that God draws and that if He did not draw a man to Christ, no man would or could believe in Christ. The Calvinist, however, uses this word "draw" to exclude (in his thinking and theology) most of the lost from ever becoming saved. It is, however, the drawing work of God that makes it possible for all unbelievers to become believers. Exactly what He does to draw us we are not told in this passage. Perhaps John 16:8 holds the answer. It is in this verse that Jesus says:

> *"When He* [the Holy Spirit] *has come, He will convict the world of sin, and of righteousness, and of judgment." (John 16:8)*

Whatever this convicting work of the Holy Spirit is, it is work on the world. He does not (in this context) have the church in focus. That is, our Lord had the lost in mind, not the saved. Shortly, I will return to the meaning of the word "draw," as it is used in John Chapter Six and elsewhere. For now, it will be helpful to consider what John records early on in his Gospel concerning our Lord's saving interest in the *world* and the condition for salvation of which he so frequently reminds his readers. Let us begin with the mission and message of John the Baptist, as John the Evangelist/Apostle defines it for us. Speaking of John the Baptist, the apostle John says:

> *This man came for a witness, to bear witness of the Light, that **all through him might believe***. *(John 1:7, emphasis added)*

The light to which John referred is, of course, Jesus Christ. Concerning the person and purpose of Jesus Christ, we are told:

> [He] *was the true Light which gives light to **every man** coming into the world. (John 1:9, emphasis added)*

When John the Baptist saw our Lord approaching he declared:

> *Behold! The Lamb of God who takes away the sin of the world! (John 1:29)*

Referring to Himself and the requirement ordained by God for salvation, Jesus says:

"... whoever believes in Him should not perish but have eternal life." (John 3:15)

Immediately following this wonderful pronouncement, our Lord adds more detail in perhaps the most memorized, as well as the most under-appreciated passage of the New Testament. That is:

> *"God so loved the world that He gave His only begotten Son, that whoever believes in Him should not perish but have everlasting life. For God did not send His Son into the world to condemn the world, but that the world through Him might be saved. He who believes in Him is not condemned; but he who does not believe is condemned already, because he has not believed in the name of the only begotten Son of God." (John 3:16–18)*

Shortly after, our Lord says:

> *"He who believes in the Son has everlasting life; and he who does not believe the Son shall not see life, but the wrath of God abides on him." (John 3:36)*

With these verses and the truths they represent firmly in mind, we can now proceed to an even better understanding of Chapter Six of John's Gospel. The Calvinist asks a reasonable question when he asks: why do people positively respond when God draws them? The Calvinist unreasonably answers that everyone who is drawn cannot help but respond positively. Sproul, appealing to *Kittel's Theological Dictionary of the New Testament*[353], argues that the word translated "draw" (i.e., a form of the word *elko*) means to *coerce, force,* or even *drag.* He notes that in James 6:2 the same word is translated *drag.* That is:

> *Do not the rich oppress you and **drag** you into the courts? (James 2:6, emphasis added)*

He also points out that in Acts 16:19, the past tense of this word is translated *dragged.* Thus we read that:

> *When her masters saw that their hope of profit was gone, they seized Paul and Silas and **dragged** them into the marketplace to the authorities. (Acts 16:19, emphasis added)*

What he does not say is that a form of this same word is also used in John 12:32, where we read:

*"... if I am lifted up from the earth, [I] will **draw** all peoples to Myself." (emphasis added)*

While the New King James Version uses the word "peoples" instead of "men," the translators supply these words in both cases. Actually it could be translated, "If I be lifted up from the earth, I will draw all [or everyone] to Myself." Thus, if the *drawing* of John 6:44 (i.e., by the Father) can be translated *forced, coerced,* or *dragged,* could we not say the same for the drawing of John 12:32 (by and to the Son)? If being drawn to Christ leads necessarily and inevitably to saving faith in Christ, it would lead to universalism (i.e. everyone will be saved), which Calvinists rightly reject. John 6:44 tells us that everyone that comes to Christ must be enabled to do so, and in fact is enabled to do so by being drawn. It does not tell us that everyone who is drawn to Christ comes to Christ. Even so, Calvin taught:

> To *come to Christ* being here used metaphorically for *believing,* the Evangelist ... says that those persons are *drawn* whose understandings God enlightens, and whose hearts he bends and forms to the obedience of Christ. The statement amounts to this ... no man will ever of himself be able to come to Christ, but God must first approach him by his Spirit; and hence it follows that all are not *drawn,* but that God bestows this grace on those whom he has elected.
>
> True, indeed, as to the kind of *drawing,* it is not violent, so as to compel men by external force; but still it is a powerful impulse of the Holy Spirit, which makes men willing who formerly were unwilling and reluctant. It is a false and profane assertion, therefore, that none are *drawn* but those who are willing to be *drawn,* as if man made himself obedient to God by his own efforts; for the willingness with which men follow God is what they already have from himself, who has formed their hearts to obey him.[354]

Being *enabled* to come to Christ, *actually coming* to Christ, and *necessarily coming* (being compelled) are not the same. The last requires the first two; the first two do not automatically or inevitably lead to the latter. If I were given one hundred dollars I would be enabled to buy a product or service that costs one hundred dollars. The ability to buy something is not the same as actually buying it. Actually buying it could be by my own decision, *or* because someone forces me to buy it.

Even so, the ability to believe is not the same as actually believing, nor is it the same as necessarily believing. A person must be able to believe in order to believe. The ability to believe, however, is no guarantee that a person will actually believe. The Calvinist wrongly assumes that to be drawn to Christ is to come to Christ. The drawing work of God is irresistible in that there is nothing a sinner can do to keep from being *drawn* to Christ. We must distinguish between being drawn to Christ, which enables us to come to Christ, and actually coming to Christ, which involves a choice to believe on our part.

The *ability* to believe is from God and God alone. The *responsibility* to believe is entirely ours. This question is not, as Calvinists suggest, "*can* a lost and spiritually impotent man *resist* an all-powerful God who has determined to save a person no matter what?" Instead, the question is "*has* God *determined* to save such a person no matter what?" The Scriptures respond with a resounding "No!"

This text in particular and the testimony of Scripture in general do not teach that God has determined that coming to Christ in faith is forced upon a person in any way whatsoever. Just the opposite is true. The challenge, appeal, and proclamation of the gospel, as well as the words of John Chapter Six, assume and state in a myriad of ways that a lost, depraved, and spiritually dead sinner must respond positively to the drawing work of God and choose to do what he is enabled to do by the drawing work of God. What a man is enabled to do by the drawing work of the Father is believe in and receive Jesus Christ. They are not *made to believe* and they are not *made believers*. In effect, a Calvinist paraphrase of John 12:32 could read as follows:

> "If I be lifted up from the earth, [I] will draw all elect men to Myself," *or* "If I be lifted up from the earth, I will draw all kinds of men (from different nations, walks of life, etc.) to Myself."

As Sproul surely knows, a single Greek word (such as *elko*) can be used to convey very different ideas depending upon the context. This is, in fact, why the translators of most translations used different English words (i.e., *draw, drag*) to translate what is essentially the same Greek word in different contexts. It is not what the word "draw" may or can mean in *some* contexts that is at stake here. It is what the word "draw" means and implies in *this* context.

Thus, if we say, as Calvinists rightly say, that the drawing itself is one hundred percent something God does, then of course, it is irresistible in the sense that man cannot keep an all-powerful God from doing what He has determined to do. Since He has determined to draw all people to Christ (John 12:32), no one can and therefore no one will stop Him from drawing people to Christ.

If we say that to be drawn to Christ implies that the one drawn necessarily or irresistibly comes to Christ and is therefore saved, as Calvinism teaches, then John 6:44, combined with John 12:32, does not teach the exclusive version of unconditional election found in Calvinism. Instead, the two passages teach an all-inclusive doctrine of unconditional election found in a *Calvinistic* version of universalism. That would be a theological oxymoron if there ever was one.

By analogy, consider the love God has for the lost. Is it resistible or irresistible? It is irresistible in that a man can't keep God from loving him if that is what God has determined to do. It is resistible in that God does not force everyone or anyone He loves to receive or reciprocate His love.

So it is with the drawing work of God. No one can keep God from drawing him. It is in this sense irresistible. Since, however those *enabled* to believe are not thereby *forced* to believe, it is in this respect resistible. Calvinists are intent on finding an irresistible grace that makes salvation inevitable for an elect caste and impossible for a reprobate caste. This colors their thinking and theology as well as their interpretation of Scripture. Calvinists are not, however, as observant of the particulars of this verse as they should be. Again, the verse reads:

> *"No one can come to Me unless the Father ... draws him; and I will raise him up at the last day." (John 6:44)*

To be raised up at the last day, two things must be true of a person:

1. He must be drawn by the Father, and

2. He must come to Christ.

That is, to believe in Christ, a lost and unable sinner must be drawn and thereby enabled by the Father to do so. To come to Christ, an enabled sinner must believe in Christ or come to Christ in faith. This is the only way a man can come to Christ. Nevertheless:

- Only in the imagination of the committed Calvinist do we see that all who are drawn by the Father come to Christ or believe in Christ.

- Only in the imagination of the committed Calvinist do we see that being drawn by the Father means that the one drawn must come to Christ.

- Only in the imagination of the committed Calvinist do we see that those who do not come to Christ were not drawn.

Again, in order for us to come to Christ, or if you prefer, in order to enable us to believe in Christ, the Father must draw us. Just as the work of salvation belongs to God and God alone, so drawing a man to Christ, thereby enabling that man to come to Christ in faith, belongs to God alone. This is not, or at least should not be, in dispute. This *enabling* to believe, however, does not negate our *responsibility* to believe in Christ as well. In fact, we are responsible to believe precisely because we are enabled to believe. If we were altogether unable to believe, then it is rather silly to talk about being responsible to believe. Believing in Christ is our responsibility and not God's. It is only the enabling work of God that makes an otherwise unable man responsible for believing. A careful reading of John 6:65, combined with John 6:37, does not provide any kind of theological silver bullet for Calvinism, as so many Calvinists contend. Again Jesus says:

> "**Therefore** I have said to you that no one can come to Me unless it has been granted to him by My Father." (John 6:65, emphasis added)

The word "therefore" in this verse takes us back to the *why* of *what* He says in verse 65. Why does He say what He says in this verse? The answer is to be found in the preceding verses. That is, our Lord says:

> "There are some of you who do not **believe**." For Jesus knew from the beginning who they were who did not believe, and who would betray Him. And He said, "**Therefore** I have said to you that no one

can come to Me unless it has been granted to him by My Father."
(John 6:64–65, emphasis added)

An important connection exists between the word "believe" and the word "therefore." If we bring our Lord's words together without the explanatory intervening words it reads:

> *"There are some of you who **do not believe**. ... **Therefore** I have said to you that no one can come to Me unless it has been granted to him by My Father." (John 64a, 65, emphasis added)*

Their problem was not that they *could not* believe in Christ. It was that they *did not* believe in Him. The drawing work of God *enables* all to come to Christ. Those God the Father gives to the Son of God (those who believe) come to Christ. Why? They come to Christ because they believe in Him. As Calvin reasoned, coming to Christ means to believe in Christ. Conversely, believing in Christ means to come to Christ. This is what God requires of the lost so that they can be saved. This is not a *contribution to* salvation but a *condition of* salvation. The enabling work of God (i.e., the Father's drawing) is a gift of the Father to the unbeliever so that he *can* believe. It should not be confused, as it is in Calvinism, with the gift of the believer to the Son. In other words, the ability to believe is a gift of God to the unbeliever. The act of believing is the responsibility of the one enabled to believe.

The sticking point for many Calvinists is found in the words "and I will raise him up at the last day," which concludes verse forty-four of Chapter Six. These words are found at the conclusion of several different statements involving the destiny of believers. Let us look very closely at what they refer to specifically in John 6:44. Again Jesus says:

> *"No one can come to Me unless the Father who sent Me draws him; **and I will raise him up at the last day**." (emphasis added)*

The Calvinist wrongly assumes that everyone whom the Father draws comes to Christ and is saved. They also wrongly believe this verse teaches that everyone the Father draws is raised up at the last day. Instead, what this text really teaches is that:

- Those that the Father draws to the Son, which we know to be *all* from John 12:32,

And:

- Those that believe in Him, which we know to be *some* from many texts in general as well as this context in particular,

… will be *raised up* or *resurrected* with the just on the last day.

A person must be drawn, which is what *God does for us,* and he must believe, which is what *God enables us to do for ourselves.* Calvinists and non-Calvinists agree that there are many who do not and will never believe in Jesus Christ. Calvinists and non-Calvinists agree that those who never believe will forever be lost. Calvinism says, however, that the reprobate do not believe and will not believe because they *cannot* believe.

In harmony with the teaching of Scripture, non-Calvinist Evangelicals say that those ultimately lost do not believe because they *will not* believe. We also say that they *could* believe because of the drawing work, which enables an unbeliever to become a believer. I agree with Calvinists when they say that without the enabling work of God, no one could believe. I disagree with Calvinists when they say that the enabling work of God is limited to those they call the elect. We will revisit this issue regarding the words "… *I will raise him up at the last day.* " For now, listen to what Jesus said about those who did not believe:

> "*I have a greater witness than John's; for the works which the Father has given Me to finish—the very works that I do—bear witness of Me, that the Father has sent Me. And the Father Himself, who sent Me, has testified of Me. You have neither heard His voice at any time, nor seen His form. But you do not have His word abiding in you, because whom He sent, Him you do not believe. You search the Scriptures, for in them you think you have eternal life; and these are they which testify of Me. But **you are not willing to come to Me** that you may have life.*" (John 5:36–40, emphasis added)*

Revisiting John 6:37–39, Jesus says:

> "*All that the Father gives Me will come to Me, and the one who comes to Me I will by no means cast out. For I have come down from heaven, not to do My own will, but the will of Him who sent Me. This is the will of the Father who sent Me, that of all He has given Me I should lose nothing, but should **raise it up at the last day**.*" (emphasis added)*

The question that must be answered is: Who is it that the Father gives to the Son? We know that those given to the Son by the Father will come to the Son and be secure in their salvation. That is, they will "by no means [be] cast out." Concerning these same people, we know that God will "lose nothing." This is also to say, we know that they will be "raised up at the last day." Who are the ones, however, whom the Father gives to the Son? Returning to verse forty, we can see that Jesus answers this question as follows:

> *"... This is the will of Him who sent Me, that everyone who sees the Son and **believes** in Him may have everlasting life; and **I will raise him up at the last day**." (John 6:40, emphasis added)*

Just as we must be *drawn* and *come,* so those who see the Son *and* believe will be raised up at the last day. It is not enough to see the Son, just as it is not enough to be drawn. You must *see* and *believe,* just as you must be *drawn to Christ* and *come to* Christ. Calvinists are *right* when they say that those who see *and* believe are one and the same as those that will never be cast out, never be lost, have everlasting life, and will be raised up at the last day. Calvinists are *wrong* when they say that if you are drawn to Christ, you will necessarily come to Christ and be raised up at the last day.

According to Calvinism, but contrary to Scripture, if God does anything to make it possible for you to be saved, you must therefore eventually become saved. The logic of this would be that if you *see* the Son (which we know from verse forty is God's will), you will *believe* in the Son (which we also know from verse forty is God's will). Calvinists agree with non-Calvinists that it is God's will that both *seeing* the Son (whatever that may mean) and *believing* in Him are God's will and that both are a characterization of the saved. It seems that everyone who believes in the Son would also have seen Him, in some sense. Will everyone, however, who has seen the Son in this necessary way also believe in the Son? Just because you must see *and* believe, does it mean that you will believe *if* you see or *because* you see? The Calvinist logic would say yes. Yet Jesus also says:

> *"I am the bread of life. He who comes to Me shall never hunger, and he who believes in Me shall never thirst. But I said to you that **you have seen Me and yet do not believe**." (John 6:35–36, emphasis added)*

Calvin himself said:

He uses the words, see and believe, in contrast with what he had formerly said; for he had reproached the Jews with not believing, even though they saw (verse 36).[355]

Thus we know:

- Some will see *and* believe and therefore will be saved.

We also know:

- Some will see *and* not believe and therefore will remain lost.

This also leads directly to verses 44 and 65, where Jesus continues to tell us what God must do, which is *enable and grant,* and what we must do, which is *believe.* God reveals the Son, so that we can see Him and therefore believe in the one we see. God draws us to His Son so that we are able to believe in the one we are drawn to. This is to say that God grants that believers, not unbelievers, come to Christ. God gives believers, not unbelievers, to Christ.

It is indisputable to all Bible believers that if we believe in Christ, God grants that we come to Christ. From the human side, this is the only bridge we need to cross. It is also indisputable, or at least should be, that all believers belong to Christ because they have been given to the Son by the Father.

NOT WILLING

If we go back in the narrative of John's Gospel, we read where Jesus addresses His opponents as follows:

> *"You do not have* [the Father's] *word abiding in you, because whom He sent, Him* **you do not believe**. *You search the Scriptures, for in them you think you have eternal life; and these are they which testify of Me. But you are* **not willing** *to come to Me that you may have life." (John 5:38–40, emphasis added)*

Here our Lord specifically tells us why these men did not have the Father's Word abiding in them. It was not because they were not elect or that they were not irresistibly or effectually called. It was not because they had not been subjected to irresistible grace. It was because they inexcusably did not believe in God's Son. Here our Lord tells us why they could not have eternal life. It was not for any of the reasons that Calvinism suggests. Rather it was because they were not willing to come to God's Son in faith. Again, consider the following verses from John Chapter Six:

> *"I am the bread of life. He who comes to Me shall never hunger, and he who believes in Me shall never thirst. But I said to you* [those that were opposing Him] *that* **you have seen Me** *and yet* **do not believe.** *" (vv. 35–36, emphasis added)*

> *"Everyone who* **sees the Son** *and* **believes in Him** *may have everlasting life; and I will raise him up at the last day." (v. 40, emphasis added)*

> *"No one can* **come to Me** *unless* **the Father who sent Me draws him**; *and I will raise him up at the last day." (v. 44, emphasis added)*

> *"Everyone who has* **heard** *and* **learned** *from the Father comes to Me." (v. 45, emphasis added)*

> *"He who* **believes in Me** *has* **everlasting life.** *" (v. 47, emphasis added)*

> *"I am the living bread which came down from heaven.* **If anyone eats of this bread, he will live forever.** *" (v. 51, emphasis added)*

> *"Most assuredly, I say to you,* **unless** *you eat the flesh of the Son of Man and drink His blood,* **you have no life** *in you." (v. 53, emphasis added)*

> *"***Whoever*** eats My flesh and drinks My blood* **has eternal life**, *and* **I will raise him up at the last day.** *" (v. 54, emphasis added)*

In an article titled, "The Place of Effectual Calling and Grace in a Calvinist Soteriology," Bruce A. Ware rightly reasons:

> If a Calvinist soteriology is to commend itself as coherent, viable, and sound, establishing the [Effectual Calling and Grace] ECG doctrine is essential. As the necessary complement and entailment of the doctrine of unconditional election, the case for the ECG doctrine must succeed. Furthermore, if a Calvinist's soteriology is to commend itself to those committed fully and unreservedly to bibli-

cal authority, the ECG doctrine must be shown to be expressive of clear biblical teaching.[356]

It is my contention that Scripture does not provide Calvinism with the support it needs to make a solid case for irresistible grace. That does not mean that many serious and devout Christians are not impressed and even persuaded by the Calvinist arguments for the so-called ECG doctrine. Obviously, many are impressed with the Calvinist case for this doctrine. Under close scrutiny, however, the ECG doctrine does not commend itself except to those who have a bias for Calvinism in the first place. Ware offers what he calls *biblical support for the ECG doctrine.* He does so by an appeal to what he refers to as three central passages that he believes teach the ECG doctrine. According to Ware, these:

> ... three central passages ... form a strong cumulative case for this Calvinist doctrine.[357]

Due to the similarity between what Ware says about John Chapter Six and what Sproul says, I will only consider two of his *three central passages* at this time.

FIRST CORINTHIANS 1:18–31

The second portion of Scripture that Ware is convinced contributes to forming "a strong cumulative case for this [ECG] Calvinist doctrine" is 1 Corinthians 1:18–31. In particular, Ware says that:

> First Corinthians 1:24 presents to us a powerful and God-honoring instance of God's calling that is at once effectual, irresistible, and selective. It reads: "but to those whom God called, both Jews and Greeks, Christ the power of God and the wisdom of God."[358]

In this connection, Ware then asks:

> How does this text support the ECG doctrine?[359]

He then goes on to correctly point out:

> The gospel or "message of the cross" (1:18), which [Paul] pur-posely refused to preach in clever, human wisdom (1:17), is, at one and the same time, God's power and wisdom for those being saved (1:18, 21, 24; cf. Rom. 1:16), while it is weakness and foolishness

to those perishing (1:18, 23, 25). It is the same gospel in both cases, but some regard it as wise, powerful, and life-giving while others see it as mere folly.[360]

Ware then says:

> The burning question, for our purposes, is why some consider it God's power and wisdom while others reject it as weakness and foolishness. That both responses to the same gospel occur is not disputed.[361]

While Ware spends a great deal of time and effort trying to demonstrate that this text teaches the ECG doctrine of Calvinism, a much better answer to his "burning question" is to be found in Romans 1:16. Ware believes that Romans 1:16 is relevant and he even references this verse for the reader. With the question he asks in mind, let us now read and consider this verse. The apostle Paul simply and clearly says:

> *I am not ashamed of the gospel of Christ, for **it is the power of God to salvation for everyone who believes**, for the Jew and also for the Greek. (emphasis added)*

The answer to Ware's question, according to the apostle Paul, is *faith*, specifically *faith in Christ*. Ware misses the point of 1 Corinthians 1:18–31 by looking for evidence of the ECG doctrine. As Ware agrees, in verse eighteen, Paul refers to two categories of people—those he says are "perishing" and those he says are "being saved." The first group believes "the message of the cross is foolishness." The same "message of the cross … is the power of God" to the second group. The whole premise of Ware's question is that the second category is a pre-elected people. It wrongly assumes that Paul is talking about why some lost people respond to a gospel presentation positively while others respond negatively. This text, however, is not dealing with *a response to* the gospel by the unsaved/elect, but *a view of* the gospel by the saved/elect.

We know that faith is the proper and positive response to the gospel and that it is required for salvation. We also know that those who respond in faith to the gospel personally discover it to be "the power of God" unto salvation. The calling of verse twenty-four is past tense. The question is this: whom has God called? Hypo-Calvinists will say that God has called everyone outwardly with a gospel proclamation/invitation and some with an additional inward, irresistible, and secret call which includes or leads to the regenerating of the lost. Because they are regenerated, they are enabled to believe and not able to "not believe" according to Reformed Theology.

Something must be made very clear to avoid confusion. The only similarity in the mind of a Calvinist between an *inward* and an *outward* call is the way the word "call" is spelled and pronounced. The difference is not, as some have suggested, an inward invitation for the elect only and an outward invitation for the elect and reprobate. For the elect, the outward invitation cannot be responded to until the inward call occurs. By definition, once the inward call occurs the outward call cannot be resisted. According to the hypo-Calvinist, for the reprobate, the invitation is somehow supposed to be a valid offer of salvation on the condition of faith, which the reprobate cannot have because he:

- Will not receive an inward call,

- Is not elect and is reprobate, and

- Christ did not die for him, etc.

For the elect, the inward call is not really an invitation to respond to, though it is or leads to a transformation of unbelievers into believers. Because the elect are unable to respond positively to the gospel in their unregenerate state, just as the reprobate are unable to respond positively, they must undergo a complete transformation, which is the result of regeneration, or even regeneration itself, according to Calvinism. I agree with Ware that there is an invitation-type call, which consists of a gospel presentation. I do not believe, however, that the calling to which Paul refers to in 1 Corinthians 1:24 is an efficacious/irresistible transformation. It should not be included in or confused with regeneration, which brings with it faith in Jesus Christ. In fact, I think such a notion is simply a theological invention of Calvinism as is unconditional election, the doctrine that necessitates it.

So what *call* is Paul referring to in this text/context? If it is *not* an irresistible call *to become a believer,* what then is it? It is *a believer's call.* That is, while God invites unbelievers to become believers through a gospel proclamation, He also calls believers to a variety of things once they come to Christ in faith. Whatever the specifics as to what we as believers are called to, this kind of calling follows faith in Christ. That is, it is a call to *believers* and not a call *to believe.* It does not lead to faith, irresistibly or otherwise.

While there is no gap between the time a person becomes a believer and the time when he is called to whatever a believer is called to, logically faith must come first. That is, God does not make a believer out of those He has called as a part of the calling process. Rather God calls, in this sense, *all those*, and *only those* who believe, *when* they believe. No one can be included among the called who does not believe in Jesus Christ. Everyone who believes is included among the called. Show me a believer and I will show someone who has this call of God on his life. Show me an unbeliever, and I will show you someone not called—at least not yet.

While this call, like election, is limited to believers, those perishing are excluded from this call, not because they are non-savable, but because they refuse to believe and thereby close the door of salvation on themselves. In this sense, God calls the saved, not the unsaved.

Keep in mind that Calvinists believe in an outward general call that can only be responded to by those who receive a corresponding inward call. This Calvinist inward call cannot be resisted. For the reprobate, the outward general call cannot be responded to because there is no corresponding inward call, which is needed to turn a will that can *only reject* into a will that can *only accept*. On the other hand, the Bible teaches that the gospel really does invite all to respond in faith, because God graciously enables unbelievers to believe. When the unbeliever becomes a believer, then and only then can he accept what God graciously offers everyone on the condition of faith.

The Bible clearly teaches that those who respond with faith in Christ, and only those who respond in faith to Christ are then called *as* believers. In this sense, we are not called to believe, but called because we believe or as believers. Sometimes the word "calling" refers to the service we are called to, such as service to God in holiness, and sometimes it refers to a calling to glory and all that implies, which we will consider shortly. The reason the apostle Peter speaks of calling and election the way he does is because all believers and only believers are *called to* what they are *elected for.* Notice that Peter says:

> *Therefore, brethren, ... make your call and election sure. (2 Pet. 1:10)*

I think it safe to say that the designation *brethren* is used here to refer to believers only. As such, the called and elect are equated with believers. There is nothing here about unbelievers being called or elect. First

Corinthians 1:26–29 puts all this in perspective. In verse twenty-six, Paul is referring to *what* we were called to, not *when* we were called. The rest of what he says in verses twenty-seven to twenty-nine bears this out. It is a call to believers—for the saved. The context suggests that it is a Christian's call to service. As Christians, we should never think that God has chosen us for service because we were or are anything special. On the contrary, by human standards, most of us would be the last ones to be chosen to serve the Lord.

Verses thirty and thirty-one remind believers who are called to the service of God that salvation itself is based on what He did and does for us and not on what we did or will do for Him. It is truly because of God that we are *in Christ Jesus* and that He is *our righteousness*, holiness, and wisdom. Truly we have no reason to boast as servants or saints. It is because of God's grace that we are both. God's saving grace is through faith. Pre-salvation grace makes saving faith possible, while saving faith itself is a prerequisite to what has been referred to as saving grace. Those called in this sense are already believers and thus already saved. Remember that faith precedes justification or righteousness, which is one of the things Christ has become to "the called" ones.

In referring to Romans 8:28–30, Ware says:

> We now come to the last, and perhaps the most straightforward, expression of God's effectual call we will examine in this chapter. The statement of greatest importance for our present concern is found in 8:30: "Those He predestined, He also called; those He called, He also justified; those He justified He also glorified."[362]

The way Ware interprets this verse is made plain by the way he paraphrases it. He says:

> We might paraphrase it in this way, "All of those whom God has predestined to become conformed to the likeness of Christ" (from 8:29), to all of these so predestined, He extends His call. And just as all the predestined are called, so too all those whom He calls heed the call to believe and are so justified. And just as all the predestined are called and all the called are justified, so too all of the justified are also glorified.[363]

Now I like a good paraphrase. Is this, however, a good paraphrase?

Notice how Ware moves from the past tense to the present tense, when it is convenient for his interpretation, while Paul only uses the past tense. We need to ask ourselves several questions. Did Paul have a purpose for using the past tense consistently? Does changing the tense change the meaning of what Paul is saying? Why does Ware conclude that this call to which Paul refers is a call to believe? Why does Ware *insert* the statement "those ... whom He calls heed the call to believe and are so justified"? I think the reason Paul stays with the past tense, concerning those predestined, called, justified, and glorified, involves the divine perspective and eternal vantage point. That is, if any of these things are true, all of these things are true, insofar as what or who God foreknows is concerned.

If God foreknows an individual from all eternity, then from the eternal perspective that person is predestined to whatever God foreknows. This is so, whether we use the Arminian or Calvinist definition of *foreknown*. From all eternity, the individuals God knows can also be referred to as *called, justified, and glorified*. Experientially we know they may not yet be called or justified, and definitely are not yet glorified. Yet, since God is speaking about the individuals He knows and not just knows about, the things that are inevitably true of those He knows can be referred to in the past tense. I agree that the things that are predestined to happen are inevitable. They are inevitable, however, in relation to each other. If something is predestined to happen, it must happen. It cannot turn out otherwise or it would not, by definition, be predestined, or the one who determined that destiny could not be in control of how things turn out and is only telling us what he would like to see happen. If you believe, as I do, that what God destines to happen actually does happen and cannot fail to happen, then what God predestines for those He foreknows must inevitably come to pass.

Paul tells us what is destined to be true for those whom God foreknows. Inevitably they will be called, justified, and glorified. Moreover they will be called according to His purpose. What is His purpose for those He foreknows? It is that ultimately and inevitably they will be glorified. Justification represents the predestined work of God in time while glorification represents the predestined work of God in eternity. From a temporal perspective justification must come first. From an eternal perspective if a person is *justified* in time, that person is also *predestined to be glorified* when time meets eternity for the believer. Spurgeon is right when he says:

Our conformity to Christ is the sacred object of predestination.[364]

While the ultimate calling (or purpose for which one is called) is to glorification, it is and must be a calling of the justified. The glorification to which the believer is destined (or if you prefer *called to*) is the resurrection of the just. The justified are believers since justification always and only follows faith in Christ. Nowhere is faith to be found in this discussion. Why doesn't Paul tell us that those same ones God foreknows are the ones pre-destined to believe? For me, the reason is simple. God only foreknows, in a relational sense, believers. You can only know God through faith in Christ. Those who know God are therefore believers. Those who do not know God are not believers. In the sense in which Paul uses the term, God only fore-knows those who know Him through faith in Christ.

If you are not aware of the Calvinist definition and understanding of *foreknow*, the distinctions I am making can be a little confusing. It becomes a little easier to understand if you look at the word in its two parts. In the Arminian sense the emphasis is on *what* is known. In the Calvinist sense the emphasis is on *who* is known. In the Arminian sense, I could say that I know tomorrow everything will be OK. In the Calvinist sense I could say tomor-row I will meet with someone I know. The former is cognitive and the latter is relational.

That God knows every hair on my head is simply a matter of fact. To say God knows me in a personal sense is to say more than He simply knows who I am. To say God foreknows (in this context) someone in the Arminian sense is to say that God knows about someone who does not as of yet exist. To say God foreknows someone (in this context) in the Calvinist sense is to say that God actually or intimately knows that someone or views that someone in relationship to Him even before he exists. Again, for our present purpose, I am assuming the Calvinist foreknowledge is contextually correct.

If no one is justified apart from faith in Christ, and the glorification to which we are ultimately called is the resurrection of the just, then faith is assumed for the justified. The related glorification is, therefore, a believer's resurrection. Thus, those called according to His purpose must also be in faith or must be believers at the time of this calling. That is, God calls those to glory who believe in Jesus Christ. Changing the tense and making this call a call *to believe* rather than a call *of the believer* changes the meaning of the message and is the reason Ware misses the actual meaning of the passage.

If Calvinists are right about the kind of knowing Paul refers to, it follows that God knew the predestined, called them, justified them, and glorified them *as believers* and not as unbelievers. Surely, Calvinists do not suggest that those God knew as justified He knew as unbelievers. Ware's paraphrase, however, would lead to that conclusion. In a different chapter in the same book in which Ware makes these comments, Packer first quotes some of what Paul said in Romans 8:30 and then makes a very pertinent comment. Pay very close attention:

> Those he called, he also justified (Rom. 8:30, NIV)—and *no one is justified who has not come to faith.*[365]

Packer rightly points out that justification always assumes faith. Why? Because faith always leads to justification and justification is always dependent upon faith. If we say someone is justified, we can also say that person has already come to faith. It matters not when, whether from an eternal or temporal perspective; we must assume the one justified or the one viewed as justified is a believer or viewed as a believer. With all of the arguments put forward by Calvinists about what it really means to be *foreknown* by God in this text, the Calvinist should be the first to recognize that all that is said of those predestined assumes that they are believers or are *viewed as* believers.

To make this verse work for or conform to the Calvinist ECG doctrine, Ware has to mix things up a bit. He needs to make the call a pre-faith event (i.e., those whom He calls heed the call to believe and are thereby justified). Why? So that it will be simultaneous to a gospel proclamation in order for him to discern an irresistible or effectual call in this text. Now, if *to be called,* like predestined, foreknown, justified, and glorified, is true only of believers, then this is not and cannot be a call to believe of any kind, resistible or otherwise. I totally agree with Ware when he says:

> One category of people is described in 8:29–30. Those foreknown are the same individuals as those predestined, those predestined are the same as those called, those called the same as those justified, and those justified the same as those glorified. That is, all the individuals spoken of in 8:29–30 are foreknown, predestined, called, justified, and glorified.[366]

Ware gets off track, however, as he goes on to say:

So then, if in Romans 8:30 all those called are justified and glorified, but if many who hear God's general gospel call to believe instead resist and so are neither justified nor glorified, it follows that the "call" of 8:30 is the effectual call (which effects the justification of all those so called) and not the general call (which does not affect the justification of those so called because it can be—and is—resisted).[367]

Ware wants to have it both ways. He wants to see the call as something related to time, logically and chronologically simultaneous to a gospel presentation corresponding to an internal call to believe, followed by a transformation or regeneration, faith, justification, and then finally glorification. He also insists that the key is to be found in what it means to be foreknown. The list of things true of certain people, specifically people that are foreknown and predestined, is too incomplete as it is found here in Romans Chapter Eight for Ware to use in defense of the Calvinist ECG doctrine. So Ware has to fill in the blanks. Thus, he selectively fills in the blanks in a way that would seem to support the ECG doctrine. If we are going to take this list of things that are true of certain people, lay them out as he does, and then insert things alongside, in front of, and behind some of them, then why not insert the rest of what can be placed in between these spiritual realities? Ware cannot do this, because to do so would destroy the whole eternal perspective of this text. Actually, Ware does this anyway as is evident in the previous quote.

If the justified, foreknown, predestined, and glorified *are believers,* why can't they be the *called?* I think they are. Now if Ware is right, and I believe he is, that *the called* are *called to* the very same thing they are *predestined to,* then it may be an irresistible call, in this instance, *for the believer.* That is, if what a believer is called to is conformity to the likeness of Christ or glorification, as I believe, then the believer can no more avoid glorification in the future than he could justification (after believing, of course) in the past. What is irresistible to the believer, because he believes, is not possible for the unbeliever because he does not believe. Faith automatically leads to justification. Justification automatically leads to glorification. Unbelief takes you in another direction.

If Ware's understanding of *foreknew* is the correct sense in this context, it must also be understood that this text also limits God's foreknowledge (not prescience but pre-relationship) to believers alone. Unbelievers will hear *"I*

never knew you." In like manner, God only predestines believers to be conformed to the image of His Son. In this text and context, Paul is telling us
about what God has ultimately predestined us to. What God has predestined
us to is the same thing that He has called us to, which is conformity to Christ
or glorification. If believers and only believers will enjoy conformity to the
likeness of Christ or glorification, then again this is a believer's calling, as it
is a believer's *pre*destination.

It is certainly possible, and I would say even certain, that there is more
than one kind of *believer's call.* There is a call on the believer's life to sanctification and service, as well as to glorification. In this text, it seems almost
too obvious that Paul had in mind a call to glorification. One of the recurring
problems with Calvinism is the false either/or category it offers. Sproul is
right when he says:

> The New Testament speaks of divine calling in more than one
> way.[370]

Sproul then explains:

> We find God's external call in the preaching of the gospel. When
> the gospel is preached, everyone who hears it is summoned to
> Christ. But not everyone responds positively. Not everyone ...
> becomes a believer. Sometimes the gospel falls upon deaf ears.
> Now we know that only those who respond to the outward call of
> the gospel in faith are justified. Justification is by faith. But again,
> not everyone whose ears hear the outward preaching of the gospel
> responds in faith. Therefore we must conclude that not all who are
> called outwardly are justified.[371]

To this point Sproul is right on target. He then says:

> But Paul says in Romans that those whom God calls, he
> justifies.[372]

What Sproul wants you to do is agree that this call to which Paul refers
is that second kind of call, the one that is irresistible and directed at the elect
unbeliever. What if, however, this is a different kind of call? What if this is
a call that is issued and has application only for the believer (i.e., the just)
and not for the unbeliever? Sproul and all Calvinists see in Romans 8 some
of the links of the Calvinist "golden" chain. They see each of the spiritual

realities, such as justification and glorification, as links in the chain. Instead of starting with unconditional election in this context, they begin with fore-knowledge. Therefore the links of the chain are:

- Foreknowledge of the *relational* kind versus foreknowledge of the *see into the future* kind,

- Predestination *to salvation* versus predestination *to damnation,*

- Calling of the *inward irresistible* kind versus the calling of the *outward resistible* kind,

- Justification that follows faith that comes with the regeneration *produced by* the call, and

- Glorification, which is *the destiny* of all the foreknown, predestined, called, and justified.

Let us assume the Calvinist is right when he argues that the foreknowledge that Paul refers to here is of the relational kind. That is, Paul is talking about people whom God *actually* knows and not just people *about whom* He knows. There is nothing in connection with these people that suggests they are predestined to salvation versus damnation *as unbelievers,* as Calvinism insists. The context leads to the conclusion that believers, not unbelievers, are predestined to be conformed to the likeness or image of Jesus Christ. I take that to mean glorification. But even if it is a reference to sanctification (an inward conformity to Christ in the life of the believer during their earthly sojourn), it is still a *believer's* destiny. Sproul perfectly represents what I believe to be the best interpretation of this text when he says:

> Predestination is expressed here in terms of being for the purpose of being conformed to the image of Christ. This is what is accomplished ultimately in our glorification. Glorification is the consummation of our sanctification, the final purification from all sin.[373]

Once again, based on the context of this passage, it is my conviction that the calling to which Paul refers is neither a call to believe (for reasons already discussed), nor an irresistible call resulting in regeneration and saving faith. Rather, it is the call of God to that which the believer has been predestined. That is, it is a call to outward conformity to Christ or glorification. It is not a call that can be left unheeded. God and God alone transforms the believer into a glorified and resurrected saint. That is our destiny as believers. The

Calvinist might object and say that Paul would in effect be repeating himself if this were the case. My response is that this is exactly what he is doing. The fact is that Paul repeats himself frequently. He says essentially the same thing in a number of different ways. It is repetition for emphasis. Consider the following:

Verse 17, *"glorified"*

Verse 18, *"the glory which shall be revealed in us"*

Verse 19, *"the manifestations of the sons of God"* (KJV)

Verse 21, *"into the glorious liberty of the children of God"*

Verse 23, *"the adoption, to wit, the redemption of our body"* (KJV)

Paul refers to the same wonderful event in the future of every believer in five different ways in just five different verses. Paul seems to be saying that all is well that ends well *for the believer.* No matter what a believer has to go through *here and now,* he needs to keep in mind what is awaiting him *there and then.* No matter what the uncertainties of this life, glorification is a certainty for the believer in the next life. The purpose of the call in this context seems to be the aim of the call, which is the destiny of the believer. The destiny of the believer is a glorious resurrection involving a complete transformation.

Glorification and justification are simply two ends of the same *applied* salvation and that is why we call glorification a *resurrection of the just.* It is evident that Paul sees justification and glorification as two ends of the same greater event, namely the complete salvation of the believer. If you are justified, you will be glorified. If you will not be glorified, you are not and never will be justified. You can't have one without the other and if you have one you ultimately must have the other. Either both belong to you or neither belongs to you. The point, however, is that everything is going to be all right in the end for the believer who is identified as the one who loves the Lord. In fact, the end is just a new and infinitely better beginning for the believer.

The real and meaningful difference between the saved and the lost is the difference between accepting Christ through faith in Him and rejecting Christ evidenced as unbelief in Him. The difference between those merely convicted by the Holy Spirit, and those who yield to the Spirit when they are drawn, is the difference between being *willing* when enabled and being *unwilling* when enabled. Jesus berates His antagonists and holds them accountable because they were "not willing" to come to Him. Had they been *unable* to do so, this would make no sense. Although Hoeksema is considered by many to be a hyper-Calvinist, he nevertheless speaks for all consistent Calvinists when he says:

> ... It is alleged [that] faith is the hand by which we take hold of the proffered salvation, the salvation proffered in the gospel ... this is not true ... the natural man has no hand whereby he is able to accept the salvation of God in Christ Jesus.[374]

According to Calvinism, the natural man cannot have faith through which he might be saved. This, however, is like saying to a man without a hand, *please, reach out with your hand and take this gift.* If you or I were to do this, knowing the man had no hand, we would be considered very cruel indeed. We would be mocking the handless man. Isn't this just what the Calvinist is saying about God's attitude toward the reprobate? That is, according to Calvinism, God is offering the reprobate salvation on the *condition of faith* knowing full well that the reprobate does not have and cannot have faith.

Moreover, the reprobate cannot have faith because God has chosen to withhold faith *from him* because He has no saving interest *in him.* Thus Calvinism not only says that God's saving grace cannot ultimately be resisted, but that the reprobate cannot positively respond to whatever sort of offer is directed at them. Paul, however, tells us that certain people perish because they *refuse* to love the truth (2 Thess. 2:10). If we are to take Calvinism seriously, we can only conclude that this is an *involuntary* or *forced refusal.* Can there be such a thing? Is it truly a *refusal* if you can't help but refuse?

For the sake of discussion, let us suppose for now that if God draws us to Himself it means He forces, coerces, or drags us to Himself irresistibly, as Calvinists say or suggest. Does this not mean then that God forced us to willingly trust Him? For the Calvinist says that regeneration actually results in a willingness to believe and a change that makes it impossible not to believe, in effect making us believe or making us believers. If you have to be forced to do something, or otherwise have no say in doing it, you are by definition not willing to do it. If you are willing, you need not be forced.

Remember what Scripture says:

"If I am lifted up from the earth, [I] will draw all peoples to Myself." (John 12:32)

Today, if you will hear His voice, do not harden your hearts. (Heb. 4:6)

"If I do not do the works of My Father, do not believe Me; but if I do, though you do not believe Me, believe the works, that you may know and believe that the Father is in Me, and I in Him." (John 10:37–38)

[God] *commands all men everywhere to repent. (Acts 17:30)*

There is no distinction between Jew and Greek, for the same Lord over all is rich to all who call upon Him. For "whoever calls on the name of the LORD shall be saved." How then shall they call on Him in whom they have not believed? And how shall they believe in Him of whom they have not heard? And how shall they hear without a preacher? And how shall they preach unless they are sent? As it is written: "How beautiful are the feet of those who preach the gospel of peace, who bring glad tidings of good things!" (Rom. 10:12–15)

"O Jerusalem, Jerusalem, ... How often I wanted to gather your children together, as a hen gathers her chicks under her wings, but you were not willing!" (Matt. 23:37)

To blame the *unwillingness* of a rebellious man to come to God on his *inability* to come to God, imposed upon man by God, is nothing less than the character assassination of God. It is (at least by implication) to *excuse* sinful man and *accuse* our Holy God!

8

TOTAL DEPRAVITY

EXPLAINED

A CCORDING to Reformed Theology, irresistible grace always leads to re-generation. If God does not irresistibly call you to regeneration in particular and salvation in general, you are inevitably and irreversibly headed for damnation. If such is the case, regeneration is simply not in the divine cards that God has dealt you. As we read in the previous chapter Sproul correctly says:

> Most Christians agree that God's work of regeneration is a work
> of grace. The issue that divides us is whether or not this grace is
> irresistible ...[375]

While this is not the only issue that divides Calvinists from non-Calvinist Evangelicals, it is certainly one of the more important differences. White says:

> ... that "irresistible grace" is a reference to God's regeneration of
> His elect: any other use of the phrase is in error.[376]

More typical of Calvinists, and with John 1:13 in mind, Van Baren says:

> It is by the irresistible grace of God that one is born again.[377]

Regeneration is also usually considered in connection with the Calvinist doctrine of total depravity, or the first point of Calvinism. Millard J. Erickson explains:

> Calvinists ... have insisted if all persons are truly sinners, totally
> depraved and incapable of responding to God's grace, no one can
> be converted unless first regenerated ...[378]

Calvinists argue that man is not free to accept the salvation offered in the gospel, except as an inevitable and irresistible consequence of being chosen by God in the first place. In Calvinism, this non-freedom of man to accept the eternal life offered in a gospel proclamation is normally, if not primarily, understood in relation to the fall of man and its consequences. This is the primary implication of a Calvinist view of total depravity.

What the Calvinist means by this term, as with other distinctives of Calvinism, is often misunderstood by outsiders. For example, in the article "Resurgent Calvinism Renews Debate Over Chance for Heaven," the author incorrectly equates the Calvinist doctrine of total depravity with the biblical truth that … *all have sinned.* As long as Christians *erroneously* assume that the Calvinist distinctive of total depravity is simply that *all have sinned,* they will continue to think erroneously that they believe in or agree with the first point of Calvinism.

All Evangelical Christians agree with the scriptural affirmation that *all have sinned.* Relatively few agree with what the Calvinist doctrine of total depravity actually means. *Christianity Today,* in the article "Calvinism Resurging Among the SBC's [Southern Baptist Convention's] Young Elites," gets it right when representing the Reformed view on total depravity. The author of this article accurately represents the Calvinist view when he says that total depravity means:

> People are spiritually dead and therefore unable to respond to God's offer of salvation unless He first regenerates them.[379]

The main thrust of the first point of Calvinism involves the relationship of faith to regeneration. In Calvinism, regeneration is the immediate *cause* of faith, or said another way, faith is the immediate *effect* of regeneration. As stated earlier, according to Calvinism, God, through regeneration, *makes you believe* and thus *makes you a believer.* Though some Calvinists do not like the sound of this, Palmer concedes that the position of Calvinism is that God:

> … makes me, who did not really want Jesus, want to love Him and believe in Him.[380]

You do not and cannot *believe to be born again,* according to Reformed Theology. You must be *born again to believe.* You will believe when and because you are born again. In Calvinism, regeneration always comes *be-*

fore faith and faith always *follows* regeneration. You cannot have the latter without the former and you cannot have the former without the latter. And as already noted, the key to understanding this point is found in the relationship and logical order of faith to regeneration. Piper represents all Calvinists when he says:

> We believe that the new birth is a miraculous creation of God that enables a formerly "dead" person to receive Christ and so be saved. We do not think that faith precedes ... the new birth. Faith is the evidence that God has begotten us anew. ... God begets us anew and the first glimmer of life in the newborn child is faith. This new birth is the effect of irresistible grace, because it is an act of sovereign creation.[381]

MacArthur reasons that:

> ... Regeneration *logically* must initiate faith.[382]

He also says:

> The unregenerate do not accept the things of the Spirit of God; spiritual things are foolishness to them. They cannot even begin to understand them, much less believe (1 Cor. 2:14). Only God can open the heart and initiate faith (cf. Acts 13:48; 16:14; 18:27).[383]

Not only so, says MacArthur, but:

> ... Genuine faith ... is granted by God ... faith is a supernatural gift of God ... it seems that what Paul had in mind [in Ephesians 2:8–9] was the entire process of grace, faith, and salvation as the gift of God ... faith is not something that is conjured up by the human will but is a sovereignly granted gift of God. (cf. Philippians 1:29) ... The faith that God begets includes both the volition and the ability to comply with His will (cf. Philippians 2:13).[384]

While I am certain that MacArthur will not concede the following and will even attempt to deny this, in effect he is saying:

- Man is not really responsible for faith or unbelief.

And:

- God is really the one who actually believes in His Son.

Sproul says:

> Regeneration is not the fruit or result of faith. Rather, regeneration precedes faith as the necessary condition for faith. We also do not in any way dispose ourselves toward regeneration or cooperate as co-workers with the Holy Spirit to bring it to pass. We do not decide or choose to be regenerated. To be sure, after we have been regenerated by the sovereign grace of God, we do choose, act, co-operate, and believe in Christ.[385]

In Calvinism, faith is not really a condition for salvation. Rather, regeneration is a pre-condition for faith, which in turn is a consequence of irresistible grace, which is a consequence of unconditional election, and so on. R. Allan Killen says:

> Reformed theologians ... place regeneration before faith, pointing out that the Holy Spirit must bring new life before the sinner can by God's enabling exercise faith and accept Jesus Christ.[386]

Sproul says that:

> A cardinal point of Reformed theology is the maxim: "Regeneration precedes faith."[387]

FROM DEATH TO LIFE WITHOUT FAITH IN CHRIST

The point is this—you go from death to life without placing faith in Christ. Faith in Christ, from a Calvinist perspective, comes with that life but is neither needed nor possible before that life begins. Sproul speaks for all five points of Calvinism when he says:

> In regeneration, God changes our hearts. He gives us a new disposition, a new inclination. He plants a desire for Christ in our hearts. We can never trust Christ for our salvation unless we first desire Him. This is why we said earlier that *regeneration precedes faith*.[388]

Sproul also says:

> The Reformed view of predestination teaches that before a person can choose Christ his heart must be changed. He must be born

again ... one does not first believe, then become reborn ...[389]

Spencer explains:

> ... The living human spirit which is "born of God" finds the living God wholly irresistible, just as a dead human spirit finds the god (Satan) of the dead irresistible. ... It is the gift of the New Nature, which makes us find Jesus Christ absolutely "irresistible." A hog, because of its very nature, loves to wallow in the muck and mire, while a lamb, because of its nature, disdains mud wallowing. "Dead in trespasses and sins," the unregenerate wallow in sin and unbelief because it is their nature to do so. Yet, when God gives His elect, who are the direct objects of His love, a "new nature," the old things pass away and all things become new! The new nature, which is a living human spirit, a new creation in Christ, finds God as irresistible as his formerly "dead" human spirit once found the devil "irresistible."[390]

Irresistible regeneration is simply a logical extension of unconditional election (second point of Calvinism) and irresistible grace (fourth point of Calvinism). As with unconditional election and irresistible grace, irresistible regeneration also has a flip side, or what I have been calling the dark side. That is, just as the elect will be born again and have no say in the matter, so the non-elect or the reprobate will not be born again and have no say in the matter. When, therefore, the Evangelist says to the reprobate lost person *you must be born again* if you are to *see* or *enter* the kingdom, he is only telling him what would irresistibly happen to him if he were one of the elect.

Most Calvinists believe that those who *can't* be born again, nevertheless, *should* be born again. In other words, hypo-Calvinists believe the reprobate ought to do what *they can't do.* They seem to think the rest of us are "stupid" for suggesting that *ought* implies *can.* Surprisingly, most Calvinists do not seem to see any problem with the view that says a person cannot do what they ought to do. Some will reason that it is because those in the reprobate caste are depraved and their depravity is their own fault. Those who argue this way do not seem to concern themselves with the fact that Calvinism teaches that the fall of man, which resulted in the depravity of man, as well as the eternal caste system they were born into, was not only *allowed* by God but also *caused* by God through His decree.

Calvinistically speaking, to appeal to the reprobate to be born again is like pouring water on a duck's back. Those who do not become born again, after we proclaim *you must be born again,* are no more responsible for not being born again than the duck is for what happens to the water that rolls so quickly off its back. Conversely, when we tell a member of the elect (but still lost) community that they must be born again, we are only telling him what will happen eventually and unavoidably. This cannot, from a Calvinist point of view, be considered a meaningful appeal to him to be born again. Rather, it is a simple statement of fact of what will eventually and inevitably happen to him.

Moreover, if the one being appealed to is *not* among the elect lost, he *does not have, cannot have,* and *is not supposed to have* the capacity to believe in Christ. Left alone, I would agree that lost and sinful man is not naturally reaching out to God. I would even agree that without God's gracious help (i.e., the Father must draw, the Spirit must convict, etc.), the unregenerate would not come to Christ in faith. However, in light of so much in Scripture that says otherwise, how can the Calvinist say that the unregenerate cannot believe the gospel unless he first becomes regenerate? Packer speaks for all Calvinists when he says:

> Without [regeneration] there is no faith in the redeemer, and there-
> fore no benefit from His death ... we are impotent to turn to Christ
> in repentance and faith; part of the effect of regeneration, however,
> is that faith dawns in our hearts.[391]

Notice the following bracketed commentary by Packer when he quotes Ephesians 2:8:

> For by grace you have been saved, through faith—this not from
> yourselves, it [either faith as such or salvation and faith together]
> is the gift of God.[392]

To Packer, and virtually all Calvinists, the word "it" (touto) in this verse must refer to either faith alone, or faith and salvation, or faith in salvation, etc. According to Reformed Theology, Paul cannot possibly be saying that faith is a means to receive and not an integral part of that which is received as well. If it did, it would mean that faith is *prior to* and a *condition for* receiving the gift of salvation. To Packer and all Calvinists, faith and repentance is a gift that comes with regeneration. No unregenerate person can believe or repent. So a call to faith and repentance cannot possibly be responded to, unless and until a person is regenerated. It is very difficult to be consistent with the implications of such a view for most mainstream Calvinists. Calvin sometimes seemed to disagree with Calvinism relative to what the "it" or "this" (touto) refers to in Ephesians 2:8–9. That is, at times Calvin clearly indicated that he believed the "it" or "gift of God" in Ephesians 2:8 refers to a salvation received *through* faith. That is, Calvin did not always seem to teach that "it" referred to faith or the faith-salvation combination that Packer and most Calvinists suggest. We will consider this further a little later.

While I am convinced that a reading of good English translations of the Greek New Testament are sufficient to provide the basis for a sound interpretation, sometimes the impression is given that if you were a New Testament Greek scholar, you would see and concede that faith is a gift in the Calvinist sense. Only someone ignorant of New Testament Greek, it is intimated, could fail to see what Calvinists see here. Such is not the case. Perhaps no passage of Scripture is more heavily relied upon by Calvinists to teach their peculiar doctrine that *faith is a gift of God* versus *a responsibility of man* than Ephesians 2:8–9. Paul reasons:

> By grace you have been saved **through faith**, and that not of your-selves; it [or "this"] is the gift of God, not of works, lest anyone should boast (emphasis added).

The New Testament Greek scholar Harold W. Hoehner, in reference to these verses, explains:

> Much debate has centered around the demonstrative pronoun "this" (*touto*). Though some think it refers back to "grace" and others to "faith," neither of these suggestions is really valid be-cause the demonstrative pronoun is neuter whereas "grace" and "faith" are feminine. Also, to refer back to either of these words specifically seems to be redundant. Rather the neuter *touto*, as is common, refers to the preceding phrase or clause. (In Eph 1:15 and 3:1 *touto*, "this," refers back to the preceding section.) Thus it re-fers back to the *concept* of salvation (2:4–8a), whose basis is grace and means is faith. This salvation does not have its source in man (it is "not from yourselves"), but rather, its source is God's grace for "it is the gift of God."[393]

The obvious point of this passage is that salvation is *by grace* versus a salvation *of works*. It is, however, *through faith*. To make faith a *part* of the gift of salvation, as opposed to the *means* through which we are to receive that gift, is to read into the text that which is not there. It is also to take away from the lost sinner the only means by which he can be saved. To suggest, as many Calvinists do, that faith, which is not a gift, is somehow a work, is to defy both Scripture and logic. The apostle Paul contrasts the *works-debt* way with the *faith-grace* way. Just as work is required to indebt an employer to an employee and thereby entitle the employee to payment of wages, so faith is required of the undeserving recipient of the salvation gift. That is, as work leads to earned wages, so faith leads to an undeserved salvation. A salvation, which is given and not earned, is a salvation by grace. Just as there is no debt without works, there can be no reception of the gift of salvation or salvation by grace without faith.

The notions that *faith is a gift* and *regeneration is before faith* and *produces faith* are logically necessitated by the Calvinist doctrine and distinctive of total depravity, as it defines the fallen nature of man. Though few, if any, will admit it, the Calvinist arguments supposedly based on a reading of the Greek are, however, theologically necessitated rather than grammatically required.

TOTAL DEPRAVITY = TOTAL INABILITY

So important to Calvinists is this notion that the unregenerate are *unable* to believe the gospel or to receive Christ in their unregenerate state, that most Calvinists use the terms *total inability* and *total depravity* interchangeably. Steele and Thomas explain:

> Because of the fall, man is unable of himself to savingly believe the gospel. The sinner is dead, blind, and deaf to the things of God; his heart is deceitful and desperately corrupt. His will is not free, it is in bondage to his evil nature, therefore, he will not—indeed he cannot—choose good over evil in the spiritual realm. Consequently, it takes much more than the Spirit's assistance to bring a sinner to Christ—it takes regeneration by which the Spirit makes the sinner alive and gives him a new nature. Faith is not something man contributes to salvation, but is itself a part of God's gift of salvation—it is God's gift to the sinner, not the sinner's gift to God.[394]

The Westminster Confession of Faith states:

> Man, by his fall into a state of sin, hath wholly lost all ability of will to any spiritual good accompanying salvation.[395]

Harold Harvey explains that in Calvinism:

> Total depravity is the cause of total inability and total inability is
> the result of total depravity.[396]

Steele and Thomas add:

> As a result of Adam's transgression, men are born in sin and by
> nature are spiritually dead; therefore, if they are to become God's
> children and enter His kingdom, they must be born anew of the
> Spirit.[397]

HARD AND SOFT

Among Calvinists, there are two schools of thought with regard to total depravity. I will call them *hard* versus *soft*. The difference between hard and
soft among authentic Calvinists on this issue is one of *degree* and not *kind*.

THE SOFT VIEW

Some Calvinists, mostly of the so-called hypo or mainstream variety,
contend that *the unregenerate* is sinful in every area of his life, but not necessarily as sinful as he can be. This could be referred to as the *comprehensive*
view of depravity. In other words, depravity affects every area of the unregenerate man's nature, but not in an absolute or exhaustive sense. Steele and
Thomas state:

> When Calvinists speak of man as being totally depraved, they
> mean that man's nature is corrupt, perverse, and sinful throughout.
> The adjective "total" does not mean that each sinner is as totally
> or completely corrupt in his actions and thoughts as it is possible
> for him to be. Instead, the word "total" is used to indicate that the
> whole of man's being has been affected by sin. The corruption ex-
> tends to every part of man, his body and soul; sin has affected all
> (the totality) of man's faculties—his mind, his will, etc.[396]

Edwin Palmer says:

> Total depravity does not mean the same as absolute depravity.
> Absolute depravity means that a person expresses his depravity
> to the nth degree at all times. Not only are all his thoughts, words,
> and deeds sinful, but they are as vicious as possible. To be totally

depraved, however, does not mean that a person is as intensively evil as possible, but as extensively evil as possible.[397]

Loraine Boettner says essentially the same thing. That is:

> This doctrine of Total Inability ... does not mean that all men are equally bad, nor that any man is as bad as he could be, nor that anyone is entirely destitute of virtue. ... His corruption is extensive but not necessarily intensive.[398]

White says:

> Man is dead in sin, completely and radically impacted by the Fall, the enemy of God, incapable of saving himself. This does not mean that man is as evil as he could be. Nor does it mean the image of God in man is destroyed, or that the will is done away with. Instead, it refers to the *all pervasiveness of the effects of sin,* and the fact that man is, outside of Christ, the enemy of God.[399]

Piper states:

> There is no doubt that man could perform more evil acts toward his fellow man than he does. But if he is restrained from performing more evil acts by motives that are not owing to his glad submission to God, then even his "virtue" is evil in the sight of God.[400]

Sproul explains:

> Total depravity is the first of Calvinism's famous five points. It is somewhat unfortunate that the doctrine is called "total depravity" because this name can be misleading. It has prevailed because it fits the familiar acrostic TULIP. Total depravity makes up the T of TULIP. The term is misleading because it suggests a moral condition of *utter* depravity. *Utter depravity* means a person is as wicked as he can possibly be. Utter suggests both total and complete corruption, lacking even in civil virtue.[401]

With virtually the same issues in view, elsewhere Sproul says:

> We know that is not the case. No matter how much each of us has sinned, we are able to think of worse sins that we could have committed. Even Adolf Hitler refrained from murdering his mother.[402]

Sproul also uses the term *radical* as a synonym for *total* (in regard to the first point). For Sproul, depravity is *radical* versus *utter.* To Sproul, the best way to express the meaning of the Reformed version of total depravity is to equate it with *humanity's radical corruption.* Sproul explains:

> The term *total depravity,* as distinguished from *utter depravity,* refers to the effect of sin and corruption on the whole person. To be totally depraved is to suffer from corruption that pervades the whole person. Sin affects every aspect of our being: the body, the soul, the mind, the will, and so forth. The total or the whole person is corrupted by sin. No vestigial "island of righteousness" escapes the influence of the fall. Sin reaches into every aspect of our lives, finding no shelter of isolated virtue.[403]

THE HARD VIEW

Other Calvinists, mostly of the hyper-Calvinist community, see the soft view of total depravity as a compromise. Hanko believes that *total* means *absolute* or what Sproul calls *utter* depravity. This is also what Boettner referred to as *intensive* versus *extensive* depravity. In contrast to the *comprehensive* view of depravity, the harder view could be called the *consummate* view of depravity. Hanko says the *Synod of Dort* intended us to understand:

> That man *is* just as bad as he can be.[404]

Hanko goes on to say:

> When Calvin and the fathers of Dort insisted that depravity was total, they knew what words mean. And they knew that "total" means precisely that.[405]

Hoeksema says:

> The distinction between absolute and total depravity has in late years been applied to men in their fallen and corrupt state. They make this distinction in order to make clear how a totally depraved sinner can still do good works. Man, according to this view, is totally depraved, but not absolutely depraved. And because he is not absolutely depraved, he is able to do good before God in his natural state. Of course, with this philosophy they fail to make clear what they really want to explain.[406]

He goes on to say:

> For a totally depraved man is after all evil and corrupt in his whole nature, in all his thinking, willing, desiring, and acting; and the problem still remains, even with the distinction between total and absolute depravity, how such a totally depraved man can bring forth good fruits. Besides, if one would make the distinction between total and absolute depravity, the distinction must certainly be applied in a different way. For by total depravity is meant that man by nature in all his existence, with all his heart and mind and soul and strength, has become a servant of sin, and that he is entirely incapable of doing good and inclined to all evil.[407]

To recap, these two views of depravity can be compared and contrasted as follows:

- Consummate versus Comprehensive

- Intensive versus Extensive

- Utter versus Radical

- Absolute versus All

What I have called the harder view sees depravity as not only affecting all areas of a man's nature but also affecting it as much as it possibly could. It is exhaustive. In other words, an unregenerate man, no matter what he does or how he behaves, is as depraved, corrupt, and sinful as he could be. The level to which he has fallen is the absolute bottom. *Intensive* is a good word for this view because it speaks of the depth of depravity to which a man has fallen or sunk and remains until he is regenerated. If he is not one of the elect, he will remain this way for the rest of his life and for all eternity as well.

What I have called the softer view, which is in some respects similar to my own view, does not see the depravity, corruption, or sinfulness of unregenerate man as necessarily the maximum degree of depravity, corruption, or sinfulness possible. While no area of an unregenerate man's life is untouched or unaffected by sin, the softer view holds that most of the unregenerate population could be even more depraved, corrupt, or sinful than they are or even will be. *Extensive* is a good word for this view because it truly sees sin *everywhere* in an unregenerate man's life, but not necessarily to the degree and depth that it could be.

If you can think of the boiling point of water as analogous to the maximum degree of depravity a man is capable of, then the harder view sees man as always and totally 212 degrees Fahrenheit (at sea level). The softer view sees the entire unregenerate man and every unregenerate man as overheated, maybe even very hot, but for most unregenerate men, maximum boil is not reached, or at least not always.

Whether a Calvinist subscribes to what I have called the hard view or the soft view, all Calvinists believe that faith is a gift and only comes *with* and *in* regeneration. They also teach that if you say that faith is a responsibility for the unbeliever (i.e., that it could be exercised before regeneration), you are guilty of synergism because you have combined the divine work of saving with the human work of believing. To say this the Calvinist must define pre-regeneration faith in Christ as a work of man. Boettner says:

> Man does not possess the power of self-regeneration, and until this inward change takes place, he cannot be convinced of the truth of the Gospel by any amount of external testimony.[408]

To characterize faith in Christ as "the power of self-regeneration" reflects either a grossly distorted view of faith or a deliberate attempt to misrepresent those who hold that faith in Christ is required for salvation. It is not *faith in Christ* that justifies, regenerates, or saves anyone, it is God—*the object of our faith*—who justifies, regenerates, and saves all those who believe. God requires that we believe as a condition for justification, regeneration, and salvation. To confuse the responsibility of man to believe with the exclusive ability of God to regenerate is simply inexcusable. Hoeksema says:

> … It is evident that regeneration is exclusively a work of God, wherein man is strictly passive in the sense that he does not and cannot cooperate in his own rebirth.[409]

Of course, "regeneration is exclusively a work of God." If Hoeksema were to pay a little closer attention to how Paul defines faith, he would see that faith is not a work at all. Piper goes so far as to claim that saying Christ provisionally died for everyone means that you believe the cross was:

> … Intended to give all men the opportunity to save themselves.[410]

Talk about misrepresentation of another's views! As is discussed elsewhere, Calvinists give lip service to the truth that salvation is conditioned upon, and follows faith. Their *order of salvation,* however, makes this impossible. That is, Calvinists, like all Evangelicals, believe that justification is necessary to salvation and that faith is necessary to justification. They say, however, that faith is dependent upon regeneration, which is unconditional and always and immediately results in or produces justification and salvation. In reality, the Calvinist view is a denial of faith alone in Christ alone for salvation. Calvinists have traded *sola fide* for *nola fide.* When I point this out, Calvinists, without clearly thinking this through, will say that I am misrepresenting them. They will say that I have confused regeneration, a link in the Calvinist chain, with salvation itself. They reason that since regeneration is before faith and faith is before justification, they can logically say that faith is a *consequence* of regeneration but a *condition* of salvation. This is, however, logical nonsense. For:

- If regeneration is requisite to faith and always results in faith,

And:

- If faith is requisite to justification and always, inevitably, and immediately results in justification,

And:

- If justification is requisite to and always, inevitably, and immediately results in salvation,

Then:

- It must follow that salvation is *not* conditioned upon faith and is an unconditional consequence of regeneration and/or that which leads to regeneration. If salvation comes before faith in Christ and if faith is required for and is prior to justification, then a person is saved even before he is justified. I would love to hear a Calvinist explain how this can be.

TOTAL DEPRAVITY

SCRIPTURALLY REFUTED

W ITH all that we considered in the previous chapter, let us now take a closer look at some of the key passages dealing with the subject of spiritual birth, especially as regeneration relates to faith in Jesus Christ. In John 1:12–13, the apostle John tells us that:

> *As many as received Him* [Jesus Christ], *to them He gave the right to become children of God, to those who believe in His name: who were born, not of blood, nor of the will of the flesh, nor of the will of man, but of God.*

Requisite to this spiritual birth, which gives us the right to become and to be called the children of God, is:

- Receiving Jesus Christ.

Receiving Jesus Christ involves:

- Believing in the name of Jesus Christ.

This spiritual birth is not a physical birth. That is, it is not of blood, of the will of the flesh, or of the will of man. To say that it is not of blood, of the will of the flesh, or of man, is to say it is not the result of procreation or accomplished by man. As we learn in John 3:6, that which is born of the flesh *is* flesh. That is, the physical procreative process produces physical beings. Likewise, that which is born of the Spirit is spiritual in nature. Since it is the Spirit of God that gives spiritual life, or spiritually regenerates the spiritually dead, the person regenerated is related to God by that means. That is, he is *born of God* and/or of the *will of God.*

The place and importance of man's will, or choice if you prefer, is discerned in the fact that we must choose to receive or believe in Jesus Christ. To say, as these verses do, that this birth is not physical but spiritual, that it relates us not to man but to God, and that it is of God and not man, is not to teach that man has no say with regard to being born again. Far from teaching, as Calvinism does, that man cannot have a say in whether or not he will be born again, this portion of Scripture teaches just the opposite. It does so in the strongest possible terms. For if we are repeatedly told we must believe and are constantly warned of the consequences of not believing, it must be assumed that we can and should believe. To receive and believe are not the words that should be used, if we are supposed to be totally *passive* in the salvation process. God is the giver, we are the receivers. God is the Savior, we are the believers. Receiving and believing is our responsibility, while giving us new life and regenerating the *spiritually dead* (a reference to everyone before receiving Christ by faith) is God's work.

SCRIPTURALLY SPEAKING, FAITH IS FIRST

Does it not seem almost too obvious that John is telling his readers that receiving Christ, which he equates with believing in Christ, is the prerequisite to becoming a child of God, or of being born of God? The Calvinist has turned this passage on its head by saying that God makes you a child of God so you can believe and receive Christ. The reason the Calvinist reverses the order is because of Reformed Theology and not what he finds in the text itself. If you are a Calvinist now, consider how, in your pre-Calvinist days, you read this passage, without anyone telling you how to read it.

The Calvinist latches onto the words "not of blood, nor of the will of the flesh, nor of the will of man." He then claims that this proves a man *cannot* receive or believe before he is born again. This is also to say that he cannot choose to receive the eternal life that comes with regeneration until after he is regenerated. It is clear that John is using these words in contrast to the words "born ... of God" to emphasize *from whom* the *receiver/believer* is directly getting this new life. That is, when you are born again, you are born *of God.*

- The first birth is physical and natural.

- The second birth is spiritual and supernatural.

- The first birth is caused by and is the result of human activity.

- The second birth is caused by and is the result of divine activity.

To say that God is the cause of that birth or the one who directly gives that life and is the only one capable of producing that life, is not to say that there is no God-ordained prerequisite to the life of regeneration. There most definitely is.

CONDITION VERSUS CONSEQUENCE

To reduce this *condition* of receiving or believing in Christ for rebirth to a mere *consequence* of rebirth:

- Reverses the obvious order in these verses,

- Flies in the face of what John says elsewhere in his writings, and

- Contradicts what Peter says about how one comes to be born again (1 Pet. 1:23, 25).

The apostle Peter says that we have:

> ... *been born again, not of corruptible seed but incorruptible, through the word of God which lives and abides forever. ... Now this is the word which by the gospel was preached to you. (1 Pet. 1:23, 25)*

Is it necessary for us to believe the gospel, through which we are born again, in order to be born again? Or must we be born again so we can and will believe the gospel as the Calvinist contends? It is clear from what Peter says that the incorruptible seed precedes rebirth. The question is this: is the seed—God's Word in the form of the gospel—received *by* faith or *without* faith? If it is received by faith, then faith is *before* and *leads to* regeneration.

LIFE BEFORE CONCEPTION?

Boice, like all other Calvinists, insists that faith must follow regeneration because of the total inability resulting from the total depravity of man. Still, in his interpretation of 1 Peter 1:23, he says:

> God *first* plants within our heart what we might call the ovum of faith. ... *Second*, He sends forth the seed of His Word, which contains the divine life within it, to pierce the ovum of faith. The result is spiritual conception.[411]

Boice is careful to point out that God gives the faith that enables a person to receive the Word. Nevertheless, he places faith before *spiritual conception* as a prerequisite to conception, which is before spiritual birth, which in turn is before saving faith. If Boice is right, then faith is before spiritual birth since it is before spiritual conception. In a conscious effort to combat what he believes to be the error of reducing saving faith to mere intellectual assent, while commenting on John 3:18, MacArthur says:

> This phrase (lit. "to believe into the name") [of Jesus Christ] means more than mere intellectual assent to the claims of the gospel. It includes trust and commitment to Christ as Lord and Savior which results in receiving a new nature (v. 7) which produces a change in heart and obedience to the Lord.[412]

Setting aside for now MacArthur's definition of saving faith, notice closely the order and relation he suggests for faith and the new nature:

True and saving faith *includes* trust and commitment.

True and saving faith *results* in a new nature.

A new nature *produces* a change of heart and obedience to the Lord.

If the new nature *results* from faith, then faith is *logically* if not *chronologically* before the new nature. If the new nature is what regeneration is all about, then faith is *before* regeneration or is what *results in* regeneration. It would seem that MacArthur wants to have it both ways. He not only says that regeneration must initiate faith but also that faith results in regeneration. This cannot be so. MacArthur also says:

> Chapter 1:12, 13, [of the Gospel of John] indicates that "born again" also carries the idea "to become children of God" through trust in the name of the incarnate Word.[413]

We cannot logically say that regeneration is through trust or faith and then turn around and say that faith is through regeneration. MacArthur needs to make up his mind concerning which way he is going to go on this.

Calvinists wrongly accuse non-Calvinists of synergism, because they (i.e., Calvinists) wrongly believe that the faith required of a man to be saved by God somehow negates the affirmation that only God saves. While it is commendable to insist that only God saves, it is unreasonable and unscriptural to make *God* responsible for that which God makes *man* responsible. No matter what their intentions, Calvinists have made God (in their thinking and theology) both the *giver* of the gift of salvation and the *one who receives* the gift of salvation on behalf of those He saves. Calvin on certain occasions said things that would lead one to conclude that he believed faith comes before and leads to regeneration. Conversely, on other occasions, he taught the exact opposite. In speaking about the fall of man in Adam, Calvin said:

> Man, when he withdrew his allegiance to God, was deprived of the spiritual gifts. … Hence it follows, that he is now an exile from the kingdom of God, so that all the things which pertain to the blessed life of the soul are extinguished in him until he recovers them by the grace of regeneration. Among these are faith …[414]

Some have suggested that this apparent conflict can be resolved by understanding that Calvin, at least some of the time, used the term *regeneration* in a very broad sense. In this broad sense the order of salvation is (supposedly) not in view. Sinclair Ferguson says:

> Calvin uses "regeneration" to denote the whole process of renewal, repentance, mortification and vivification (new life), in contrast to later Evangelical theology's use of the term in an inaugural sense (new birth).[415]

Hoeksema distinguishes between what he refers to as:

> … regeneration in the narrowest sense of the word …[416]

And:

> … regeneration in the broader sense of the word.[417]

This simply does not solve the problem since contemporary Calvinism says that regeneration, in this narrower sense, precedes faith and Calvin at times said just the opposite:

> … Christ confers upon us, and we obtain by faith, both free reconciliation and newness of life.[418]

Thus, sometimes Calvin taught that faith comes before newness of life. Whether that newness of life was in the narrow or broad sense, you still have faith first. Even so, in keeping with mainstream Calvinism, Wilson says:

> The first indications of the Spirit's quickening are repentance and belief. The new birth does not result from repentance and belief, as many mistakenly imagine. It is the other way around. Repentance and faith are gifts from God that He bestows through the Spirit. ... No one can have faith unless it is first given by God. That way no one can take credit for his own salvation.[419]

If Wilson is right, it would mean, for example, that if he gave me a copy of the book in which he said this, I could take part of the credit for writing that book, assuming he required me to accept this book as his gift to me. According to Calvinism, to view faith as man's responsibility would be to give man a legitimate reason for boasting. The consequence of this would mean that you could thank yourself for the gifts that were given to you because your voluntary reception of the gifts made you a co-giver of the gifts. Sound silly? Boettner explains:

> If any person believes, it is because God has quickened him; and if any person fails to believe, it is because God has withheld that grace ...[420]

God is, therefore, just as responsible for unbelief as He is for faith, according to this view. *The Canons of Dort* say:

> This conversion is that regeneration, new creation, resurrection from the dead, making alive, so highly spoken of in the Scriptures, which God works in us without us. But this regeneration is by no means brought about only by outward preaching, by moral persuasion, or by such a mode of operation that, after God has done his part, it remains in the power of man to be regenerated or not regenerated, converted or not converted ... regeneration is not inferior in power to creation or the resurrection of the dead. Hence all those in whose hearts God works in this amazing way are certainly, unfailingly, and effectually regenerated and do actually believe.[421]

According to Reformed Theology, to *enable* a man to believe (John 6:44) without *making* a man believe or *making* him *a believer*, would be "the power of man to be regenerated or not." This is the equivalent of saying that if a man has the ability to accept a gift, he has the power to give the gift. To the contrary, merely because I have the ability to accept an abundance of money and thereby become rich, it does not follow that I have the power to make myself rich. In the same way, if someone makes me rich by giving me a fortune, I could not, by virtue of my ability and choice to accept that money, take credit for my new and welcomed wealth. And yet this is the logic of *The Canons of Dort* in particular and of Calvinism in general.

In John 3:1–8, Jesus carries on a conversation with a man named Nicodemus, some of which we have already considered. During this conversation, Jesus told Nicodemus that the only hope of *seeing* or *entering* the kingdom of God was to be born again. In verse 3, Jesus said to Nicodemus:

> *"Most assuredly, I say to you, unless one is born again, he cannot see the kingdom of God."*

In verse 7, He said:

> *"Do not marvel that I said to you, 'you must be born again.'"*

Sproul is right when he says:

> It was Jesus who first declared that spiritual rebirth was an absolute necessity for entering the kingdom of God. ...[422]

Sproul then correctly says:

> The word *unless* in Jesus' teaching signals a universally necessary condition for seeing and entering the kingdom of God. Rebirth then is an essential part of Christianity; without it, entrance to God's kingdom is impossible. ... Just as birth is our initiation, our first entrance into life outside the womb, so rebirth is the starting point of our spiritual life.[423]

Crenshaw, however, asks:

> But where in the passage did the Lord tell Nicodemus *how* to be born again? Some say that it is necessary or one could not enter the kingdom, which is true. The word for "must" in John 3 (*dei*) means "it is necessary," but it is not a command to do so. Even if it were, a command does not mean one would have the ability to obey.[424]

Most Calvinists say you *should* be born again, even if you are in the reprobate caste and cannot be born again. They cannot say that any reprobate person *can* be born again. Gerstner, in his commentary on John 1:12 and 13, says:

We must not get the notion that people come to Jesus, and as a result of that they are "born again." ... Those who do come to Jesus
are not therefore born again, but on the contrary indicate that they
have been born again. In other words, they are not born again because they have come to Jesus but they have come to Jesus because
they have been born again.[425]

Gerstner is right in stride with the way Calvin handled this passage. As
is so typical of Calvin, however, he begins his commentary on this portion of
Scripture suggesting that he believes one way but then quickly corrects that
initial impression. Thus he says:

... The Evangelist ... says that by faith they obtain this glory of
being reckoned the sons of God ... the Evangelist adds, that they
become the sons of God, not by the will which belongs to the flesh,
but when they are born of God. But if faith regenerates us, so that
we are the sons of God, and if God breathes faith into us from heav-
en, it plainly appears that not by possibility only, but actually—as
we say—is the grace of adoption offered to us by Christ. ... He
expresses briefly the manner of receiving Christ, that is, believing in him. Having been engrafted into Christ by faith, we obtain
the right of adoption, so as to be the sons of God. The Evangelist
declares that this power is given to those who already believe. ...
Now it is certain that such persons are in reality the sons of God.
... They detract too much from the value of faith who say that, by
believing, a man obtains nothing more than that he may become a
son of God ...[426]

The error Calvin was combating was the notion that faith in Christ only
made it *possible* for a man to be a child of God. Calvin rightly reasoned
that faith in Christ resulted not in the mere *possibility* of becoming a child
of God, but the *actuality* of becoming a child of God. Nevertheless, what
Calvin gave, he then inconsistently took away. That is, while he said that
believing leads to spiritual rebirth, which in turn makes the new believer a
child of God, he also said that rebirth must come first. Thus he said:

The Evangelist says that those who *believe* are already *born of God*
... faith ... is the fruit of spiritual regeneration; for the Evangelist
affirms that no man can believe, unless he be begotten of God; and
therefore faith is a heavenly gift. It follows ... that faith is not bare

or cold knowledge, since no man can believe who has not been renewed by the Spirit of God.[427]

Calvin was well aware of the logical problems he posed by affirming a *regeneration* that both precedes and produces *faith*, and also a *faith* that precedes and produces *regeneration*. He said:

> It may be thought that the Evangelist reverses the natural order by making regeneration to precede faith, whereas, on the contrary, it is an effect of faith, and therefore ought to be placed later. *I reply, that both statements perfectly agree;* because by faith we receive the incorruptible seed (1 Peter 1:23) by which we are born again to a new and divine life. And yet faith itself is a work of the Holy Spirit, who dwells in none but the children of God. So then, in various respects, faith is a part of our regeneration, and an entrance into the kingdom of God, that he may reckon us among his children. The illumination of our minds by the Holy Spirit belongs to our renewal, and thus faith flows from regeneration as from its source; but since it is by the same faith that we receive Christ, who sanctifies us by his Spirit, on that account it is said to be the beginning of our adoption.[428]

According to Calvin, in terms of an order of salvation, this first solution is as follows:

- The gift of faith is first, enabling us to receive the incorruptible seed.

- Regeneration is second, resulting from the implanted seed that we are enabled to receive by the gift of faith.

- Active faith in Christ is third, in that it is produced by regeneration and in a sense is a part of the regeneration/salvation package.

Stated differently, we have a *received* gift of faith, *followed* by an implanted seed, *resulting* in regeneration, *producing* an exercised faith. The other solution Calvin suggests involves an appeal to the *hidden* methods of God. Thus he said:

> Another solution, still more plain and easy, may be offered; for when the Lord breathes faith into us, he regenerates us by some method that is hidden and unknown to us; but after we have

received faith, we perceive, by a lively feeling of conscience, not only the grace of adoption, but also newness of life and the other gifts of the Holy Spirit. For since faith, as we have said, receives Christ, it puts us in possession, so to speak, of all his blessings. Thus so far as respects our sense, it is only after having believed that we begin to be the sons of God.[429]

This second solution is really not another solution, but simply another way to state the first solution. Insofar as the order is concerned, the gift of faith is first, and regeneration is second. It begins with the implanted seed, and is followed by a conscious expression of faith. This is also what might best be considered the *phenomenological* explanation of the order of salvation. That is, just as the sun appears to rise and set (and yet we know that really the earth rotates on its axis), we can, for all practical purposes, speak of the sun rising and setting at a particular time each day (without forfeiting our scientific credibility).

According to Calvinism, the apostle John (in John 1:12–13) is teaching the exact opposite of what he appears to be teaching. To use John 1:12–13 to prove that regeneration must precede faith in Christ is like using a sphere to prove the earth is flat. No one coming to this passage without a Calvinist bias could interpret it as does the Calvinist. In fact, just the opposite is true. Unless one is wearing Calvinist-colored glasses, the Calvinist interpretation of this passage (i.e., rebirth before faith in Christ) is completely unobtainable. White is right when he says in reference to John 1:12 and 13:

> ... God is the one who causes the new birth in contrast to any action of the will of man.[430]

He is wrong to suggest that what God causes is not and cannot be conditioned upon faith in Christ. It would be like saying that since justification is caused by God, justification is not and cannot be conditioned upon faith in Christ. Non-Calvinists do not say the will of man can regenerate a man. Man's will is simply incapable of doing such a thing. Faith is not capable of regenerating a man. Not even faith in Christ is capable of such a thing. No non-Calvinist I know believes it is the will of man or the decision of a man to believe, or for that matter, that it is believing that gives a spiritually dead man new life in Christ. Only God gives this new life because only God is capable of giving life to the spiritually dead. While Calvinists constantly complain they are being misrepresented, they attribute views to non-Calvinist

Evangelicals they should know cannot accurately or fairly represent us. Concerning John 3:11–21, even MacArthur says:

> The key word in these verses is "believe," used 7 times. The new birth must be appropriated by an act of faith.[431]

MacArthur cannot have it both ways. Either regeneration initiates faith and therefore precedes faith, or regeneration is appropriated by faith, or through faith, making faith first.

According to Sproul, Ephesians 2:1–10 represents:

> … A predestinarian passage *par excellence* …[432]

He then goes on to say:

> This passage celebrates the newness of life that the Holy Spirit has created in us.[433]

Keep in mind that it is newness of life that is obtained by faith, according to Calvin. Sproul then clarifies:

> What is here [in Eph. 2:1–10] called quickening or being made alive is what is elsewhere called rebirth or regeneration … the beginning of spiritual life.[434]

We have already considered this passage relative to the Calvinist contention that faith is the gift of God or is included with the gift of God that Paul is talking about in Ephesians 2:1–10. This time we focus on what the text says relative to the logical relationship of faith to regeneration. The apostle Paul tells us that salvation is not only *by grace* but that it is also *through faith*. Even though the system of Calvinism that Calvin is responsible for helping create denies this, commenting on these verses, Calvin rightly said that the apostle Paul:

> … Asserts that the salvation of the Ephesians was entirely the work, the free work, of God but they had obtained this grace by faith. On one side, we must look at God; and on the other, at men. God declares that He owes us nothing; so that salvation is not a reward or recompense, but mere grace. Now it may be asked how men receive the salvation offered to them by the hand of God? I reply by faith. Hence he concludes that there is nothing of our own, if on

the part of God, it is grace alone, and if we bring nothing but faith, which strips of all praise, it follows that salvation is not of us.[435]

If the obtaining of a gracious salvation is dependent upon faith, then logically speaking faith must be first. This could not possibly imply that the believer is a co-savior. It does not allow a man to take any credit for his salvation. The greatly respected Calvinist professor J. Gresham Machen says:

> Faith consists not in doing something but in receiving something.[436]

And:

> Faith is no more than an activity of reception contributing nothing to that which it receives.[437]

Charles Spurgeon is right when he says:

> Faith excludes all boasting. The hand which receives charity does not say "I am to be thanked for accepting the gift"; that would be absurd.[438]

While it must be emphasized that we bring *nothing but* faith, it must also be emphasized that we *must bring* faith. Calvin is absolutely right when he suggests that because we only bring faith, we have nothing to boast about. Requiring the lost to bring faith is not to ask the lost to make a contribution to their salvation, but it is a constant reminder that salvation is *all of God* and *not at all of man.*

NO CHOICE?

Many Calvinists will admit that they came to Christ, or at least thought they did, when they believed the gospel that someone proclaimed to them. And yet the Calvinist view must imply that their act of believing was, from beginning to end, God's act and not their own; that the only reason they believed was because they were in the elect caste—otherwise they would have been unable to believe, consigned to the non-elect caste forever. They are also saying that many unbelievers are not now and will never be able to come to Christ.

A few years ago at a Harvest Crusade, some hyper-Calvinist zealots showed up with T-shirts that had the word *choice* circled with a diagonal line through it, indicating that no one has a choice. These people actively sought to discourage people from making a choice to accept Jesus Christ as Savior. Admittedly, this is not the typical behavior of Calvinists, certainly not mainstream Calvinists. It is easy, however, to see how a Calvinist could justify such an attitude. Even among mainstream Calvinists, however, the faith people place in Christ at such events is often assumed to be spurious. This is often described, within mainstream Calvinism, by the theologically pejorative term *decisionalism.* Taking Calvinism to its logical extreme makes the Calvinists like men that safely and easily cross over a deep and dangerous canyon on the only bridge provided for that purpose. Then they tell others that there may not be a bridge for them to cross over on, and if there is, they will simply find it under them some day.

Although John 1:12–13 makes it clear that a person is born again upon believing in Jesus Christ, it will still be helpful to consider the question asked by Nicodemus about *how* one can be born again. There are two *how* questions and answers to consider. One could simply answer that this is what God does supernaturally. God gives us life. When He does, we become His spiritual children. That, of course, does not really tell us *how* He does it. It is enough for most of us to know *that* He does it. From the perspective of the lost, we might also ask, "How can I make *sure* that I am one of those to whom God gives this new life or new birth?"

A consistent Calvinist would answer that there is nothing you can do to determine whether you will or will not be born again. There are some things that may help you to *discover* that you are one of the elect. There is nothing, says the consistent Calvinist, that you can do to *determine* you are one of the elect. That is, if you become a believer and follow through with a reasonably holy life, that is a pretty good indication (though not solid proof) that you are one of the elect. If you really want proof of election, that will have to wait until you have persevered in faith and righteousness to the end of your life on earth. There is nothing you can do, however, if Calvinism is true, to *determine* if you are elect or reprobate. That was settled long before you were born, and you simply have no say in the matter. This is despite the fact that John 3:3 and 3:7 clearly express the need and necessity for spiritual rebirth in two of the most famous statements from the New Testament.

The Calvinist tells us that our Lord was only telling Nicodemus what *must* happen if he is to see or enter the kingdom, not that Nicodemus could do anything about it. He was not, according to Calvinism, telling Nicodemus that he *ought* to be born again, as if Nicodemus could choose to be born again. The Calvinist *must* is not a command, but merely the inevitable result of election, Christ's death for the elect alone, and irresistible grace leading to regeneration. Regeneration then results in or produces faith for the elect. Even to the most careless student, however, it should be obvious that Jesus is still talking to Nicodemus when He says:

> *"For God so loved the world that He gave His only begotten Son, that whoever believes in Him should not perish but have everlasting life." (John 3:16)*

JOHN 3:16 SAYS IT ALL

John 3:16 is the answer to Nicodemus' question of *how* one can be born again—both in terms of the cause (God) and condition (faith). Jesus, in this most beloved of all verses, tells us:

- How God feels about the world (He loves it).

- The extent to which He loves it (He gave His Son for it).

- What He offers to the world through His Son (He offers eternal life).

- Who can receive what He offers (whoever, all or everyone who believes can receive it).

To say that *John 3:16 says it all* is not to suggest that this is all we need to know about salvation, as some have simplistically charged us with asserting. Rather, it is to say that John 3:16 speaks clearly and with finality on this matter of *how* one can move from the category of the unregenerate to the category of the regenerate. Stated differently, John 3:16 unambiguously tells us how the spiritually dead can become spiritually alive and how the unbelieving lost can become the eternally saved. It says that you *must* believe and clearly implies you *ought* to believe and *can* believe. Remember that the context of John 3:16 is within the context of John 3:3 and 3:7. Our Lord did not say what He said (recorded in Chapter 3, verse 16) in a vacuum.

John 3:16 is to be understood in the context of a conversation with Nicodemus about the absolute necessity of regeneration. Our Lord told Nicodemus what must happen, what ought to happen, and what can happen. Rebirth is both caused and commanded by God. He causes it to happen when we meet the *God-ordained* condition for it to happen. That is, we are born again when we believe in or receive Jesus Christ. The Calvinist then asks: how can a person who is spiritually dead make a spiritual decision (i.e., believe in or receive Christ)? Boettner reasons:

> If a man were dead, in a natural and physical sense, it would at once be readily granted that there is no further possibility of that man being able to perform any physical actions. A corpse cannot act in any way whatever, and that man would be reckoned to have taken leave of his senses who asserted that it could. If a man is dead spiritually, therefore, it is surely equally as evident that he is unable to perform any spiritual actions ...[439]

If Boettner was consistent, he could not propose that John 3 represents an argument by Jesus to Nicodemus, since it would be useless to attempt to reason with a spiritually dead man about spiritual things—a spiritually dead man cannot even hear what Jesus is saying to him (according to what Boettner thinks "spiritually dead" means). There would be no reason for Jesus to talk to a spiritually dead man about spiritual things, knowing that the spiritually dead man could not even hear what He was saying to him. Although the analogy of physical and spiritual death and life is valid for our Lord's limited purpose, Calvinists go beyond the limits of the analogy to argue that spiritually dead men are effectively spiritually insentient. If it were the case that the physical unresponsiveness of physical death mandates spiritual unresponsiveness for those spiritually dead, then it would be the case that those who have "died to sin" (*all* Christians according to Rom. 6:3) would be insentient to sin—in other words, no longer able to sin. And yet the Bible tells us that if we say we have no sin, we are liars (1 John 1:8). Since we know that John does not contradict Jesus, spiritual death must not imply the inability to respond assumed by Boettner and other Calvinists.

All Calvinists would agree that Adam spiritually died the instant he sinned against God. Yet all Calvinists will admit that the same spiritually dead Adam was able to hear the living God and carry on a conversation with Him sometime after his spiritual demise. That strikes me as a very spiritual interaction that demonstrates a spiritual capacity on the part of the spiritually dead. Thus, just because a person is spiritually dead does not mean he cannot believe the gospel when it is presented to him. In fact, since it is to all the lost and only the lost (the spiritually dead of this world) that the gospel is to be preached, it should be assumed that they can believe. Scripture, however, more than assumes that a lost person can believe. It commands and requires that he believe as a condition of becoming a saved person. That is also why Scripture holds an unbeliever accountable for rejecting the gospel and remaining in unbelief. In fact, it is precisely because a man is spiritually dead that it is so vital that we get the offer of life and the message concerning the absolute necessity of regeneration to him. The spiritually alive (i.e., the regenerated) do not need the life offered in the gospel. They already have it.

Believing for the unregenerate is not, according to Calvinism, a command to obey but a gift that is involuntarily received. When they say the elect are regenerated so they *can* believe, they mean that the elect are regenerated and *will* believe and are in fact made believers. Some Calvinists make a distinction (intentional or otherwise) between the faith that is received involuntarily (and that comes with the gift of regeneration) and the faith that is exercised in Christ after faith is *placed in* the believer as a part of the regenerating work of God.

Suppose I wanted to turn a poor man into a rich man. I could offer him money that he could refuse and thereby remain poor. This is the way salvation is offered according to Scripture. What if, however, I simply put the money in this poor man's bank account (or pocket)? This is salvation according to Calvinism. You must (and will) first *involuntarily* receive faith when you are born again. Then you must (and will) irresistibly and freely place that faith in Christ because you have been turned into a believer by the regenerating work of God. God irresistibly makes you freely receive what He offers you in Christ, according to Calvinism. If you have trouble reconciling such a contradiction of terms, you are not alone.

According to Reformed Theology, God causes the elect lost to receive regeneration (which comes with faith) involuntarily so that he can voluntarily accept all that is available to him and that is his and is obtained through faith. Thus, we have an involuntarily received faith, followed by a voluntarily exercised faith to accept all that comes to us through that faith. But that would mean that there is a gift of faith that is not equal to (though it does lead to) believing in Christ. In other words, as money must be spent, so faith must be exercised. Can biblical faith, which is also a saving faith, be viewed as anything less than, or short of, faith *in* Jesus Christ?

If the Calvinist says that the faith we are given is faith *in* Jesus Christ, it would be like putting money in a man's pocket and spending it for him at the same time. But if the one who gives us the faith gives us an exercised faith (a faith in Christ), then it is not the newly regenerated that is doing the believing, but God. That is, the regenerated one is not simply enabled to believe, but is made a believer and unable not to believe as a result of regeneration. Despite the protest of Calvinists, they have implied that saving faith in Christ is the result of God the Father believing in His Son through a regenerated man.

I realize that it sounds silly to say someone affirms the proposition that saving faith is God believing in His Son through us. According to Calvinism, however, the faith that comes with regeneration is irresistibly exercised just as it is irresistibly received. If it is irresistibly exercised, it is effectively God doing the believing. Sound ridiculous? It is. All this just tends to complicate, distort, and confuse what is in Scripture a very straightforward proposition. That is, before we become Christians, we are lost in our sins and in need of a Savior. Jesus Christ died on the cross to save us from our sins and then triumphed over death. We simply need to turn to Him in faith. He then gives us a new life, making us His children. The same faith in Christ that enables us to receive Him is the faith by which we are justified (declared righteous) and through which we are saved. Sound simple? It actually is. It is certainly not as complicated as Calvinism makes it.

Rising almost to the level of a mantra, the Calvinist constantly repeats the misleading sentiment that the spiritually dead cannot do anything of a *positive* spiritual nature. The lost are spiritual corpses, according to Calvinism, with no more capacity for believing in Christ than a cadaver has for choosing what the mortician will dress it in for its funeral. As already stated, this is not, however, what the Bible means when it says a man is spiritually dead before and until he is given life in Christ.

Calvinists love to use Lazarus as their example of lostness. Like Lazarus, they say, the Lord raises the spiritually dead without their consent. As Lazarus passively received life from our Lord, without believing in Christ, they also say the unbeliever, without believing, receives life and then faith with that life. They insist that he does not, and indeed cannot, believe before he receives new life in Christ and from Christ.

In contrast, Jesus gives us an example of what it means to be spiritually lost and spiritually dead. He also makes it clear that the way to life and salvation for the spiritually dead and spiritually lost man is anything but passive.

Jesus prefaces His story of a spiritually dead and spiritually lost man with two other stories. Here is Chapter Fifteen of Luke to give the complete context:

Then all the tax collectors and the sinners drew near to Him to hear Him. And the Pharisees and scribes complained, saying, "This Man receives sinners and eats with them." So He spoke this parable to them, saying:

"What man of you, having a hundred sheep, if he loses one of them, does not leave the ninety-nine in the wilderness, and go after the one which is lost until he finds it? And when he has found it, he lays it on his shoulders, rejoicing. And when he comes home, he calls together his friends and neighbors, saying to them, 'Rejoice with me, for I have found my sheep which was lost!' I say to you that likewise there will be more joy in heaven over one sinner who repents than over ninety-nine just persons who need no repentance.

"Or what woman, having ten silver coins, if she loses one coin, does not light a lamp, sweep the house, and search carefully until she finds it? And when she has found it, she calls her friends and neighbors together, saying, 'Rejoice with me, for I have found the piece which I lost!' Likewise, I say to you, there is joy in the presence of the angels of God over one sinner who repents."

Then He said: "A certain man had two sons. And the younger of them said to his father, 'Father, give me the portion of goods that falls to me.' So he divided to them his livelihood. And not many days after, the younger son gathered all together, journeyed to a far country, and there wasted his possessions with prodigal living. But when he had spent all, there arose a severe famine in that land, and he began to be in want. Then he went and joined himself to a citizen of that country, and he sent him into his fields to feed swine. And he would gladly have filled his stomach with the pods that the swine ate, and no one gave him anything.

"But when he came to himself, he said, 'How many of my father's hired servants have bread enough and to spare, and I perish with hunger! I will arise and go to my father, and will say to him, "Father, I have sinned against heaven and before you, and I am no longer worthy to be called your son. Make me like one of your hired servants." '

"And he arose and came to his father. But when he was still a great way off, his father saw him and had compassion, and ran and fell on his neck and kissed him. And the son said to him, 'Father, I have sinned against heaven and in your sight, and am no longer worthy to be called your son.'

"But the father said to his servants, 'Bring out the best robe and put it on him, and put a ring on his hand and sandals on his feet. And bring the fatted calf here and kill it, and let us eat and be merry; for this my son was dead and is alive again; he was lost and is found.' And they began to be merry.

"Now his older son was in the field. And as he came and drew near to the house, he heard music and dancing. So he called one of the servants and asked what these things meant. And he said to him, 'Your brother has come, and because he has received him safe and sound, your father has killed the fatted calf.'

"But he was angry and would not go in. Therefore his father came out and pleaded with him. So he answered and said to his father, 'Lo, these many years I have been serving you; I never transgressed your commandment at any time; and yet you never gave me a young goat, that I might make merry with my friends. But as soon as this son of yours came, who has devoured your livelihood with harlots, you killed the fatted calf for him.'

"And he said to him, 'Son, you are always with me, and all that I have is yours. It was right that we should make merry and be glad, for your brother was dead and is alive again, and was lost and is found.' "

Before discussing the implications of the road to life and salvation for the prodigal son, it should be noted that while sheep may be passive in the process by which they are rescued, the Lord does not allow us to see a non-involved sinner in the analogy. For He says:

"There will be ... joy in heaven over one sinner who repents." *(Luke 15:7)*

Thus, repentance was requisite from the sinner's side, as seeking and finding was requisite from the shepherd's side. Likewise, even though a lost coin does not and cannot help a lady find it, the Lord again does not allow us to conclude that lost people have no responsibility in being found. For once again He follows this story with the telling words:

> *"There is joy in the presence of the angels of God over one sinner who repents." (Luke 15:10)*

In both stories, while the saving or finding is outside the ability of the lost sheep and lost coin respectively, a sinner repenting is cause for celebration. The Calvinist will say that the sinner only repents because he has been found and is not found because he repents. This, however, misses the point of the stories. When the focus is on man's responsibility versus God's desire to find and rescue that which was lost, we can clearly see the way to life and salvation from the human side of the salvation equation. That is:

> *"When he came to himself, he said, 'How many of my father's hired servants have bread enough and to spare, and I perish with hunger! I will arise and go to my father, and will say to him, "Father, I have sinned against heaven and before you, and I am no longer worthy to be called your son. Make me like one of your hired servants." 'And he arose and came to his father."*

Finally, the father said of his repentant son that he …

> " '… was dead and is alive again, and was lost and is found.' "

So much for the Calvinist contention that the spiritually dead can do nothing of a positive spiritual nature while yet spiritually dead! God wants you to know what you *must do* to be born again, which is to believe in Jesus Christ. Spiritual deadness is your problem. Spiritual life is God's solution. Faith in Jesus Christ is the means by which God has ordained that you should avail yourself of the life He offers you. Calvinist pastor Dr. D. James Kennedy seems to concede this very point. In his book, *Why I Believe,* in a chapter stressing the necessity of rebirth, he says:

> We have an imperative, that is true, but it contains within itself the germ of a promise. For if it is true that we must be born again, then it is also true that we *may* be born again. … We can be forgiven. We can be recreated. We can have new hearts, new affections, new life, new power, new purpose, new direction, and new destinations. Yes we *may* be born again. That, my friends, is the *good news.*[440]

Kennedy even seems to concede that faith comes *before* and results *in* regeneration when he invites his readers:

> Place your trust in [Christ]. Ask Him to come in and be born in you today.[441]

When Kennedy uses the pronoun *we,* are we to understand that he is only referring to the *elect* who happen to hear or read these words? What kind of good news is this to the reprobate who may *not* (in fact *cannot*) be born again? Why would Kennedy ask *anyone* to "place your trust in" Christ? If *all* the elect will and cannot do otherwise and if *none* of the reprobate can, it seems a very odd thing for a Calvinist to make such an appeal.

Perhaps one reason Kennedy's *Evangelism Explosion* has prompted millions of "decisions" worldwide over the time it has been in use is because his Calvinist view of the lost is artfully disguised to look like the very un-Calvinist (but biblical) view that God genuinely invites *any* lost person to "place your trust" in Christ and "ask Him to come in," resulting in Him being "born in you today."

It should be evident that Calvinism has its theological cart before the biblical horse. Thus to accept the first of the five points of Calvinism is to reject—no matter how unwittingly—a reasonable interpretation of John 3:3 as well as many other portions of Scripture.

The Calvinist cannot help but win the argument, however, if the way he frames the issue is left unchallenged. In fact, I believe the Calvinist often establishes or *rigs* the rules for debate in such a way so as to ensure a favorable outcome for Calvinism. The Calvinist gives you two choices, as if they are the only two choices possible. One choice is to accept what he says is true. In this case, *regeneration precedes and even produces faith.* The other choice he gives you is to say that you are able, in one way or another, to save yourself. Another way of stating this is to say that you must admit:

- Calvinism is right.

Or:

- You believe what you know is not true (that you can save yourself).

The Calvinist knows that if you are an Evangelical, you do not believe you can save yourself. He knows that you believe God is the Savior and that only God can legitimately get credit for saving you. As we have repeatedly documented, the Calvinist also believes that if a person could have faith in Christ without regeneration preceding and producing that faith, it would mean he is at least partially his own savior. Since no thoughtful Christian would say such a ridiculous thing, he has got you *over a theological barrel*—or so he thinks.

Suppose someone asks you, "Have you stopped beating your wife?" You could answer, "I have never beaten my wife." What if, however, you were in a court of law and the judge instructed you to answer only with a *yes* or *no?* If you say *yes,* it means you *were beating her.* If you say *no,* it means you still *are beating her.* The problem with the question asked by the Calvinist is with the options you are given to answer the question. You need that additional option—"I have never beaten my wife." Even so, the Calvinist gives you the Calvinist option and only one other option that is equally wrong. From my perspective, we are being shortchanged by at least one option—the option I have suggested. Carefully consider the way the discussion is framed by Calvinists:

> Faith is not something man contributes to salvation ...[442]

Would our placing faith in Christ, without being regenerated first, mean we contribute something to salvation? Is it not possible that an unregenerate person would turn in faith to Christ precisely *because* he had nothing to contribute? Remember what Machen says. That is, although he incorrectly believed that faith itself is a gift, he correctly says:

> Faith consists not in doing something but in receiving something.[443]

And:

> Faith is no more than an activity of reception contributing nothing to that which it receives.[444]

The Calvinist says:

> Faith is ... not the sinner's gift to God.[445]

Would putting your faith in Christ be *giving* a gift to God? Could it not be that faith is simply the means by which we *receive* the gift of God without our reception being considered a gift itself? How does believing in Christ, which John equates with *receiving* (John 1:12) become synonymous to the Calvinist with *giving?* In his notes concerning John 1:12, MacArthur says:

> **As many as received Him ... to those who believe in His name**. The second phrase describes the first. To receive Him who is the Word of God means to acknowledge His claims, place one's faith in Him. ...[446]

Elsewhere he says:

> "You do not receive" and "you do not believe" mean the same thing.[447]

The Calvinist view takes the means by which we *receive* the gift that God gives and says that it is "the sinner's gift to God," if indeed it comes before regeneration or as a condition of regeneration. Calvinists rightly reason:

> Man does not possess the power of self-regeneration ...[448]

If, however, we could have faith in Christ before regeneration, would it constitute the power of self-regeneration, as Calvinists charge? Is it not possible that faith is simply the condition that God, the giver of life, requires of the sinner before He will give him that life? Calvinists rightly reason:

> ... regeneration is exclusively a work of God ...[449]

If, however, God regenerates the spiritually dead on the condition of faith in Christ, that does not and cannot mean that He does not do all the work of regeneration, as Calvinists charge. Remember what Calvin said:

> If we bring nothing but faith, which strips us of all commendation, it follows that salvation does not come from us.[450]

If we do not pay attention to how the issues have been framed, we will fall into the *either/or* trap that has been set for us. I am not suggesting that the advocates of Calvinism are intentionally setting a trap. Their intention or motivation, however, is not the issue. The issue is that they have set a false either/or trap and a lot of people seem to be falling into it, not the least of whom are those advocating Calvinism. They have fallen into the proverbial pit that they themselves have dug.

The Calvinist argument boils down to the following. God alone regenerates the unregenerate. If the unregenerate must exercise faith in Christ in order to be born again, then the regenerate can take some credit for regeneration. It would not therefore be *all of God*. It would therefore be *some of man*. If you agree that it is all of God, then to be consistent, you should also agree that faith is *not required* for regeneration, but is instead a *result* of regeneration.

Is justification *all of God* or is it *some of man?* All Calvinists would agree that it is also *all of God*. Yet, every Calvinist would also agree that justification is by faith. Justification does not lead to faith, but faith leads to justification according to all Evangelicals, including Calvinists. Remember the question asked by the apostle Paul:

Who shall bring a charge against God's elect? (Rom. 8:33)

He then says:

It is God who justifies. (Rom. 8:33)

Paul also says:

Having been justified by faith, we have peace with God through our Lord Jesus Christ. (Rom. 5:1)

The Calvinist could say faith can precede and lead to justification and still not allow a man to take credit for justification because the faith that leads to justification is a gift from God. Scripturally speaking, however, since faith is neither a work nor a meritorious act of any kind, God can require a man to believe as a condition of justification, or regeneration for that matter, without surrendering any of the credit to man.

The Calvinist could say that the reason faith is not a work or a meritorious act is because it is a gift from God in the first place. Faith, however, is not scripturally viewed as work or a meritorious act simply because it is by definition something different. The writer to the Hebrews says:

He who comes to God must believe that He is. (Heb. 11:6)

It sounds very much like he is saying that *coming to God* is conditioned upon or is even synonymous with *faith in God*. The Calvinist reverses this by saying that coming to God is a prerequisite to faith. If regeneration is before faith and is a prerequisite to faith, the writer of Hebrews should have said:

He who comes to God must be born again so he can and will believe.

A Calvinist can say:

Every biblical command to people to undergo a radical change of character from self-centeredness to God-centeredness is, in effect, an appeal to be "born again."[451]

He can also say:

In regeneration a person's sinful nature is changed, and that person is enabled to respond to God in faith.[452]

What many cannot seemingly see is how absurd this sounds. It puts God in the position of appealing to many, if not most, people to radically change, but not ever intending that they should or even could change. With all this in mind, let us look once again at the Calvinist reasoning that seems so intimidating to some.

- Faith is not something man contributes to salvation.

- Faith ... is not the sinner's gift to God.

- Man does not possess the power of self-regeneration.

- Regeneration is exclusively a work of God.

It is true that faith is not something man contributes to salvation. Faith as *a condition,* however, is very different from faith as *a contribution.*

It is true that faith is not the sinner's gift to God. The exercise of faith to receive *the gift from God* does not, however, constitute *a gift to God.*

It is true that man does not possess the power of *self-regeneration.* If God requires a sinner to believe before He regenerates that sinner, it does not follow that man possesses and exercises some of the power involved in, or required for, regeneration.

It is true that regeneration is *exclusively* the work of God, but that does not mean that we would be sharing in the work of regeneration if God were to insist that we believe in Christ as a condition of regeneration.

Suppose I said (and I do):

- Man does not possess the power of self-justification (instead of *self-regeneration*).

Or:

- Justification (instead of regeneration) is *exclusively* a work of God.

Would that mean that I could not believe faith is before justification? If faith can be before justification, and if justification can be totally of God, then it can be before regeneration without giving man credit for that for which only God deserves credit. Remember the words of Romans 3:27:

> *Boasting ... is ... excluded ... by ... faith.*

In their theology Calvinists have turned faith into something we could boast about by suggesting that a pre-regeneration faith would make the believer a co-savior. They have also effectively made God the believer by their misguided notion of faith as a gift. Is it really possible that many (if not most) of those who need to be born again *cannot* be born again, and they cannot be born again because God has so *decreed and designed* that they cannot be born again? Remember what Scripture says:

> *"... you must be born again." (John 3:7)*

> *"As many as received Him* [Jesus Christ], *to them He gave the right to become children of God, to those who believe in His name: who were born, not of blood, nor of the will of the flesh, nor of the will of man, but of God." (John 1:12–13)*

> *Whoever believes that Jesus is the Christ is born of God. (1 John 5:1)*

> *"God so loved the world that He gave His only begotten Son, that whoever believes in Him should not perish but have everlasting life." (John 3:16)*

> *These* [miracles recorded in the Gospel of John] *are written that you may believe that Jesus is the Christ, the Son of God, and that believing you may have life in His name. (John 20:31)*

> *These things* [truths of John's first letter] *I have written to you who believe in the name of the Son of God, that you may know that you have eternal life. (1 John 5:13)*

He who has the Son has life. (1 John 5:12)

God ... commands all men everywhere to repent. (Acts 17:30)

"There will be ... joy in heaven over one sinner who repents." (Luke 15:7)

"There is joy in the presence of the angels of God over one sinner who repents." (Luke 15:10)

10

PERSEVERANCE OF THE SAINTS

EXPLAINED

R ELATIVE to the five points, the Calvinist view of sanctification is very close to, and in the minds of many, the same as the Calvinist doctrine of perseverance. This is the fifth point of Calvinism. Some Calvinists have a tough time embracing the third point, or limited atonement, although many non-Calvinists believe they can and do embrace the fifth point—perseverance of the saints. Usually, when non-Reformed Evangelicals say they believe in perseverance of the saints, they have something altogether different in mind than does the Calvinist. Many believers are simply confused about the meaning of the fifth point. As is the case with other distinctives of Calvinism, such confusion is not limited to the so-called lay community of believers. In the article "Resurgent Calvinism Renews Debate Over Chance for Heaven," the author says:

> Most Southern Baptists would have little quarrel with …
> Perseverance of the Saints *(once saved always saved).*[453]

As long as Christians *erroneously* assume that the Calvinist distinctive of *perseverance* means the same thing as the affirmation *"once saved always saved,"* they will continue to *incorrectly* think of themselves as in agreement with the fifth point. The Calvinist writing team of Talbot and Crampton rightly state that:

> It should be obvious that the Calvinist doctrine of the perseverance
> of the saints is not one and the same thing as "once saved, always
> saved."[454]

While it is true that Calvinists believe in *once saved always saved,* so do many non-Calvinists. What most Southern Baptists would have little quarrel with has little or nothing to do with the fifth point of Calvinism. I do not point this out to be critical of Southern Baptists. From what I can tell, the Southern Baptist Convention is doing a very good job of keeping the Calvinists from taking over. I am, however, concerned that a misunderstanding of Calvinism makes the non-Calvinist community vulnerable to the errors of Calvinism. The article "Calvinism Resurging Among the SBC's Young Elite" is a little more helpful, but it still misses the primary meaning Calvinists give to *perseverance of the saints*. The author of this article says:

> God will preserve in salvation and eternal life those He saves.[455]

If such a misunderstanding can be published in a reputable Christian magazine like *Christianity Today,* it is little wonder that so many Christians are so confused about the meaning of the fifth point. Perseverance of the saints in Calvinism is really about what I call the *inevitability principle.* The inevitability principle says:

- The way a Christian is supposed to live, throughout the course of his life as a saved person, he does so *inevitably.*

And:

- If someone, who is called a Christian, does not live the way a Christian is supposed to live, for the most part, it simply means he was never really saved.

Calvinists and non-Calvinist Evangelicals have no argument about how a Christian *should* live. According to Reformed Theology, however, there is no difference between the way a Christian *should* live and the way a Christian *will* live.

Much in *The Canons of Dort* and *The Westminster Confession of Faith* seem at first glance to contradict what I have just said. A thorough reading of these and other Reformed explanations of what Calvinism means when it talks about perseverance of the saints will clarify those general statements and thereby support my contention. Sproul explains:

> The Reformed view of eternal security is called "perseverance of the saints." ... The idea here is ... "If you have it, you never lose it; if you lose it you never had it."[456]

There is a distinctive view of eternal security that can be called "The Reformed view of eternal security." Not all views of eternal security are

Reformed. In fact, the scriptural view of eternal security is not Reformed. Sproul also says:

> I prefer to use the term preservation of the saints. ... Preservation is what God does. We persevere because God preserves.[457]

According to Calvinism, the elect do not persevere because God enables them to persevere *as if* they have a choice to persevere or not. Reformed Theology says that the preservation of God is the cause and perseverance of the saint is the effect and is therefore inevitable for the saint.

There are basically three views among Evangelicals concerning the doctrine of eternal security. The *Arminian view* says that once you are truly saved, it is possible to lose your salvation. In effect, the Arminian says that once you are saved, you need to live as though you are saved or you will lose your salvation. Sproul quotes from the Arminian Conference of the Remonstrants as follows:

> Persons truly regenerate, by neglecting grace and grieving the Holy Spirit with sin, fall away totally, and at length finally, from grace into eternal perdition.[458]

The *Calvinist view*:

> If we have it we never lose it; if we lose it, we never had it.[459]

A *third view* (which is my view and the view of millions of other non-Arminian, non-Calvinist Evangelicals) says that once you are saved you are always saved. It does not, however, confuse the importance and need for sanctification with the "faith alone in Christ alone" requirement for justification. Like the Arminian, we do not see sanctification as automatic or inevitable, however desirous that might be. Like the Calvinist, we do not believe a regenerate child of God can be lost.

If you are a Calvinist, you could speak of *inevitability* from the point of *regeneration, saving faith,* or *justification.* In a manner of speaking, the Calvinist sees *the inevitabilities* built into unconditional election, irresistible grace, the atonement, regeneration, saving faith, and justification. Thus Calvinism says:

- If you are born again, you will live the new life (mostly) for the rest of your life, because you are born again and *cannot do otherwise.*

- If you have saving faith, which is a living faith, you will *automatically* have a *working faith* or a *faith that works* (mostly) for the rest of your life.

- If you are justified positionally or legally, you will *unavoidably* be sanctified practically or experientially, and remain so (mostly) for the rest of your life.

- What that *new life, works,* and *sanctification* amounts to or equals, according to Calvinism, is *perseverance in faith and righteousness* (mostly) *to the end.*

If you ask about the Christian who does not persevere in faith and righteousness to the very end, you have missed the meaning and implication of perseverance or the fifth point of Calvinism. That is, the true believer perseveres and cannot do otherwise. MacArthur contends that:

> Those whose faith is genuine will prove their salvation is secure by persevering to the end in the way of righteousness. ... True believers *will* persevere. If a person turns against Christ, it is proof that person was never saved.[460]

According to MacArthur:

> Genuine believers may stumble and fall, but they *will* persevere in the faith. Those who later turn completely away from the Lord show that they were never truly born again.[461]

Boice says:

> The mark of true justification is perseverance in righteousness—to the very end.[462]

The inevitability principle is not so much about what *should be,* but what *will be* and what *cannot be otherwise.* While it is often expressed in terms of persevering in faith or righteousness, it can also be understood in terms of ongoing fruitfulness. MacArthur says:

> I do believe without apology that real salvation cannot and will not fail to produce works of righteousness in the life of a true believer. ... God's work of salvation includes a change of intent, will, desire, and attitude that inevitably produces the fruit of the Spirit. The very

essence of God's saving work is the transformation of the will that results in a love for God. Salvation thus establishes the *root* that will surely produce the *fruit*.[463]

The inevitability principle is also evident in the way Calvinism relates *practical sanctification* to saving faith in Jesus Christ. *Positional* justification is that righteousness which is imputed to us through faith. *Practical* sanctification refers to righteous living. All thoughtful Evangelicals agree that positional justification always and immediately follows faith in Jesus Christ. Calvinists contend that while practical righteousness may be incomplete and progressive in the life of those who have true faith, it is inevitable that they will (mostly) live righteously. MacArthur says:

> The Apostle Paul ... saw practical righteousness as the necessary and inevitable result of true faith.[464]

In similar fashion, MacArthur says:

> Righteous living is an inevitable by-product of real faith (Romans 10:10).[465]

We will consider Romans 10:10 a little later to see if it in fact teaches what MacArthur says it does. For now, it should be noted that MacArthur rightly explains:

> Justification is distinct from sanctification because in justification God does not *make* the sinner righteous; He *declares* that person righteous (Rom. 3:28; Gal. 2:16). Justification *imputes* Christ's righteousness to the sinner's account (Rom. 4:11b) ... justification is an event, sanctification a process.[466]

Crenshaw asks:

> What is the relationship of justification to sanctification?[467]

MacArthur agrees when Crenshaw answers:

> Sanctification follows inevitably on the heels of justification. ... The Spirit irresistibly enables the saint himself to do good works. ... There is, of course, an inherent and inseparable connection between legal justification and moral sanctification, the former being the cause and the latter being the effect. Justification always

comes first logically and is always followed by sanctification automatically.[468]

Those who hold to the Calvinist view that *obedience, faithfulness, fruitfulness, perseverance in righteousness to the end* are *inevitable and automatic* for the true believer are troubled by the suggestion that a true Christian could possibly fail in these matters.

In fact, one of the more troubling ideas held by some non-Calvinists, according to MacArthur, is the view that says:

> Heaven is guaranteed to believers … but Christian victory is not.[469]

MacArthur is not saying that the *possibility* of *Christian victory* is *guaranteed to believers* but the *actuality* of Christian victory in this lifetime (at least mostly) is inevitable. In other words, the true believer cannot fail to be victorious (at least mostly) in a practical or experiential sense this side of heaven. Speaking on behalf of all *true* Christians, MacArthur says:

> … God Himself guarantees our perseverance in righteousness …[470]

A CARNAL CHRISTIAN?

The very idea that a true believer could be characterized as a carnal Christian is anathema to many of those who believe in the fifth point. MacArthur refers to what he calls "The Myth of the Carnal Christian." He says:

> The whole idea is based on a misunderstanding of 1 Corinthians 2:14–3:3.[471]

MacArthur's explanation of the behavior of at least some Christians in Corinth, however, actually supports this notion of a carnal Christian. He says:

> Paul told them their divisive behavior was unworthy of Christians: "You are still fleshly."[472]

Then in brackets, MacArthur gives us a short lesson in Greek as follows:

> [Gr. *sarkikos*, 'pertaining to the flesh, carnal'].[473]

He goes on to say:

> Clearly Paul was accusing the Corinthians of behaving like non-Christians. Factions were not the only problem at Corinth. ... Some were drunk and disorderly in the communion service ...[474]

If these are Christians, they must have been carnal Christians. Nevertheless, Reisinger goes so far as to say:

> This theory [concerning carnal Christians] is one of the most perverse teachings in our generation. It is so dangerous and self-deceiving that in many cases it is damning.[475]

Given the Calvinist doctrines of unconditional election/reprobation, definite atonement, etc., it is difficult (if not impossible) to understand how any doctrine could be damning or put at risk anyone who was not already doomed from the womb. According to Reformed Theology, just as *faith in Christ is irresistible* for the elect, so *a consistent lifelong faithfulness to Christ* (mostly) *is inevitable* for the regenerated. Calvinist John Murray argues:

> A believer cannot abandon himself to sin; he cannot come under the dominion of sin; he cannot be guilty of certain kinds of unfaithfulness.[476]

Note carefully that he does not say a Christian *should not* abandon himself to sin, come under the dominion of sin, or be guilty of certain kinds of unfaithfulness, but that he *cannot*. Richard Alderson, in his book *No Holiness, No Heaven,* gives this notion a very Calvinist-sounding spin when he says:

> By this lack of holiness they prove they were not so predestined.[477]

This brings us full circle. The Calvinist reasons that since God is sovereign:

- Man has been predestined to heaven or hell and has no say in where he ends up. This also means the reprobate have no responsibility for where they go.

- If a man has the advantage to be among the elect, he will be regenerated irresistibly.

- If a man has been regenerated, he will have a saving faith.

- If a man has a saving faith, he will be justified.

- If a man has been justified, he will persevere in faith and righteousness (mostly) to the end, proving he was among the elect and so predestined to be among the elect.

- If a man does not persevere in faith and righteousness to the end (at least mostly), he simply proves he had the disadvantage of never being among the elect but was instead one of the reprobate.

ASSURANCE WITHOUT SECURITY?

The Calvinist doctrine of perseverance of the saints allows for a formal recognition of a true believer's security of salvation. And yet according to Calvinism, no true believer can have assurance of salvation because full assurance cannot come until you arrive at the end of your earthly sojourn. That is, a believer can only have certain proof of divine preservation and election *after* he has persevered to the very end. That is why John Piper says:

> We do not breathe easy after a person has prayed to receive Christ.
> ... There is a fight of faith to be fought. We must endure to the end
> in faith if we are to be saved.[478]

This does not mean that the elect ultimately can be lost according to Reformed Theology. For in keeping with all Calvinists, Piper also says:

> God's elect cannot be lost. This is why we believe in eternal secu-
> rity—namely, the eternal security of the elect. The implication is
> that God will so work that those whom he has chosen for eternal sal-
> vation will be enabled by him to persevere in faith to the end ...[479]

This enablement Piper refers to, however, does not simply make perseverance *possible*. It makes perseverance *inevitable*. The person, therefore, who does not persevere to the end proves he is not elect and therefore not saved or a true believer after all. Since no one except God can know for a certainty that a person will persevere to the end, full assurance of salvation is not possible this side of glory, according to Calvinism. Now if regeneration, and the saving faith that comes with it, inevitably leads to a persevering righteousness, then all we can do is try to ensure that someone has really placed a saving faith in Jesus Christ, and righteous living will automatically and inevitably be the result.

There is no need for exhortation, warning, or ministry of any kind to the saved, except as a matter of obedience to God. Why? Because if we are trying to encourage godliness in the life of the believer in our ministry to the believer, and yet the true believer inevitably and unavoidably will persevere in righteousness to the end, it is clear that our efforts are not really needed. And if we are trying to encourage godliness in the life of someone we mistakenly think is a believer, we are encouraging him to do what he absolutely cannot do.

These matters were settled in eternity past, and we are altogether helpless to make a difference, according to Reformed Theology. When you think about it, Christians are really quite useless when it comes to affecting the destiny of the lost and when it comes to making much of a difference in the life of the saved *if* Reformed Theology is an accurate reflection of biblical theology.

This is not the picture painted by Scripture. While Scripture never divorces sanctification *from* justification, just as clearly, it distinguishes *between* them. While God gives us all we need for a victorious life, victory is not guaranteed or inevitable. By suggesting otherwise, the Calvinist view undermines the very thing it claims to be trying to accomplish in the Christian community. That is, if you want to see more godliness among believers, the last thing you should be doing is telling them that godliness is inevitable, automatic, or guaranteed. This is not the approach the writers of the New Testament embraced.

It is certainly true that not everyone who professes to be a Christian is a Christian. Some are mistaken. Some are pretending. At the risk of belaboring the point, however, if all true believers persevere to the end, why does Scripture so often encourage the saints to persevere and just as often warn them of the consequences of not persevering?

Surely Calvinists should understand that if saints persevere because they are saints and cannot do otherwise, then no lack of exhortation or warning is going to prevent them from persevering. If one cannot be a saint because he has not been elected to salvation, no amount of encouragement or warning is going to help him persevere in a faith he does not, cannot, and should not have to persevere in.

Nothing, however, could be more obvious than this: Christians are repeatedly encouraged to persevere. Just as clearly, they are constantly warned of the consequences for not persevering throughout the pages of the New Testament. To challenge perseverance of the saints in the Calvinist sense is not to deny eternal security. To affirm the Calvinist type of perseverance is, however, to deny the believer real assurance.

PERSEVERANCE AND ASSURANCE

It must also be stressed that a challenge to the Calvinist view of perseverance of the saints is not to deny the importance of saints persevering—even to the end. Scripture is replete with exhortations and warnings regarding perseverance. Still, according to Calvinism, salvation, justification, and sanctification are hardly distinguishable. Thus, the problem with Calvinist perseverance is not in its overemphasis, but in its *mis*-emphasis. Not only so, but a case can be made for the fact that Calvinism can actually result in an *under*-emphasis on sanctification. That is, since perseverance is a foregone conclusion for the elect, the one who believes he is elect and born again may pay less attention to exhortations and warnings about perseverance. Why? If he is saved, he *will* persevere. Since you cannot do anything about being elected or not elected, you cannot do anything about all that is inevitable because you are elected or not elected. This includes perseverance.

As a side note, there is a little known dark secret of Calvin that further undermines anyone's assurance that he is one of the elect. Calvin actually taught that someone who is not elect, who is reprobate, who is damned from all eternity for all eternity, could actually and sincerely believe he is elect and loved by God. This "false work of grace" ultimately is caused, not by the individual's own flawed thinking, but by God's own work in his darkened heart:

> Experience shows that the reprobate are sometimes affected in a way so similar to the elect, that even in their own judgment there is no difference between them. ...

> The Lord, the better to convict them, and leave them without excuse, instills into their minds such a sense of his goodness as can be felt without the Spirit of adoption. ...

> Still it is correctly said, that the reprobate believe God to be propitious to them, inasmuch as they accept the gift of reconciliation,

though confusedly and without due discernment. ... Nor do I even deny that God illumines their minds to this extent, that they recognize his grace; but that conviction he distinguishes from the peculiar testimony which he gives to his elect in this respect, that the reprobate never obtain to the full result or to fruition. ... Thus we dispose of the objection, that if God truly displays his grace, it must endure for ever. There is nothing inconsistent in this with the fact of his enlightening some with a present sense of grace, which afterward proves evanescent.[480]

In Calvin's commentary on Hebrews he said that the same kinds of spiritual blessings that are given by God to the elect can be given to the reprobate:

But I cannot admit that all this is any reason why he should not grant the reprobate also some taste of his grace, why he should not irradiate their minds with some sparks of his light, why he should not give them some perception of his goodness, and in some sort engrave his word on their hearts. Otherwise where would be the temporary faith mentioned by Mark 4:17? There is therefore some knowledge even in the reprobate, which afterwards vanishes away, either because it did not strike roots sufficiently deep, or because it withers, being choked up.

And by this bridle the Lord keeps us in fear and humility; and we certainly see how prone human nature is otherwise to security and foolish confidence.[481]

Where, then, is the "assurance" of Calvinism? It cannot come to anyone until the moment of death—when one has finished the race without falling away. It can only come when one's sincere experience of salvation is finally confirmed by God and one finally knows for sure that he is truly elect, and not merely a reprobate confused by God into falsely believing that he is a true believer.

When we define perseverance (at least as it is worked out behaviorally) as faithfully following Christ, being obedient to God's Word, and walking in the light, we can see that perseverance is what *ought* to be true for every Christian. Believers are encouraged to do this and warned about failing to, precisely because we have a *tendency* or *inclination* to not do it.

PERSEVERANCE OF THE SAINTS

SCRIPTURALLY REFUTED

D OES the apostle Paul teach us that righteous living is inevitable for those who have true faith in Jesus Christ? Is that what Paul was telling us in Romans 10:10? Paul says:

> *With the heart one believes unto righteousness, and with the mouth confession is made unto salvation.*

Is this the righteous living that comes from faithfully following Christ? Or is this the imputed righteousness that comes to those who believe with faith alone in Christ alone? In other words, is Paul talking about justification or sanctification? Is he talking about coming to Christ in faith, or persevering in faith for Christ? Consider the exhortation of Paul to the believers in the Colossian church:

> *As you therefore have received Christ Jesus the Lord, so walk in Him. (Col. 2:6)*

Now if it is a foregone conclusion that a true believer will always continue to walk in Christ in the sense in which Paul is speaking, why encourage him to do so? With this in mind, consider Romans 12:1–2 (NASB):

> *I urge you therefore, brethren, by the mercies of God, to present your bodies a living and holy sacrifice, acceptable to God. ... do not be conformed to this world, but be transformed ... that you may prove what the will of God is, that which is good and acceptable and perfect.*

It seems clear that Paul exhorts the believer this way because:

- This is what the believer *ought to do.*

- The believer, without such exhortation, *is less inclined to do this.*

The fact that perseverance to the end is not inevitable for true believers, as Calvinists want us to believe, is acknowledged, perhaps unwittingly, by Calvinist John Piper when he says:

> The fact that such a thing is possible is precisely why the ministry of the Word in every local church must contain many admonitions to the church members to persevere in faith and not be entangled in those things which could possibly strangle them and result in their condemnation.[482]

Persevering in faith assumes that one has faith in which to persevere. If so, these words of Piper not only deny the Calvinist doctrine of perseverance, but also the biblical doctrine of a believer's security. My guess is that he did not really mean to say what he said or that he did not think it through very well. Regardless, he is right about the need for "admonitions to the church members to persevere in faith and not to be entangled ..." With at least this much I agree.

THE CASE OF THE CARNAL CHRISTIAN

Is it impossible for a true Christian to live in a manner that would justifiably earn him the label of *carnal Christian,* as the Calvinist contends? The Calvinist view, based on the inevitability factor, says that there can be no such person. Yet Reisinger, who so vehemently opposes the idea that one could be a *carnal Christian,* also says that:

> ... Those [in Corinth] who fell into strife, division, and contentions over ministers in chapters 1–3 [of 1 Cor.] were carnal, resembling the unregenerate, in that particular respect.[483]

If they resemble the unregenerate and yet they are not unregenerate, they must be regenerate. If they are regenerate, they are Christians. If they are Christians living like non-Christians, that makes them carnal Christians. In addition to MacArthur's earlier admission from Chapter Ten, MacArthur also concedes that:

> Although Corinthian believers were no longer "natural," they were not "spiritual" (fully controlled by the Holy Spirit). In fact, they were "carnal" (controlled by the fallen flesh).[484]

This is exactly what is meant by the words "carnal Christian." No Christian I am aware of is condoning carnality. No Christian I know of has anything good to say about carnal behavior among Christians. The question is not, *should* Christians be carnal? Of course they should not. The question is, *can* they be? Is there scriptural evidence to suggest that Christians sometimes do behave in a carnal fashion? And, most importantly, what is the best way to discourage carnality in the life of a believer or in the church as a whole?

The Calvinist must be very careful how he answers this question. Every believer knows other believers they would consider to be carnal Christians according to Paul's definition. Every earnest minister would want to do everything possible to keep this from becoming a long-term pattern in the life of that Christian. If that person remains carnal for a prolonged period of time, however, then it is clear, according to Calvinism, that he is not persevering in righteousness. Surely MacArthur does not believe that being controlled by the "fallen flesh" is persevering in righteousness. If a person claiming to be a Christian is not persevering in righteousness, either he is not a Christian, or perseverance in righteousness is not inevitable. If the Calvinist throws out the inevitability principle, he virtually denies the essence of the fifth point and by extension all five points of Calvinism.

One thing is certain from the record of Scripture and from the common experience of Christians throughout history and everywhere. Despite the way a Christian ought to live, despite all the spiritual help and resources at our disposal, some Christians do not live the way they should. None of us always lives the way we should. Calvinists and non-Calvinists agree on this much. The Calvinist, however, contends that all true Christians persevere to the end in righteousness and faith. I only wish that were so. Paul was very troubled that some in the church of Corinth were not only causing strife and division—and therefore earned the label *carnal*—but that some were even engaged in an outrageous display of immorality.

Nowhere in this text is there the slightest hint that the guilty parties are not real Christians. In fact, just the opposite is true. It was this very fact that gave Paul such concern. Paul expected and accepted that unbelievers would live lives of immorality. Christians, however, were not supposed to do so. To the Corinthians he says:

It is actually reported that there is sexual immorality among

you, and such sexual immorality as is not even named among the
Gentiles—that a man has his father's wife! (1 Cor. 5:1)

Paul went on to refer to these people and the activities in which they were engaged as *leaven.* He chides:

Do you not know that a little leaven leavens the whole lump?
Therefore purge out the old leaven, that you may be a new lump.
(1 Cor. 5:6–7)

From the context of this passage, we are given every reason to believe that this particular display of immorality was so troubling precisely because the guilty party was a true Christian. That is, the one "named a brother" was indeed a brother.

Some of what troubled Paul was the way the Corinthian church responded or failed to respond to this immorality. He says that they were *puffed up* and their *glorying* was *not good.* Whatever he meant by *glorying,* we know that it was *not good.* This just demonstrates that individual Christians and whole congregations of believers can behave, to varying degrees, as carnal Christians.

To recognize carnality among believers is not to condone it. A failure to admit that Christians are capable of being carnal Christians may be one reason why some Christians can seemingly get away with or excuse carnality in their lives. After all, if they are true Christians, they cannot be carnal Christians, according to the Calvinist view. They can then look at their lives with Calvinist-colored lenses and reason, "since I am a Christian, I cannot be carnal." A denial of carnality among Christians does not promote spirituality, but it can cause self-delusion among believers. Reisinger never tells us how it is that the Corinthian Christians can be carnal in the way that he admits they were, "in that particular respect," and at the same time deny that a true Christian can be carnal.

It is certain, however, that they did, according to Reisinger, "resemble the unregenerate, in that particular respect." This is not the only reference to Christians resembling non-Christians in Scripture. So much that is said in Scripture challenges the inevitability principle in general, and the *no such thing as a carnal Christian* contention of the Calvinist view in particular. For example, if persevering in righteousness is inevitable for the true believer, there is no need for the apostle Paul to tell the Corinthian believers to:

Flee sexual immorality. (1 Cor. 6:18)

There is no need to flee from something that cannot hurt or overcome you. Now at this point, the Calvinist will argue that they do not deny that a Christian can fall into a serious sin such as represented by sexual immorality. And, of course, it is true that they allow for such spiritual lapses. If, however, we are to take the inevitability principle seriously, we must conclude that no matter how serious that fall may be, it will only be temporary. According to the inevitability principle, righteous behavior will always characterize the greater part of a true believer's life, from the point of regeneration on. So while it may be grieving to see a brother fall, it poses no lasting threat, according to the fifth point.

According to the fifth point of Calvinism, if someone who *seems* to be a Christian does not recover from what *appears* to be a fall for a prolonged period of time, it proves he was not really a brother in the first place. The very passages, however, that advocates of Calvinism use to *prove* a true Christian cannot fall into a long-term or even a lifetime pattern of sinful behavior prove just the opposite. For example, consider the following words of the apostle Paul in his letter to the church in Ephesus:

Therefore be imitators of God as dear children. And walk in love, as Christ also has loved us and given Himself for us, an offering and a sacrifice to God for a sweet-smelling aroma.

But fornication and all uncleanness or covetousness, let it not even be named among you, as is fitting for saints; neither filthiness, nor foolish talking, nor coarse jesting, which are not fitting, but rather giving of thanks. For this you know, that no fornicator, unclean person, nor covetous man, who is an idolater, has any inheritance in the kingdom of Christ and God. Let no one deceive you with empty words, for because of these things the wrath of God comes upon the sons of disobedience. Therefore do not be partakers with them.

For you were once darkness, but now you are light in the Lord. Walk as children of light (for the fruit of the Spirit is in all goodness, righteousness, and truth), finding out what is acceptable to the Lord. And have no fellowship with the unfruitful works of darkness, but rather expose them. For it is shameful even to speak of those things which are done by them in secret. But all things that

are exposed are made manifest by the light, for whatever makes
manifest is light. Therefore He says: "Awake, you who sleep, arise
from the dead, and Christ will give you light."

See then that you walk circumspectly, not as fools but as wise,
redeeming the time, because the days are evil. Therefore do not
be unwise, but understand what the will of the Lord is. And do not
be drunk with wine, in which is dissipation; but be filled with the
Spirit. (Eph. 5:1–18)

A number of things relevant to our present discussion are stated in these
verses of Scripture.

- It is "not fitting" for a saint to commit sin. Whether it is "fornication" or "coarse jesting," it is "not fitting." That is, it is entirely inap-
  propriate and unacceptable behavior for a Christian.

- A fornicator in particular or an unclean person in general (i.e., sinners of all kinds) forfeits "any inheritance in the kingdom of Christ
  and God."

- These sins result in the "wrath of God" coming upon "the sons of
  disobedience."

- Christians are commanded not to be "partakers with" the children of
  "disobedience."

- Christians are called upon to act in accordance with what they are
  now (i.e., light in the Lord) as opposed to what they once were (i.e.,
  darkness).

- Christians are exhorted to "walk circumspectly, not as fools but as
  wise."

- Christians should be "redeeming the time … understand[ing] what
  the will of the Lord is."

- Christians are told, "Do not be drunk with wine … but be filled with
  the Spirit."

It would seem very reasonable to assume that Christians are warned
about sin of all kinds precisely because they are capable of falling into sin
of all kinds. Due to the deceptive and enslaving capacity of sin, spiritual

recovery and restoration is not a foregone conclusion as the Calvinist view maintains. It would also seem reasonable to assume that the reason Christians are encouraged to go in the right direction, as opposed to the wrong direction, is because going in the right direction, or living righteously, is not inevitable for Christians. Those things which are *not fitting* for a saint, however tragic, are *possible*. Likewise, those things which are *fitting* are *not inevitable*. Both a scriptural and a reality check will confirm the truth of what I am saying. Consider also the severe warnings of 1 Corinthians 10:1–14. Paul says:

> *I do not want you to be unaware that all our fathers were under the cloud, all passed through the sea, all were baptized into Moses in the cloud and in the sea, all ate the same spiritual food, and all drank the same spiritual drink. For they drank of that spiritual Rock that followed them, and that Rock was Christ. But with most of them God was not well pleased, for **their bodies** were scattered in the wilderness.*

> *Now these things became **our** examples, to the intent that we should not lust after evil things as they also lusted. And do not become idolaters as were some of them. As it is written, "**The people sat down to eat and drink, and rose up to play.**" Nor let us commit sexual immorality, as some of them did, and in one day twenty-three thousand fell; nor let us tempt Christ, as some of them also tempted, and were destroyed by serpents; nor complain, as some of them also complained, and were destroyed by the destroyer. Now all these things happened to them as examples, and they were written for our admonition, upon whom the ends of the ages have come.*

> *Therefore let him who thinks he stands take heed lest he fall. No temptation has overtaken you except such as is common to man; but God is faithful, who will not allow you to be tempted beyond what you are able, but with the temptation will also make the way of escape, that you may be able to bear **it**. Therefore, my beloved, flee from idolatry. (emphasis added)*

As most Calvinists would agree, if Paul is speaking to and warning Christians, then it follows that Paul believed Christians were capable of committing that which he warned them about. If he were speaking to non-Christians, then he would have preached to them a message of salvation. It is or should be clear, however, that he assumed that those he was writing to and was concerned about were already saved. The message is not about justification by faith but the need for sanctification through faithfulness. Notice what Paul says:

> *These things* [that occurred in the wilderness] *became **our** examples, to the intent that we should not lust after evil things as they also lusted. ... Now all these things happened to them as examples, and they were written for **our** admonition. (1 Cor. 10:6, 11a, emphasis added)*

The recording of these terrible things serves the Christian community as a reverse or negative example, says Paul. Instead of the, "Do as I do" kind of example, in effect he says, "Do not do as they did." "If you do, you will also be judged accordingly."

If

- The Calvinist view is right and a true believer cannot lose his salvation,

And if

- It is true that a true Christian can be guilty of the kind of behavior Paul warns against,

Then

- Whatever is lost or forfeited (i.e., the inheritance) for such behavior is not justification or glorification, but some or even most of the benefits and blessings available, but not guaranteed to the saved. This applies to time and eternity. In other words, just as Christian victory is not guaranteed, so Christian rewards are not guaranteed to the non-victorious.

If it were inevitable or automatic that the true Christian would live righteously, there would hardly have been a need for Paul to tell believers:

> *Put off all these: anger, wrath, malice, blasphemy, filthy language. ... (Col. 3:8)*

These kinds of things should not be tolerated in the Christian community. They are wrong and unacceptable. To say, however, that no real

Christian is capable of a pattern of behavior that is characterized as sinful or carnal is simply unscriptural and unrealistic. Paul exhorts those born of God to:

> **Put off,** *concerning your former conduct,* **the old man** *which grows corrupt according to the deceitful lusts, and be renewed in the spirit of your mind, and* [...] **put on the new man** *which was* **created** *according to God,* **in true righteousness and holiness.** *(Eph. 4:22–24, emphasis added)*

And:

> **Put on the new man who is renewed in knowledge according to the image of Him** *who created him. (Col. 3:10, emphasis added)*

These are exhortations and admonitions to the saved, encouraging them to live a sanctified life. Nothing is taken for granted in this regard.

EXHORTATIONS TO ABIDE—MEANINGLESS?

In John Chapter Fifteen, where Jesus is talking to the disciples concerning their relationship to Him as the true vine, He exhorts them to abide in Him that they might bear fruit. He then, in verse six, brings up the possibility of not abiding in Him and the subsequent consequences. This warning is totally meaningless and unnecessary if the Calvinist position on perseverance is correct. Sproul, who spends a considerable amount of time defending the Calvinist view of perseverance, asks:

> If no one falls away, why even bother to warn people against it?[485]

Sproul also admits:

> It seems frivolous to exhort people to avoid the impossible.[486]

While Sproul attempts to explain why it is not frivolous to warn people of the impossible, he at least seems to understand why non-Calvinists might find the Calvinist view of perseverance fraught with problems. In the opening verses of the Second Epistle of Peter, we read:

> *Simon Peter, a bondservant and apostle of Jesus Christ, to those who have obtained like precious faith with us by the righteousness of our God and Savior Jesus Christ:*

Grace and peace be multiplied to you in the knowledge of God and of Jesus our Lord, as His divine power has given to us all things that pertain to life and godliness, through the knowledge of Him who called us by glory and virtue, by which have been given to us exceedingly great and precious promises, that through these you may be partakers of the divine nature, having escaped the corruption that is in the world through lust.

But also for this very reason, giving all diligence, add to your faith virtue, to virtue knowledge, to knowledge self-control, to self-control perseverance, to perseverance godliness, to godliness brotherly kindness, and to brotherly kindness love. (1:1–7)

SPIRITUAL BUILDING BLOCKS

The things Christians are told to add to faith, including *perseverance,* are not *automatically* added to the life of the true believer. If they were, there would be no need to exhort the true believer to add them. To say they are not inevitable is not to say they are not important. Just the opposite is true. That is, that which will come to pass inevitably is nothing to be concerned about. If we can liken each of these additions to our faith as important building blocks for a truly spiritual and productive life, we can see why Peter says *"giving all diligence, add to your faith ..."* This is exactly the point Peter is making and why he goes on to say:

For if these things are yours and abound, you will be neither barren nor unfruitful in the knowledge of our Lord Jesus Christ. For he who lacks these things is shortsighted, even to blindness, and has forgotten that he was cleansed from his old sins.

Therefore, brethren, be even more diligent to make your call and election sure, for if you do these things you will never stumble; for so an entrance will be supplied to you abundantly into the everlasting kingdom of our Lord and Savior Jesus Christ.

For this reason I will not be negligent to remind you always of these things, though you know and are established in the present truth. Yes, I think it is right, as long as I am in this tent, to stir you up. (2 Pet. 1:8–13)

The apostle John says:

> *He who says he abides in Him* [Christ] ***ought*** *himself also to walk*
> *just as He walked. (1 John 2:6, emphasis added)*

There is nothing inevitable about what *ought* to be. If it were inevitable, the apostle would have used the word *will,* instead of the word *ought.* The apostle John also says:

> *By this we know love, because He* [Christ] *laid down His life for*
> *us. And we also* ***ought*** *to lay down our lives for the brethren.*
> *(1 John 3:16, emphasis added)*

We know what to do for each other because of what He did for us. We know what we *ought* to do. The question is, will we do it? The apostle Peter does not seem to take righteous living for granted when he says:

> *Beloved, I* ***beg*** *you as sojourners and pilgrims, abstain from*
> *fleshly lusts which war against the soul, having your conduct*
> *honorable among the Gentiles. (1 Pet. 2:11, emphasis added)*

If we are unconditionally guaranteed a victorious Christian life as true Christians, then nothing we do or fail to do will alter this fact. There certainly would have been no need for Peter to resort to begging them to stay away from these sinful activities. Holy living is not guaranteed because we are Christians. Rather, it is guaranteed if we yield to the Holy Spirit and live in accordance with God's holy Word. We need to take advantage of what is available to us and walk in the Spirit. As the apostle Paul told the church in Galatia:

> *Walk in the Spirit, and you shall not fulfill the lust of the flesh.*
> *(Gal. 5:16)*

Ware rightly reasons:

> … When believers are admonished to "live by the Spirit, and you
> will not gratify the desires of the sinful nature" (Gal. 5:16), clearly
> the implication is that they may choose not to live by the Spirit's
> power, thus resisting the gracious and transforming work he wishes
> to accomplish in their lives. Not all grace, then, is irresistible.[487]

Although it may not seem so to Ware, such reasoning contradicts the heart of the Calvinist view of perseverance.

THE CHALLENGE AND THE GOAL

The apostle Paul constantly warns believers about the serious consequences of a sinful pattern of behavior. By reducing perseverance to an *inevitability,* as does the fifth point, all of these words of encouragement and warning are in a very real sense wasted. In Scripture, however, *perseverance in faith and holiness* to the end is seen as the sacred challenge and reasonable goal of our earthly sojourn on our way to our heavenly home. Perseverance in faith and righteousness should be sought after earnestly. In fact, to say that perseverance is what we *will* do because we are true believers is to radically redefine the meaning of perseverance. Instead, we need to see perseverance as what we *ought* to do because we are true believers. God is more than able and always willing to help us persevere in faith and righteousness. We must, however, yield to the work of God's Holy Spirit in concert with God's holy Word.

Perseverance of the saints as defined by Calvinism says that a Christian is eternally secure, or that once a Christian is saved, he will always be saved. The doctrine of eternal security, or "once saved, always saved," is not, however, unique to Calvinism. As already noted, it is possible to have a doctrine of eternal security, one which conforms to what Scripture says, without sacrificing the believer's assurance of salvation. Compare the following two very different versions of eternal security:

- The Calvinist says that you are eternally secure *for* all eternity because you have been eternally secure *from* all eternity. Faith in Christ during your sojourn in this life is a mere consequence of unconditional election, irresistible grace/the effectual call, regeneration, and Christ's death on behalf of the elect. Your response to the gospel is an eternally foregone conclusion. It does not *make* a difference so much as it *reflects* a difference. The difference it reflects is your unconditional election to salvation.

- The non-Calvinist who believes in eternal security believes you are eternally secure because you met the sole, sufficient, and necessary condition for salvation. That sole, sufficient, and necessary condition for salvation is faith alone in Christ alone. Your believing response to the gospel, therefore, makes an eternal difference.

- For the Calvinist, once you are saved, you are really no more eternally secure than you were before you were saved. By placing your faith in Christ, you merely prove you were one of the elect that Christ died for. It is election and atonement that guarantees your security. Faith in Christ simply proceeds directly, irresistibly, and inevitably from unconditional election, effectual grace, and the atonement.

- For the non-Calvinist, once you are saved, you then, and only then, become eternally saved and can say with confidence that you will always be saved.

- The Calvinist says that what you do after you are saved is merely the necessary proof that you are saved and have always been destined for salvation.

- The non-Calvinist says that what you do after you are saved is proof of your love for God or evidence of your failure to love Him, and therefore very important. Loving God results in obedience to Him and is rewarded both in time and eternity. A failure to love and obey God for the believer results in a serious loss both in time and eternity.

Typical of Calvinism, Paul Enns equates perseverance of the saints with the Calvinist doctrine of the believer's security.

He then immediately explains:

> Those whom Christ chose and died for are eternally secure in their salvation; they can never fall away or be lost once they are saved.[488]

Notice that for the Calvinist, eternal security is connected to election and the atonement. Faith in Christ is merely an unavoidable result. It would be just as accurate to say that the lost who are elect can never perish and are therefore never at risk. Even their lostness is only apparent. Calvinists usually give some kind of formal acknowledgment of the role man plays in coming to faith in Christ and in continuing in faithfulness to Him. As noted many times, however, this does not amount to much more than theological lip service. Allow me to explain. On the surface, to say saints must persevere in faith and righteousness to the end seems to place a serious and sobering responsibility on the believer. In the New Testament, of course, perseverance is a serious and sobering responsibility, though we are not left without divine resources and help in rising to this sacred challenge.

Calvinists, however, make it clear that what may sound like human perseverance is really divine preservation. As a believer, you are not really persevering in faith and righteousness, but God is preserving you in faith and righteousness to the end. This perseverance in faith and righteousness to the end must not be thought of as merely positional but practical as well. That is, what you must do to persevere in faith and righteousness, God does in and through you, according to the fifth point. But still, since you cannot be sure that you are one of the elect until you have persevered in faith and righteousness to the end, the Calvinist doctrine of salvation provides no more assurance of salvation than Arminianism does, and perhaps less. As a result of the Calvinist doctrine of perseverance, Boettner believes:

> We can never know that we are elected of God to eternal life except by manifesting in our lives the fruits of election—faith and virtue, knowledge ... love of brethren. It is idle to seek assurance of election outside of holiness of life.[489]

Compare this with the words of the apostle John:

> *Whoever believes that Jesus is the Christ is born of God. ... (1 John 5:1)*

> *God has given us eternal life, and this life is in His Son. (1 John 5:11)*

> *He who has the Son has life. ... (1 John 5:12)*

> *These things I have written to you who believe in the name of the Son of God, that you may know that you have eternal life. ... (1 John 5:13)*

As important as faithfulness to Christ is, biblically based assurance of salvation is linked to *faith in* Christ, not *faithfulness to* Christ. The Reformed doctrine of perseverance of the saints, for all practical purposes, confuses *faith in Christ,* which is requisite to justification with *faithfulness to Christ,* which is requisite to sanctification.

12

THE SIXTH POINT OF CALVINISM

CALVINISTS sometimes seem to affirm freedom of choice for a lost man regarding where he will spend eternity. Calvinism as a system, however, will not allow it. The primary reason Calvinism denies man this freedom is found in a seriously flawed definition of sovereignty. Despite the fact that Calvinists see themselves as the vanguards of divine sovereignty, the concept of sovereignty as found in Calvinism undermines and degrades the concept of sovereignty found in Scripture.

One of the ways in which Calvinism undermines the biblical concept of divine sovereignty is by confusing it with the biblical concept of divine freedom. For some Calvinists, such as James White, God's sovereignty and God's freedom are practically synonymous. It is truly doubtful that any thoughtful Evangelical would disagree with the fact that God is absolutely free because He is absolutely sovereign—and He is absolutely sovereign if, and only if, He is absolutely free. According to White, however, the problem is:

> Sin causes man to constantly seek to insert himself into the work of God in salvation, so every generation has to be reminded of their complete dependence upon Him and of His perfect salvation. That is one reason why I do not believe the common "Five Points" ... is enough for today. There is a sixth point that lies at the head of the list, which must be firmly proclaimed and defended today: the freedom of God. While it may have been taken for granted a few centuries ago, today it is surely a belief under fire. But since it lies at the very heart of the debate, we need to begin with a discussion of what it means.[490]

On one hand, the Calvinist doctrine of sovereignty teaches us that everything is as it ought to be. In other words, things are as the sovereign God desired, determined, and even decreed them to be. Thus, according to Calvinism, if God is on the throne, in charge, and in control, things could not be other than they are, unless He had determined or decreed them to be some other way.

On the other hand, Calvinists constantly bemoan the fact that man (especially those pesky Arminians) does not accept God's sovereignty but openly denies and even attempts to resist that sovereignty. They do this without even noticing how inconsistent this view is. Assuming Calvinism is true, how can man (even an Arminian man) do anything to offend God, or please Him for that matter, that God did not sovereignly predestine that he would and should do?

Calvinists may speak of sin causing this or that thing to happen in a secondary sense, but in the primary and morally responsible sense, a consistent Calvinism teaches that God causes everything, including sin and the refusal of some men to embrace Calvinism. Some Calvinists may not mean to teach this and may even deny that this is what they are teaching. In such cases, however, these Calvinists are failing to understand the implicit and sometimes even explicit teachings of Reformed Theology. In fact, according to a consistent Calvinism, God "… causes man to constantly seek to insert himself into the work of God in salvation." God does so by His own irresistible determination and decree, which caused the "sin" that "causes man to constantly seek to insert himself into the work of God in salvation." A consistent Calvinism also holds that God caused James White, for example, to complain about what God caused by His irresistible decree. And according to this way of thinking, I could not escape being caused by God to point out how silly all this sounds.

In mainstream Calvinism in general, and for White in particular, the meaning of God's freedom can be stated as follows:

- God can and does as He pleases in all matters, including with man and his eternal destiny. God has the *only say* in what He does with man. Conversely, man has *no say* in what God does with him.

In more picturesque terms, the divine potter shapes the human clay into any form He pleases to use and (in the case of some) to dispose of as He pleases. Ultimately, the human clay cannot meaningfully *assist* or *resist* the way he or his future shapes up. The divine potter does as He pleases with the human clay and the human clay does as the divine potter pleases. *Period!* Even the things that we are told in Scripture that displease God are decreed by God in accordance to His own pleasure, according to a consistent Calvinism.

Focusing heavily upon the image of a potter and his clay (Romans 9), Calvinists misinterpret Paul's use of this image by going far beyond Paul's intended purpose. In fact, Calvinists not only go too far but they take you in the wrong direction. How would a consistent Calvinist answer the question "why have You made me this way?" The Calvinist could, and probably should, logically and theologically, say that even this question, along with the sinful rebellion they say it represents, is really determined and decreed by God. Not only so, but a consistent Calvinist could and should also be able to say that even the non-Calvinist misunderstanding of the biblical doctrines of salvation and damnation and the non-Calvinists' rejection of Calvinism are also determined and decreed by God. The fact that no Calvinist suggests such an interpretation for the potter and the clay only proves that Calvinists cannot go all the way down the interpretive road they are asking others to travel on. Nevertheless, for White, at least one of the issues he believes is at stake is the affirmation that:

> God truly can do as He pleases, without getting permission from anyone, including man ...[491]

Given the basic and faulty premise of Reformed Theology, how could a man object to God doing what He pleases, unless God determined and decreed that he would object to God doing what He pleases? If Reformed Theology is true, God had to decree even that.

If Calvinism's view of God's sovereignty is true, then every thought (correct or in error), every feeling (good or bad), and every statement (either for or against Calvinism) have been sovereignly determined and decreed by God. If Calvinism's view of God's sovereignty is true, we could never actually know it, test it, or argue its merits—we could only "go through the motions" that *look like* real thinking and arguing but which are actually merely the sovereignly determined and decreed acts or thoughts of God working themselves in, through, and out of us.

I have described and defined this Calvinist dilemma repeatedly because once one understands the dilemma, it seems absurd and unbelievable. Why would anyone believe such a thing? The fact is, even to have a meaningful discussion of Calvinism, some central tenets of Calvinism cannot be true and for all practical purposes must be assumed not to be true.

DEFINING DOWN SOVEREIGNTY

What if God, however, simply chose to give man a choice in where he spends eternity? Not possible, says the consistent Calvinist. For as there can be only one will that truly accomplishes anything, according to Calvinism, so there can only be one being who is free. White likes to say that he believes in libertarian free will, but only for God. Earlier I referred to this as mono-volitionism. Richard Phillips, vice president of *The Alliance of Confessing Evangelicals,* perfectly identifies the Calvinist concern by asking:

> Who is free? Man or God? Which is sovereign?[492]

For Phillips, White, and the Calvinism they represent, the answers to these questions are the theological bottom line. *God is free. Man is not.* For White, this is also to say that *God is sovereign. Man is not.* It is true that a sovereign being is by definition a free being. It is not true, however, that a free being is necessarily a sovereign being. Therefore, while it is true that an absolutely sovereign God would have to be absolutely free, as the one and only true God is, one does not have to be absolutely free to be meaningfully free. A being that is meaningfully and relatively free is not thereby *relatively sovereign,* if I may use an oxymoron to illustrate my point.

Calvinism is simply guilty of muddying the theological waters. Many hypo-Calvinists want to dance around this issue because Scripture often affirms that man is both free and responsible. They often state their view in a way that makes it *seem like* they really believe that both man and God can be free. Given enough time to explain what they mean or what is implied by their view, however, they end up denying that man is free in any meaningful or responsible way.

Mainstream Calvinists want to be able to say that both God and man are free, but object when the Biblicist does so. For when a Calvinist says that un-regenerate man is free to reject the gospel, as they often do, they mean something very different than does the non-Calvinist Evangelical. *Free* to reject, according to Calvinism, actually means exactly the same thing as *bound* to reject. When *freedom* and *bondage* mean the same thing, they mean *nothing.* When a reprobate *freely* rejects God's offer of eternal life on the condition of faith in Christ, it is, according to the Calvinist, because of his *bondage* to sin. That is, the reprobate is only free to reject, not free to accept *or* reject. Some freedom! This kind of convoluted thinking has led some very bright and godly men to say some pretty incongruent things. For example, Charles Spurgeon says:

> Free agency we may believe in, but free will is simply ridiculous.[493]

I suggest that what is really ridiculous is to believe you are a free agent in any meaningful sense, unless you have a will that is meaningfully free. In theological lockstep with Spurgeon, George Bishop says:

> Man is a free agent. But man has no free will.[494]

Pardon me if I cannot distinguish between the Calvinist definition of a free agent and my definition of a non-free agent. I fail to see how a man with no free will can still be a free agent. How can there be such a thing as free agency, without a will that is free through which the agent can express freedom or act freely? Spurgeon says:

> I believe in [the Calvinist version of] predestination ... its very jots and tittles. I believe ... that every word and thought of man ... is foreknown and foreordained [in the Calvinist sense].[495]

He also says everything:

> ... is ordained and settled by a decree which cannot be violated.[496]

Spurgeon goes on to say:

> ... I believe in the free agency of man, that man acts as he wills, especially in moral operations—choosing the evil with a will that is unbiased by anything that comes from God, biased only by his own depravity of heart and the perverseness of his habits ...[497]

Perhaps unconsciously, Spurgeon reduces the decree of God to no effect on man by saying that man's choice to commit evil is "unbiased by anything that comes from God, biased only by his own depravity of heart and the perverseness of his habits." Spurgeon asks:

> Can you understand it, for I cannot, how a man is a free agent, a responsible agent, so that his sin is his own sin and lies with him and never with God? ... I cannot comprehend it: without hesitation I believe it, and rejoice to do so, I never hope to comprehend it. I worship a God I never expect to comprehend ...[498]

The Reformed professor Douglas J. Wilson is right when he says:

> From cover to cover, the Bible teaches that divine sovereignty and
> human responsibility are compatible with one another; nowhere
> does the Bible even suggest that the affirmation of divine sover-
> eignty leads to the denial of human liberty.[499]

R. Laird Harris represents the hypo-Calvinist view as follows:

> Calvinism does not deny free will. It declares that God's sover-
> eignty extends to all things and persons, but that His sovereign
> control in some inscrutable way does not deny man's free moral
> agency and responsibility. ... Calvinism does not claim to solve the
> problem, but only to put it in the Scripture focus and leave it there,
> not going beyond what is written.[500]

Feinberg goes as far as to say:

> Common sense, let alone Scripture, suggests that we are free and
> morally responsible for our actions.[501]

To be "free and morally responsible" in Reformed Theology is, however, to be neither free nor morally responsible. Man becomes excused from
moral culpability by any view that sees man only doing what God makes
him do (by His hidden decrees). While not recognizing what they are doing, or recognizing it and not admitting it, some hypo-Calvinists engage
in a serious redefinition and defining down of the meaning of freedom to
avoid coming into conflict with the contradictions imposed by their views of
human depravity and divine sovereignty. Sometimes Calvinists will simply
accept conflicting definitions of divine sovereignty and human freedom and
leave the resulting logical problems unresolved. In fact, Calvinist Thomas
Schreiner admits:

> The scandal of the Calvinist system is that ultimately the logical
> problem posed cannot be fully resolved. The final resolution to the
> problem of human responsibility and divine justice is beyond our
> rational capacity.[502]

The example I provided earlier for the kind of Calvinist that
Feinberg refers to is Edwin Palmer. According to Palmer, a true Calvinist
embraces:

... both sides of the antinomy. He realizes that what he advocates is ridiculous.[503]

Palmer goes on to admit:

It is impossible to harmonize these two sets of data [divine sovereignty and human responsibility].[504]

The Calvinist creates and introduces this apparent paradox, with all its awful ramifications concerning the character of God and the destiny of men. He then berates us for wanting to take a probing look at the arguments and evidence offered upon which it precariously rests. While Palmer apparently does not see the utter impossibility of what he is affirming, at least he concedes that it comes across as "impossible," "ridiculous," and "nonsense." As far as concessions go, this should raise some eyebrows. What it all leads to, according to Palmer and Calvinism, is that:

This is the awesome biblical asymmetry. God ordains sin and man is to blame.[505]

"Asymmetry!" This is a nice way of saying that it is "nonsense" or "ridiculous" to say that "God ordains sin and man is to blame." If God ordains sin in the Calvinist sense, how can man be blamed in any sense? Logically and legitimately, he can't. If the Calvinist view of sovereignty and predestination did not at least *appear* to clash with human responsibility and divine justice, which Calvin and others clearly admitted it does, there would be no problem to solve or classify it as a mystery.

As we have repeatedly seen, a common defense of the contradictions of Calvinism is that we simply do not have enough information to understand the solution to the problem of reconciling divine sovereignty and human freedom and responsibility. That is not the case. Instead, the contradictions appear not because we do not have enough information. The problem for the Calvinist and for Calvinism is that we have too much information. That is why Calvinists, like many if not most non-Calvinists, simply cannot leave this matter alone. Too much scriptural information about both divine sovereignty and human responsibility are on the theological table.

What we can and should know from Scripture makes Calvinism appear to be unscriptural (as it really is). Feinberg's affirmation that sovereignty and free will are compatible is clearly defensible from a scriptural point of view.

His explanation of what it means to be free undermines and even contradicts his affirmation. For Feinberg:

> The best way out of this dilemma is for Calvinists to begin by reexamining what free will means.[506]

What Feinberg does is radically redefine and define down what it means to be free. Shortly, we will allow Feinberg to explain exactly what is involved in his reexamination of "what free will means." Before we do so, consider the following analogy, which admittedly is mine and not Feinberg's:

Suppose you have a married couple we will call Bob and Sue who cannot get along together. So you decide to *reconcile* them by replacing one of them with someone who can get along with the one you do not replace. While it may result in harmony, the original two are not reconciled but separated.

In the same way, redefining freedom as some Calvinists do does not reconcile sovereignty with freedom but instead removes meaningful freedom from the discussion. Something I will call *nominal freedom* is introduced in the place of *real freedom.*

Using our analogy of the married couple who cannot get along, let us suppose that Bob represents sovereignty and Sue represents freedom. Since it is believed that Sue cannot peacefully coexist with Bob, we replace her with Sally, whom we rename Sue, and then claim we have resolved the differences between Bob and Sue and saved the marriage.

If we did this to a married couple, everyone would see right through it. By redefining freedom, however, the Calvinist, who feels a need to reconcile divine sovereignty with human freedom, can tell everyone that this is what he has done and few seem to notice.

Some Calvinists, while defining sovereignty and freedom in a contradictory way, do not try to reconcile them. Instead, they just say that the problem of affirming both divine sovereignty and human freedom represents an irresolvable mystery for the mind of man. Still others, especially of the hyper-Calvinist camp, simply deny that unregenerate man is free in any meaningful way.

A Calvinist would go theologically ballistic if an Arminian were to define down divine sovereignty to reconcile it with a misguided notion of human freedom (as Open Theists do). While I agree that it is wrong to redefine and define down sovereignty to conform to a particular and misguided view of free will, it is equally wrong to take the *free* out of the will. Ironically, in their misguided attempt to rescue God's sovereignty from the supposed damage done by a view that accepts that man is morally free and a morally responsible agent, Calvinists actually define down sovereignty as well as freedom. Just as important, it is not necessary to do this for either scriptural or logical reasons.

Feinberg's proposed solution to the problem Calvinism has created is no solution at all. Pay very close attention to how he believes he has resolved this matter:

> People are morally responsible for their actions because they do them freely. I agree that no one can be held morally accountable for actions that are not free. … If the acts are constrained, then they are not free and the agent is not morally responsible for them. But if the act is according to the agent's desire, then even though the act is causally determined [by God], it is free and the agent is morally responsible.[507]

Feinberg is one of many Calvinists who say they believe that sovereignty and freedom are compatible. He believes in a certain kind of Calvinist determinism (i.e., what he calls "soft determinism") that says God causally determines things to happen that are at the same time freely done by morally responsible agents. The kind of causal determinism he describes, however, does not really allow for any real freedom on the part of the agent. Why? Because this so-called "non-constraining" cause involves "sufficient conditions, which incline the will *decisively* in one way or the other."[508] Feinberg is right when he reasons:

> If … the agent is causally determined by constraining forces on a particular occasion … his act on that particular occasion was [not] free.[509]

Feinberg is wrong when he reasons that if an agent is "causally determined" to act under the influence of "conditions sufficient to incline the will *decisively* in one way or the other," "his act" is free. This is like saying a man chose to commit suicide by jumping off a cliff where he was pushed with sufficient force to ensure that he would actually end up on the canyon floor below. If a police investigation were to follow the death of this man, assuming the police could determine the facts of the case, would they call it a suicide or a homicide? Would they determine the man killed himself or that someone else murdered him? The fact is, if the man was pushed hard enough to *ensure* that he would actually fall to his death, it is murder.

In like manner, if God causally determines in the way that Feinberg suggests, the agent is not really free and cannot really be morally accountable for what he was causally determined by God to do. A sufficient condition that "decisively inclines the will" is a condition that forces the agent to do what the agent does. Some Calvinists, such as Feinberg, believe they can get around this problem by saying that the agent is only doing what the agent desires and is therefore morally responsible for what he does. In the Calvinist scheme of things, this only pushes the problem back one level. Why does the agent desire to do what the agent does? Feinberg says that the agent's desire is causally determined and his will is "decisively" inclined. If such is the case, there is no rational way to deny that the agent's will and desire are under a divine and irresistible "constraining force." Feinberg, as well as many hypo-Calvinists, wants what Calvinism cannot give him. The Biblicist faces no such problem. God's absolute sovereignty does not deny human freedom but is in fact the basis for real and meaningful human freedom. If we should admit an apparent problem, it is certainly solved by the very implications of the meaning of divine sovereignty. Admittedly, there are some things even God cannot do. For example, God cannot lie because He is by nature *true*. He cannot cease to exist because He is by nature *eternal*. As Hank Hanegraaff points out:

> God is limited in His activities only in this way—He accomplishes what He wants (or wills) to accomplish. In other words, because God always acts in accord with His nature, He does not (and indeed cannot) desire to lie or deny Himself. While it is agreed that God is completely sovereign over His creation, He performs only what sovereign power can actually accomplish. To make a nonsense statement and add the words "God can ..." in front of them does not change the fact that the statement is nonsense. ... Simply because God is unable to create a hypothetical absurdity, such as a square circle, does not mean that He is not omnipotent. Instead it means that there is no such thing [and cannot be] as a square circle. The same can be said with the "heavy rock" question often asked of Christians [e.g., can God create a rock so heavy He can't lift it?]. God can lift any rock He actually creates. But there is no such thing as [and cannot be] a rock so big that an all-powerful and sovereign

Being could not lift it. So the probability of God creating one is naturally zero.[510]

Such an admission says nothing that diminishes the concepts of absolute sovereignty and omnipotence. By definition, nothing could diminish the absoluteness of God's sovereignty and omnipotence. Either He is or He is not absolutely sovereign. *Period!* Of course, men can and do deny that God is absolutely sovereign and all-powerful, but the idea of a reduced level of absolute sovereignty or omnipotence is itself absurd. It would be like saying that a man has all the money in the world in his safe, but others have some in their safes as well.

While questions such as "Can God create a rock so heavy He can't lift it?" may sound clever to the people asking them, they say nothing at all about what God can or cannot really do. In no way should they lead to an admission that God may not be sovereign or omnipotent after all. Questions like these merely reflect the inability of some men to seriously think through the questions they sometimes ask, or to see how intellectually silly questions like these really are.

Unless we say that God sovereignly determines that men will deny His sovereignty (which in some sense Calvinism does), it is evident that divine sovereignty does not cancel out human freedom. There is no definitional, logical, or scriptural reason to suggest that divine sovereignty makes it impossible for an unregenerate man, while in an unregenerate state, to make a real choice between either of two eternal destinies. The fall of Adam and the resultant depravity of man imply nothing that could possibly limit the options open to a sovereign God.

God is just as sovereign over the unregenerate as He is over the regenerate. All this is to say that an acknowledgment of divine sovereignty, consistent with what is affirmed in Scripture, overcomes any problems that might otherwise be *posed* by the limitations *imposed* by the many and serious consequences of the fall, such as *spiritual death*. To say otherwise is not to *protect* the doctrine of sovereignty, as is often claimed, but to *undermine* it. Thus, one should not appeal to the facts of either divine sovereignty or human depravity as proof that an unregenerate man can have no say in where he spends eternity. Neither divine sovereignty nor human depravity should be used as a basis for denying that a man can have a say in where he spends eternity. Sovereign power is the solution to the problems faced by the unregenerate and not a problem itself, as Calvinism has made it out to be.

The Calvinist agrees that sovereign power is the solution in that God regenerates the unregenerate. Man is spiritually dead. That is the problem. God gives life to the spiritually dead. That is the solution. There is nothing about the concept of sovereignty or the unregenerate nature of man that prevents God from enabling a spiritually dead man, while spiritually dead, to make a choice between heaven and hell. Everything about the scriptural concept of divine sovereignty says that God can make it possible for a spiritually dead man to turn in faith to Jesus Christ if that man so chooses. The question is not what *can* God do, but what *has* He done or what *will* He do?

It would not be misleading or an overstatement to say that everything Calvinism teaches about salvation and damnation can be traced to the Reformed doctrines of sovereignty and predestination. It is equally clear that it is the way that Calvinists have *defined the doctrines of sovereignty and predestination* that is responsible for so many thorny theological and logical problems. The concepts of sovereignty and predestination do not in themselves pose any real problems, especially as they are defined in light of what Scripture says about the sovereign God and the way He administers sovereign control. It is either the height of arrogance or the depth of ignorance (or both) that moves Calvinists like Leonard Coppes to say:

> Only the Calvinist ... recognizes the absolute sovereignty of God.[511]

On many different occasions, I have been asked, mostly by Calvinist acquaintances and friends, the twin questions: *Do you believe God is sovereign?* And: *Do you believe everyone and everything (acts, words, thoughts, intentions, motives, events, etc.) is according to God's sovereign will?* It might surprise some and anger others that I, as a non-Calvinist, would say *yes* to both questions. In fact, I would say that if you say yes to the first question, you must also logically say yes to the second question, as I know my Calvinist friends would agree. Where the Calvinist goes wrong is in *the way* he believes God sovereignly governs the universe.

Despite the fact that many Calvinists may and do deny this, the Calvinist view of divine sovereignty and predestination makes God, through the nature of His sovereign control of all things that come to pass, the morally responsible agent, not only of everything *moral* that comes to pass, but also of everything *immoral* that comes to pass. As most Calvinists will agree, this simply cannot be if what Scripture says about the holy nature of the sovereign God is true. Gunn is right when he says:

> The sovereignty of God also teaches that God is not the responsible author of [moral] evil, that man is a free moral agent who is not forced to sin and who is responsible for what he does.[512]

Pay very close attention, however, to how Jay Adams addresses this same issue. He says:

> God is neither the author of sin, nor sanctions it (approves of it). He is not responsible for sin, *though He decreed it.* Those guilty of sin are responsible.[513]

Can God decree sin in the Calvinist sense and not be responsible for what follows inevitably from and because of that decree? If you understand the Calvinist concept of decree, such a statement logically must be recognized for the contradiction that it is. I agree with *The Canons of Dort* when it says:

> The cause or guilt of ... unbelief and all other sins, is in no wise in God.[514]

Once, however, you take into account the meaning and implications of a divine decree as defined by Calvinists, this statement should also be recognized for the impossible contradiction that it is. I would say that if God is truly sovereign, then everyone and everything must be under God's sovereign control, and therefore everything happens *according to* the sovereign will of God. That does mean that everything that happens, happens *because* of God's sovereign control.

Whatever happens must, by definition, always be under the sovereign control of God, if God is absolutely sovereign. This is like saying a circle must be round to be a circle. If something is not round it would not be a circle. Even so, if a sovereign God administers sovereign control over everything, then nothing is or could be outside His sovereign control.

Even Calvinists, however, recognize that a sovereign God can and does command that some things should happen that do not actually happen. Needless to say, God does this without surrendering His sovereignty. Otherwise, the Calvinist would have to admit that when God commands things to happen that do not happen, He must not be commanding sovereignly.

Conversely, God can and does command that some things *should* not happen, that in fact, do happen. Those sinful or immoral things that have happened or will happen can and do happen as a result of what I will call *other* morally responsible agents. By this I mean that morally responsible agents other than God can be morally responsible for moral things that happen, under the sovereign control of God. They can and do happen without implicating God in immorality or suggesting that God is morally responsible for that immoral behavior.

Whereas Calvinists unwittingly define down human freedom to accommodate an unbiblical view of divine sovereignty, they should define up their lower view of sovereignty to accommodate for what Scripture really says about the nature of God and His sovereign control of everything. In fact, a scripturally informed doctrine of sovereignty says that everything that is under God's sovereign control (which is everything) takes place in such a way that only morally good things can be legitimately traced to God.

The decretive will of God is predictably in accord with His nature. Thus, whatever God is morally responsible for is by definition morally defensible. Conversely, if something occurs that is morally reprehensible, God cannot, by definition, be morally responsible for that something.

A scripturally informed doctrine of divine sovereignty does not say that God is morally responsible for everything that is under His sovereign control. Again, if something is morally reprehensible, it cannot rightly be traced to God in a way that suggests God is the morally responsible agent of that activity or decision. Why? It is because God is absolutely holy and only decides or acts in ways that are consistent with His holiness.

While we can and should distinguish between the will and nature of God, we should not pit the one against the other. God's decretive will is predictably and inevitably holy because God is absolutely holy. Anything that happens that is not holy must be attributed to someone other than God. Anyone who commits an immoral act must already be immoral or become immoral at the time they commit such an act. Since God is absolutely moral, He cannot do immoral things and cannot legitimately be viewed as morally responsible for immorality.

It may be helpful at this point to consider an entirely different aspect of the nature of God. Consider the omniscience of God as it is brought to bear on the future. God knows everything that will happen. What He knows will happen must happen in accordance with what He knows. Otherwise, He would not and could not have known they were going to happen. His foreknowledge, however, of what will happen is not the cause of what happens. Even Calvin admitted that foreknowledge of the future is not the cause of future events. Calvin, however, got off track by saying that God knows the future because He determined the future (in a Calvinistic sense) and all that takes place in the future.

If God determines or decides something will happen, that something has to happen. Otherwise, God would not be *omnipotent.* God, however, knows the future not simply because He determines future events by a decree. He knows *future* events because He knows *all* events—past, present, and future. God knows the future because He is *omniscient.* Some things happen because God determines they will and must happen. Some things happen because God determines to allow them to happen. The relationship to God of those things that happen differs, depending upon whether He causes or allows them to happen. The kind of responsibility God has for those things also differs depending upon whether or not He causes or allows them to happen. You can allow a thing to happen and thereby become complicit with the one that is the cause.

For example, suppose you witness a bank robbery from the safety of a secure room and choose not to report the robbery until the bank robber has left the scene of the crime. You were not the cause of the robbery, but you could have and should have prevented the robbery. You would be morally, even if not legally, culpable. Suppose, however, that you knew that by calling the police, innocent people would unnecessarily die during their intervention. In such a case, even if you were legally culpable, you certainly would not be morally culpable. Even so, God can allow things (given what He knows—which is everything) without being morally responsible for what He knows. To judge God, we would have to know what He knows and know that what He did was wrong in light of all relevant factors. If God is absolutely holy, as Scripture declares Him to be, we could only find out (if we also knew everything) that what He did was the right thing to do.

Knowing an event *is going to* occur (or even allowing for an event to occur) is no more the cause of that event occurring than is knowing an event *has occurred* is the cause of an event which has already occurred. In effect, Calvin made the divine attribute of *omniscience* a mere by-product of *omnipotence.* That is, Calvin taught that God only knows what will happen because He makes it happen by His irresistible decree. This is a fallacy of the first magnitude.

If God only knows what will happen in the future because He causes the future to occur by His irresistible decree, it would make God the primary and morally responsible cause of everything bad, wrong, and wicked, just as He is the morally responsible cause ultimately of everything that is good, right, and righteous. Such a view of God does not square with what we know of the God of Scripture and of our Lord Jesus Christ. The Psalmist tells us:

> *The LORD is righteous in all His ways. ... (Ps. 145:17)*

Job's comforters were not always right. But surely young Elihu is right when he says:

> *Far be it from God to do wickedness, and from the Almighty to commit iniquity. (Job 34:10)*

So then, how can it be said that God is in sovereign control of all things without being morally responsible for the immoral things that happen during His sovereign reign? My contention is that God is responsible for everything only in the sense that He is the uncreated Creator or the uncaused cause of everything and everyone in the original and sinless created state. He causes beings to exist who are meaningfully free and morally responsible. He does not determine all the decisions made or actions taken by those free beings He has created. As philosopher-theologian Norman Geisler says, God is the author of the *fact* of freedom without being the author of the *acts* of freedom.[515]

God is not morally responsible for the immorality of those He created. God is responsible for *creating beings that became immoral* but He is not responsible for *creating immoral beings.* In fact, no such beings were ever created. God, therefore, cannot be morally responsible for creating that which was never created. God created moral beings who, by their own choices, became immoral. God is responsible for creating the capacity for immorality but not immorality itself. Creating the capacity for immorality does not make the Creator guilty of creating immorality.

By way of analogy, suppose I were to give my daughter the keys to my car and then send her to the store. Suppose then that she deliberately runs a red light on her way there. If I had not given her keys to the car and then sent her to the store, she would not have run the red light. A link then can be made to me, but not a link which makes me legally or morally responsible for her illegal and immoral act. So it is between the sin of a sinner and the God who made the one who becomes a sinner. As long as God does not make the sinner a sinner or make the sinner sin, He cannot legitimately be viewed as morally responsible for the sin or sinfulness of the sinner.

At this juncture, it may be helpful to revisit the creation of the first man. God sovereignly created man and therefore is fully responsible for creating man and for creating man the way man was created. God is even responsible for creating man with the capacity to sin, for that is the way He created man. God is therefore responsible for the sinful capacity of the first man. However, unless you can demonstrate that there is something immoral about creating a being capable of sin, you have nothing to blame God for in His creation of man. If you could successfully argue that God created man with a *necessity* (not mere *capacity*) to sin, you could legitimately charge God with wrongdoing. For if God created man with the necessity to sin, He would be the responsible cause of sin.

Despite some non-reality based denials, Calvin makes God out to be guilty of creating a man who *had to* sin, and had to sin because God *determined, decreed,* and *willed* that he would sin. God, according to Calvin, effectively *forced* the pre-fallen Adam to sin. According to Calvin, we can only discern purpose in the fall if we see it as a push from God. At this point, it will be helpful to hear what Calvin said to his detractors regarding this matter. Calvin complained:

> They deny that it is ever said in distinct terms, God decreed that Adam should perish by his revolt. As if the same God, who is declared in Scripture to do whatsoever he pleases, could have made the noblest of his creatures without any special purpose. They say that, in accordance with free-will, he was to be the architect of his own fortune, that God had decreed nothing but to treat him according to his desert. If this frigid fiction is received, where will be the omnipotence of God, by which, according to his secret counsel on which every thing depends, he rules over all? But whether they will allow it or not, predestination is manifest in Adam's posterity.

> It was not owing to nature that they all lost salvation by the fault of one parent. Why should they refuse to admit with regard to one man that which against their will they admit with regard to the whole human race? Why should they in cavilling lose their labor? Scripture proclaims that all were, in the person of one, made liable to eternal death. As this cannot be ascribed to nature, it is plain that it is owing to the wonderful counsel of God.[516]

In truth and according to Scripture, you cannot blame God for wrongdoing because He did nothing, does nothing, and can do nothing wrong. It is not wrong to create someone *capable of sinning*. It would be wrong to create someone *incapable of not sinning*. But only in the mind of Calvin and in the theology of Calvinism was such a man ever created by God. God is responsible for creating Adam, but not morally responsible for the immorality of Adam as Calvin and Calvinism make Him out to be.

The sinful Adam was no less under God's sovereign control than was the sin-free Adam. By definition he could not be. And assuming a sinful Adam could do good things (e.g. tell the truth) after becoming a sinner, his sinful acts (e.g. lying) could be no less in God's sovereign will than his sin-free acts. I doubt a sinful man could ever do something that subjectively speaking was totally free from the influence of sin. Objectively, however, bad men can do good things. The bad things, however, that a man does cannot be traced back to God, and do not have a relationship to God the way we can trace good things to God.

Adam's immoral or sinful acts, insofar as moral culpability is concerned, can only be traced back to Adam and perhaps to the influence of his wife and Satan. Despite what Calvin taught, God, in no sense, can be viewed legitimately as a morally responsible party (directly or indirectly, primarily or secondarily) of Adam's fall. He is not the cause of Adam's sin. God created Adam with the capacity to sin but also with a capacity to resist sin. God also gave Adam incentive not to sin in the form of a command not to sin and a warning which spelled out consequences if he did sin.

The real influence of God was in opposition to sin. God is innocent, therefore, of any charge that He is somehow the morally responsible cause or even a morally co-responsible cause of the sin that Adam committed or that anyone commits. God's sovereignty works in perfect concert with His absolutely holy nature and character. Just as God cannot surrender His sovereignty, He cannot sovereignly do anything contrary to His holiness. God simply does not and cannot work in conflict with His nature, which is absolutely holy.

Consider the relationship you have with the rest of humanity. (This is admittedly a narrow, limited analogy, but in the following sense, it is applicable.) You are related to everyone through Adam. You are closer (relationally) to some people than you are to others. You are closer to your sister than to your third cousin, though you are related to both. The kind of relationship you have with one person is also very different from the kind of relationship you have with another person. I have a close relationship with my daughter and a close relationship with my wife. The nature of the relationship I have with each is, however, very different. The relationship I have with a casual acquaintance, an enemy, or even someone I have never met is even more different. Even so, all things are related to God in *some sense,* but not all things are related to God in the *same sense.* This is why the apostle James says:

> *Let no one say when he is tempted, "I am tempted by God"; for God cannot be tempted by evil, nor does He Himself tempt anyone. But each one is tempted when he is drawn away by his own desires and enticed. Then, when desire has conceived, it gives birth to sin; and sin, when it is full-grown, brings forth death.*

> *Do not be deceived, my beloved brethren. Every good gift and every perfect gift is from above, and comes down from the Father of lights, with whom there is no variation or shadow of turning. (1:13–17)*

God does not lose any control when a man rebels. God is just as sovereign over the wicked as He is over the righteous. If something could come to pass that was not under the sovereign control of God, then that something would happen, by definition, independently of God. Even the free action of a free moral agent happens because God sovereignly has determined that such freedom exists. As noted earlier, the Calvinist needs to define sovereignty and predestination up, in accordance with Scripture, and not define human freedom down.

God can and does determine everything in *one sense,* and yet is not morally responsible for some things in *any sense.* Nevertheless, the immoral acts, which immoral men do, are on His perfectly sovereign and moral watch. God's sovereign will *permits* things to happen that God does not *de-*

sire to happen, or that He even *commands* not to happen. For example, God desires that every Christian man love his wife as Christ loves the church. He even commands every Christian man to love his wife as Christ loves the church (Eph. 5:25). Yet, not every Christian man loves his wife as God desires and commands. The very fact that God feels a necessity to command us to do something, such as repent, suggests the very real possibility that we may not do it, especially without such a command as a motivator to comply with what He desires.

Even with such motivation as a divine command, men, including very devout men, do not always do what God desires and commands. God *allows* them to disobey Him without *causing* them to disobey Him. There is, however, no conflict between what God sovereignly allows (which is the only way a sovereign God can allow anything), and the painfully apparent fact that people defy God's moral and expressed will. A consistent Calvinism would have us believe that God ultimately causes man's sinful rebellion.

In fact, to a Calvinist, sinful rebellion is a manifestation of a man involuntarily yielding to the sovereign decree of God for that man's life. It should be obvious that not everything under God's sovereign control happens in relation to God in the same way. In fact, the God who sovereignly controls everything, as we have already seen, may and does allow things to happen that He disapproves of. This list of the divinely disapproved of and forbidden things in this wicked world is very long. Sproul is right when he says:

> That God in some sense foreordains whatever comes to pass is a necessary result of his sovereignty. *In itself it does not plead for Calvinism.* It only declares that God is absolutely sovereign over his creation. God can foreordain things in different ways. But everything that happens must at least happen by his permission. If he permits something, then he must decide to allow it. If he decides to allow something, then in a sense he is foreordaining it. ... To say that God foreordains all that comes to pass is simply to say that God is sovereign over his entire creation. If something could come to pass apart from God's sovereign permission, then that which came to pass would frustrate his sovereignty. If God refused to permit something to happen and it happened anyway, then whatever caused it to happen would have more authority and power than God.[517]

Ironically, it is the Calvinist who places logically unnecessary as well as unscriptural restrictions (in his thinking and theology) on the freedom and sovereignty of God. It is the Calvinist who says or suggests that not even a sovereign God could ordain that an unregenerate man would be able to choose between two separate eternal destinies while still unregenerate. For God to bring to life a spiritually dead man on the condition he believes in Jesus Christ is not, however, the equivalent of trying to create a square circle, as Calvinists insist. There is nothing about spiritual deadness that prevents God from sovereignly requiring and enabling the unregenerate to put his faith in Jesus Christ without actually placing faith *in* the man *for* the man.

Hypothetically, God certainly could regenerate a spiritually dead man unconditionally if He chose to do so. Scripturally speaking, however, God chooses to regenerate spiritually dead men on the condition they believe in Jesus Christ. Calvinism unscripturally and illogically requires God to create faith in a man in order for a man to place that faith in Christ. According to Scripture, God gives man reasons for believing in Christ, enables a man to believe in Christ, and then leaves it up to the man to believe or not believe.

Much of what Calvinism says about the sovereignty of God is, of course, true. Insofar as it goes, I agree with the definition of sovereignty found in a Calvinist dictionary of theological terms which defines sovereignty as:

> The right of God to do as He wishes (Psalm 50:1; Isaiah 40:15; 1 Tim. 6:15) with His creation. This implies that there is no external influence upon Him and that He also has the ability to exercise His power and control according to His will.[518]

There is no external force that can influence God to act contrary to His will *or* nature. There is no force that can cause God to do anything. He does, however, have an absolutely holy character, which ensures that all of His decisions or decrees will be holy. God's holiness ensures that all of His acts and interactions will be holy. Hypothetically, if we could get out in front of God's decrees, knowing what we know about God from Scripture, we could predict with absolute accuracy that all of God's decrees or sovereign determinations would be in accord with His absolute holiness. Therefore, whatever is determined by God to come to pass is determined by God in such a way so as to ensure that He is not morally responsible for immoral things. Boettner is right when he says:

It has been recognized by Christians in all ages that God is the Creator and Ruler of the universe, and that as the Creator and Ruler of the universe He is the ultimate source of all power that is found in the creatures. Hence nothing can come to pass apart from His sovereign will ...[519]

Boettner is also correct when he says:

By virtue of the fact that God has created everything which exists, He is the absolute Owner and final Disposer of all that He has made. He exerts not merely a general influence, but actually rules in the world that He has created. The nations of the earth, in their insignificance, are as the small dust of the balance when compared with His greatness; and far sooner might the sun be stopped in its course than God be hindered in His work or in His will. Amid all the apparent defeats and inconsistencies of life, God actually moves on in undisturbed majesty. Even the sinful actions of men can occur only by His permission. And since He permits not unwillingly but willingly, all that comes to pass—including the actions and ultimate destiny of men—must be, in some sense, in accordance with what He has desired and purposed.[520]

The question is in *what sense?* In the Calvinist sense, God is effectively blamed for the sin of man, just as He is credited with the saving of some of the sinful men He caused to be sinners in the first place. In *What is the Reformed Faith?* John R. de Witt, while noting agreement with Prof. G. C. Berkouwer, says:

The Calvinist insists that God is Lord, and that He reigns in history, over all the universe; that He knows the end from the beginning; that He created, sustains, governs, directs; that in the day of the Lord the marvelous design which He has had from the beginning will be fully manifest—complete, perfect at last.[521]

Without a doubt, all thoughtful Christians could and would affirm the same. In his now classic *Evangelism and the Sovereignty of God,* J. I. Packer goes so far as to say:

I do not intend to spend any time at all proving to you the general truth that God is sovereign in His world. There is no need; for I know that, if you are a Christian, you believe this already. ... Nor, again, am I going to spend time proving to you the particular truth that God is sovereign in salvation. For that, too, you believe already.[522]

Sproul could not be more right than when he says:

If God is not sovereign, God is not God.[523]

And,

Without sovereignty God cannot be God.[524]

For as Sproul also says:

We know God is sovereign because we know that God is God.[525]

Sproul even says:

Every Christian gladly affirms that God is sovereign. God's sovereignty is a comfort to us. It assures us that He is able to do what He promises to do.[526]

According to Sproul:

Rarely, if ever, does a professing Christian deny the thesis of the sovereignty of God. It is axiomatic to Christianity that God is sovereign. Manifestly, a God Who is not sovereign is no God at all.[527]

Despite what Sproul says elsewhere, he is right when he says that:

We must hold tight to God's sovereignty. Yet we must do it in such a way so as not to violate human freedom.[528]

It is not just human freedom that must be guarded in this discussion. Calvinism also calls into question God's holiness. Technically speaking, in the Calvinist scheme of things, not even Adam before the fall could have a real say in where he would spend eternity. For, as we have already established, Calvin believed that the first man sinned because God decreed with an irresistible decree that Adam would and should sin. If you follow Calvin's reasoning, you will note that freedom, even for pre-fallen Adam, was only an appearance of reality and not reality itself. If the decree of God is the ultimate cause of man's first sin, then man was never really free not to commit that first sin. Some Calvinists quote Calvin only when what he says substantiates or represents their version of Calvinism.

For example, I recently read an article posted on the Internet that quoted Calvin as follows:

> In this upright state, man possessed freedom of will, by which, if he chose, he was able to obtain eternal life. ... Adam, therefore, might have stood if he chose, since it was only by his own will that he fell; but it was because his will was pliable in either direction and he had not received constancy to persevere, that he so easily fell. Still he had a free choice of good and evil. ...[529]

The Calvinist who posted this quote was attempting to prove the often-repeated contention that Calvinism allows for both the sovereignty of God and freedom for at least the first man. Knowingly or otherwise, a sentence was left out of the paragraph which denies the very thing it is being used to affirm. Let us now consider this paragraph with this important sentence included:

> In this upright state, man possessed freedom of will, by which, if he chose, he was able to obtain eternal life. *It were here unseasonable to introduce the question **concerning the secret predestination of God, because we are not considering what might or might not happen**, but what the nature of man truly was.*[530]

In other words, *if we do not factor in* "the secret predestination of God," it would *appear* that Adam had a choice to sin or not sin, because he was not sinful the first time he did sin. Once you take the secret counsel into account, however, you can see that Adam's freedom not to sin that first time *was only an illusion* created by our inability to see "the secret predestination of God." In other words, Adam *had to sin* because of the decree of God that determined he would. According to Calvinism then, the real reason everything happens, the guiding and controlling force in time and eternity, is that God, mostly working behind the scenes, ensures that everything will happen in accordance with this secret and irresistible decree.

Some Calvinists want you to feel theologically shallow if you cannot see how this can be so or theologically arrogant for even pointing out how contradictory all of this is. Consider the very convoluted reasoning of Calvin in his commentary on Genesis with regard to why Adam fell into sin:

> I understand that [God] had appointed whatever he wished to be done. Here, indeed, a difference arises on the part of many, who

suppose Adam to have been so left to his own free will, that God would not have him fall. They take for granted, what I allow them, that nothing is less probable than that God should be regarded as the cause of sin, which he has avenged with so many and such severe penalties. When I say, however, that Adam did not fall without the ordination and will of God, I do not so take it as if sin had ever been pleasing to him, or as if he simply wished that the precept which he had given should be violated. So far as the fall of Adam was the subversion of equity, and of well-constituted order, so far as it was contumacy [stubborn rebelliousness] against the Divine Law-giver, and the transgression of righteousness, certainly it was against the will of God; yet none of these things render it impossible that, for a certain cause, although to us unknown, he might will the fall of man. *It offends the ears of some, when it is said God willed this fall; but what else, I pray, is the permission of him, who has the power of preventing, and in whose hand the whole matter is placed, but his will?*[531]

Thus, according to Calvin:

- God is not the cause of sin.

- The fall of Adam was the subversion of equity.

- The transgression of righteousness was ... against the will of God.

- Sin is not pleasing to God.

Yet:

- Adam was not left to his own free will.

- Adam fell according to the ordination and will of God.

- God willed this fall.

- Sin is among the things God wished to happen.

Sproul says:

If it is true that in some sense God foreordains everything that comes to pass, then it follows with no doubt that God must have foreordained the entrance of sin into the world. That is not to say that God forced it to happen or that he imposed evil upon his creation. All that means is that God must have decided to allow it to happen.[532]

It is hard for me to imagine that Sproul could say (with a straight face) that all foreordination "means" to a Calvinist "is that God must have decided to allow [all things] to happen." If that was all Calvinists meant by foreordination there would be no difference between Calvinists and Biblicists (such as myself). Even Arminians agree that "God must have decided to allow [all things] to happen." Sproul knows that to the Calvinist foreordination means God is the cause of everything that is foreordained, which to the Calvinist is everything that comes to pass. Still, Sproul is right when he says:

> God gave us [in Adam] free will. Free will is a good thing. That God gave us free will does not cast blame on him. In creation man was given an ability to sin and an ability not to sin. He chose to sin.[533]

Because all men since pre-fallen Adam (with the exception of our Savior) are born in an unregenerate or spiritually dead state, I will restrict myself here to a consideration of sovereignty and predestination as it relates to the unregenerate. What must be understood is that Calvinists separate themselves from most of the rest of the Evangelical community in the way they answer what Sproul calls the *big question.* That is:

> How is God's sovereignty related to human freedom?[534]

In Calvinism, human freedom with regard to eternal destinies is not so much *related* to divine sovereignty as it is *negated* by divine sovereignty. In order for God to have a "free will," or to be sovereign, Calvinists say or imply that a lost man can have no say in whether or not he will be saved. According to Best:

> The ideas of free grace and free will are diametrically opposed. All who are strict advocates for free will are strangers to the grace of the sovereign God.[535]

In Calvinism, if man were free to accept or reject salvation, God could neither graciously give salvation nor could He be sovereign in the salvation He gives. The Calvinist cannot even entertain the possibility that a sovereign, omniscient, and omnipotent God could, of His own absolutely free will:

- decree that fallen man must or could exercise a relatively free will to freely choose the salvation God freely offers fallen men.

In fact, Calvinists say or imply that there is nothing, short of regeneration, that even God could do to make an unregenerate man able to choose heaven over hell. As we read earlier, according to Reformed Theology:

It takes much more than the Spirit's assistance to bring a sinner to Christ—it takes regeneration by which the Spirit makes the sinner alive and gives him a new nature.[536]

SOVEREIGNTY VERSUS AUTONOMY

It is true that the lie and illusion of *human autonomy* is incompatible with the truth and reality of divine sovereignty. Sproul is right when he says:

If God is sovereign, man cannot possibly be autonomous. If man is autonomous, God cannot possibly be sovereign. These would be contradictions.[537]

Sproul correctly says:

It is not freedom that is cancelled out by sovereignty; it is autonomy that cannot coexist with sovereignty.[538]

He is also right when he reasons:

One does not have to be autonomous to be free. Autonomy implies absolute freedom. There are limits to our freedom.[539]

While this is true, the Calvinist definition of sovereignty does not allow for any meaningful freedom for man. That is why so few Calvinists try to harmonize or reconcile these concepts. For example, I found the following and typically hypo-Calvinist sentiments on the Internet:

Human free moral agency and the sovereignty of God are both clearly taught in the Bible. They cannot be understood or harmonized by the human mind, yet they are true. One side of the truth does not cancel the other side. They both are true, yet God is the only One who can explain this and will, when we see Him in Heaven, not before. If we attempt to harmonize these clearly revealed truths in this life we run the risk of distorting the Word of

God. Let's get it right; our logic must bow to the ultimate authority of God's revealed truth, not the other way around.[540]

On the surface, such a view may sound very spiritual. It is, however, also very superficial. The one who wrote these words apparently takes comfort or is satisfied with the words of another theologically and logically "conflicted" hypo-Calvinist who says:

> It is true that verses like John 6:44–45, Acts 13:48, and Ephesians 1:4–5 teach that we cannot come to God unless He first draws us to Himself. Such passages make it clear that those who choose Christ are people destined beforehand to be the eternal children of God. Other passages teach that the human will is so fallen and captured by sin that only the Spirit of God can give a person a desire to know God and be freed by Him.

> This is a difficult claim, and not only for people of faith. The principle of determinism is one side of a greater paradox that has defied explanation not only by Christian theologians but by atheistic philosophers as well. Both sides have struggled with two seemingly irreconcilable aspects of human experience: freedom and determinism.

> The Bible holds both sides in tension without trying to resolve the problem for us. While teaching that God is in control of His universe, the Scriptures make it equally clear that He offers salvation to all and holds all accountable for the real choice of accepting or rejecting His genuine offer. [541]

The problem with this well-intended but misguided reasoning is that the doctrine of determinism, as defined in Calvinism, contradicts what Scripture says about human freedom and responsibility. It is not that we cannot understand and therefore cannot reconcile Calvinistic determinism (hard or soft) and human freedom. We can understand them both. We cannot reconcile them with each other because they cannot by definition be reconciled.

Some Calvinists and even some non-Calvinists argue that we can actually have two parallel lines that eventually meet. One line represents Calvinistic determinism. The other line represents human freedom in the biblical sense. In time, these two parallel lines never merge *because* in fact they are parallel. In eternity, they are supposedly able to merge *despite* the fact that they are parallel. Calvinistic determinism, however, cancels out human freedom of the biblical kind. The most famous and most respected hypo-Calvinist of all time, Charles Spurgeon, insists:

> The [Calvinist] system of truth is not one straight line, but two. No man will ever get a right view of the gospel until he knows how to look at the two lines at once ...[542]

Spurgeon, like most hypo-Calvinists, does not believe it is possible for two truths to be in contradiction. They could appear to be in contradiction but they could not in fact be in contradiction. They could be irreconcilable *in time* and *for us*. That does not mean that they are irreconcilable to God or for us in eternity. Spurgeon even scolded those that believed it was beyond God's ability to reconcile what appeared to be impossible contradictions to us. He argued that it was our duty to believe whatever Scripture teaches, no matter how impossible it is for us to understand how Calvinist determinism and biblical freedom could both be true. He even looked at this kind of problem as a test to see if we are going to believe God and His Word no matter what our logic tells us. Iain Murray, a disciple of Spurgeon (if I may use that term in the most positive way possible), probably expresses this view as well as anyone when he says:

> ... however unable we may be to reconcile the calls and invitations addressed to all sinners with God's purpose of electing grace, we may be assured that *to the eye of God they are reconcilable* like many other things in His unsearchable works and ways which seem to our limited minds to be equally mysterious. For our part, we find ourselves necessitated *to believe both the one and the other* (although we cannot discern on what principle they are to be harmonized) on the clear Scriptural grounds that may be severally assigned for them. We do well to be exceedingly diffident in our judgments respecting matters so unsearchable as the secret purposes of God.[543]

There is simply no logical way, however, for eternity to reconcile that which by definition is irreconcilable. It would be like saying that we cannot reconcile the idea of a square circle in time, but in eternity, we will have no such problem. Sproul prefers to say, "I don't know," when responding to the questions related to a Calvinist view of sovereignty and predestination and a biblical view of human freedom and moral responsibility. Sproul correctly reasons:

> If the lines meet, then they are not ultimately parallel. If they are ultimately parallel, they will never meet. ... To say that parallel lines meet in eternity is a nonsense statement; it is a blatant contradiction.[544]

Keep in mind that Sproul is himself a hypo-Calvinist and probably very much aligned with Spurgeon on many other matters of importance to the greater Calvinist community. The question that must finally be answered is: can we be freely living our lives according to the Calvinist understanding of a divine script? Suppose that the writer of a play writes a scene in his play in which an evil man commits a terrible crime. Suppose the writer of the script exercises the kind of control over the play that ensures the actor playing the evil man does exactly as the script says he will do. From the vantage point of the audience, within the context of the play, the evil character, played by the actor, is responsible for the crime. From the perspective of the writer of the script, the writer is in reality responsible for the crime committed in the play by the actor playing the evil man.

If we were to call God the writer of the play, and a sinful human becomes the actor/evil man, then it would be appropriate to say that God committed the terrible crime (since He is the writer), and yet to also say that the evil man/actor committed the terrible crime (since that was written into his role). When all the theological fog is cleared away, Calvinism asserts that God is really the one responsible for whatever happens, good or bad, while man only appears to be the one responsible for his actions (that were in actuality "scripted" for him). Since, however, we are in this divinely written play, and it appears to be reality to us, and is in fact *our reality*, the Calvinist says we are free. The Calvinist also believes that we will ultimately be held accountable for what Calvinism says or suggests that God is really responsible for. Many will object to my analogy of the play. They argue that this is not really what Calvinism says or suggests. To the contrary, Calvinist Wayne Grudem says:

> The analogy of an author writing a play may help. ... In the Shakespearean play Macbeth, the character Macbeth murders King Duncan. Now (if we assume for a moment that this is a fictional account), the question may be asked, "Who killed King Duncan?"

On one level, the correct answer is "Macbeth." Within the context of the play he carried out the murder and is rightly to blame for it. But on another level, a correct answer to the question, "Who killed King Duncan?" "William Shakespeare:" he wrote the play, he created all the characters in it, and he wrote the part where Macbeth killed King Duncan.[545]

Although Grudem's theology makes mankind *less* than actors in a divine play (an actor can always quit or *ad lib* his lines)—mere puppets controlled by divine strings—he still attempts to rescue Calvinism from the charge of fatalism as follows:

> Sometimes those who object to the [Calvinist] doctrine of election say that it is "fatalism." ... By fatalism is meant a system in which human choices and human decisions really do not make any difference. In fatalism, no matter what we do, things are going to turn out as they have been previously ordained. Therefore, it is futile to try to influence the outcome of events or the outcome of our lives by putting forth any effort or making any significant choices, because these will not make any difference anyway. In a truly fatalistic system, of course, our humanity is destroyed for our choices really mean nothing, and the motivation for moral accountability is removed.[546]

Grudem rightly argues that Scripture paints no such picture and in many ways contradicts such a view of reality and humanity. Yet, this is exactly the picture painted by Calvinism in general and Grudem in particular. Everything said in the above quote could be and is said by Calvinists about the Calvinist version of sovereignty and predestination.

In the Jim Henson animated Disney movie *The Dark Crystal,* the forces of light and darkness, good and evil, finally meet to see who or what will ultimately triumph. To the delight of New Agers everywhere, as it turned out, the ultimate victory, according to the creator of the Muppets, was not good over evil but the realization that these were mere illusions. That is, ultimately there was no good or evil, right or wrong. Unwittingly, the Calvinist view of the sovereign decrees of God accomplishes essentially the same thing.

If evil can be traced to God the way good can, if God is responsible for everything the way Calvinism says He is, if man is just an actor in a divine play (a tragedy at that), then the Hindu concept of Maya, which says (among other things) that human morality is just an illusion, is not that far off after all. A well thought-out understanding of Calvinist logic actually leads to views which are more in keeping with Hinduism than with biblical Christianity. I do not say these things to inflame the Calvinist. I do not believe Calvinists are Hindus. I do believe, however, that the Calvinist view of sovereignty and predestination logically lead to ideas which are as foreign to Scripture as is Hinduism. Some ideas in Calvinism lead logically to other ideas that should be *anathema* even to the most staunch and extreme Calvinist.

PREDESTINATION REVISITED

No doctrine of Calvinism is more closely associated with the Calvinist doctrine of sovereignty than is the Calvinist doctrine of predestination. In fact, they are so closely related in Reformed Theology that what is said about one is often said about the other. Since, however, predestination is such a key concept in Calvinism, even at the risk of some repetition, it is needful that we look even closer at this concept in light of Scripture. As with so many other matters, it is not the Calvinists' affirmation of predestination that distinguishes Calvinists from non-Calvinist Evangelicals. Rather, it is the Calvinist *doctrine* of predestination (which in turn is based upon the Calvinist *definition* of predestination) that sets Calvinists apart from the rest of us. As Sproul says:

> Virtually all Christian churches have some formal doctrine of pre-destination. ... If the Bible is the Word of God, not mere human speculation, and if God himself declares that there is such a thing as predestination, then it follows irresistibly that we must embrace some doctrine of predestination.[547]

In like manner, Sproul correctly reasons that:

> Almost every church has developed some form of the doctrine of predestination simply because the Bible teaches predestination. Predestination is a biblical word and a biblical concept. If one seeks to develop a theology that is biblical, one cannot avoid the doctrine of predestination.[548]

And as Sproul also says:

> The idea of predestination is rooted in the Bible. This is why all churches historically have found it necessary to formulate some

doctrine of predestination in an effort to be Biblical in their theology. The issue is not does the Bible teach the doctrine of predestination or election but *what* or *which* doctrine of predestination does it teach.[549]

And Sproul is right when he says:

It is not enough to have any view of predestination. It is our duty to seek the correct view of predestination, lest we be guilty of distorting or ignoring the Word of God.[550]

I have no argument with Sproul when he says:

Our destination is the place we are going. In theology it refers to one of two places: either we are going to heaven or we are going to hell. In either case, we cannot cancel the trip. God gives us but two final options. One or the other is our final destination.[551]

According to Sproul, however, the problem is that the Calvinist definition of predestination:

… seems to cast a shadow on the very heart of human freedom. If God has decided our destinies [in the Calvinist sense] from all eternity, that strongly suggests that our free choices are but charades, empty exercises in predetermined playacting. It is as though God wrote the script for us in concrete and we are merely carrying out His scenario.[552]

One reason the Calvinist definition and doctrine of predestination "seems to cast a shadow on the very heart of human freedom" is that in Calvinism, God *does not really* give man "two final options," as Calvinists repeatedly remind us. To say that men will either go to heaven or to hell is not to say that heaven and hell are options. An option suggests a choice for the person with options. No such choice exists for man *in Calvinism.* In Calvinism, it is not *you are going to hell, but you can go to heaven if you believe in Jesus Christ.* Rather, it is *you can only believe in Jesus if God predestines you to believe.* Conversely, the dark side of Calvinism says that some are unconditionally and from all eternity predestined for hell and cannot cancel the trip.

To believe otherwise is to deny the very heart of the Calvinist doctrine(s) of sovereignty, predestination, redemption, and reprobation. Calvinists should step up to the plate and admit as much. In mainstream Calvinism, embracing predestination, and all that follows in the Calvinist scheme of things, and embracing real human freedom of choice, especially with regard to spiritual and eternal matters, is, according to Sproul and effectively all Calvinists, embracing a:

> "You can have your cake and eat it too" system.[553]

That is, if you are divinely predestined in the Calvinist sense, *you* cannot be meaningfully free. This is the essence of the so-called sixth point of Calvinism. In fact, the five separate points of Calvinism are merely particularizations of the sixth point as it is brought to bear on the various matters addressed in each of the respective points. As the Calvinist view of sovereignty leads to the Calvinist view of predestination, so the Calvinist view of predestination leads to theistic fatalism. In Reformed Theology, divine freedom leaves no room for human freedom.

Before going further, it is important that we make a distinction between what is the biblical doctrine of predestination and the way the term is used in a broader theological and philosophical context. Sproul is right when he says that predestination is taught in Scripture. He is wrong in saying or suggesting that the biblical doctrine of predestination is equivalent to the Calvinist doctrine of predestination. The Calvinist doctrine of predestination is deduced not from what is clearly taught in the scriptural usage of the word *predestination* or its cognates, but from a distinctive and erroneous understanding of the nature and administration of God's sovereign control of everything. By this, I mean that if you actually examine those passages that use the word predestination or similar terms, they do not teach, explicitly or implicitly, the Calvinist doctrine of predestination. When the Bible uses the word predestination, it is always with regard to the future of a believer. Never is the future of an unbeliever referred to as predestined in the Calvinist sense, one way or the other. We will come back to this matter at the end of this chapter.

THE CAUSE OF SIN

Those of us who do not fault God with anything immoral or wrong must recognize that when something immoral or wrong occurs, someone other than God is responsible. We must also recognize that there is something about those who are responsible that makes them responsible. That *something* God sovereignly included or predestined for man, we call *volition.* A moral (and morally culpable) man must by definition be more than a volitional being.

He cannot, however, be less than a volitional being. The volition of a man must *by definition* and *actually* allow a man to really choose between good and evil. No matter how depraved a sinful man is, he is still morally responsible for what he does because the immoral things he *does*, he does not *have* to do, but *chooses* to do.

One could argue that a time may come when an immoral being, due to his enslavement to sin or to the effect of sin on the will, may not even "know" that he is doing something bad when he does it. He is still morally responsible because he is responsible for the immoral behavior that leads to this serious consequence of immorality. Somewhere behind and before this, this man had a choice to sin or not to sin. He was not forced to sin. Not even his sinful nature forces the sinner to sin. The sinful nature of the sinner does not make the sinner sin. The sinner makes himself sin. It is not the other way around. God's sovereign decrees do not force or even influence man to sin. God's power (if we disregard His holiness) could force a person to *act* against God's holy standard, but that coerced action would not meet the biblical definition of *sin* any more than a man being pushed to his death off a bridge could be defined as a suicide. God's holy nature guarantees that no such thing would or could ever happen.

Consider a *vicious attack* by a pit bull on an innocent letter carrier. The result of that attack can be horrible and even lead to a painful death for the letter carrier. All the letter carrier was trying to do was his job. Now we might call that a *bad* dog and even put him to death. I know I would. But we would not consider that dog immoral or sinful. A dog is amoral and therefore incapable of sin. Why? It is because a dog does not have the capacity for sin, because a dog cannot make moral choices. He has no moral *volition*. He can do awful things but he cannot do wicked things as a moral/immoral man can do.

If we say a man has no capacity for real moral choices, or that he can only do immoral things, we do not thereby deny his ability to do terrible harm. We would not, however, be able to morally judge him for the terrible acts he might commit *as if* those acts were sinful or immoral acts. The fall of man into sin and its consequent state of spiritual death does not change the fact that man can and must make moral choices. Both the Calvinist view of an all-encompassing decree and the Calvinist view of fallen nature make man amoral—not immoral.

Again, most Evangelicals believe that one of the reasons things happen that are relationally distant from God, such as all sinful deeds, is that sinful man, even in his spiritually dead state, is still a moral creature capable of morally defensible behavior as well as morally reprehensible behavior. This capability of man legitimately provides a moral shield, so to speak, for God so that whatever happens by the hand of man does not reach back to God in a way that makes God morally responsible for the immorality of man. If God is absolutely moral and only God was responsible (or even primarily responsible) for all things that happen, then only moral things could happen. But since immoral things happen in a world under the absolute sovereign control of an absolutely moral God, it is evident that God does not relate to everything in the same way. It cannot be overemphasized that some things can legitimately be traced to immoral beings in a way they cannot be traced to God. God is not thereby less than in control of all things. Control of all things is not the issue. Cause is the issue. To say God is in sovereign control of all things is not to say that He is the responsible cause of all things.

Even though all immoral activity is repugnant to God and cannot be traced to God in a way that allows us to legitimately blame Him for that immorality, we still believe it happens on His watch, under His sovereign control, and in accordance with what He has sovereignly allowed to occur from all eternity. Is God not to blame for immoral acts just because He is God and can do as He pleases? Or do we say that He makes the rules so that whatever God does is, by definition, not immoral? Unless we recognize that man, even fallen and spiritually dead man, possesses and retains something that allows him to make decisions which are really his decisions and not God's (or causally determined by God in the Calvinist sense), then God by definition is morally responsible for all of the ungodly conduct of ungodly men.

If Calvinists became as zealous for the holiness of God as they are for the sovereignty of God, Calvinism might soon cease to exist as a theological system. Calvinists like to say or suggest that you must either accept a God-centered theology and their view on divine sovereignty or a man-centered theology and the Arminian view of human autonomy. What Calvinists have really done, however unintentionally, is asked us to embrace a view of divine sovereignty that is dissociated with the moral attributes of God, such as holiness and righteousness.

Fortunately, the solution to the so-called problem of relating divine sovereignty to human freedom is far simpler than what many theologians and philosophers would have us believe. That is, the God who sovereignly controls everything determined us to be meaningfully free, even after the fall of Adam. It is God who factored in volition. God is absolutely sovereign and His sovereignty is not, and cannot, be limited by our relative but meaningful freedom. Our freedom in no way restricts His sovereignty, but is dependent upon His sovereignty. The Calvinist is not doing God any favors by placing unnecessary restrictions on what God can and cannot do. The question is not (or at least should not be): could God make it possible for a sinful and un-regenerate man to choose heaven over hell while that man is in a spiritually dead state, but: did He? To believe that a sovereign God (the only kind of God there can be) can make it possible for a man (regenerate or unregener-ate) to make a real choice between heaven and hell is not the equivalent of suggesting God can make an *honest liar,* as Calvinists have charged.

If, therefore, we are to establish the notion that man is not really free to choose heaven over hell, as Calvinism says, we must seek to do so outside a discussion of divine sovereignty and human depravity as such. We would have to demonstrate that God sovereignly decided that man would not be able to make such a choice. Keep in mind that the concept of sovereignty tells us what God *can* do, which is everything not contrary to His nature or of a contradictory nature. It does not tell us what God *cannot* do.

Most philosophers and some theologians insist that a meaningful dis-cussion of God's sovereign rule over man cannot occur without a long and complicated definition of what is meant by the *free will* of man. I think this is misleading at best. Just as we must assume some things to have a meaning-ful discussion, such as *words have meaning and can be understood,* we must also assume that a person is free to have a meaningful discussion about free-dom. Otherwise, our very discussion is not actually meaningful, but merely determined. Most people, even people who formally do not believe man has a really free will or that he can make really free decisions, know what is meant by free will or free decisions, and even act as if they have a free will. To even engage in a discussion about free will presumes that a person is free to actually have such a discussion.

For many mainstream Calvinists, such as Feinberg, Sproul, and Wilson, who formally agree that divine sovereignty and human freedom are not in-compatible, the question is not, is man free? Rather the questions are, how can a man be free and in what sense is he free? While I disagree with their particular attempts to answer this question, I agree with them that the question can be answered and that the right answer must and does affirm both the absolute sovereignty of God and a meaningful freedom for man. The view I hold and that I believe is the biblical view is called "moral self-determinism." The Christian philosopher and Evangelical theologian Norman Geisler has stated this view as well as I think anyone could. Because Geisler has done such a great job in this regard, I will not reinvent this same theological and philosophical wheel. First, it must be understood, as explained by Geisler, that "moral self-determinism" holds:

> Moral acts are not uncaused or caused by someone else. Rather, they are caused by oneself.[554]

In agreement with Geisler I believe:

> This view best fits both the biblical and rational criteria.[555]

As Geisler says:

> There are several philosophical objections [to moral self-determinism]. The first has to do with the principle of causality—that *every* event has an adequate cause. If this is so, then it would seem that even one's free will has a prior cause. If one's free will has a prior cause, then it cannot be caused by oneself. Thus self-determinism would be contrary to the principle of causality which it embraces.[556]

In defense of moral self-determinism, Geisler explains:

> There is a basic confusion in this objection. This confusion results in part from an infelicitous expression of the self-determinism view. Representatives of moral self-determinism sometimes speak of free will as though it were the efficient cause of moral actions. This would lead one naturally to ask: what is the cause of one's free will? But a more precise description of the process of a free act would avoid this problem.[557]

Geisler goes on to explain:

> Technically, free will is not the efficient cause of a free act; free will is simply the power through which the agent performs the free act. The efficient cause of the free act is really the free *agent,* not the free will. Free will is simply the power by which the free agent

acts. We do not say that humans *are* free will but only that they *have* free will. Likewise, we do not say that humans are thought but only that they have the power of thought. So it is not the power of free choice which causes a free act, but the *person* who has this power.[558]

Geisler then reasons:

If the real cause of a free act is not an act but an *actor,* then it makes no sense to ask for the cause of the actor as though the actor were another act. The cause of the performance is the performer. It is meaningless to ask what performance caused the performance. Likewise, the cause of a free act is not another free act. Rather, it is a free agent. And once we have arrived at the free agent, it is meaningless to ask what caused its free acts. For if something else caused its actions, then the agent is not the cause of them and thus is not responsible for them. The free moral agent is responsible for the free moral actions. And it is as senseless to ask what caused the free agent to act as it is to ask who made God? The answer is the same in both instances: nothing can cause the first cause because it is the first. There is nothing before the first. Likewise, humans are the first cause of their own moral actions. If humans were not the cause of their own free actions, then the actions would not be *their* actions.[559]

Geisler anticipates and answers critics of this view as follows:

If it is argued that it is impossible to claim that humans can be the first cause of their moral actions, then it is also impossible for God to be the first cause of his moral actions. Tracing the first cause back to God does not solve the problem of finding a cause for every action. It simply pushes the problem back farther. Sooner or later theists will have to admit that a free act is a self-determined act, which is not caused by another. Eventually it must be acknowledged that all acts come from actors, but that actors (free agents) are the first cause of their actions, which therefore have no prior cause. The real question, then, is not whether there are agents who cause their own actions but whether God is the only true agent (that is, person) in the universe.[560]

James White in his challenge to (some would say attack on) Geisler and

Chosen but Free, a book in which Geisler sets forth and defends this view, takes the very position that Geisler refers to. That is, according to White, "God is the only true agent (that is, person) in the universe." This is the error (some might say heresy) of monovolitionism.

Geisler also identifies and effectively answers three important philosophical objections to moral self-determinism. I highly recommend reading the book *Predestination and Free Will: Four Views of Divine Sovereignty and Human Freedom* (David Basinger and Randall Basinger, eds., InterVarsity Press, 1986), in which Geisler does this, and carefully considering what he has to say.

As much as I appreciate that Geisler and others from different theological persuasions have grappled with this topic for us, I do not really think it is all that difficult to accept either the concept that God is *absolutely sovereign* or that man is *responsibly free* (and therefore morally responsible for a whole host of important and even eternal matters). The fact that you may not be able to articulate your convictions in precise theological or philosophical terms makes little or no difference in your day-to-day living. Most Christians simply do not have trouble reconciling sovereignty and free will because they see no natural conflict between them.

What matters most, for most of us, is that we take God's sovereignty seriously and use our God-given freedom to submit to His sovereignty so that we *do the right thing.* You may not understand how it is that God can be absolutely sovereign while you are truly free and morally responsible. That, however, does not necessarily constitute a paradox or even rate as a mystery. It may just be that you have been misled into believing the two concepts cannot be reconciled this side of glory. The very fact that a sovereign God says He is going to hold us accountable for how we use our freedom should settle the matter for all practical purposes for the believer. Both concepts are true and are of the greatest practical importance to our life, both temporally and eternally.

> *For we shall all stand before the judgment seat of Christ. For it is written: "As I live, says the LORD, every knee shall bow to Me, and every tongue shall confess to God." So then each of us shall give account of himself to God. (Rom. 14:10–12)*

> *God ... has highly exalted Him and given Him the name which is above every name, that at the name of Jesus every knee should*

> bow, of those in heaven, and of those on earth, and of those under
> the earth, and that every tongue should confess that Jesus Christ
> is Lord, to the glory of God the Father. Therefore, my beloved, as
> you have always obeyed, not as in my presence only, but now much
> more in my absence, work out your own salvation with fear and
> trembling; for it is God who works in you both to will and to do for
> His good pleasure. (Phil. 2:9–13)

If you believe that ultimately you will bow your knee to the King of kings and Lord of lords, you need no further proof that God really is absolutely sovereign, not just over all, but over *you*. The fact that we will have to give account to Him for how we have lived the life He has given us, with all the gifts and resources needed to bring honor and glory to Him, is all the proof that we should need that we are free and really are morally responsible to Him. Divine sovereignty and human freedom are not antithetical to one another, as Calvinism at least implies. It is the very freedom that our sovereign God gives us and for which He will hold us accountable that allows us to appreciate and appropriately respond to God's sovereignty. If we were not free to submit to or reject God's sovereign rule over our lives in a practical manner, knowledge of His sovereignty would have no real or practical value to us. In other words, a denial of freedom, such as is found in Calvinism, makes the very emphasis placed on sovereignty unnecessary at best.

As noted earlier, when Scripture uses the word predestination, it limits the discussion to the destiny of the believer. Perhaps this is because God realizes how easy it is for some to falsely conjure up extreme and unwarranted notions about man having no real say as to where he will spend eternity and thus no real responsibility for where he ends up. For whatever reason or reasons, it is a very conspicuous fact that nothing is said about the destiny of the unbeliever relative to the use of this word in any of its several forms. Sproul seems to admit as much (at least in one of the primary texts dealing with predestination) when he says, in the context of a discussion of Ephesians 1:3–12:

> Paul speaks of believers being predestined according to the counsel
> of God's will.[561]

While Sproul clearly believes that God unconditionally predestines unbelievers to be saved from all eternity, what he says here is indisputable. It is believers who are predestined to heavenly glory and all that this implies.

Nothing is taught about the unbeliever being predestined, unconditional or otherwise, to salvation or damnation. As Herbert Lockyer says:

> What must be born in mind is the fact that *predestination* is not God's predetermining from past ages who should and who should not be saved. Scripture does not teach this view. What it does teach is that this [biblical] doctrine of predestination concerns the future of believers. Predestination is the Divine determining the glorious consummation of all who through faith and surrender become the Lord's. He has determined beforehand that each child of His will reach *adoption,* or the "son-placing" at his resurrection when Christ returns. It has been determined beforehand that all who are truly Christ's shall be conformed to His image. (Romans 8:29; Ephesians 1:5).[562]

H. A. Ironside concurs as follows:

> Nowhere in the Bible are people ever predestined to go to hell, and nowhere are [pre-saved] people predestined to heaven. ... Predestination is always to some special place of blessing.[563]

Elsewhere, Ironside exhorts:

> Turn to your Bible and read for yourself in the only two chapters in which the word "predestinate" or "predestinated" is found. The first is Romans 8:29–30. The other chapter is Ephesians 1:5, 11. You will note that there is no reference in these four verses to either Heaven or Hell, but to Christlikeness eventually. Nowhere are we told in Scripture that God predestined one man to be saved and another lost.[564]

I will conclude this discussion with a consideration of one of the two passages referenced by Lockyer and Ironside and among the most frequently used by Calvinists to suggest their distinctive doctrines of salvation and damnation or redemption and reprobation. The other (Rom. 8:29) has already been considered in some detail. In Paul's opening salutation to the church at Ephesus he says:

> *Paul, an apostle of Jesus Christ by the will of God,* **to the saints** *who are in Ephesus, and* **faithful in Christ Jesus***: Grace to you and peace from God our Father and the Lord Jesus Christ.*

*Blessed be the God and Father of our Lord Jesus Christ, who has **blessed us** with every spiritual blessing in the heavenly places **in Christ**, just as **He chose us in Him** before the foundation of the world, that we should be holy and without blame before Him in love, **having predestined us to adoption as sons** by Jesus Christ to Himself, according to the good pleasure of His will, to the praise of the glory of His grace, by which He made us accepted in the Beloved.*

In Him *we have redemption through His blood, the forgiveness of sins, according to the riches of His grace which He made to abound toward us in all wisdom and prudence, having made known to us the mystery of His will, according to His good pleasure which He purposed in Himself, that in the dispensation of the fullness of the times He might gather together in one all things in Christ, both which are in heaven and which are on earth—in Him.*

In Him *also we have obtained an inheritance, being **predestined according to the purpose of Him who works all things according to the counsel of His will**, that we who first trusted in Christ should be to the praise of His glory. In Him **you also trusted, after you heard the word of truth, the gospel of your salvation**; in whom also, **having believed**, you were sealed with the Holy Spirit of promise, who is the guarantee of our inheritance until the redemption of the purchased possession, to the praise of His glory. (Eph. 1:1–14, emphasis added)*

- First, it should be noted that those chosen were chosen *in* Christ and not *outside* of Christ.

- Second, it should be noted that those chosen in Christ were not chosen for salvation but for holiness, blamelessness, and love.

- Third, it should be noted that those chosen in Christ for holiness, blamelessness, and love were predestined to adoption as sons. They were not predestined to salvation as non-sons to be sons. They were predestined to adoption *as sons*. Adoption in this context does not bring a non-family member into the family but a family member into his inheritance.

- Fourth, predestination here relates to those who first trusted Christ.

- Fifth, the Ephesian believers trusted Christ after they heard the gospel.

- Sixth, those who trusted Christ were then sealed with the Holy Spirit of promise.

- Seventh, the promise of the Holy Spirit is that those who trust Christ are guaranteed that they will receive their inheritance.

- Eighth, the guarantee is given until the redemption (the resurrection of the just or glorification) of the believer.

Once again, only in Ephesians 1:5 and 1:11 does Scripture use the term *predestinated,* and only in Romans 8:29–30 does Scripture use the term *predestinate* (KJV). This does not suggest that this is not an important concept and that it does not refer to important truths. It does mean that we should not go beyond what Scripture says in our definition of a biblically based predestination. As Vance points out:

> There are several problems with the Calvinists' understanding of these verses that immediately come to mind. First, in none of these verses is predestination ever called a decree of God. Second, there is no mention in any of these verses of predestination taking place before the foundation of the world. Third, none of these verses mention any angels. Fourth, there is no mention in any of these verses of anyone being predestinated to salvation. Fifth, none of these verses contain any reference to judgment, condemnation, reprobation, or everlasting death. It is apparent that what the Bible says about predestination is irreconcilable with what the Calvinists say about predestination.[565]

I have no problem with calling a decision by God to do something a decree of God. I have no problem thinking of God's decisions as eternal decisions. The issues are not *that* God makes decisions or *when* He makes them. The issue is about the *kind* of decisions attributed to God by Calvinists. The theological landscape would be a very different place today if Calvin would have heeded his own words when he said:

> Let it ... be our first principle ... [not] to desire any other knowledge of predestination than that which is expounded by the word of God ...[566]

13

MATTERS THAT MATTER

CALVINISM AND EVANGELISM

I realize that there are some Calvinists who are great evangelists. In light of what Calvinism teaches about salvation and damnation, however, I am convinced that Calvinists who evangelize do so *in spite of* Calvinism, and *not because of* Calvinism. That is, there is not one distinctive of Reformed doctrine that encourages or promotes evangelism of the lost. Just the opposite is true. A thorough understanding of what Calvin taught has been a great discouragement to reaching the lost with the saving knowledge of Jesus Christ.

The great evangelist Charles Spurgeon is a man that hypo-Calvinists love to point to as proof that Calvinism does not undermine the Great Commission. A careful reading of all that Spurgeon believed, however, shows that he was at best an inconsistent Calvinist. He was a soul winner *despite* Reformed Theology and *not because of* Reformed Theology. In fact, as documented earlier, Spurgeon held to some views that actually undermine some of the most basic tenets of the Reformed faith. These same views contributed greatly to his effectiveness as an evangelist. Spurgeon also chose to preach to the lost as if Calvinism were not true. That is, he was willing to say to everyone that they could be saved. Yet he believed that only the elect could be saved. That is, although he may have (mostly) believed like a Calvinist, he often preached like a Biblicist.

The Calvinist doctrines of sovereignty, predestination, election, reprobation, limited atonement, irresistible grace, regeneration before faith, total depravity, etc. all make evangelism *incidental* and *not essential,* despite what some Calvinists would like you to believe. Just as one who holds to antinomianism may live a very moral life, so one who holds to the anti-evangelistic doctrines of Calvinism may still be effective as an evangelist. Nevertheless, evangelism is neither encouraged by nor consistent with the Calvinist doctrines of salvation and damnation. This should be obvious to anyone who truly understands the distinctives of the Reformed faith.

WHY WITNESS?

Other than evangelizing simply because God tells you to, why would a Calvinist evangelize? The evangelist cannot, in the Calvinist scheme of things, really make a difference. As has been documented, *both sides of Calvinism* mitigate against a commitment to evangelism:

THE LIGHT SIDE OF CALVINISM	THE DARK SIDE OF CALVINISM
God the Father unconditionally elects some to salvation.	God the Father unconditionally reprobates some to damnation.
God the Son redemptively died for some.	God the Son did not die redemptively for some.
God the Spirit irresistibly regenerates some.	God the Spirit refuses to regenerate some.
If God the Father elects a person to salvation, that person will be saved.	If God the Father does not elect a person to salvation, that person will be damned.
If God the Son die for the salvation of a person, that person will be saved.	If God the Son did not die for the salvation of a person, that person will be damned.
If God the Spirit produces saving faith in a person, that person will be saved.	If God the Spirit does not produce saving faith in a person that person will be damned.

If all this is true, it seems legitimate to ask: *Why witness?* After all, the elect will be *saved* regardless, and the non-elect will be *damned* regardless. What difference, if any, will or can our witnessing for Christ make? A Calvinist may answer this question in two different ways. Sproul says:

> Evangelism is our duty. God has commanded it. That should be enough to end the matter.[567]

This answer really gets to the heart of the Reformed view. Now the Calvinist has a nicer-sounding answer to this question as well. It does not, however, add anything of substance to the more abrupt answer, "God commands it." To think it does is to miss the point. Admittedly, however, it does sound more appealing to say, as Sproul also says:

> Evangelism is not only our duty; it is also a privilege. God allows us to participate in the greatest work in human history, the work of redemption.[568]

Taken by itself, what Sproul says here is perfectly scriptural. According to Calvinist logic, however, this statement would make Sproul a synergist, because if we can participate in *the work of redemption* we are at least in some sense helping God in the work of saving the lost. To the Calvinist, this is synergism. Getting back to the issue at hand, this soft answer does not change the meaning of the first and more abrupt statement. For Sproul also says:

> God not only foreordains the end of salvation for the elect, he also foreordained the means to that end.[569]

The *means* to that end, in Reformed Theology, is not a *means* that makes a difference. In Calvinism, the means is just as void of a free and meaningful choice as is the end. In other words, those who do witness cannot, by this logic, do anything but witness. As the salvation of a man does not *require* a man to choose to be saved, so the means to the end (evangelism) does not *require* that a man evangelize. As surely as some will be *saved*, some will *evangelize*. Any apparent choice to be saved, or to evangelize so others can be saved, is only an illusion according to the logic of Reformed doctrine.

It seems especially reasonable to ask the Calvinist why he would witness to reprobates, since reprobates cannot be saved. Calvinists say they should do this out of obedience *and because* they are ignorant of who the savable elect are versus the unsavable reprobate. Spurgeon, who was unquestionably a great soul winner, admits that it at least seems logically inconsistent, not to mention a waste of time, to evangelize the reprobate. Nevertheless he says:

> Our Savior has bidden us to preach the gospel to every creature (Mark 16:15). He has not said "Preach it only to the elect," and though that might seem to be the most logical thing for us to do, yet since he has not been pleased to stamp the elect in their foreheads or put any distinctive upon them, it would be an impossible task for

us to perform. When we preach the gospel to every creature, the gospel makes its own division, and Christ's sheep hear his voice, and follow him.[570]

I don't know why it would be such an impossible task to identify the elect. God could surely direct us to them in the same way Calvinists say He directs, determines, and decrees everything that was, is, or will be. Spurgeon understood the logic of what I am saying. He just chose to ignore what Calvinism teaches or implies on this matter. Perhaps one of the seven wonders of the theological world is a conviction held by some and expressed so clearly by Spencer. He says:

> Once the basic teachings of Calvinism are correctly understood, the heart becomes warm and the urgency of sharing the gospel with others becomes almost overwhelming.[571]

Did I miss something? How does one get a sense of urgency about evangelizing the lost when "what will be, will be"? Iain Murray represents the position of most hypo-Calvinists in general and Spurgeon in particular as follows:

> How can sinners be offered a salvation which Christ did not fulfill on their behalf? Spurgeon set that question aside as something which God has not chosen to explain.[572]

Despite the fact that Spurgeon tenaciously affirmed the Calvinist version of sovereignty, predestination, and election, which leaves no real room for human freedom or culpability, he still believed that a man would have no one to blame but himself if he ends up in hell. According to Iain Murray, Spurgeon insists that:

> Those who hear the gospel and reject the Savior will not be able to plead that sovereignty prevented them from exercising the obedience of faith. None will be able to claim that God excluded them. No, it is on account of sin alone, including the sin of unbelief, that unrepentant sinners will finally be condemned and lost forever. Asked to explain such a mystery, Spurgeon constantly replied that it was not his business to do so.[573]

The culpability of the repentant sinner could only be "such a mystery" if the Calvinist doctrines of sovereignty, predestination, and election/

reprobation are true. There should be no doubt that Spurgeon fully realized how contradictory his position was. Spurgeon even says that:

> I believe that man is as accountable as if there were no destiny whatsoever. Where these two truths [of divine sovereignty and human responsibility] meet I do not know, nor do I want to know. They do not puzzle me, since I have given up my mind to believing them both.[574]

Just because Spurgeon does not care to resolve this problem, the problem for Calvinism does not go away. What Spurgeon says is that if I do not let it bother me, it is not really a problem after all. It is intellectually, if not spiritually, dishonest to view a man who faces the Calvinist version of a destiny as if he has the scriptural kind of freedom and responsibility with which he can respond to the gospel of Jesus Christ. It is the kind of "destiny" that Spurgeon believes in that makes a contradiction out of the kind of responsibility he also believes in. Calling it a mystery or a paradox or saying that it will be resolved in the next life will simply not do. If God, by definition, cannot make a square circle, then for exactly the same reason, God cannot reconcile the Calvinist version of destiny with the scriptural version of responsibility. The following quotes demonstrate the silly predicament in which the Calvinist doctrine has left the Calvinist.

> ... Unconditional election ... does not contradict biblical expressions of God's compassion for all people, and does not nullify sincere offers of salvation to everyone who is lost among all the peoples of the world.[575]

> We believe that sovereign election does not contradict or negate the responsibility of man to repent and trust Christ as Savior and Lord.[576]

> The question [of limited atonement] does not relate to the universal offer in perfect good faith in a saving interest, in Christ's work on the condition of faith.[577]

> ... Our duty is, to embrace *the benefit which is offered to all* that each of us may be convinced that there is nothing to hinder him from obtaining reconciliation in Christ, provided that he comes to him by the guidance of faith ...[578]

> God in the gospel expresses a bona fide wish that all may hear, and
> that all who hear, may believe and be saved.[579]

Have some Calvinists discovered a new kind of logic that allows contradictory propositions to be reconciled? The only kind of logic I am familiar with says that if the *wish* is *bona fide* and *all may believe and be saved,* then the distinctives of Calvinism cannot be true. If a man *has* no faith and *cannot have* faith, anything offered on the condition of faith cannot, by any stretch of the imagination, be a valid offer.

It is simply irrational to say that salvation is offered in all seriousness to all who hear the gospel on condition of faith and repentance, and yet, say that these same people, by God's decree, *cannot* meet the condition of faith and repentance. You cannot reasonably affirm that faith is a consequence of unconditional election and the result of an irresistible grace and then say it is also a condition for salvation. How can a man have no say in *anything* and yet reasonably be blamed and punished for *everything?*

In an "Overview of Theology," MacArthur says:

> We teach that sovereign election does not contradict or negate
> the responsibility of man to repent and trust Christ as Savior and
> Lord.[580]

He goes on to say:

> Nevertheless, since sovereign grace includes the means of receiv-
> ing the gift of salvation as well as the gift itself, sovereign election
> will result in what God determines.[581]

A sovereign God (if we hypothesize discounting God's justice, holiness, mercy, and love) can hold men responsible for what they cannot do, and what He has sovereignly determined that they will be incapable of doing. Can, however, a sovereign God do so in accordance with justice? Does might make right? Suppose the President and Congress of the United States declare that all young men between the ages of 18 and 24 must join the military and then fight in a particular war. Suppose also that the President and Congress send buses to pick up all Hispanic men and have them driven to a camp away from the war where they are not released until after the war has ended. Now suppose that after the war has ended, the Hispanic young men are prosecuted for not fighting in the war.

The President and Congress may have the power to hold these men responsible for not doing what they were unable to do, but can it be said that they are really responsible? The power of the Presidency and Congress may enable the President and Congress to hold men responsible for what they cannot do, and even what the President and Congress prevented them from doing. Can we say, however, that under such circumstances these Hispanic men are morally responsible for not defending their county? And more importantly, don't such actions prove that the President and Congress are unjust and unreasonable? Essentially, this is the long and short of the Calvinist doctrines of unconditional election and damnation.

If the Calvinist doctrine of limited atonement in particular and the Calvinist doctrines of salvation and damnation in general are true, the whole idea of a sincere offer is bogus at best. So why evangelize? The Calvinist contention that ignorance of who is and who is not among the elect is a good reason for preaching the gospel to all (as if it were for all and all could believe the gospel) simply does not work.

How does the fact that we are ignorant of who will or will not be saved make an offer that cannot be accepted any more valid than if we knew who is or is not elect? Ignorance may seem like a good excuse for evangelizing people who will be saved or lost regardless of whether or not you evangelize them, but it is not a very compelling reason. If the God who saves has no saving interest in a person, did nothing of a saving nature for that person, then the offer cannot be a valid offer when made to that person. Our ignorance is simply irrelevant to the validity of an offer.

To illustrate the predicament the Calvinist version of evangelism poses, suppose we have a Calvinist believer I will call Carl and an unbelieving neighbor I will call John who are engaged in a conversation about spiritual matters. Suppose that John asks Carl some very basic questions that turn the conversation directly to the Calvinist doctrines of salvation and damnation. Suppose also that Carl decides to lay it all out on the table for his unbelieving neighbor, something I have never known a Calvinist to do. Imagine that as you enter the room, you hear the following:

> John: Carl, I have heard many times that God loves me. I have also been told that because of His love for me, He sent His Son to die on the cross for my sins. Not only so, but I have also been told that if I believe in Him, I will go to heaven. Is this what you believe?

Carl: Well John, it is not quite that simple. I know God loves me and that Christ died for me. So I also know that I am going to heaven. I cannot, however, be sure that God has a saving interest in you, and, therefore, I cannot know if He loves you with a saving love or if He has chosen to save you as He chose to save me.

John: I do not understand. Are you saying that God does not have a saving interest in everyone? Are you saying that God has chosen to save some people and not others? Are you saying that Christ died for some people and not others?

Carl: Yes, I am saying just that. I am not, however, saying that *I know* God has no saving interest in you, or that *I know* He did not choose to save you or that Christ did not die for you. I am only saying that I do not know that God has a saving interest in you, or that He has chosen to save you or that Christ died for you. As far as I know, He has a saving interest in you, has chosen to save you, and that Christ did die for you.

John: But as far as you know, it may just as well be the case that He has no saving interest in me, has not chosen to save me, and that Christ did not die for me.

Carl: Exactly.

John: Is there anything I can do to be chosen?

Carl: No. That was settled in eternity past.

John: But doesn't the Bible say that if I choose to believe, I can be saved?

Carl: No. It says if you believe, you will be saved.

John: What is the difference?

Carl: The difference is that believing is not a choice of man, but a gift from God.

John: So how do I get that gift of faith so that I can believe and be saved?

Carl: You will get that gift in time, whether you do anything or not, if you were chosen by God in eternity. If God chose to save you in eternity, then He will irresistibly draw or call you to Himself in time. If He did not choose to save you in eternity, He will not draw or irresistibly call you in time, whether you do anything or not.

John: What does it mean to be drawn or called?

Carl: It means you will be raised spiritually from the dead. When you are raised from the dead spiritually, you will be given a new life in Christ with a new nature. With that new life and new nature comes faith in Christ. In effect, you will be made a believer when you are born of the Spirit. On the other hand, if you were not chosen in eternity, you will not be drawn, raised from spiritual death, or given a new life, and, therefore, you cannot receive the gift of faith and thereby be saved.

John: It sounds like you are saying that I just have to accept whatever cards God has dealt me, and that there is nothing I can do to determine where I will spend eternity.

Carl: Exactly.

I know that most Calvinists, especially those who consider themselves mainstream, will not appreciate this little dialogue and will say that it is a terrible misrepresentation. It does, however, accurately reflect the implications of Calvinism, even though it will be met by protests from Calvinists. Packer rightly reasons that:

> The saving ministry of Jesus Christ is summed up in the statement that he is the "mediator between God and men."[582]

While this is true, Packer could, though I doubt he would, say that the saving ministry of Jesus Christ is summed up in the statement that "He is the mediator between God and *some men*" or "God and *elect men*," or "God and *all kinds of men*," etc. Packer is also right when he says that:

> The mediator's present work, which he carries forward through human messengers, is to persuade those for whom he achieved reconciliation actually to receive it (see John 12:32; Romans 15: 18; 2 Corinthians 15:18–21; Ephesians 2:17).[583]

Second Corinthians 5:18–21 is especially relevant to this discussion. In these verses Paul says:

> *Now all things are of God, who has reconciled us to Himself through Jesus Christ, and has given us the ministry of reconciliation, that is, that God was in Christ reconciling the world to Himself, not imputing their trespasses to them, and has committed to us the word of reconciliation.*
>
> *Now then, we are ambassadors for Christ, as though God were pleading through us: we implore you on Christ's behalf, be reconciled to God. For He made Him who knew no sin to be sin for us, that we might become the righteousness of God in Him.*

Notice that the *ministry* of reconciliation is to *the world*. This then must also be the *message* of reconciliation, or as Paul called it, the word of reconciliation. Calvinism in general and Packer in particular would have us believe that God was in Christ reconciling the elect, and only the elect of the world. The Calvinist ministry and message is, therefore, a ministry and message to the elect of the world but not the world itself. An unbiased reading of Scripture does not support the Calvinist view of an efficient gospel to the elect only, but a powerful gospel as sufficient to save Gentiles who believe as it is to save Jews who believe. Consciously or not, Calvinists are *only* looking for *the elect* of this world. By contrast, Jesus sent us to *all* the lost of this world.

THE EVANGELIST AND SALVATION

In Romans 10:13–17, it is evident that God expects the lost to believe so that they can become saved. According to the apostle Paul, God also connects the evangelistic efforts of the evangelist to that salvation as a necessary part of the pre-salvation process. That is, God uses the saved to reach the lost. The lost have a responsibility to God to believe, and the saved have a responsibility to God *and* the lost to proclaim the glorious good news of God's grace and love.

Paul taught that what the lost do or do not do (such as believe or remain in unbelief) is the difference between getting saved or remaining lost. He also went a step further. That is, Paul also taught that what the saved are supposed to do, such as go to the lost and preach the gospel to them, is also essential to the process of getting them saved. To even think such thoughts makes a Calvinist very uneasy. In a universe where everything is already decided, allowing anyone but God to have a say in the outcome of anything, much less the salvation of a lost person, is a very disturbing and unsettling concept. Paul evidently did not feel this way at all.

More than once, Paul explicitly says that what he did was done to bring about the salvation of the lost and even the new birth of the spiritually dead. Paul saw no conflict in working to save those whom ultimately God alone can and does save. Paul had no trouble reconciling the fact that only God can and does raise the spiritually dead with the fact that in his ministry, and through his message to the lost, he had given new life through the new birth. That is, in fact, the essence of what evangelism is and does. Paul refers to what could accurately be called a ministry of provocation that was meant to lead to the regeneration and salvation of the unbelieving Jews. He even sees himself involved in the process of reconciling the world to God.

The Calvinist is right to insist that ultimately only God can reconcile the spiritually alienated, regenerate the spiritually dead, and save the spiritually lost. He is wrong to say that our part in this divine process is passive, and by implication ineffective. In his letter to the Romans, Paul says:

> *For I speak to you Gentiles; inasmuch as I am an apostle to the Gentiles, I magnify my ministry, if by any means **I** may provoke to jealousy those who are my flesh and save some of them. For if their being cast away is the **reconciling of the world**, what will their acceptance be but **life from the dead**? (11:13–15, emphasis added)*

In his first letter to the Corinthians Paul was so bold as to say:

> *I have made myself a servant to all, that **I might win** the more; and to the Jews I became as a Jew, that **I might win Jews**; to those who are under the law, as under the law, that **I might win those who are under the law**; to those who are without law, as without law (not being without law toward God, but under law toward Christ), that **I might win those who are without law**; to the weak I became as weak, that **I might win the weak**. I have become all things to all men, that **I might by all means save some**. (9:19–22, emphasis added)*

Who does Paul think he is? Does he actually believe that by preaching the gospel of Christ, he has the right to say that he is winning people to God and thereby helping them get saved? What audacity to think that his efforts could lead to the salvation of the lost! Of course, Paul did not die on the cross for the sins of anyone. Paul did not see himself as a co-savior. Nevertheless, Paul confidently used the language of winning and saving in relationship to his evangelistic efforts. Can the Calvinist?

Paul knew better than most that the power was in the gospel and not in the preacher. He also knew, however, that preaching the powerful and precious gospel, the gospel that is the power of salvation to everyone *who believes,* was a necessary and effective means by which to get the lost saved. While he took none of the glory for the salvation of the lost to himself, giving it to the only One who deserves it, he did not minimize or undermine the role of the saved in reaching the lost. Earlier in 1 Corinthians Paul says:

> *Though you might have ten thousand instructors in Christ, yet you do not have many fathers; for in Christ Jesus **I have begotten you through the gospel**. (4:15, emphasis added)*

Paul did not think of himself as the source and giver of life. He did not think that he regenerated the Corinthian believers. He did, however, realize and stress how important our part is, as saved believers, in reaching the unbelieving lost. He could not have used stronger language to do so. Like Jesus, Paul spent much of his time declaring facts that encouraged faith in unbelievers. In other words, he gave unbelievers reasons to believe in Christ. In this way he was assisting God in the pre-salvation process that sometimes led to the salvation of the lost. Calvin seemed to recognize the importance and place of the evangelist, when he said in reference to Romans 11:14:

> Observe here that the minister of the word is said in some way to save those whom he leads to the obedience of faith. So conducted indeed ought to be the ministry of our salvation, as that we may feel that the whole power and efficacy of it depends on God, and that we may give him his due praise: we ought at the same time to understand that preaching is an instrument for effecting the salvation of the faithful, and though it can do nothing without the Spirit of God, yet through his inward operation it produces the most powerful effects.[584]

With 1 Corinthians 4:15 in mind, Calvin said that Paul:

... called himself father, and now he shows that this title belongs to him peculiarly and specially, inasmuch as he alone has begotten them in Christ ... he alone ought to be esteemed as the father of the Corinthian Church—because he had begotten it. And truly it is in most appropriate terms that he here describes spiritual generation, when he says that he has begotten them in Christ, who alone is the life of the soul, and makes the gospel the formal cause. Let us observe, then, that we are then in the sight of God truly begotten, when we are engrafted into Christ, out of whom there will be found nothing but death, and that this is effected by means of the gospel ... it is the incorruptible seed by which we are renewed to eternal life. Take away the gospel, and we will all remain accursed and dead in the sight of God. That same word by which we are begotten is afterwards milk to us for nourishing us, and it is also solid food to sustain us forever.[585]

Though I disagree with Calvin on many important issues, I would not accuse him of synergism because he recognizes a sense in which a man can save the lost and regenerate the spiritually dead. I understand what he means by the use of such terms because of the context in which he uses them. Calvinists owe non-Calvinists the same consideration.

CALVINISM AND PRAYER

In a debate I had with a Calvinist, we were both asked the question: Does prayer change things? Predictably, the Calvinist, with only one exception, said *no*. The one exception was the impact that prayer has on the believer himself who prays. Admittedly, it does sound a lot better and much more spiritual to say that prayer changes the one who prays, than to say it changes nothing at all. As with evangelism, Calvinists will say with the rest of us that we are supposed to pray. They will also say that God has called us to pray. The consistent Calvinist, at least in theory, when he does pray, only does so in obedience to the God who says we should pray.

I do not want to give the impression that it is not good to do something out of simple obedience to the Lord. As with everything else, however, when God tells us to do something, there are usually a lot of good reasons for doing it. When God says not to do something, we can be sure that it is to our own detriment or even destruction if we do it anyway. If God says to do something, we can be sure it is to our benefit, ultimately if not temporally, if we do it. I do not think that it is controversial to say that whatever is to the glory of God is also to our good.

The sheer emphasis on prayer in Scripture, in addition to what Scripture says about prayer, should serve as a very solemn correction, if not rebuke, to the implications of Calvinism relative to prayer. As with evangelism, I am not saying that Calvinists do not pray. Nor am I saying that Calvinist pastors and preachers do not encourage, urge, and even plead with believers within their sphere of influence to pray and to do so earnestly and regularly. I am sure many, if not most, do. I am saying that when Calvinists pray and encourage others to pray, and especially when they make biblical claims and promises relative to the value and rewards of praying, they do so in spite of, and not because of Calvinism. Many Calvinists will not like the way Joseph Wilson represents them and Calvinism. Nevertheless, it is easy to see how he can say what he says, given his commitment to the Calvinist doctrine of predestination.

> No man can believe in the glorious, Biblical doctrine of absolute predestination, and believe that prayer changes things. The two are incompatible. They do not go together. If one is true, the other is false. Since predestination is true, it follows as night follows day, that prayer does not change things.[586]

Given the Calvinist definition of absolute predestination, I would have to agree with Wilson. This issue alone should be enough to get a serious student of Scripture to reconsider the Calvinist version of predestination. It is too bad that this does not seem to concern many Calvinists. Perhaps less bluntly, but leaving the same impression, Calvinist James Wilmoth says that:

> We know that God has predestined all things that happen. He works all things after the counsel of His own will. It is difficult to reconcile prayer and the unchanging will of God.[587]

David West is not so cautious. With extraordinary bluntness, he says:

> Prayer does not change things, nor does it change God or His mind.[588]

Prayer does not change God or His mind. That is a red herring if there ever was one. It is to confuse God Himself with the things that God does in relationship to prayer. What about the contention of the Calvinist who says that while prayer does not change things, it does change us? Calvinist Dan Phillips puts it this way:

> What God has predestinated to be will always come to pass as He has purposed, all the praying one can muster will not change that. No, prayer does not change things, however, it does change us.[589]

Would this mean that God has not predestined us to be the way we are without the assistance of our prayer? If the Calvinist says that God predestined that we would change and predestined we would change by means of prayer, why cannot the same be said for all things? How did we get out from under the predestination of God? Why can we say that prayer changes the one who prays, but that it cannot change that for which he prays? What if the one who prays, prays that he would change? If he changes, is it that he changed by virtue of the fact that he prayed, and not in answer to his prayer? Did God ignore his prayer because He had predestined to change him anyway, relative to the fact that, through prayer, He changes those who pray? I know all this sounds silly. It sounds silly because it is silly. Calvinists are theologically forced to alter so much that Scripture says to conform to so much that Scripture does not say. Ironically and so wrongly, Calvinist Robert Selph says:

> Everyone is a Calvinist when on his knees in prayer.[590]

The fact is, virtually every Christian I know, including many Calvinists who may not admit as much, pray with the expectation that God hears and answers prayer. Many Calvinists will pray as if they believe it does change things, even if their theological convictions contradict them. Most Christians, Calvinists included, would not pray nearly as much if they did not really believe that God changes things through prayer. Contrary to praying in accordance with Calvinist convictions, most Christians, when on their knees, pray as if Calvinism is not true, Calvinists included. Calvinists, like the rest of us, have some good reasons to pray besides expecting God to change things.

Prayer should be and can be a wonderful time of communion. Prayer can and should be used to express our gratefulness and thankfulness to the Lord for all He has done for us, and what He has yet in store for us. During prayer, we can and should confess our sins, reflect on our ways, meditate on His Word, grace, goodness, and so much more. In effect, Calvinists have taken away, in their thinking and theology, an effective tool that God can and does use to accomplish His will in and through our lives and through our ministries. Consider for a moment what the apostle James said relative to prayer:

> *Is anyone among you suffering? Let him pray. Is anyone cheerful? Let him sing psalms. Is anyone among you sick? Let him call for the elders of the church, and let them pray over him, anointing him with oil in the name of the Lord. And the prayer of faith will save the sick, and the Lord will raise him up. And if he has committed sins, he will be forgiven. Confess your trespasses to one another, and pray for one another, that you may be healed. The effective, fervent prayer of a righteous man avails much. Elijah was a man with a nature like ours, and he prayed earnestly that it would not rain; and it did not rain on the land for three years and six months. And he prayed again, and the heaven gave rain, and the earth produced its fruit. (5:13–18)*

Is prayer able to alleviate some suffering, or just divert our attention away from our suffering? If James was just trying to get suffering believers to think about something else, there were a lot of other ways for him to do this. Whatever kind of suffering we experience, prayer can help. It also sounds like James is saying that if you are *sick* and *down,* prayer can be used to get you *well* and *up.* Combined with confession, prayer can also result in forgiveness. If James is right, I'd say that prayer does change things, and for the better. Wouldn't you?

When prayer is said to be *effective* or that it *avails much,* it sounds as though God is getting something done through prayer. While I have no doubt that prayer does change the one who prays, James seems to believe it changes a lot of other things as well. Elijah is an exception to the old joke that says, *"Everyone complains about the weather, but no one does anything about it."* It would appear that through righteous and fervent prayer, God used Elijah to actually change the weather. Commenting on this portion of Scripture, Calvin said:

> There is no time in which God does not invite us to himself. For afflictions ought to stimulate us to Pray. ... This custom of praying over one was intended to shew, that they stood as it were before God; for when we come as it were to the very scene itself, we utter prayers with more feeling; and not only Elisha and Paul, but Christ

himself, roused the ardor of prayer and commended the grace of God by thus praying over persons ...

But it must be observed, that he connects a promise with the prayer, lest it should be made without faith. ... Whosoever then really seeks to be heard, must be fully persuaded that he does not pray in vain. ... That no one may think that this is done without fruit, that is, when others pray for us, he expressly mentions the benefit and the effect of prayer. But he names expressly the prayer of a righteous or just man. ... Then James testifies that the righteous or the faithful pray for us beneficially and not without fruit.

But what does he mean by adding effectual or efficacious? ... For if the prayer avails much, it is doubtless effectual ... the sentence may be thus explained, "It avails much, because it is effectual". As it is an argument drawn from this principle, that God will not allow the prayers of the faithful to be void or useless, he does not therefore unjustly conclude that it avails much. But I would rather confine it to the present case: for our prayers may properly be said to be working, when some necessity meets us which excites in us earnest prayer.

We pray daily for the whole Church, that God may pardon its sins; but then only is our prayer really in earnest, when we go forth to succor those who are in trouble. But such efficacy cannot be in the prayers of our brethren, except they know that we are in difficulties. Hence the reason given is not general, but must be specially referred to the former sentence. There are innumerable instances in Scripture of what [James] meant to prove; but he chose one that is remarkable above all others; for it was a great thing that God should make heaven in a manner subject to the prayers of Elias, so as to obey his wishes.

Elias kept heaven shut by his prayers for three years and a half; he again opened it, so that it poured down abundance of rain. Hence appeared the wonderful power of prayer. Well known is this remarkable history, and is found in 1 Kings 17 and 1 Kings 18. And though it is not there expressly said, that Elias prayed for drought, it may yet be easily gathered, and that the rain also was given to his prayers. But we must notice the application of the example. ...

We must then observe the rule of prayer, so that it may be by faith. He, therefore, thus accommodates this example,—that if Elias was heard, so also we shall be heard when we rightly pray. ... Lest any one should object and say, that we are far distant from the dignity of Elias, he places him in our own rank, by saying, that he was a mortal man and subject to the same passions with ourselves.[591]

Despite the implications of the system he championed, Calvin could not deny the potency of prayer. If believing that prayer can change things is incompatible with the Calvinist version of predestination, then it would seem we have an easy choice. If something has to be given up, let us hold fast to what Scripture says about prayer. Putting the power of prayer together with the need for evangelism, Jesus said to His disciples:

> *"The harvest truly is plentiful, but the laborers are few. Therefore pray the Lord of the harvest to send out laborers into His harvest."* *(Matt. 9:37–38)*

I could easily cite dozens of examples where prayer is encouraged precisely because it can and does accomplish things. God could win the lost without us. He has chosen to do otherwise (Rom. 10:13–17). God can do whatever He wants to do, whether we pray or not. He has chosen to use prayer to change things. Who are we to invent a theological system which pits God's purposes in general against what God wants, wills, and does through His peoples' prayers?

JUSTIFICATION BY FAITH

God *imparts* righteousness with the new nature. The new nature comes with the new life in Christ. New life in Christ comes with the new birth, when a spiritually dead sinner is raised from spiritual death by the exclusive and omnipotent power of God. Knowledgeable Calvinists will agree with what I have just said. Calvinists, however, cannot accept the scripturally based view that says God has determined to raise the spiritually dead sinner to life when and only when the lost sinner turns in faith to Jesus Christ for salvation. God also *imputes* righteousness to a guilty sinner when, and on condition, the guilty sinner turns in faith to Christ. It is that wonderful and it is that simple. The Calvinist *order of salvation,* by placing faith after regeneration and before justification, has, theologically speaking, defeated the very purpose of justification by faith as articulated by Paul, and later championed by Luther.

Allow me to explain. The Judaizers of Paul's day were putting theological roadblocks between the lost and the justification they so desperately needed. This was, by the way, the charge made by Luther and other Reformers against Rome. Justification is absolutely essential for a condemned sinner to stand with confidence before the infinitely holy and perfectly just Judge of the universe—namely God.

For the Jews of Paul's day, the roadblock between justification and the sinner came in the form of a requirement to keep the law in some form or fashion. The Judaizers argued that faith was necessary, but that it was not enough to make a sinner right before God. Therein is the problem. The sinner was unable to really keep the law, at least he was unable to keep it in a manner that would be pleasing to God and satisfy a perfectly holy God. There are other issues at stake in a legalistic approach at trying to obtain justification this way. The bottom line, however, was that instead of making it possible for a condemned sinner to be justified before God and accounted righteous, legalism kept the condemned sinner from the true and only way of justification and salvation, which is faith alone in Christ alone. By definition, if something is added to a sole requirement, the requirement cannot be met. If you are told that you can enter a building with only one briefcase, a second briefcase will bar you from the building. Even so:

If:

- It is faith alone that is the means by which God justifies us through the righteous merits of Christ and what He accomplished in His life and death on our behalf,

Then:

- Bringing something else with us—such as our supposed good works, fidelity to the law, or whatever is supposed to be a necessary or helpful complement to faith, actually makes faith alone in Christ alone impossible.

One reason these other supposed requirements represent such a serious error is that they keep the sinner from meeting the requirement of faith alone, thereby keeping the sinner from being justified. It was Paul's desire that nothing stand between the lost and justification. If something stood between the sinner and justification, it would keep the sinner from the Savior and the full and free salvation He provides through His cross and offers in and through His gospel. It was as if Paul was saying, as to justification, forget and forsake everything but faith. Faith alone in Christ alone is not only all you need, it is all you can have. The Calvinist will agree with this. So how is it that I can say that Calvinism hinders the sinner from becoming justified by faith alone in Christ alone? If you believe that faith alone in Christ alone is all you need and all you can have, is that not enough? As a formula, it is enough, and in fact, it is scripturally perfect.

The faith alone in Christ alone that is required for, and results in, justification is not, however, a mere formula. To be justified, the sinner does not simply agree that it is faith alone in Christ alone that results in justification. Rather, the sinner must *have* faith alone in Christ alone to be justified. I believe it is possible, and probably quite common, for a person to be justified by faith alone in Christ alone without understanding or articulating this formula. On the other hand, a person may understand and be convinced of this formula without personally placing faith in Christ for justification. The important thing, from an evangelistic point of view, is to let the sinner know what the sinner has to do to become justified. What the sinner has to do to be justified is to believe in Christ. Nothing more and nothing less will do. We may need to give the sinner reasons to believe, but we must also encourage the sinner *to believe* in Christ in order that the sinner can by justified by God.

As Paul tells the believers in Rome:

> But the righteousness of faith speaks in this way, "Do not say in your heart, 'Who will ascend into heaven?'" (that is, to bring Christ down from above) or, "'Who will descend into the abyss?'" (that is, to bring Christ up from the dead). But what does it say? "The word is near you, in your mouth and in your heart" (that is, the word of faith which we preach): that if you confess with your mouth the Lord Jesus and believe in your heart that God has raised Him from the dead, you will be saved. For with the heart one believes unto righteousness, and with the mouth confession is made unto salvation. For the Scripture says, "Whoever believes on Him will not be put to shame." For there is no distinction between Jew and Greek, for the same Lord over all is rich to all who call upon Him. For "whoever calls on the name of the LORD shall be saved."
>
> How then shall they call on Him in whom they have not believed? And how shall they believe in Him of whom they have not heard?

> *And how shall they hear without a preacher? And how shall they preach unless they are sent? As it is written:*
>
> *"How beautiful are the feet of those who preach the gospel of peace, who bring glad tidings of good things!" (Rom. 10:6–15)*

To be justified, God *is not asking* you to do what is impossible for you to do (*i.e., ascend into heaven, descend into the abyss*). God *is requiring* that you do what you can and should do, which is to *believe in Jesus Christ.* By placing regeneration before faith and then saying God may not have decreed that you be born again, the Calvinist could be asking you to do the impossible. According to Calvinism, it is certain that some people were not decreed to be born again. It is equally certain, therefore, that they will not and cannot be born again. Thus, according to Calvinism, to say they must be born again is to ask of them the impossible. I am very doubtful that this is what Luther had in mind when speaking of the doctrine of justification by faith. I am absolutely certain this is not what Paul had in mind.

SYNERGISM—THE RED HERRING OF REFORMED THEOLOGY

In *The History of Christian Doctrine,* Calvinist Louis Berkhof represents the *Synod of Dort's* view of regeneration as follows:

> Regeneration is regarded as strictly monergistic, and not at all the work of God and man. Without regenerating grace no one can turn to God, and none can accept the offer of salvation apart from an efficient act of God founded on election. Yet salvation is offered in all seriousness to all who hear the gospel on condition of faith and repentance. They who are lost will only have themselves to blame.[592]

The first two sentences of this statement cannot be true if the second two sentences of this statement are true. It is simply amazing that the hypo-Calvinist cannot see this as the contradiction that it is. Regeneration is also "strictly monergistic," according to the non-Calvinist, if monergism does not exclude pre-regeneration faith as a condition of salvation. However, monergism, as Calvinists define the term, does just that. That is, Calvinists insist that if you do not believe regeneration comes before faith, then you are not a monergist.

Only God can redeem the lost, forgive the sinner, regenerate the spiritually dead, or justify the ungodly. In short, only God can and therefore only God does do anything of a saving nature in this most foundational and fundamental sense. Despite the loud and frequent protests of many Calvinists, anyone who understands and agrees with what I have just said is a biblical *monergist.* That is, if monergism is defined as the view that says God and God alone is the Savior and does all the saving of the sinner by grace and through faith, then all non-Calvinist Evangelicals are true monergists of the biblical kind. Monergism can, however, be defined unscripturally—as it is in Reformed Theology. The same can be said for just about any theological term. In the wrong hands, an otherwise good term can be used to convey a bad concept. So it is with monergism in the hands of a Calvinist.

The Calvinist falsely accuses those who teach that faith is before regeneration of synergism. They commit the real fallacy of confusing faith with works. Doing so, they *effectively* make God the believer *and* the Savior of those He believes through. I would never deny that Calvin believed in a form of monergism. The kind of monergism that Calvinists embrace is, however, an unscriptural kind. By analogy, all true Trinitarians are monotheists, but not all monotheists are Trinitarians. Even so, all monergists believe that God and God alone saves, but not all monergists believe that God saves on condition of faith alone in Christ alone.

The Calvinist error is in thinking that only those who deny faith as a condition of regeneration, and by extension salvation, are monergists. This represents a logical, definitional, and scriptural error. To affirm that salvation is the work (*energeo*) of only one (*mono*) is to affirm monergism. This assumes that we allow the meaning of the two parts of the word to determine the meaning of the whole word. Even if I were to concede that there is room for a legitimate debate as to who should be allowed to call themselves monergists, when Calvinists call non-Calvinist Evangelicals *synergists,* it is either due to ignorance, or to a desire to deliberately malign and grossly misrepresent the views of those with whom they disagree. That is, even if we concede that monergism excludes faith as a condition of salvation (something I don't do), it would still not mean that a non-Calvinist is a synergist. To be a synergist you must hold that two or more agents make a contribution to whatever it is the agents are working to accomplish.

If you take two different chemicals and combine them to produce a certain result different from what you would get with either one of them alone, you have an illustration of a synergistic work. Two artists working on one painting would also be an example of synergism. Even if one artist contributes only one percent of the artistic effort, the final product would still be synergistic. Two or more voices in a song, or two or more musical instruments used together, make a synergistic sound. Even so, if God did almost all of the saving work and man contributed only a small fraction of the saving work in salvation, it could legitimately be said that salvation was accomplished synergistically. The person holding to such a view of salvation could legitimately be called a synergist. *The Webster's Dictionary of the English Language* says that synergism is the:

> Joint action of agents, as drugs, that when taken together increase each other's effectiveness.[593]

According to *The American Heritage Dictionary,* synergism is:

> The action of two or more substances, organs, or organisms to achieve an effect of which each is individually incapable.[594]

The meaning is difficult to miss. If the believer, by believing, increased the effectiveness of God to save him, then faith as a condition would indeed make faith a contribution and constitute a synergistic view of salvation. If God relied upon or needed the faith of the believer to regenerate a person, then believing would be a work and salvation would be accomplished synergistically. Then those who hold to the view that says salvation is just as much *through faith* as it is *by grace* would be synergists. Conversely, they could not, by definition, be monergists.

Along with millions of other mainstream Evangelicals, I affirm that God and God alone can and does save the lost. I also explicitly and implicitly deny that a lost man can or does make any saving contribution to his own salvation. Still, as already noted, many Calvinists, either ignoring these facts or being ignorant of this truth, choose to pejoratively label all non-Calvinist Evangelicals as synergists. It is not just about being sticklers for self-serving definitions of theological terms. It is about distorting, knowingly or otherwise, the position of millions of non-Calvinist Evangelicals. One apparent advantage of this for Calvinists is that they feel they do not need to refute their theological opponents in a legitimate debate, because they have dismissed them by attributing views to them that every knowledgeable student of Scripture knows and agrees are unscriptural.

It would be the equivalent of me saying that Calvinists do not believe that God loves or cares for *anyone*. I would not say this because it is, in fact, not true. If I said it loud and often, however, some might believe me and dismiss authentic Calvinism for this faulty reason. In truth, Reformed Theology says that God only savingly loves *some*. Conversely, it says God does not savingly love some or He does not savingly love *everyone*. While I would like to see Christians reject the Calvinist doctrines of salvation and damnation, because I believe them to be unscriptural, I do not believe misrepresenting Calvinism and its doctrines can serve any legitimate purpose. Although I believe Calvinists are wrong, it would be dishonest of me to represent their view that says that God does not have a saving love for *some* by saying that Calvinists teach God does not have a saving love for *any*.

By referring to non-Calvinist Evangelicals as synergists, Calvinists have committed the exact same kind of fallacy. It is very difficult for me to imagine that they do not know better. Mainstream non-Calvinist Evangelicals agree with Calvinists when they affirm that God alone is the Savior of the lost, or they would not be Evangelicals. On the other hand, if it can be proved that monergism cannot allow for a faith that leads to regeneration, then monergism must go because it denies what Scripture affirms. Conversely, if it is true that a biblically consistent monergism requires that a lost person believe in Jesus Christ in order to become a new creation in Christ Jesus, the Calvinists cannot legitimately claim to be biblical monergists, any more than Jehovah Witnesses can rightly claim to be biblical monotheists.

Ultimately, it simply does not matter how Calvinists define the term monergism. What matters is that salvation is *through faith* just as it is *by grace*. For the record, in Isaiah 43:11, the Lord said to Israel:

> *I ... am the LORD, and besides Me there is no savior.*

In Hosea 13:4, the Lord said to Israel:

> *I am the LORD your God ... and you shall know no God but Me; for there is no savior besides Me.*

In 1 Timothy 4:10, the apostle Paul says to Timothy:

> *We trust in the living God, who is the Savior of all men, especially of those who believe.*

- Since there is only one savior, only one can and does save.

- Since God is the only Savior, it follows that only God can and does save.

- There are no *other* saviors and there are no *co*-saviors.

This is *biblical* monergism, if indeed monergism can be biblical. If a person has to deny the scriptural truth that faith is a pre-regeneration condition, then I will gladly disown this label and will leave it to the Calvinist who commits such a serious scriptural error. I am convinced, however, that it would be premature to surrender such a term to the Calvinist. I am willing to distinguish between a biblical monergism and a Calvinist monergism just as I am willing to concede the existence of a Unitarian monotheism as well as a biblical or Trinitarian monotheism.

Assuming there is something we can call biblical monergism, it must say that one and only one God can and does any work of a truly saving nature. Just as clearly, monergism, if it is to be biblical, must affirm that faith is a precondition to regeneration. Although Calvinists have tried to hijack the term monergism to be used exclusively for their distinctively Calvinist doctrines of salvation and damnation, anyone who believes that only God can and does save is a biblical monergist and cannot by definition be a synergist. Anyone who says that faith is a consequence of regeneration as opposed to a condition of regeneration cannot be a Biblicist or a biblical monergist.

- God and God alone *regenerates* the spiritually dead. In Ephesians 2:4–5 we read:

  God, who is rich in mercy, because of His great love with which He loved us, even when we were dead in trespasses, made us alive together with Christ (by grace you have been saved).

Paul, however, goes on to say:

  *By grace you have been saved **through faith**, and that not of yourselves; it is the gift of God, not of works, lest anyone should boast. (Eph. 2:8–9, emphasis added)*

- God and God alone *justifies* the ungodly. The apostle unequivocally says that:

  It is God who justifies. (Rom. 8:33)

The apostle also asks and scripturally answers the question as to how and why God justifies those He justifies:

> *What does the Scripture say? "Abraham believed God, and it was accounted to him for righteousness." Now to him who works, the wages are not counted as grace but as debt. But to him who does not work but believes on Him who justifies the ungodly, his faith is accounted for righteousness. (Rom. 4:3–5)*

- God and God alone *redeems* the lost. In Colossians 1:13–14 we read that God:

> *... has delivered us from the power of darkness and conveyed us into the kingdom of the Son of His love, in whom we have redemption through His blood, the forgiveness of sins.*

The appropriation, however, of the redemptive, forgiving, and cleansing blood of Christ is conditioned on faith in Christ. That is, God justifies those who believe. God justifies *only* those who believe and *all* those who believe. The apostle Paul explains the relationship of faith to justification, redemption, and forgiveness as follows:

> *Now the righteousness of God apart from the law is revealed, being witnessed by the Law and the Prophets, even the righteousness of God, **through faith in Jesus Christ**, to all and on **all who believe**. For there is no difference; for all have sinned and fall short of the glory of God, being justified freely by His grace through the redemption that is in Christ Jesus, whom God set forth as a propitiation by His blood, **through faith**, to demonstrate His righteousness, because in His forbearance God had passed over the sins that were previously committed, to demonstrate at the present time His righteousness, that He might be just and the justifier of the one who has **faith in Jesus**.*

> *Where is boasting then? It is excluded. By what law? Of works? No, but by the law of faith. Therefore we conclude that a man is justified by faith apart from the deeds of the law. Or is He the God of the Jews only? Is He not also the God of the Gentiles? Yes, of the Gentiles also. (Rom. 3:21–29, emphasis added)*

There are many legitimate and substantial areas of disagreement between Calvinists and other mainstream Evangelicals. I, for one, am not only willing to acknowledge these differences but to shout them from the rooftops. It serves no good purpose, however, to manufacture areas of disagreement that do not in fact exist. Just because only God can and does save, does this mean, as Calvinists want us to believe, that man has no say in whether or not he goes to heaven or hell? That, of course, is what the Calvinist kind of monergism says. Because it is God's job alone to save, does that mean the lost cannot be responsible to believe in God the Savior? Does unconditional election necessarily follow from a monergism that would pass the test of Scripture? Because man cannot make a *contribution* to the end that he might be saved, does it follow that he cannot meet a God-ordained *condition* so that he may be saved?

By way of analogy, suppose a mother of a kindergarten-age child says that the child must choose between two different amusement parks before she will take the child to the one the child chooses. Suppose the child chooses amusement park *A* over amusement park *B*. Although the choice made by the child is necessary to getting to the amusement park, the ability to actually get the child to the amusement park belongs to the mother.

So it is with the will of man or the faith required of a man to get saved and go to heaven. The fact that God requires that we choose to believe does not mean that our choice or faith in Christ gives us the ability to save ourselves or to get into heaven. Neither choosing to believe in Christ nor believing in Christ saves a lost person. That is, there is no power in our choice. Why should Calvinists argue with God over the way He chooses to do that which only He can and in fact does do? Why should the Calvinist deny God the divine prerogative to save the lost by grace *through faith?*

POWER IN PREACHING THE GOSPEL

The apostle Paul says:

> *I am not ashamed of the gospel of Christ, for it is the power of God to salvation for everyone who believes. ... (Rom 1:16)*

In his comments on Romans 1:16, Calvin says:

> ... Observe how much Paul ascribes to the ministry of the word, when he testifies that God thereby puts forth his power to save; for he speaks not here of any secret revelation, but of vocal preaching.

It hence follows, that those as it were willfully despise the power of God, and drive away from them his delivering hand, who withdraw themselves from the hearing of the word.[595]

Admittedly it sounds like Calvin gets it. No *secret revelation*, hidden counsel, or deeper truth involved. The gospel proclaimed to the lost is the power to save the lost—right? But Calvin immediately goes on to say:

At the same time, as [God] works not effectually in all, but only where the Spirit, the inward Teacher, illuminates the heart, he sub-joins, "To every one who believeth". The gospel is indeed offered to all for their salvation, but the power of it appears not everywhere: and that it is the savor of death to the ungodly, does not proceed from what it is, but from their own wickedness. By setting forth but one Salvation he cuts off every other trust. When men withdraw themselves from this one salvation, they find in the gospel a sure proof of their own ruin. Since then the gospel invites all to partake of salvation without any difference, it is rightly called the doctrine of salvation: for Christ is there offered, whose peculiar office is to save that which was lost; and those who refuse to be saved by him, shall in find him a Judge.[596]

THE UNBELIEF OF THE UNBELIEVING

In John 10:26, we hear Jesus saying to the unbelieving Jews in His audience:

"You do not believe, because you are not of My sheep."

At the heart of the Calvinist interpretation of this verse is the misguided notion that the still-unbelieving elect, which is a theological oxymoron, be-long to Christ before they actually believe. The Calvinist could say (though I doubt most would say this) that although certain men do not believe, they are still Christ's sheep. Suppose Jesus is standing in front of an elect man who is still an unbeliever. Would Jesus have said to him: "Although you do not yet believe, because you are one of the elect, you are nonetheless one of My sheep"?

Probably no verse of Scripture is used more by Calvinists to *prove* un-conditional election and the Reformed *order of salvation*, which says that faith in Christ follows regeneration in Christ, than John 10:26. Hagopian speaks for all Calvinists when he says:

Note that Jesus does not say that they are not His sheep because they do not believe, but rather, that they do not believe because they are not His sheep ...[597]

It is true that they do not believe because they are not His sheep. That is not in dispute. There is, however, a more basic question. Why are they not His sheep? Are they not His sheep because He did not elect them? And of course, does this mean, as Calvinists contend, that they cannot believe because they are not elect or because they were born into an *irreversibly unable to believe* caste? A closer look at this context makes such an interpretation very unlikely. Reasoning and pleading with the same people that He says are not His sheep, Jesus also says:

> *"If I do not do the works of My Father, do not believe Me; but if I do, though you do not believe Me, believe the works, that* ***you may know and believe*** *that the Father is in Me, and I in Him." (John 10:37–39, emphasis added)*

The works that Jesus did served as a stepping stone to faith in Him for those willing to examine the significance of what He had done. In light of what our Lord was doing in full view of these men, which they could not deny, He is asking them to put their trust in Him. He is appealing to these unbelievers *to become* believers. He is giving them reasons *for* believing. If they were incapable of becoming believers because they were not His sheep, this appeal would make no sense. If it is possible for them to "know and believe," then those that are not His sheep because of unbelief could, through faith in Christ, become His sheep. What is the answer to the question, *why are they not His sheep?* It is to be found earlier in this same book. As Jesus says to them:

> *"You do not have* [the Father's] *word abiding in you, because whom He sent, Him* ***you do not believe****. You search the Scriptures, for in them you think you have eternal life; and these are they that testify of Me. But you are not willing to come to Me that you may have life." (John 5:38–40, emphasis added)*

Their problem was that they did "not believe." The Calvinist interpretation of this verse makes unbelief the *fruit* of their problem as opposed to the *root* of their problem. It makes reprobation the root of their problem, of which unbelief is merely the fruit. The fact is, they were "not willing to come to" Christ. They were not unable, as Calvinism insists. To say, "You do not believe because you are not My sheep," is the equivalent of saying "You do not believe Me because you are not a Christian, or are not one of Christ's disciples." Faith is a condition for becoming a Christian. Faith is a characterization of being a Christian. In other words, if you were a Christian or one of Christ's disciples, you would believe in Christ. No matter what else may be said of a Christian, a disciple of Christ, or one of Christ's sheep, it can be said that they *believe*. That is why the word *believer* is a synonym for the word *Christian* or the words *Christian disciple*. If you do not believe in Christ, however, you are not a Christian, a disciple of Christ, or one of Christ's sheep. Show me one of our Lord's sheep and I will show you a person who believes in Jesus Christ. Show me someone who does not believe in Jesus Christ and I will show you someone who is not one of His sheep.

From the human side of the salvation transaction, faith is *how* we are saved, or as Paul and Silas said, it is what a man must do to be saved (Acts 16:27–31). You do not become one of our Lord's sheep, a Christian, or a disciple of Christ *before* you believe, but *when* you believe. Calvinism would have us believe that the elect, and the elect alone, are His sheep even while they are lost unbelievers. The rest are not really sheep at all. They were, therefore, never really lost sheep. Instead they were goats, are goats, and will always be nothing but goats. Calvinists love to quote the Scripture which says:

> *"... the sheep hear his voice; and he calls his own sheep by name and leads them out. And when he brings out his own sheep, he goes before them; and the sheep follow him, for they know his voice." (John 10:3–4)*

This passage of Scripture, however, poses some serious problems for Reformed Theology. First of all, Calvinists believe that the elect are:

- spiritually dead until they are born again,

- guilty and condemned sinners until they are justified, and

- lost in every conceivable way until the Lord finds them.

In other words, they are just as totally depraved and just as totally unable to believe as any of the lost who are not among the elect. So how then can a person in such a deplorable condition hear anything? According to Calvinism, dead men, and I must assume dead sheep, cannot hear anything the Lord might say to them while dead. Notice, however, that the text does not say that His sheep will hear His voice *after* they are raised from spiritual death, justified by faith, or saved by God.

Calvinists tell us that it is absurd to think the spiritually dead could believe in Christ while still dead. If His sheep can only hear His voice after He raises them to spiritual life in Christ, however, then the sheep that hear His voice are saved sheep. Thus, His sheep that hear His voice are one and the same as Christian believers that are already saved. This text says four very positive things about His sheep. Not even one of these four important things is true of unbelievers.

1.   His sheep *hear his voice.*

2.   His sheep *know his voice.*

3.   He *leads* his sheep.

4.   His sheep *follow* him.

Calvinists admit that the unsaved elect are incapable of hearing and knowing the Lord's voice. Calvinists admit that the unsaved are not led by the Lord and do not follow the Lord. Once an unbeliever becomes a believer, however, he hears and knows the Lord's voice. Once an unbeliever becomes a believer, the Lord does begin to lead him and he does begin to follow the Lord. The Calvinist has it exactly backwards. What Jesus is telling His detractors is that their unbelief in Him is responsible for excluding them from this special relationship to Him. The only thing that stands between them and Him is their unbelief in Him. The only bridge to Christ is faith in Him.

It is true that our Lord can and does view people as His *own* even before they come to Him in saving faith. This passage does not, however, say what the Calvinist needs it to say to support the Calvinist doctrine of an unconditional election. The Good, Great, and Chief Shepherd does love His sheep with a saving love, and did die as a Lamb without spot or blemish for them. He did this for them before they were His sheep so that they could become His sheep. He did the same, however, even for those who will never be among His sheep.

OUR LORD'S MIRACLES AND FAITH IN HIM

Let us now consider the reason John said he recorded the miracles found in his gospel. He says:

These are written that you may believe that Jesus is the Christ,
the Son of God, and that believing you may have life in His name.
(John 20:31)

Commenting on this verse, Calvin goes even further than what I am suggesting when he refers to eternal life as the:

... effect of faith ... what is sufficient for obtaining life.[598]

This means that eternal life follows faith and does not precede it. Calvin also says:

Here John repeats the most important point of his doctrine, that we
obtain eternal life by faith, because, while we are out of Christ, we
are dead, and we are restored to life by his grace alone.[599]

While I do not believe faith is the cause and eternal life the effect, as seems to be said here, I do believe that as a *cause* precedes an effect, faith comes before eternal life and leads to eternal life—not as a cause of eternal life but as a *condition* for eternal life. Notice that the signs of John's Gospel are recorded so we can:

- *Believe Jesus is the Christ, the Son of God.*

We believe that Jesus is the Christ, the Son of God, so that we:

- *May have life in His name.*

REPENTANCE AND FAITH

If, as many Calvinists would agree, faith and repentance are two sides of the same coin, then it must follow that if an unregenerate man is unable to believe, he must also be unable to repent. As to faith and repentance, at least in the initial sense, I would agree with those Calvinists who believe that when a man believes in Christ, he also necessarily repents. Conversely, I also believe that when a man repents, he also necessarily believes. You cannot do one without doing the other. On the Day of Pentecost, the apostle Peter, while preaching to the Jews that were gathered, said:

"Let all the house of Israel know assuredly that God has made this
Jesus, whom you crucified, both Lord and Christ."

Now when they heard this, they were cut to the heart, and said to

Peter and the rest of the apostles, "Men and brethren, what shall we do?"

Then Peter said to them, "Repent, and let every one of you be baptized in the name of Jesus Christ for the remission of sins; and you shall receive the gift of the Holy Spirit. For the promise is to you and to your children, and to all who are afar off, as many as the Lord our God will call."

And with many other words he testified and exhorted them, saying, "Be saved from this perverse generation." Then those who gladly received his word were baptized; and that day about three thousand souls were added to them. (Acts 2:36–41)

Peter's call to repentance was a call *from unbelief,* evidenced as a rejection of Christ as the Jewish Messiah and Savior of the world. It was also a call *to faith in Christ* as their Messiah and Savior. This does not suggest that Christians are not supposed to repent of particular sins, when they commit them, or of a sinful pattern, if and when they fall into such a pattern. Only that in this initial and primary sense, a person is to repent *from* unbelief and rejection of Jesus Christ *to* faith in and acceptance of Jesus Christ. This was essentially the same message delivered by Paul and Silas to the suicidal jailor in Philippi (Acts 16:27–31).

Paul tells us that God:

... commands all men everywhere to repent. (Acts 17:30)

Is it really possible, as the Calvinist would have us believe, that God does not really intend for many to repent; that He was commanding them to do what He knew they were incapable of doing and had no interest in making it possible for them to do it? Conversely, are we supposed to believe that He was commanding the elect to do what they could not help but do? This would be like commanding rain from cloudless skies and from clouds filled with moisture. In both cases, you would be wasting your words. In the first case, the commandment is meaningless because it cannot happen. In the second instance, the commandment is meaningless because it would happen anyway.

Or could it be that God is only commanding all kinds of men everywhere to repent? Can this mean that God only means for some men to repent? Could it be that He is not really commanding all men to repent? Or could it be that God is really commanding all men everywhere to do what they cannot do by His design and decree? Calvinism will simply not let a Calvinist accept what the text says and implies by what it says. Namely, that all men everywhere are commanded to repent, should repent, and can repent if they choose to do so.

WHY DO THE LOST PERISH?

In light of Calvinism, it would also seem reasonable to ask why Paul would say concerning those ultimately lost that:

> ... [they] *perish, because they did not receive the love of the truth, that they might be saved. (2 Thess. 2:10)*

Commenting on this verse, Calvin says:

> Lest the wicked should complain that they perish innocently, and that they have been appointed to death rather from cruelty on the part of God, than from any fault on their part, Paul shews on what good grounds it is that so severe vengeance from God is to come upon them— ... of their own accord they refused salvation. ... And unquestionably, while the voice of the Son of God has sounded forth everywhere, it finds the ears of men deaf, nay obstinate, and while a profession of Christianity is common, yet there are few who have truly and heartily given themselves to Christ. ... It is asked whether the punishment of blindness does not fall on any but those who have on set purpose rebelled against the gospel. I answer, that this special judgment by which God has avenged open contumacy, does not stand in the way of his striking down with stupidity, as often as seems good to him, those that have never heard a single word respecting Christ ...[600]

THE FAITH FACTOR

Repeatedly in the preceding chapters we have seen how Reformed Theology undermines and even denies the importance and place that Scripture gives to faith in the salvation of the lost. In contradistinction, the apostle Peter says to Cornelius and company:

> *Whoever believes in* [Jesus Christ] *will receive remission of sins. (Acts 10:43)*

According to this verse, Peter doesn't concern himself or his hearers with which of them are elect and which are reprobate. His only concern—and the only concern Cornelius and company should have—is about how they are going to respond to Jesus Christ—His provision for salvation and His offer of eternal life. The apostle Paul also tells us:

> *Whoever believes on* [Jesus Christ] *will not be put to shame. (Rom. 9:33)*

Faith in Christ makes all the difference and insofar as the responsibility of the lost is concerned, it is the only difference that really matters. Nowhere are we told we will suffer eternal damnation if we are not elect, as the Calvinist tells us (at least by implication). All throughout the New Testament, however, it is clear that we will be held accountable if we choose not to believe in Jesus Christ. If you are familiar with the passage just referenced (Acts 16:27–31) and the story of the Philippian jailer, you will remember that God had opened the prison doors where Paul and Silas were being held. Luke tells us:

> *The keeper of the prison, awaking from sleep and seeing the prison doors open, supposing the prisoners had fled, drew his sword **and was about to kill himself**. But Paul called with a loud voice, saying, "Do yourself no harm, for we are all here."*
>
> *Then he called for a light, ran in, and fell down trembling before Paul and Silas. And he brought them out and said, "**Sirs, what must I do to be saved?**"*
>
> *So they said, "**Believe on the Lord Jesus Christ, and you will be saved, you and your household**." (emphasis added)*

It does not matter which translation you read. The question is always directly to the point. The answer is always simple, sufficient, and the same.

Q-What must I do to be saved?

> *A-Believe on the Lord Jesus Christ, and thou shalt be saved.* (KJV)

Q-What must I do to be saved?

> *A-Believe in the Lord Jesus, and you will be saved.* (NIV)

*Q-*What must I do to be saved?

A-Believe on the Lord Jesus, and you will be saved. (NRSV)

*Q-*What must I do to be saved?

A-Believe in the Lord Jesus, and you will be saved. (NASB)

George Ricker Berry, in his *Interlinear Greek-English New Testament,* translates this all-important question:

What is necessary for me to do, that I might be saved?[601]

According to Berry, the answer Paul and Silas gave to that question is (not surprisingly):

Believe on the Lord Jesus Christ …[602]

Calvin says:

This is but a short, and, to look to [sic], a cold and hungry definition of salvation, and yet it is perfect to believe in Christ. For Christ
alone hath all the parts of blessedness and eternal life included in
him, which he offers to us by the gospel; and by faith we receive
them, as I have declared. … And here we must note two things;
first, that Christ is the mark where faith must aim. … Secondly, we
must note, that after we have embraced Christ by faith, that alone
is sufficient to salvation.[603]

If faith in Christ is the sole *and* sufficient condition for salvation, an
unconditional election to salvation in the Calvinist sense must simply be an
unscriptural invention of Calvinism. Calvinists would have us believe that
this suicidal jailer, by asking this question, was manifesting the new birth.
This is because Calvinists teach that no one will (or even can) want Christ
until after they have been born again. If so, the proper Calvinist rendering
should be something like:

Since you are asking the question you must already be born again.
Since you are already born again, you already have faith in Christ.
Since you already have faith, which is the result of regeneration
and necessary to justification, you need not do anything. You do
not even need to be saved. Your very question, assuming you are
sincere, makes clear that you are already saved.

Spurgeon saw the fallacy in this kind of thinking:

> If I am to preach faith in Christ to someone who is regenerated, then the man who is regenerated is saved already, and it is an unnecessary and ridiculous thing for me to preach Christ to him and bid him to believe in order to be saved when he is saved already, being regenerate. ... This is preaching Christ to the righteous and not to sinners.[604]

Spurgeon parts company here with his Calvinist friends, but his point is well taken. That is, if a person has to be regenerated to believe, then they cannot respond to the gospel until after they are born again. Once the person is born again, he is given faith, according to Calvinism. Once he has faith, he is justified, and once justified, he is saved. Let the Calvinist protest all he wants, as he no doubt will. This is not a misrepresentation of Reformed Theology. Even emphatic denials cannot change the fact that this is the Calvinist view, no matter how strange it may seem.

Now, would all or even most Calvinists state their views in the way I have just described? Of course not! But if you put all the pieces of the Calvinist puzzle together, this is the only picture that emerges. How sad and tragic a picture it is! The apostle Paul would have us contrast the plight of unbelievers with God's promise to a believer. Whereas the believer can and will obtain to glory, unbelievers will:

> ... *perish, because they did not receive the love of the truth, that they might be saved. And for this reason God will send them strong delusion, that they should believe the lie, that they all may be condemned who did not believe the truth but had pleasure in unrighteousness. (2 Thess. 2:10–12)*

Those said to perish are perishing because *they did not receive the love of the truth.* They are left under condemnation because *they did not believe the truth.* Logically speaking, these people perish or remain condemned because they do not believe. If they would believe, they would not perish and would therefore be free of condemnation. To say someone will not perish is also to say they will be saved. Unbelievers are justified *by* or *through* faith in Christ, and thus, are saved by God on the *condition* of faith in Christ. Sometimes this is referred to as salvation from the *penalty of sin.* It can be said that God's decision to save is the most important factor. If God did not choose to save, no one would ever be saved.

MORE ON NEW TESTAMENT GREEK
AND FAITH AS A GIFT

As stated earlier, Calvinists argue that those who know New Testament Greek well agree with the Calvinist view concerning faith as a gift, thus supporting the Calvinist doctrine of unconditional election. Ephesians 2:8–10 usually serves as a scriptural *star witness* on behalf of Calvinism. Normally, I would not argue for or against a scriptural view based upon the reading of the Greek since I believe that our standard translations are more than adequate to represent the meaning and message of the Greek New Testament. Since, however, many Calvinists insist that New Testament Greek makes an even stronger case than any English translation for the Calvinist interpretation of Ephesians 2:8–10, I will include some relevant comments from recognized New Testament Greek scholars. For example, A. T. Robertson, in *Word Pictures in the New Testament,* says in reference to the words "is the gift of God," that Paul has salvation itself in mind, which is graciously given by God. He says that it is not a reference to the faith by which that salvation is received.[605]

Alford says:

> It (the salvation) has been effected by grace and apprehended by faith. The word "that" is *touto,* "this," a demonstrative pronoun in the neuter gender. The Greek word "faith" is feminine in gender and therefore *touto* could not refer to "faith." It refers to the general idea of salvation in the immediate context. The translation reads, "and this not out from you as a source, of God (it is) the gift." That is, salvation is a gift of God. It does not find its source in man. Furthermore, this salvation is not "out of a source of works." This explains salvation by grace. It is not produced by man nor earned by him. It is a gift from God with no strings tied to it. Paul presents the same truth in Romans 4:4,5 when speaking of the righteousness which God imputed to Abraham, where he says: "Now, to the one who works, his wages are not looked upon as a favor but as that which is justly or legally due. But to the one who does not work but believes on the One who justifies the impious, his faith is imputed for righteousness."[606]

Terry L. Miethe explains that:

In the Greek text of Ephesians 2:8 ("by grace you have been saved through faith, and that not of yourselves, it is a gift of God") there is only one pronoun, not two ... the pronoun is neuter in gender, while "faith" is feminine. According to all grammatical rules, the gift to which the verse refers cannot be faith. The gift is salvation, which none can merit.[607]

In Kenneth Wuest's *Word Studies in the Greek New Testament,* concerning Ephesians 2:8–10, we read that:

The words "through faith" speak of the instrument.[608]

That is, faith is the means by which we receive the gift. It is not and should not be confused with the gift itself, as it is in Reformed Theology. J. I. Packer concedes:

Whether "this" refers to faith simply, or to salvation-through-faith as a whole, is not quite certain.[609]

Even so, he immediately goes on to say:

... On either view Paul is saying that faith springs from spiritual co-resurrection with Christ ...[610]

Where does it say this? This passage says that salvation is *by grace* and that it is *through faith.* It does not say that faith is by grace, as Packer and Reformed Theology insist. What if someone said that, "grace is not really that *by* which we are saved but it comes with salvation"? The Calvinist would argue that this misses the point. The Calvinist would say that Paul wants the Ephesian believers to know that they were saved *by grace* and therefore plainly says so. This is no different, however, than a Calvinist saying that we are not really saved through faith, but that faith is a part of the total salvation package. Just as God wanted the Ephesian believers to know they were saved *by grace,* He wanted them to know they were saved by grace *through faith.* Thus, He plainly says they were saved ... *through faith,* just as He plainly says they were saved *by grace.*

In effect, what Packer has done is to say that even if I cannot use the "faith is a gift" argument by an appeal to Greek grammar, I can still use the argument. The argument then is not based on what the text says, but on what Calvinism, *apart from the text,* says it must mean if Calvinism is true. Now, I do not believe you need to be a Greek scholar to understand and appreciate what Paul is teaching in Ephesians 2:8–10. Nor do I believe that a Greek scholar's understanding or appreciation of this text is necessarily better than that of a non-Greek scholar. Since Greek scholars disagree among themselves, just as do non-Greek scholars, one should not let the fact that someone says they know Greek settle matters of great biblical and theological importance.

Most (if not all) of the first century heretics knew Greek quite well. I only quote these men to dispel a common myth that seems to carry weight with some and is promoted by many Calvinists. The myth to which I refer says that an understanding of New Testament Greek necessarily leads to the Calvinist conviction that faith is a gift in the Calvinist sense.

Conclusion

I<small>N</small> the preceding chapters, I have marshaled a great deal of Scripture and scripturally based arguments against the doctrinal distinctives of Calvinism. The Lord knows that in the process I made every effort to be fair in my representation of Calvinism. If you are a Calvinist and are troubled by what you have read, it will be tempting to become upset with me. Remember, however, that while this book serves as the canvas, the picture painted belongs to Calvin and his leading proponents from the days of Calvin to the present. Most troubling, of course, is what Feinberg calls the Calvinist "portrait of God." In stark contrast to what we know about God from Scripture, Calvin and his followers have made God out to be the primary and responsible cause of all misery on this planet. While it is difficult (if not impossible) for some Calvinists to admit this (especially to a non-Calvinist), Calvin and Calvinism point a very slanderous finger at God.

Recently, I was a guest on the *Bible Answer Man* radio program with Hank Hanegraaff. I was invited to the program to represent a non-Reformed view of God while James White was on the program to defend the Calvinist "portrait of God." After the program, Calvinists of all kinds typically contributed many unflattering things about me to their favorite Reformed web sites. No offense taken. They also gave many glowing reviews of James White's defense of Calvinism and the superiority of the Calvinist view over what they conveniently (though not accurately) referred to as my Arminian, semi-Pelagian and even Pelagian view of God and salvation. Not all Calvinists, however, were as enamored with White and his representation of Calvinism as he and his fans might want you to think. For example, on the Reformed site called "Third Millennium Ministries," one contributor asks:

> What do you think about James White? I know others on the Reformed forums who give him glowing endorsements, but I was disappointed with him in today's BAM radio program. ... White more or less agreed that God is the author of sin in the debate. And,

since White is presented as the spokesman for Calvinism, the part I heard didn't speak well of us.[611]

Even more pointed, in comments found on the Internet in a section called "Whilin' Away the Hours," the Calvinist John Rabe offers what he calls:

"A loose paraphrase from the James White and George Bryson debate on the *Bible Answer Man:*

"begin paraphrase:

"BRYSON: Calvinists believe that God is an evil potentate who causes sin and tyrannically damns people for no good reason and causes babies to be raped.

"WHITE: Yes, and here's why I believe that. Genesis 50 says ...

"end paraphrase[.]

"Yikes! With friends like this who needs enemies?"[612]

Remember what the apostle James says:

Every good gift and every perfect gift is from above, and comes down from the Father of lights, with whom there is no variation or shadow of turning. (James 1:17)

If the Calvinist is right, then James could and perhaps should also have said:

Every good and bad gift is from above, and comes down from the Father of lights and darkness.

I can understand why the admission of White is so disturbing to Calvinists. In his defense, however, White is only admitting what should be obvious to all Calvinists. Remember that according to Calvin:

All are not created on equal terms, but some are preordained to eternal life, others to eternal damnation; and, accordingly, as each has been created for one or other of those ends, we say that he has been predestined to life or death.[613]

I ... ask how it is that the fall of Adam involves so many nations with their infant children in eternal death without remedy unless that it so seemed meet to God? ... The decree, I admit, is, dreadful; and yet it is impossible to deny that God foreknew what the end of man was to be before he made him, and foreknew, because He had so ordained by his decree. ... God not only foresaw the fall of the first man, and in him the ruin of his posterity; but also at his own pleasure arranged it.[614]

It offends the ears of some, when it is said God willed this fall [of Adam]; but what else, I pray, is the permission of him, who has the power of preventing, and in whose hand the whole matter is placed, but his will?[615]

They deny that it is ever said in distinct terms, God decreed that Adam should perish by his revolt. ... They say that, in accordance with free-will, he was to be the architect of his own fortune, that God had decreed nothing but to treat him according to his desert. If this frigid fiction is received, where will be the omnipotence of God, by which, according to his secret counsel on which everything depends, he rules over all? But whether they will allow it or not, predestination is manifest in Adam's posterity. It was not owing to [Adam's] nature that they all lost salvation by the fault of one parent. ... Scripture proclaims that all were, in the person of one, made liable to eternal death. As this cannot be ascribed to [Adam's] nature, it is plain that it is owing to the wonderful counsel of God.[616]

... God ... arranges all things by his sovereign counsel, in such a way that individuals are born, who are doomed from the womb to certain death ...[617]

The word hardens, when applied to God in Scripture, means not only permission, (as some washy moderators would have it,) but also the operation of the wrath of God: for all those external things, which lead to the blinding of the reprobate, are the instruments of his wrath; and Satan himself, who works inwardly with great power, is so far his minister, that he acts not, but by his command. ... Paul teaches us, that the ruin of the wicked is not only foreseen by the Lord, but also ordained by his counsel and his will ... not only the destruction of the wicked is foreknown, but that the wicked themselves have been created for this very end—that they may perish.[618]

What all of this amounts to is nothing less than the character assassination of God. Can you really square this with the words of our Lord Jesus when He says:

> *God so loved the world that He gave His only begotten Son, that whoever believes in Him should not perish but have everlasting life. For God did not send His Son into the world to condemn the world, but that the world through Him might be saved. (John 3:16–17)*

Can you honestly reconcile the Calvinist portrait of God with the picture painted by the apostle Peter when he says:

> *The Lord is ... longsuffering toward us, not willing that any should perish but that all should come to repentance. (2 Pet. 3:9)*

What about the words of the apostle Paul when he says:

> *... God our Savior ... desires all men to be saved and to come to the knowledge of the truth. (1 Tim. 2:3–4)*

Do you truly believe that the "all men" that God desires to save can be reduced to "all kinds of men" or "all elect men"?

If you do believe this, you are indeed a true Calvinist. If you do not believe this, no matter what you call yourself, you are not a Calvinist and do not believe in Reformed Theology. If you are thinking about becoming a Calvinist, you must embrace the dark side of Calvinism along with its light side. You cannot have an unconditional election without an unconditional reprobation any more than you can have one side of a coin without the other also.

NOTES

FOREWORD

[1] John Calvin, *Institutes of the Christian Religion,* translated by Henry Beveridge (Grand Rapids, Mich.: Wm. B. Publishing Company, Electronic Edition, reprinted 1993), iii, xxi, sec. 5, 1030–1031.

[2] James R. White, *The Potter's Freedom* (Amityville, N.Y.: Calvary Press Publishing, 2000), 39.

INTRODUCTION: THE CASE AGAINST CALVINISM

[3] Calvin, *Institutes of the Christian Religion,* iii, xxiii, sec. 7, 1063.

[4] Ibid, iii, xxi, sec. 5, 1030–1031.

[5] Ibid, iii, xxiii, sec. 6, 231.

[6] R. Laird Harris, "Calvinism," *The Wycliffe Bible Encyclopedia A–J* (Chicago, Ill.: Moody Press, 1975), 293.

[7] John S. Feinberg, "God, Freedom, and Evil in Calvinist Thinking." Thomas R. Schreiner and Bruce A. Ware, eds. *The Grace of God, the Bondage of the Will* (Grand Rapids, Mich.: Baker Book House, 1995), 459.

[8] John S. Feinberg, Ed. by Basinger and Basinger, *Predestination & Free Will* (Downers Grove, Ill.: InterVarsity Press, 1986), 24.

[9] Edwin H. Palmer, *The Five Points of Calvinism* (Grand Rapids, Mich.: Baker Book House, 1999), 85–87.

[10] Ibid.

[11] Paul Enns, *The Moody Handbook of Theology* (Chicago, Ill.: Moody Press, 1989), 475.

[12] R. C. Sproul. *Chosen by God* (Wheaton, Ill.: Tyndale Publishing House, 1986), 13.

[13] Ibid.

[14] Ibid, 9–10.

[15] Lawrence M. Vance, *The Other Side of Calvinism* (revised edition) (Pensacola, Fla.: Vance Publications, 1999), 278.

[16] Wayne Grudem, *Systematic Theology* (Grand Rapids, Mich.: Zondervan, 1995), 674.

[17] Loraine Boettner, *The Reformed Doctrine of Predestination* (Phillipsburg, N.J.: Presbyterian and Reformed Publishing Company, 1932), 348.

[18] Ernest C. Reisinger and D. Matthew Allen, *A Quiet Revolution,* online edition (Cape Coral, Fla.: Founders Press, 2000), "Walk Without Slipping, Instructions for Local Reformation," Ch. 4. Retrieved March 25, 2004, from www.founders.org/library/quiet/quiet4.html.

[19] John MacArthur, *Introduction to Biblical Counseling* (Dallas, Tex.: Word Publishing, 1994), 378.

[20] Ibid.

[21] Ibid.

[22] CURE is the acronym for a very aggressive Calvinist organization. It stands for Christians United for a Reformed Evangelicalism.

[23] Boettner, *The Reformed Doctrine of Predestination,* 95 (italics added).

[24] Sproul, *Chosen by God,* 14.

[25] *The Canons of Dort, The Westminster Confession of Faith,* and the *Heidelberg Catechism* make up what are called *The Three Forms of Unity,* subscribed to by most mainstream Reformed communities.

[26] St. Augustine was the first notable figure in church history to promote many of the ideas found in Calvin and Calvinism. Many Calvinists refer to Calvin as an Augustinian. Jonathan Edwards was an early and very influential American theologian who embraced a form of Reformed Theology called Puritanism. His teachings and views are still very influential among many Calvinist Christians today.

[27] David N. Steele and Curtis C. Thomas, *The Five Points of Calvinism* (Philadelphia, Penn.: Presbyterian and Reformed Publishing Company, 1975), 24.

[28] Boettner, *The Reformed Doctrine of Predestination,* 51.

[29] Ibid.

[30] Charles Hodge quoted by Loraine Boettner in *The Reformed Doctrine of Predestination,* 50.

[31] C. H. Spurgeon, *The Spurgeon Sermon Collection,* Ages Electronic Library, Vol. 2, 223.

[32] Douglas J. Wilson. "Here and There." *Credenda Agenda* (Vol. 10, Issue 3). Retrieved April 21, 2004, from www.credenda.org/issues/10-3meander.php.

[33] While there is no one representative church or church-related movement today that represents all forms of Arminian theology, Bible-believing Methodists, Wesleyans, Nazarenes, mainstream Pentecostal churches, and even some Baptist groups, specifically the Free-will Baptist denomination, all carry on the tradition

(for the most part) of the Remonstrance and the teachings of James Arminius, relative to the doctrine of salvation.

[34] Boettner, *The Reformed Doctrine of Predestination,* 333.

[35] William G. T. Shedd, *Calvinism: Pure and Mixed* (Edinburgh: The Banner of Truth Trust, 1986), xviii.

[36] Ibid, 149.

[37] The Remonstrance was a theological reaction and challenge to the extremes of Calvinism that were mostly based on the teachings of the Reformer James Arminius. In turn, Calvinists answered back with what has become known as the five points of Calvinism, condemning the position and the people of the Remonstrance in the process.

CHAPTER 1: IS CALVINISM THE GOSPEL?

[38] C. H. Spurgeon, *Spurgeon's Sovereign Grace Sermons* (Edmonton: Still Waters Revival Books, 1990), 129.

[39] John Piper, *Tulip, The Pursuit of God's Glory in Salvation* (Minneapolis, Minn.: Bethlehem Baptist Church, 2000), back cover.

[40] H. Hanko and H. C. Hoeksema and J. Van Baren, *The Five Points of Calvinism* (Grand Rapids, Mich.: Reformed Free Publishing Association, 1976), 45.

[41] Professor David J. Engelsma, *A Defense of Calvinism as the Gospel* (South Holland: The Evangelism Committee, Protestant Reformed Church). Retrieved May 11, 2004, from www.prca.org/pamphlets/pamphlet_31.html

[42] Arthur C. Custance, *The Sovereignty of Grace* (Phillipsburg, N.J.: Presbyterian and Reformed Publishing Company, 1979), 302.

[43] Boettner, *The Reformed Doctrine of Predestination,* 1.

[44] Ibid, 7.

[45] Ibid, 52.

[46] Taken from an article in The Founders Journal, "What Should We Think of Evangelism and Calvinism," by Ernest Reisinger, Issue 19/20, no citation provided.

[47] Kenneth G. Talbot and W. Gary Crampton, *Calvinism, Hyper-Calvinism, and Arminianism* (Edmonton: Still Waters Revival Books, 1990), 3.

[48] Loraine Boettner, *The Reformed Faith* (Phillipsburg, N.J.: Presbyterian and Reformed Publishing Company, 1983), 2.

[49] Boettner, *The Reformed Doctrine of Predestination,* 353.

[50] Ibid, 353–354.

[51] Ibid, 354.

[52] Ibid, 353.

[53] C. H. Spurgeon, *Spurgeon at His Best,* Ed. Tom Carter (Grand Rapids, Mich.: Baker Book House, 1988), 27.

[54] Ibid.

[55] Spurgeon, *The Spurgeon Sermon Collection,* Vol. 1, 86.

[56] Ibid.

[57] Ibid, 196.

[58] D. James Kennedy, *Why I Am a Presbyterian* (Fort Lauderdale, Fla.: Coral Ridge Ministries, n.d.), 1.

[59] Norman Geisler, *Predestination and Free Will* (Downers Grove, Ill.: InterVarsity Press, 1986), 68.

[60] Vance, *The Other Side of Calvinism,* 37–68.

[61] Hanko, Hoeksema, and Van Baren, *The Five Points of Calvinism,* 10.

[62] Boettner, *The Reformed Doctrine of Predestination,* 3–4.

[63] Charles F. Pfeiffer, Howard F. Vos, and John Rea, eds. *The Wycliffe Bible Encyclopedia A–J.* R. Laird Harris, "Calvinism." (Chicago, Ill.: Moody Press, 1975), 293.

[64] Boettner, *The Reformed Doctrine of Predestination,* 367.

[65] J. I. Packer, "The Love of God: Universal and Particular." Schreiner and Ware, eds. *The Grace of God, the Bondage of the Will,* 420.

[66] Palmer, *The Five Points of Calvinism,* Foreword.

[67] Boettner, *The Reformed Doctrine of Predestination,* 4.

[68] Ibid, 5.

[69] Spurgeon, *The Spurgeon Sermon Collection,* Vol. 2, 216.

[70] William S. Reid, "Calvinism," *Evangelical Dictionary of Theology,* Ed. Walter A. Elwell (Grand Rapids, Mich.: Baker Book House, 1984), 186–188.

[71] Bruce L. Shelley, *Church History in Plain Language* (Dallas, Tex.: Word Publishing, 1995), 257.

[72] www.baptistfire.com.

[73] Boettner, *The Reformed Doctrine of Predestination,* 59.

[74] Sproul, *Chosen by God,* 204.

[75] Ibid.

[76] Boettner, *The Reformed Doctrine of Predestination,* 6.

[77] Joseph M. Wilson. "How is the Atonement Limited?" *The Baptist Examiner* 9 December 1989, 1.

[78] Charles W. Bronson, *The Extent of the Atonement* (Pasadena, Tex.: Pilgrim Publications, 1992), 19.

[79] Grover E. Gunn, *The Doctrines of Grace* (Memphis, Tenn.: Footstool Publications, 1987), 4.

[80] Hanko, Hoeksema, and Van Baren, *The Five Points of Calvinism,* 91.

[81] Custance, *The Sovereignty of Grace,* 71.

[82] Palmer, *The Five Points of Calvinism,* 27.

[83] Hanko, Hoeksema, and Van Baren, *The Five Points of Calvinism,* 28.

[84] J. I. Packer (and O. R. Johnston), "Historical and Theological Introduction" to Martin Luther's *Bondage of the Will,* as quoted in *The Five Points of Calvinism,* David N. Steele and Curtis C. Thomas, (Phillipsburg, N.J.: Presbyterian and Reformed Publishing Co., 1963), 22–23.

[85] Fred Phelps, *The Five Points of Calvinism,* The Berea Baptist Banner (Mantachie, Miss.: Berea Baptist Church, 1990), 21.

[86] Ibid, 26.

CHAPTER 2: UNCONDITIONAL ELECTION/REPROBATION EXPLAINED

[87] *All Nations English Dictionary,* published by All Nations Literature, P.O. Box 26300, Colorado Springs, CO 80936, 1992).

[88] Ibid.

[89] Phillip Schaff, *History of the Christian Church* (Albany, Ore.: The Ages Digital Library, Books for the Ages, Ages Software, Version 1.0, 1997), Book 8, Ch. 14, sec. 114.

[90] Ibid.

[91] Ibid.

[92] Sproul, *Chosen by God,* 23.

[93] Calvin, *Institutes of the Christian Religion,* iii, xxi, sec. 5, 1030–1031.

[94] Herman Hoeksema, *Reformed Dogmatics* (Grand Rapids, Mich.: Reformed Free Publishing Association, 1966), 159.

[95] Boettner, *The Reformed Doctrine of Predestination,* 104.

[96] Ibid, 87.

[97] Hanko, Hoeksema, and Van Baren, *The Five Points of Calvinism,* 28.

[98] Ibid, 29.

[99] Ibid.

[100] Ibid.

[101] Ibid, 34.

[102] White, *The Potter's Freedom,* 39.

[103] Sproul, *Chosen by God,* 154–155.

[104] Ibid, 156.

[105] H. Wayne House, *Charts of Christian Theology & Doctrine* (Grand Rapids, Mich.: Zondervan, 1992), 91.

[106] Ibid.

[107] Ibid, 92.

[108] Steele and Thomas, *The Five Points of Calvinism,* 30.

[109] W. R. Godfrey, "Predestination," *New Dictionary of Theology* (Downers Grove, Ill.: InterVarsity Press, 1988), 528.

[110] Steele and Thomas, *The Five Points of Calvinism,* 16.

[111] Jay Adams, *Counseling and The Five Points of Calvinism* (Phillipsburg, N.J.: Presbyterian and Reformed Publishing Co., 1981), 11.

[112] Duane Spencer, *TULIP, The Five Points of Calvinism in the Light of Scripture* (Grand Rapids, Mich.: Baker Book House, 1979), 30.

[113] Steele and Thomas, *The Five Points of Calvinism,* 16–17.

[114] Calvin, *Institutes of the Christian Religion,* iii, xxiii, sec. 8, 1064.

[115] Ibid, italics added.

[116] Ibid.

[117] R. C. Sproul, *Almighty Over All* (Grand Rapids, Mich.: Baker Book House, 1999), 54.

[118] Palmer, *The Five Points of Calvinism,* 25, italics added.

[119] Calvin, *Institutes of the Christian Religion,* iii, xxiii, sec. 6, 1061.

[120] Ibid.

[121] George Bryson, *The Five Points of Calvinism, Weighed and Found Wanting* (Costa Mesa, Calif.: The Word For Today, 1996), 37.

[122] Calvin, *Institutes of the Christian Religion,* iii, xxii, sec. 11, 1052–1053.

[123] Calvin, *Institutes of the Christian Religion,* book three, chapter one, page 1056, Electronic Edition.

[124] Ibid, 1057.

[125] Hanko, Hoeksema, and Van Baren, *The Five Points of Calvinism,* 35.

[126] Spurgeon, *The Spurgeon Sermon Collection,* Vol. 2, 221.

[127] Calvin, *Institutes of the Christian Religion,* iii, xxiii, sec. 7, 1063.

[128] Sproul, *Chosen by God,* 141.

[129] R. C. Sproul, *Essential Truths of the Christian Faith* (Wheaton, Ill.: Tyndale House, 1998), 165.

[130] Sproul, *Chosen by God,* 142.

[131] Ibid.

[132] Ibid.

[133] Ibid.

[134] Ibid, 144–145.

[135] J. Oliver Buswell, *A Systematic Theology of the Christian Religion* (Grand Rapids, Mich.: Zondervan Publishing House, 1962), Vol. 1, 164.

[136] John Gill, *Body of Divinity*, Third Reprint (Atlanta, Ga.: Turner Lassetter, 1965), 174.

[137] John L. Giradeau, *Calvinism and Evangelical Arminianism* (Harrisonburg, Va.: Sprinkle Publications, 1984), 9–10.

[138] Sproul, *Essential Truths of the Christian Faith,* 166.

[139] Ibid.

[140] Douglas J. Wilson, contributor, "Back to Conversion." *Back to Basics: Rediscovering the Richness of the Reformed Faith* (Phillipsburg, N.J.: Presbyterian and Reformed Publishing Company, 1996), 35.

[141] John Calvin, *Calvin's New Testament Commentaries* (Romans 9:18) (Grand Rapids, Mich.: Wm. B. Eerdmans Publishing Company, 1965) (Ages Digital Library).

[142] Calvin, *Institutes of the Christian Religion,* iii, xxiii, sec. 8, 1063.

[143] Ibid, 1063–1064.

[144] Ibid, i, xvi, secs. 3, 8, 175, 179.

[145] Ibid, iii, xxiii, sec. 6, 231.

[146] Alister MacGrath, *Reformation Thought,* 2nd Edition (Grand Rapids, Mich.: Baker Book House, 1993), 125.

[147] A. A. Hodge, *The Atonement* (Memphis, Tenn.: Footstool Publications, 1987), 389.

[148] Boettner, *The Reformed Doctrine of Predestination,* 126–127.

[149] Calvin, *Institutes of the Christian Religion,* iii, xxiii, sec. 1, 225.

[150] Ibid.

[151] Ibid, iii, xxi, sec. 5, 206.

[152] Ibid, iii, xxiii, sec. 7, 98.

[153] Sproul, *Almighty Over All,* 54, italics added.

[154] Sproul, *Chosen by God,* 36.

[155] Ibid, 37.

[156] Ibid, 32, italics added.

[157] Gill, *Body of Divinity,* 472.

[158] Iain H. Murray, *Spurgeon V. Hyper-Calvinism* (Carlisle, Penn.: The Banner of Truth Trust, 1995), 98.

[159] Ibid.

[160] John MacArthur, *The God Who Loves* (Nashville, Tenn.: W Publishing Group, 2001), 16–17.

[161] Ibid.

[162] Ibid, 12.

[163] Ibid.

[164] Ibid, 13.

[165] John MacArthur, *The Love of God* (Dallas, London, Vancouver, Melbourne: Word Publishing, 1996), in the note section for chapter 1.

[166] Ibid, 15.

[167] Ibid.

[168] MacArthur, *The God Who Loves,* 107.

[169] Ibid, 110.

[170] Spurgeon, *The Spurgeon Sermon Collection,* Vol. 1, 522.

[171] Ibid.

[172] MacArthur, *The God Who Loves,* 102.

CHAPTER 3: UNCONDITIONAL ELECTION/REPROBATION SCRIPTURALLY REFUTED

[173] Murray, *Spurgeon V. Hyper-Calvinism,* 150.

[174] John MacArthur, *The MacArthur Study Bible,* The New King James Version (Word Publishing, 1977), 1862 (notes on 1 Tim. 2:4).

[175] *Calvin's New Testament Commentaries* (1 Tim. 2:4).

[176] John Piper, "Are There Two Wills in God? Divine Election and God's Desire for all to be Saved." Schreiner and Ware, eds. *The Grace of God, the Bondage of the Will,* 107.

[177] John Piper, *The Legacy of Sovereign Joy: God's Triumphant Grace in the Lives of Augustine, Luther, and Calvin* (Wheaton, Ill.: Crossway Books, 2000), 73.

[178] Ibid.

[179] Piper, "Are There Two Wills in God? Divine Election and God's Desire for all to be Saved." Schreiner and Ware, eds. *The Grace of God, the Bondage of the Will,* 109.

[180] Piper, *Legacy of Sovereign Joy,* 73.

[181] David Hagopian, ed. *Back to Basics: Rediscovering the Richness of the Reformed Faith* (Phillipsburg, N.J.: Presbyterian and Reformed Publishing Company, 1996), 49.

[182] Ibid, 50.

[183] White, *The Potter's Freedom,* 141.

[184] *Calvin's New Testament Commentaries* (1 Tim. 2:4).

[185] Ibid.

[186] Murray, *Spurgeon V. Hyper-Calvinism,* 150.

[187] John Piper and Pastoral Staff, *Tulip: What We Believe about the Five Points of Calvinism:* (Minneapolis, Minn.: Desiring God Ministries, 1997), 16–17.

[188] Charles Spurgeon, *Good News for the Lost,* #1100, a sermon delivered on the Lord's Day, March 9, 1873, at the Metropolitan Tabernacle, Newington. Retrieved April 6, 2004, from http://www.spurgeongems.org/vols19-21/chs1100.pdf.

[189] Ibid.

[190] Murray, *Spurgeon V. Hyper-Calvinism,* 81.

[191] Spurgeon, *Spurgeon at His Best,* 63.

[192] Sproul, *Chosen by God,* 195, 197.

[193] Ibid, 197.

[194] *The MacArthur Study Bible,* 1959 (notes on 2 Peter 3:9).

[195] Spencer, *Tulip,* 39.

[196] Ibid.

[197] White, *The Potter's Freedom,* 146.

[198] Ibid, 147–148.

[199] *Calvin's New Testament Commentaries* (2 Pet. 3:9).

[200] Ibid.

[201] Ibid.

[202] Joseph M. Wilson. "I'm Going to Heaven Someday." *The Baptist Examiner* 24 June 1989, 2.

[203] Wilson, contributor, "Back to Conversion." *Back to Basics: Rediscovering the Richness of the Reformed Faith,* 32.

[204] Boettner, *The Reformed Doctrine of Predestination,* 87.

[205] Spencer, *Tulip,* 31.

[206] Sproul, *Chosen by God,* 137.

[207] Ibid, 69

[208] White, *The Potter's Freedom,* 201.

[209] *The MacArthur Study Bible,* 1593 (see notes on John 6:70).

[210] *Calvin's New Testament Commentaries* (John 6:70).

[211] Ibid (2 Pet. 2:1–12).

[212] John MacArthur, "The Sovereignty of God in Salvation." Retrieved April 6, 2004, from http://www.gty.org/Broadcast/transcripts/80-46.htm.

[213] Robert Jamieson, A.R. Fausset, and David Brown. *A Commentary: Critical, Experimental, and Practical on the Old and New Testaments* (Grand Rapids, Mich.: Wm. B. Eerdmans Publishing Company, 1976 reprint of 1880 edition), Acts, 95.

[214] 1599 *Geneva Bible* Notes (see notes on Acts 13:48).

[215] Murray, *Spurgeon V. Hyper-Calvinism*, page xi.

[216] *The MacArthur Study Bible,* 1658 (see notes on Acts 13:48).

[217] *Nelson's Quick Reference Vine's Dictionary of Bible Words* (Nashville, Tenn.: Thomas Nelson Publishers, 1997), 28.

[218] Henry Alford, *New Testament for English Readers* (Grand Rapids, Mich.: Baker Book House, 1983), 745.

[219] Archibald Thomas Robertson, *Word Pictures in the New Testament* (Nashville, Tenn.: Broadman Press, 1930), Vol. III, 200.

[220] R. J. Knowling, *Acts of the Apostles, the Expositor's Greek New Testament* (New York, N.Y.: Dodd, Mead & Company, 1900), 300.

[221] Buswell, *A Systematic Theology of the Christian Religion,* Vol. 2, 152.

[222] Albert Barnes, *Barnes' Notes on the New Testament* (Grand Rapids, Mich.: Kregel Publications, 1962), 463.

[223] Ibid.

[224] Ibid, 464.

[225] Francois Wendel, *Calvin: The Origins and Development of His Religious Thought* (New York, N.Y.: Harper & Row, 1963), 264.

[226] Williston Walker, *John Calvin* (New York, N.Y.: Schocken Books, 1969), 417.

[227] Murray, *Spurgeon V. Hyper-Calvinism,* 99.

CHAPTER 4: LIMITED ATONEMENT EXPLAINED

[228] Sproul, *Chosen by God,* 204.

[229] Ibid.

[230] Sproul, *Essential Truths of the Christian Faith,* 175.

[231] Ibid.

[232] Sproul, *Chosen by God,* 207.

[233] Palmer, *The Five Points of Calvinism,* 50.

[234] *The Canons of Dort,* 2:8.

[235] John Owen, "The Death of Christ," Vol. 10 of *The Works of John Owen,* ed. William H. Gold, (Edinburgh: The Banner of Truth Trust, 1967), 245.

[236] Louis Berkhof, *Systematic Theology* (Grand Rapids, Mich.: Wm. B. Eerdmans Publishing Company, fourth edition, 1941), 394.

[237] Ibid, 395.

[238] Boettner, *The Reformed Doctrine of Predestination,* 150.

[239] Tom Ross, *Abandoned Truth* (Chesapeake, Ohio: Mt. Pleasant Baptist Church, 1991), 134.

[240] *Calvin's New Testament Commentaries* (Mark 14:29).

[241] Ibid (Col. 1:14).

[242] Garner Smith, The Berea Baptist Banner Forum, *The Berea Baptist Banner,* 5 November 1992, 211.

[243] Boettner, *The Reformed Doctrine of Predestination,* 155.

[244] Godfrey, *New Dictionary of Theology,* 57.

[245] Ibid.

[246] Boettner, *The Reformed Doctrine of Predestination,* 151

[247] Sproul, *Chosen by God,* 204.

[248] Ibid, 205.

[249] White, *The Potter's Freedom,* 232.

[250] John Murray, *Redemption Accomplished and Applied* (Grand Rapids, Mich.: Wm. B. Eerdmans Publishing Company, 1955), 73–74.

[251] John Owen, *The Works of John Owen,* ed. Thomas Cloutt (London: J.F. Dove, 1823), V, 290–291.

[252] Boettner, *The Reformed Doctrine of Predestination,* 160.

[253] Ibid, 157.

[254] Hoeksema, *Limited Atonement,* 61.

[255] Hanko, Hoeksema, and Van Baren, *The Five Points of Calvinism,* 46.

[256] Spencer, *Tulip,* 37.

[257] Reid, *Evangelical Dictionary of Theology,* 98.

[258] Boettner, *The Reformed Doctrine of Predestination,* 150–151.

[259] Charles H. Spurgeon, quoted by A. A. Hodge, *The Atonement,* Appendix 39.

[260] Spurgeon, *Autobiography of Charles H. Spurgeon,* Vol. I, 175.

[261] Spurgeon, *Spurgeon at His Best,* 17.

[262] Ibid.

[263] J. I. Packer, *Knowing God* (Downers Grove, Ill.: InterVarsity Press, 1973), 182.

[264] Steele and Thomas, *The Five Points of Calvinism,* 17.

[265] Ibid, 39.

[266] Ibid.

[267] Hodge, *The Atonement,* 357.

[268] Ibid.

[269] Hanko, Hoeksema, and Van Baren, *The Five Points of Calvinism,* 48.

[270] Ibid, 48–49.

[271] Custance, *Sovereignty of Grace,* 156.

[272] Boettner, *The Reformed Faith,* 98.

[273] Grudem, *Systematic Theology,* 595.

[274] Millard J. Erickson, *Christian Theology* (Grand Rapids, Mich.: Baker Book House, 1996), 835.

[275] Curtis I. Crenshaw, quoted in A. A. Hodge, *The Atonement,* Appendix 4.

[276] Ibid, Appendix 4–5.

[277] Ibid, Appendix 5.

CHAPTER 5: LIMITED ATONEMENT SCRIPTURALLY REFUTED

[277] Ibid, Appendix 5.

[278] Owen, "The Death of Christ," Vol. 10 of *The Works of John Owen,* 245.

[279] *The MacArthur Study Bible,* 1863 (see notes on 1 Tim. 2:6).

[280] Ibid, 1965 (see notes on 1 John 2:2).

[281] *Calvin's New Testament Commentaries* (1 John 2:2).

[282] Ibid.

[283] *The MacArthur Study Bible,* 1965 (see notes on 1 John 2:2).

[284] Gill, *Body of Divinity,* 473.

[285] *Barnes' Notes on the New Testament,* 1471. (from Barnes' Notes, Electronic Database. Copyright © 1997 by Biblesoft.)

[286] R. C. Sproul, *Grace Unknown* (Grand Rapids, Mich.: Baker Book House, 1997), 176.

[287] *The MacArthur Study Bible,* 1965 (see notes on 1 John 2:2).

[288] Ibid, 1867 (see notes on 1 Tim. 4:10).

[289] White, *The Potter's Freedom,* 273–274.

[290] James Montgomery Boice, *The Epistles of John, an Expositional Commentary* (Grand Rapids, Mich.: Zondervan Publishing, 1979), 52.

[291] *Calvin's New Testament Commentaries* (Heb. 2:9).

[292] *The MacArthur Study Bible,* 1899 (see notes on Heb. 2:9).

[293] Palmer, *The Five Points of Calvinism,* 44-45.

[294] Steele and Thomas, *The Five Points of Calvinism,* 46.

[295] *The MacArthur Study Bible,* 1955 (see notes on 2 Pet. 2:1).

[296] Hoeksema, *Reformed Dogmatics,* 555.

[297] Ibid.

[298] John Calvin, *The Mysteries of Godliness* (quoted from *Chosen But Free,* by Norman Geisler, 157), 83.

[299] Gill, *Body of Divinity,* 474.

[300] *Barnes' Notes On The New Testament,* 1448.

[301] *Calvin's New Testament Commentaries* (John 1:29).

[302] *The MacArthur Study Bible,* 1772 (see notes on 2 Cor. 5:19).

[303] Charles H. Spurgeon September 6, 1874, "For Whom Did Christ Die?" [Online version]. Retrieved March 26, 2004, from http://www.spurgeon.org/sermons/1191.htm.

[304] Godfrey, *New Dictionary of Theology,* 57.

[305] Hodge, *The Atonement,* 388.

[306] White, *The Potter's Freedom,* 231.

[307] Curtis I. Crenshaw, quoted in A. A. Hodge, *The Atonement,* Appendix 4.

[308] John Calvin, *The Mysteries of Godliness* (quoted from *Chosen But Free,* by Norman Geisler, 157), 83.

[309] Sproul, *Chosen by God,* 207.

[310] Palmer, *The Five Points of Calvinism,* 50.

[311] MacArthur, *The God Who Loves,* 104.

CHAPTER 6: IRRESISTIBLE GRACE EXPLAINED

[312] Spurgeon, *Spurgeon at His Best,* 89.

[313] Sproul, *Essential Truths of the Christian Faith,* 169.

[314] Ibid, 169–170.

[315] Ibid.

[316] Ibid.

[317] Ibid.

[318] Piper, *What We Believe About the Five Points of Calvinism,* 10.

[319] Erickson, *Christian Theology,* 932.

[320] Sproul, *Chosen by God,* 120–121.

[321] Spencer, *Tulip,* 44.

[322] Curtis I. Crenshaw, *Lordship Salvation: The Only Kind There Is!* (Memphis, Tenn.: Footstool Publications, 1994), 191.

[323] Ibid, 41.

[324] Ibid, 42.

[325] W. E. Best, *Free Grace Versus Free Will* (Houston, Tex.: W. E. Best Book Missionary Trust, 1997), 46.

[326] Steele and Thomas, *The Five Points of Calvinism,* 18.

[327] David J. Engelsma, *Is Denial of the "Well Meant Offer" Hyper-Calvinism?* [Online version]. Retrieved March 26, 2004, from, www.prca.org/pamphlets/pamphlet_35.html.

[328] Steele and Thomas, *The Five Points of Calvinism,* 48.

[329] Boettner, *The Reformed Doctrine of Predestination,* 62.

[330] Erickson, *Christian Theology,* 910.

[331] Spurgeon, *Spurgeon at His Best,* 26–27.

[332] Crenshaw, *Lordship Salvation: The Only Kind There Is!* 40.

[333] Sproul, *Chosen by God,* 34.

[334] Ibid.

[335] Ibid.

[336] Ibid, 75.

[337] Berkhof, *Systematic Theology,* 397.

[338] Ibid.

[339] Ibid.

[340] Ibid, 398.

[341] House, *Charts of Christian Theology & Doctrine,* 102.

[342] Ibid.

CHAPTER 7: IRRESISTIBLE GRACE SCRIPTURALLY REFUTED

[343] White, *The Potter's Freedom,* 138.

[344] Ibid.

[345] John Gill, *The Cause of God and Truth* (Paris, Ark.: The Baptist Standard Bearer, 1992), 29.

[346] *Calvin's New Testament Commentaries* (Matt. 23:38).

[347] R. C. Sproul, *Loved by God* (Nashville, Tenn.: Word Publishing, 2001), 123.

[348] Sproul, *Chosen by God,* 68.

[349] Ibid.

[350] Ibid.

[351] Ibid, 68–69.

[352] Steele and Thomas, *The Five Points of Calvinism,* 16.

[353] Sproul, *Chosen by God,* 69.

[354] *Calvin's New Testament Commentaries* (John 6:44).

[355] Ibid, (John 6:36).

[356] Bruce A. Ware, "The Place of Effectual Calling and Grace in a Calvinistic Soteriology." Schreiner and Ware, eds. *The Grace of God, the Bondage of the Will,* 362.

[357] Ibid, 347–348.

[358] Ibid, 356.

[359] Ibid.

[360] Ibid.

[361] Ibid, 357.

[362] Ibid, 361.

[363] Ibid.

[364] Charles H. Spurgeon, *Treasury of the New Testament* (Grand Rapids, Mich.: Zondervan Publishing, 1950), II: 72.

[365] Packer, "The Love of God: Universal and Particular." Schreiner and Ware, eds. *The Grace of God, the Bondage of the Will,* 419, italics added.

[366] Ware, "The Place of Effectual Calling and Grace in a Calvinistic Soteriology." *The Grace of God, the Bondage of the Will,* 361–362.

[367] Ibid, 362.

[368] Sproul, *Chosen by God,* 131.

[369] Ibid.

[370] Ibid, 132.

[371] Sproul, *Loved By God,* 122.

[372] Hoeksema, *Reformed Dogmatics,* 479.

CHAPTER 8: TOTAL DEPRAVITY EXPLAINED

[373] Sproul, *Chosen by God,* 120.

[374] White, *The Potter's Freedom,* 137.

[375] Hanko, Hoeksema, and Van Baren, *The Five Points of Calvinism,* 77.

[376] Erickson, *Christian Theology,* 932.

[377] Keith Hinson, "Calvinism Resurging Among the SBC's Young Elites." *Christianity Today,* October 1997.

[378] Palmer, *The Five Points of Calvinism,* 21.

[379] Piper, *What We Believe about the Five Points of Calvinism,* 11–12.

[380] John MacArthur, *Faith Works* (Dallas, Tex.: Word Publishing, 1993), 62.

[381] Ibid, 199.

[382] John MacArthur, *The Gospel According to Jesus* (Grand Rapids, Mich.: Zondervan Publishing House, 1988), 172–173.

[383] Sproul, *Essential Truths of the Christian Faith,* 172.

[384] R. Allan Killen, *The Wycliffe Bible Encyclopedia K-Z* (Chicago, Ill.: Moody Press, 1975), 1449.

[385] Sproul, *Chosen by God,* 72.

[386] Ibid, 118.

[387] Ibid, 72.

[388] Spencer, *Tulip,* 45.

[389] J. I. Packer, *Great Grace* (Ann Arbor, Mich.: Vine Books, 1997), 67.

[390] Ibid.

[391] Harold W. Hoehner, *The Bible Knowledge Commentary, New Testament* (Colorado Springs, Colo.: Chariot Victor Publishing, 1983), 624.

[392] Steele and Thomas, *The Five Points of Calvinism,* 16.

[393] *The Westminster Confession of Faith,* chapter 9, section 3.

[394] Harold Harvey, The Berea Baptist Banner Forum, *The Berea Baptist Banner,* 5 October 1989, 190.

[395] Steele and Thomas, *The Five Points of Calvinism,* 25.

[396] Ibid.

[397] Palmer, *The Five Points of Calvinism,* 9.

[398] Boettner, *The Reformed Doctrine of Predestination,* 61.

[399] White, *The Potter's Freedom,* 39.

[400] Piper, *What We Believe about the Five Points of Calvinism,* 5.

[401] Sproul, *Grace Unknown,* 117.

[402] Sproul, *Chosen by God,* 104.

[403] Sproul, *Grace Unknown,* 118.

[404] Hanko, Hoeksema, and Van Baren, *The Five Points of Calvinism,* 17, italics added.

[405] Ibid, 18.

[406] Hoeksema, *Reformed Dogmatics,* 253.

[407] Ibid.

[408] Boettner, *The Reformed Doctrine of Predestination,* 68.

[409] Hoeksema, *Reformed Dogmatics,* 462.

[410] Piper, *What We Believe about the Five Points of Calvinism,* 17.

CHAPTER 9: TOTAL DEPRAVITY SCRIPTURALLY REFUTED

[411] James Boice, *Foundations of the Christian Faith* (Downers Grove, Ill: Intervarsity Press, 1986), 407.

[412] *The MacArthur Study Bible,* 1582 (see notes on John 3:18).

[413] Ibid, 1580 (see notes on John 3:3).

[414] Calvin, *Institutes of the Christian Religion,* ii, ii, sec. 12, 233.

[415] Ferguson, *New Dictionary of Theology,* 480.

[416] Hoeksema, *Reformed Dogmatics,* 462–463.

[417] Ibid, 463.

[418] Calvin, *Institutes of the Christian Religion,* iii, iii, sec. 1, 509.

[419] Wilson, contributor, "Back to Conversion." *Back to Basics: Rediscovering the Richness of the Reformed Faith,* 55–56.

[420] Boettner, *The Reformed Doctrine of Predestination,* 166.

[421] *Synod of Dort,* Article 14.

[422] Sproul, *Essential Truths of the Christian Faith,* 171.

[423] Ibid, 171–172.

[424] Crenshaw, *Lordship Salvation: The Only Kind There Is!* 36.

[425] John H. Gerstner, A *Predestination Primer* (Grand Rapids, Mich.: Baker Book House, 1960), 9.

[426] *Calvin's New Testament Commentaries* (John 1:12-13).

[427] Ibid, (John 1:12-13).

[428] Ibid, (John 1:12-13), italics added.

[429] Ibid.

[430] White, *The Potter's Freedom,* 186.

[431] *The MacArthur Study Bible,* 1581 (see notes on John 3:11–21).

[432] Sproul, *Chosen by God,* 113.

[433] Ibid.

[434] Ibid, 113–114.

[435] *Calvin's New Testament Commentaries* (Eph. 2:8–10).

[436] J. Gresham Machen, *What Is Faith?* (Grand Rapids, Mich.: Wm. B. Eerdmans Publishing Company, 1925), 172.

[437] Ibid.

[438] Roger T. Forster and V. Paul Marston, *God's Strategy in Human History* (Great Britain: Highland Books, 1989), 37.

[439] Boettner, *The Reformed Doctrine of Predestination,* 66.

[440] Dr. D. James Kennedy, *Why I Believe* (Dallas, Tex.: Word Publishing, 1980), 138.

[441] Ibid, 140.

[442] Steele and Thomas, *The Five Points of Calvinism,* 16.

[443] Machen, *What Is Faith?* 172.

[444] Ibid, 172.

[445] Steele and Thomas, *The Five Points of Calvinism,* 16.

[446] *The MacArthur Study Bible,* 1574 (see notes on John 1:12).

[447] MacArthur, *The Gospel According to Jesus,* 44.

[448] Boettner, *The Reformed Doctrine of Predestination,* 68.

[449] Hoeksema, *Reformed Dogmatics,* 462.

[450] *Calvin's New Testament Commentaries* (Eph. 2:8–10).

[451] "Regeneration," Gen. Ed. Ronald Youngblood, *Nelson's New Illustrated Bible Dictionary* (Nashville, Tenn.: Thomas Nelson Publishers, 1995–1996), 1075.

[452] Ibid, 1074.

CHAPTER 10: PERSEVERANCE OF THE SAINTS EXPLAINED

[453] Bryson, *The Five Points of Calvinism, Weighed and Found Wanting,* 13–14.

[454] Talbot and Crampton, *Calvinism, Hyper-Calvinism, and Arminianism,* 52.

[455] Hinson, "Calvinism Resurging Among the SBC's Young Elites." *Christianity Today,* October 1997.

[456] Sproul, *Chosen by God,* 174.

[457] Ibid, 174–175.

[458] Ibid, 176.

[459] Ibid, 180.

[460] MacArthur, *The Gospel According to Jesus,* 98.

[461] MacArthur, *Faith Works,* 217.

[462] MacArthur, *The Gospel According to Jesus,* xii (from the foreword).

[463] Ibid, xiii, italics added.

[464] Ibid, 214.

[465] Ibid, 176.

[466] MacArthur, *Faith Works,* 90, italics added.

[467] Crenshaw, *Lordship Salvation: The Only Kind There Is!* 95.

[468] Ibid, 96–98.

[469] MacArthur, *Faith Works,* 28.

[470] Ibid, 130.

[471] Ibid, 125.

[472] Ibid, 126.

[473] Ibid.

[474] Ibid.

[475] Ernest C. Reisinger, *Lord and Christ: The Implications of Lordship for Faith and Life* (Phillipsburg, N.J.: P & R Publishing, 1994), 79.

[476] Murray, *Redemption Accomplished and Applied,* 154–155.

[477] Richard Alderson, *No Holiness, No Heaven* (Edmonton: Banner of Truth, 1986), 88.

[478] Piper, *What We Believe about the Five Points of Calvinism,* 23.

[479] Ibid, 24.

[480] John Calvin, *Institutes of the Christian Religion* (Grand Rapids, Mich.: Wm. B. Eerdmans Publishing Company, 1993) reprint, III.11.478–479.

[481] John Calvin, *Epistle to the Hebrews* (Grand Rapids, Mich.: Baker Book House, 1981 reprint), 138.

CHAPTER 11: PERSEVERANCE OF THE SAINTS SCRIPTURALLY REFUTED

[482] Piper, *What We Believe about the Five Points of Calvinism,* 25.

[483] Reisinger, *Lord and Christ,* 85.

[484] *The MacArthur Study Bible,* 1732 (see notes on 1 Cor. 3:1).

[485] Sproul, *Chosen by God,* 186.

[486] Ibid.

[487] Schreiner and Ware, eds. *The Grace of God, the Bondage of the Will,* 347.

[488] Paul Enns, *The Moody Handbook of Theology,* 643.

[489] Boettner, *The Reformed Doctrine of Predestination,* 309.

CHAPTER 12: THE SIXTH POINT OF CALVINISM

[490] White, *The Potter's Freedom,* 40–41.

[491] Ibid, 41.

[492] Ibid, "Praise for the Potter's Freedom" section.

[493] Charles Spurgeon, *Free Will—A Slave* (Canton, Ga.: Free Grace Publications, 1977), 3.

[494] George S. Bishop, *The Doctrines of Grace* (Grand Rapids, Mich.: Baker Book House, 1977), 146.

[495] Murray, *Spurgeon V. Hyper-Calvinism,* 82–83.

[496] Ibid, 83.

[497] Ibid.

[498] Ibid, 83–84.

[499] Wilson, contributor, "Back to Conversion." *Back to Basics: Rediscovering the Richness of the Reformed Faith,* 9.

[500] R. Laird Harris, "Calvinism," *The Wycliffe Bible Encyclopedia A–J,* 293.

[501] John Feinberg, "God, Freedom, and Evil in Calvinist Thinking." Schreiner and Ware, eds. *The Grace of God, the Bondage of the Will,* 462.

[502] Schreiner, "God, Freedom, and Evil in Calvinist Thinking." Schreiner and Ware, eds. *The Grace of God, the Bondage of The Will,* 381.

[503] Palmer, *The Five Points of Calvinism,* 85–87.

[504] Ibid.

[505] Ibid, 97–100.

[506] Feinberg, "God, Freedom, and Evil in Calvinist Thinking." Schreiner and Ware, eds. *The Grace of God, the Bondage of the Will,* 463.

[507] Ibid, 37.

[508] Ibid, 23–24.

[509] Feinberg, *Predestination & Free Will* (see note 16), 25.

[510] Hank Hanegraaff, *Christian Research Report,* Vol. 13, Issue 4, October 2000, 4.

[511] Leonard J. Coppes, *Are Five Points Enough? The Ten Points of Calvinism* (Manassas, Va.: Reformation Educational Foundation, 1980), 15.

[512] Gunn, *The Doctrines of Grace,* 14.

[513] Jay Adams, *The Grand Demonstration* (Santa Barbara, Calif.: EastGate Publishers, 1991), 62 (italics added).

[514] *The Canons of Dort,* Divine Predestination, I, 3.

[515] Norman L. Geisler. *Chosen But Free: A Balanced View of Divine Election* (Minneapolis, Minn.: Bethany House Publishers, 1999), 23.

[516] Calvin, *Institutes of the Christian Religion,* iii, xxiii, sec. 7, 987.

[517] Sproul, *Chosen by God,* 26 (italics added).

[518] Christian Research and Apologetics Ministry, www.carm.org/dictionary.htm.

[519] Boettner, *The Reformed Doctrine of Predestination,* 30.

[520] Ibid.

[521] John R. de Witt, *What is the Reformed Faith?* (Edmonton: Banner of Truth Trust, 1981), 9.

[522] J. I. Packer, *Evangelism and the Sovereignty of God* (Downers Grove, Ill.: InterVarsity Press, 1961), 11–12.

[523] Sproul, *Chosen by God,* 26.

[524] Ibid, 27.

[525] Ibid, 31.

[526] Ibid, 39.

[527] Sproul, *Loved by God,* 70.

[528] Sproul, *Chosen by God,* 27.

[529] Ronald W. Leigh, Ph. D., *Calvin and Arminius.* Retrieved May 12, 2004, from http://theology.home.att.net/calarm/ in section D.2 entitled "Sovereignty and Free Will."

[530] Calvin, *Institutes of the Christian Religion,* i, xv, sec. 8, 223 (italics and bold face added).

[531] *Calvin's Old Testament Commentaries* (Gen. 3), (italics added).

[532] Sproul, *Chosen by God,* 31.

[533] Ibid, 30.

[534] Ibid, 39.

[535] Best, *Free Grace Versus Free Will,* 22.

[536] Steele and Thomas, *The Five Points of Calvinism,* 16.

[537] Sproul, *Chosen by God,* 42.

[538] Ibid, 41.

[539] Ibid, 42.

[540] "Is God in Control?" *The Hard Truth.* Retrieved March 23, 2004, from www.geocities.com/rerb2000/index.

[541] Dan Vander Lugt, RBC Ministries (2003). "Predestination and Election."

Answers to Tough Questions. Retrieved March 23, 2004, from www.gospelcom.net/
rbc/questions/answer/bible/predestine/predestined.xml.

[542] Murray, *Spurgeon V. Hyper-Calvinism,* 82.

[543] Ibid, 147–148.

[544] Sproul, *Chosen by God,* 40.

[545] Grudem, *Systematic Theology,* 321–322.

[546] Ibid, 674.

[547] Sproul, *Chosen by God,* 10–11.

[548] Sproul, *Grace Unknown,* 139.

[549] Sproul, *Loved by God,* 86.

[550] Sproul, *Chosen by God,* 11.

[551] Ibid, 22.

[552] Ibid, 51.

[553] White, *The Potter's Freedom,* 16 (from R. C. Sproul's Foreword).

[554] Geisler, *Predestination and Free Will,* 75.

[555] Ibid, 75–76.

[556] Ibid, 76.

[557] Ibid.

[558] Ibid.

[559] Ibid.

[560] Ibid, 77.

[561] Sproul, *Grace Unknown,* 140.

[562] Herbert Lockyer, *All the Doctrines of the Bible* (Grand Rapids, Mich.: Zondervan
Publishing House, 1964), 153.

[563] H. A. Ironside, *In the Heavenlies, Addresses on Ephesians* (New York, N.Y.:
Loizeaux Brothers, 1937), 34.

[564] H. A. Ironside, *Full Assurance* (Chicago, Ill.: Moody Press, 1937), 93–94.

[565] Vance, *The Other Side of Calvinism,* 382.

[566] Calvin, *Institutes of the Christian Religion,* iii, xxi, 2.

CHAPTER 13: MATTERS THAT MATTER

[567] Sproul, *Chosen by God,* 209.

[568] Ibid.

[569] Ibid, 210.

[570] Spurgeon, *Spurgeon at His Best,* 63.

[571] Spencer, *Tulip,* 7.

[572] Murray, *Spurgeon V. Hyper-Calvinism,* 74.

[573] Ibid, 81–82.

[574] Ibid, 83.

[575] Piper, "Are There Two Wills in God? Divine Election and God's Desire for All to Be Saved." Schreiner and Ware, eds. *The Grace of God, the Bondage of the Will,* 107.

[576] Eds. Thomas R. Schreiner and Bruce A. Ware, *Still Sovereign: Contemporary Perspectives on Election, Foreknowledge, and Grace* (Grand Rapids, Mich.: Baker Book House, 2000), 94.

[577] Ibid.

[578] *Calvin's New Testament Commentaries* (John 1:29).

[579] Packer, "The Love of God: Universal and Particular." Schreiner and Ware, eds. *The Grace of God and the Bondage of the Will,* 419.

[580] *The MacArthur Study Bible,* 2194 (from the "Overview of Theology" section).

[581] Ibid.

[582] Packer, *Great Grace,* 57.

[583] Ibid, 58.

[584] *Calvin's New Testament Commentaries* (Rom. 11:14).

[585] Ibid (1 Cor. 4:15).

[586] Joseph M. Wilson. "Does Prayer Change Things?" *The Baptist Examiner* 8 June 1991, 8.

[587] James O. Wilmoth. "Does Prayer Change Things?" *The Baptist Examiner* 18 February 1989, 5.

[588] David S. West. "Does Prayer Change Things?" *The Baptist Examiner* Forum II, 18 February 1989, 5.

[589] Dan Phillips, "Does Prayer Change Things?" *The Baptist Examiner* Forum II, February 18, 1989, 5.

[590] Robert B. Selph, *Southern Baptists and the Doctrine of Election* (Harrisonburg, Va.: Sprinkle Publications, 1998), 144.

[591] *Calvin's New Testament Commentaries* (James 5:13–18).

[592] Louis Berkhof, *The History of Christian Doctrine* (Grand Rapids, Mich.: Baker Book House), 152-153.

[593] "Synergism," *The Webster's Dictionary of the English Language, Classic edition* (New York, N.Y.: Random House, 1983), 909.

594 "Synergism," *The American Heritage Dictionary* based on the New 2nd College Edition (New York, N.Y.: Dell Publishing, 1983), 691.

595 *Calvin's New Testament Commentaries* (Rom. 1:16).

596 Ibid.

597 Hagopian, ed. *Back to Basics: Rediscovering the Richness of the Reformed Faith,* 46.

598 *Calvin's New Testament Commentaries* (John 20:31).

599 Ibid.

600 Ibid (2 Thess. 2:10).

601 George Ricker Berry, *Interlinear Greek-English New Testament* (Nashville, Tenn.: Broadman Press, 1978), 363.

602 Ibid.

603 *Calvin's New Testament Commentaries* (Acts 16:27–31).

604 Charles Spurgeon, *The Warrant of Faith* (Pasadena, Tex.: Pilgrim Publications, 1978), 3. Single sermon booklet from 63-volume set.

605 Robertson, *Word Pictures in the New Testament,* Vol. IV, 525.

606 Alford, *New Testament for English Readers,* 69.

607 Terry L. Miethe, *The Compact Dictionary of Doctrinal Words* (Minneapolis, Minn.: Bethany House Publishers, 1988), 139.

608 Kenneth Wuest, *Word Studies in the Greek New Testament* (Grand Rapids, Mich.: Wm. B. Eerdmans Publishing Company, 1961), see comments on Eph. 2:8–10.

609 Packer, *Great Grace,* 72.

610 Ibid.

611 Retrieved December 2003 from www.thirdmill.org. Quote may no longer exist on the web site listed.

612 Retrieved May 11, 2004, from http://scarecrowsheaves.blogspot.com/2003_12_01_scarecrowsheaves_archive.html.

613 Calvin, *Institutes of the Christian Religion,* iii, xxi, sec. 5, 1030–1031.

614 Ibid, iii, xxiii, sec. 7, 1063.

615 *Calvin's New Testament Commentaries* (Gen. 3).

616 Calvin, *Institutes of the Christian Religion,* iii, xxiii, sec. 7, 987.

617 Ibid, sec. 6, 231.

618 *Calvin's New Testament Commentaries* (Rom. 9:18).

Made in the USA
Monee, IL
15 January 2023

25304738R10223